Reidar Visser

D1826321

Basra, the Failed Gulf State

POLITIK

Forschung und Wissenschaft

Band 22

LIT

Reidar Visser

Basra, the Failed Gulf State

Separatism and Nationalism in Southern Iraq

LIT

Cover illustration: Iraqi soldier guarding oil installations near Basra, May 2005. Photo by Essam al-Sudani (AFP).

Bibliographic information published by Die Deutsche Bibliothek
Die Deutsche Bibliothek lists this publication in the Deutsche Nationalbibliografie; detailed bibliographic data are available in the Internet at http://dnb.ddb.de.

ISBN 3-8258-8799-5

A catalogue record for this book is available from the British Library

© LIT VERLAG Münster   2005
Grevener Str./Fresnostr. 2   D- 48159 Münster
Tel. +49/(0)251-62 03 20   Fax +49/(0)251-23 19 72
e-Mail: lit@lit-verlag.de   http://www.lit-verlag.de

Distributed in the UK by:
Global Book Marketing
38 King Street, London WC 2E 8JT
Phone: +44 (0) 207 240 6649 – Fax: +44 (0) 20 7497 0309
http://www.globalbookmarketing.co.uk

Distributed in North America by:

Transaction Publishers
New Brunswick (U.S.A.) and London (U.K.)

Transaction Publishers
Rutgers University
35 Berrue Circle
Piscataway, NJ 08854

Tel.: (732) 445 - 2280
Fax: (732) 445 - 3138
for orders (U. S. only):
toll free (888) 999 - 6778

Contents

1. The Shatt al-'Arab
2. 'Ashar River
3. Iraq pamphlet
4. Letter from Basra merchant to India
5. Indian sepoys in Basra
6. Basrawis at donkey race
7. Ahmad al-Sani' and 'Abd al-Latif al-Mandil
8. Muharram in Basra
9. The ziggurat at Ur
10. Abadan oil refinery
11. 'Ashar
12. Basra coffee shop
13. RAF airplane on mission
14. The Iraq Museum
15. Shi'i anti-federalism demonstration
16. Wa'il 'Abd al-Latif

All photographs are from private collections unless annotated otherwise.

Preface and Acknowledgements

When I started working on this book in the mid 1990s, Europe was experiencing war in its midst. Multi-ethnic Yugoslavia was disintegrating, giving way to successor states based on narrow and exclusivist conceptions of national identity. Many wondered whether the Middle East would follow suit: If the authoritarian systems in place in states like Lebanon, Syria and Iraq collapsed, would they too become subjected to Balkanisation and fall apart?

I became fascinated by this question, but soon realised that the Middle East, for all its own problems, contrasted sharply with the Balkans in its approach to multi-ethnic realities. Although parallels were often drawn between the ethno-religious labyrinths of Bosnia and Lebanon, the arrangements that eventually brought an end to hostilities in these two countries actually marked opposite poles: whereas the 1995 Dayton accord cemented ethno-sectarian divisions within Bosnia between the Serb republic and the Muslim-Croat federation, the 1989 Ta'if agreement consecrated the indivisibility of Lebanon and pointed towards a withering away of sectarian politics. True, there came the subsequent problems of applying such lofty principles to the Lebanese context – but this was nevertheless a deliberate attempt to *restore* multi-ethnic complexity in areas affected by the war instead of succumbing to the logic of pure ethnic zones. Its bloody past notwithstanding, Lebanon of the mid 1990s did seem to possess a kernel of hope for mosaic-like societies, a sort of limit to separatist instincts and the boundless prosecution of ethnic wars of liberation – elements of an antithesis to the old European practice of enforcing neatness on political maps through religious and linguistic standardisation.

With a population made up of Shi'i Arabs, Sunni Arabs, Kurds (mostly Sunnis) and several smaller ethno-religious communities, Iraq was similar to Lebanon in exhibiting a kind of uneasy pride in its own complex make-up. In the 1990s, the Ba'th regime's rhetorical support for ideals of coexistence was savagely compromised by its actual deeds, but large groups within the opposition staunchly continued to defend the concept of a unitary, multi-ethnic Iraq, even in the face of repeated suggestions from Western think-tanks about partitioning the country in the best interests of all. Above all, the Shi'i refusal to create a sectarian separatism in the south of Iraq made a strong impression on me – it seemed the epitome of an alternative approach to ethnicity, a paradigm for living together from which Europeans stood a good deal to learn.

I began reading works on Iraqi history to try to understand the background to this Iraqi predilection for the intricate – and particularly the apparent Shi'i non-assertiveness vis-à-vis the vast oil resources concentrated their core areas, a detached attitude almost anomalous to many European minds. Clearly there appeared to be intellectual links from modern-day ideals of coexistence to the practices of the old Islamic empires, which had accommodated groups of different religions within a single polity. Pioneering studies published in the 1990s also refuted the traditional view of the Iraqi Shi'is as fifth columnists for Iran, and explained how they maintained a distinctly Arab identity. But what still puzzled me was how the particular borders of the modern state of Iraq had achieved such a sacrosanct position in Shi'i and Sunni discourse alike, less than a century after the country had formally come into being. What were the roots of this omnipresent and yet elusive idea of "Iraqi unity"?

When I accidentally came across a reference to a Basra separatist project dating from the 1920s, my immediate reaction was that this might be a key to understanding the absence of Shi'i separatism in southern Iraq for much of the rest of the twentieth century: whatever this project had been, its almost complete absence from cursory texts on Iraqi history suggested that it had failed to thrive and had subsequently disappeared completely. I speculated that the only recorded example of southern separatism would reveal the Iraqi nationalist forces of anti-separation in a brilliant, translucent picture – surely they would have been closer to the surface than ever during this period, in some of the finest hours of their odyssey.

I was to encounter many surprises in the subsequent study – not least that the Basra separatist project of the 1920s was not really a *Shi'i* bid for secession. My analysis came to focus instead on a cosmopolitan form of separatism that sought to embrace the entire ethno-religious patchwork of Basra: Sunnis and Shi'is, Christians and Jews, Mandaeans and Shaykhis, Arabs and Indians. Not until the late 1920s did some kind of separatism with a distinctive Shi'i flavour materialise; it soon proved even more ephemeral than the original movement for an autonomous Basra. But in both cases, it was possible to detect how anti-separatist ideals and Iraqi nationalism grew stronger – if sometimes in ways more opaque than I had initially expected. That interplay between separatist and nationalist forces, and ultimately the triumph of ideologues in favour of a large centralised state with Baghdad as its capital, is what this book is all about.

One multi-ethnic vision of the nation thus came to defeat another, and separatism was to remain in the background in southern Iraq for the rest of the twentieth century. Even after the 2003 Iraq War, similar patterns can be seen. Many southerners still support ideals of Iraqi unity, and to the extent that the model of a single, centralised state is coming under pressure, the attention is on regionalist visions (for Basra and its two neighbouring provinces to form a separate entity in a new federal Iraq) rather than on sectarian Shi'i separatism. The remarkably widespread persistence of southern loyalty to Baghdad beyond the authoritarian era of the Ba'th disproves the notion that Iraqi nationalism can be reduced to propaganda imposed by a ruthless regime during the height of its power, and even the new and more radical federalist trend in the south has so far held on to the vision of a unified country (albeit in a more decentralised incarnation) as well as the language of anti-sectarianism.

It is a paradox, though, that Iraqi nationalism, with its emphasis on an inclusivist and tolerant approach to ethnicity, has fostered a school of historians so set against any schemes that might cast doubt on their narrative of the unified nation state – where no space for the Basra separatist movement has been allowed and considerable energy has been devoted to rejecting it as a sheer falsification. After all, Iraqi nationalism is itself also a form of separatism from the larger Arab and Islamic wholes to which it so frequently refers, but the act of isolating Iraq from other Arab countries like Syria has generally met with silent acceptance among Iraqi historians, quite unlike the denigration meted out to the Basra non-conformists of the interwar years. And whilst the steady support for the territorial integrity of Iraq comes across as an admirable trend simply because population movements and redrawing of borders tend to beget bloodshed, the darker flip-side of the "unity" coin – the rigid focus on intellectual conformity – remains an important challenge to Iraqi nationalists today as they set about building a new Iraq after the Ba'th. In that context, simply allowing for the articulation of alternative stories (such as that of the Basra separation movement) could be a good thing in itself. Opening for a more pluralistic debate on the past would only serve to reinforce existing currents of ethno-religious tolerance in Iraqi public discourse – and the democratic value of this would probably outweigh the risks of any straying from the standard nationalist epic being exploited by intrigue-prone outsiders. Perhaps in this context, ideas from other regions of the world about *historiographical* pluralism might also serve some constructive purpose: in the case of Basra such pluralism can help uncover long forgotten ideas about alternative state models for the Mesopotamian valleys and plains (including visions that can mediate between the extreme centralism associated with the Ba'th and the black-and-white separatism often propagated by Western political scientists as a solution for Iraq), as well as versions of Iraqi nationalism that were much more tolerant and pacific than the propaganda of the post-1958 authoritarian era. These indigenous ideas and visions deserve to be taken seriously in the ongoing debate about a new democratic future for Iraq, where there has so far been a peculiar preoccupation with concepts and models of government imported from abroad.

It took many years to complete this book, and I have received much valuable assistance and support underway. I am particularly grateful to the supervisor for my doctoral thesis at Oxford, Eugene Rogan, who encouraged me to go beyond the diplomatic aspects of the Basra question to further explore its local dimensions. Eugene's inspiring advice and constructive criticisms were administered in concentrated doses at key junctures, and although I spent much of my study time in archives away from Oxford, it is fair to say that this study would have looked completely different had it not been for his guidance. I would also like to thank the examiners for my thesis, John Darwin and Peter Sluglett. Both generously employed their expertise on British imperialism and Iraq to make specific suggestions for how I could develop and elaborate my project. Furthermore I am grateful to Paul Dresch, Derek Hopwood and Ahmed al-Shahi, who all offered stimulating comments and suggestions on individual chapters and essays related to my thesis work. During the work with preparing my revised study for publication I have benefited greatly from the support of my commissioning editor at LIT Verlag in Berlin, Veit D. Hopf, who was able to offer efficient production and prompt release of the book at a time when developments in southern Iraq were once more beginning to make a radical political impact.

Others have been of invaluable assistance in signposting the widely dispersed corpus of sources that relate to twentieth-century southern Iraq. Yitzhak Nakash and Meir Litvak were forthcoming with advice on work with the files relating to Iraq in the National Archives of India in advance of my visit there; Tamara Agha-Jaffar, Meer S. Basri and Basil S. Faidhi unsparingly gave of their time and knowledge and enabled me to work with the private documents of relatives who played important roles in political developments in Basra during the Iraqi monarchy; David Sagiv kindly made available information from his unpublished research on the Jewish community of Basra; whereas Russ Gasero of the Reformed Church of America gave me the opportunity to work with missionary archives from stations in and around Basra. I am grateful to all of them for the help and personal advice they have provided.

At the Norwegian Institute of International Affairs, where I have been based for much of this period, I would like to thank Tore Gustavsson, Hazel M. Henriksen and Dagfrid Hermansen, all of the library; Haakon Gunnerud and Ivar Windheim, who helped with graphics; Susan Høivik, our in-house copy editor and gentle enforcer of clarity and logic; and most of all Daniel Heradstveit, who has been a paragon of patience and far-sightedness since the early days of my project. I am also thankful to the Norwegian Research Council, whose Petropol programme made available financial support and created avenues for the exchange of ideas – Halvdan Buflod, Tor Kartevold and Kjetil Visnes have been particularly important in this regard. Special thanks to Yngve Nedrebø and Atle Thowsen, who long ago inspired me to pursue university studies in history, and to my parents, Gunvor and Pieter, who have supported my excursions into mysteries of the past for as long as I can remember.

Note on Transliteration

Words of Arabic, Persian or Turkish origin are treated in one of three ways in this book. Words which have acquired a commonly accepted form in English and occur in unabridged dictionaries are written in the standard English form, following *The New Oxford Dictionary of English* (Oxford: Oxford University Press, 1998). This relates to certain titles (e.g. pasha, aga, haji, sayyid), administrative and occupational terms (vilayet, ulama, mullah etc.) and well-known place names (for instance Kuwait, Fao and Mosul). For words in Arabic or Persian, the transliteration system of the *International Journal of Middle East Studies* has been adopted, with ' for *'ayn* and with ' representing the *hamza*, but diacritical signs specifying emphatic consonants and long vowels have been omitted. Ottoman Turkish is transliterated according to *Osmanlıca Türkçe Sözlük* (Istanbul: İnkilâp Kitabevi, 1987).

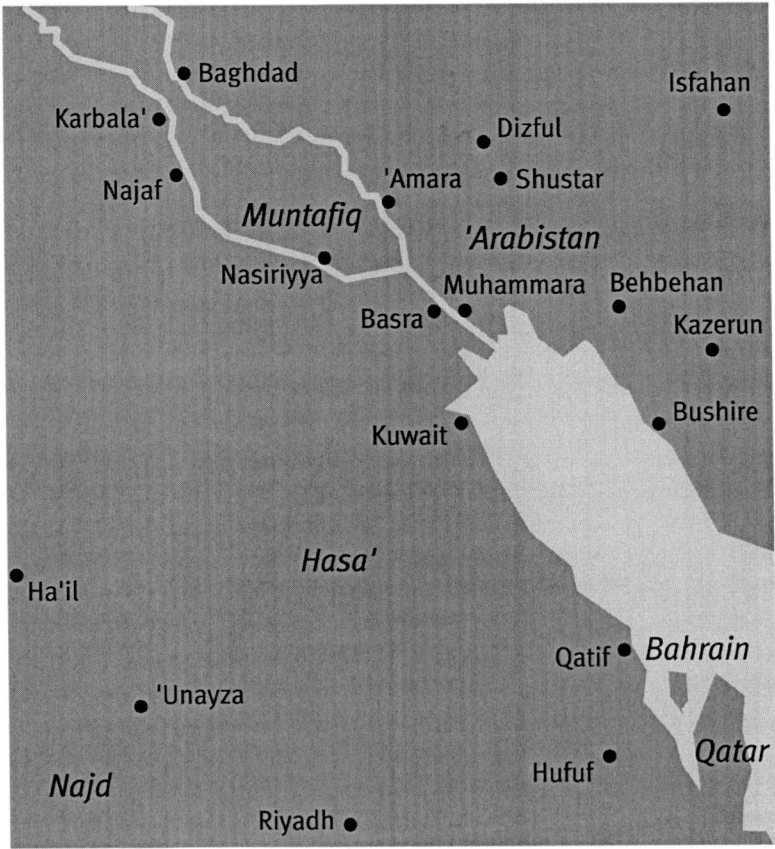

Map of population centres in the Persian Gulf region in the early twentieth century (scale 1: 8,500,000).

1 Introduction

This book is driven by a single question: Why did the oppressed population of oil-rich southern Iraq refrain from separatist activities for most of the twentieth century?

Analysts have frequently predicted that southern Iraq might break free from Baghdad. Some have based their views on historical factors, describing Iraq as a recent, fragile and "artificial" creation, a hotchpotch of former Ottoman provinces randomly assembled after the First World War.[1] Others have simply assumed that coexistence between Shi'is in "the south" and Sunnis in "central" Iraq in a single polity is impossible and that Shi'i "separatist" ambitions are a perennial latent feature of Iraqi politics.[2]

In historical perspective, however, any manifestations of a separatist current in the south have been of scant consequence. In contrast to the northern areas of Iraq, where separatism or calls for a loose federative state model have been frequent, projects challenging the territorial integrity of the Iraqi state in the south have been limited to unconfirmed rumours – a pattern that persisted from Iraq's independence in 1932 to the fall of the Ba'th regime in 2003. Despite decades of extreme political pressure, there was little in the way of definitive projects of territorial separation: no such scheme materialised in the south during the eight-year long war with Iran; the uprising against the regime after the 1991 Gulf War aimed at taking over control of the entire Iraqi state rather than isolating the south; and during the build-up to the 2003 Iraq War, Shi'is from the south figured among the most vocal critics of even a limited project of territorial devolution in the shape of federal arrangements.[3] True, "separatism in the south" was used as a tag by the Ba'th regime to justify repressive policies in the area, and outsiders occasionally called for foreign intervention to divide Iraq – in the belief that political tension would be reduced by lopping off the south and the north from Baghdad.[4] But the inhabitants of the area themselves failed to show much interest in such projects.

There has been one significant exception to the general historical tendency of non-separatism in the south. During the crucial years of transformation after the First World War, when Britain held a League of Nations mandate to create the modern state of Iraq from former Ottoman territories, a separatist initiative did materialise in the city of Basra. Referring to the area's unique position in international trade as well as its strategic location at the head of the Gulf, local elites argued for a special relationship with the British and a virtually independent position vis-à-vis the projected Iraqi state. For several years, this project remained influential at the local level, and many notables of Basra opted to stay aloof from the new Iraqi regime with its capital in Baghdad. As the British mandate drew towards a close in the late 1920s, however, the calls for separation had silenced. In this period, the office of the League of Nations in Geneva was flooded with representations from various parts of Iraq, all presenting alternative schemes challenging the vision of a unitary, independent Iraqi state. But the project of making Basra a separate Gulf state had disappeared from the list of problems that faced the Iraqi state-builders. In 1932, Iraq formally achieved independence without any effective protests from the southern Gulf city, and the subsequent years of political upheaval in Iraq saw no resurgence of the old separatist plan.

The southern secessionist bid of the 1920s has hardly received any attention by historians writing on modern Iraq. With all the speculation about separatism in the south representing a threat to Iraqi unity, this is a remarkable omission. The Basra separatist movement is the only twentieth-century historical manifestation of a southern project to challenge Baghdad's supremacy, and constitutes an ideal case for studying both local autonomist ambitions as well as their limitations. Additionally, it forms an excellent historical example for focusing on the dynamics of Iraqi nationalism – as the anti-separatist forces became mobilised to a maximum extent precisely during this episode of radical challenge. In this book, I will utilise the Basra separatist movement of the 1920s to explain why southern separatism went on to disappear completely from Iraqi politics for the rest of the twentieth century, and how Iraqi nationalism so successfully supplanted it. Finally, I will ask whether this apparent supersession can be considered to be truly complete. Today, there are interesting new political trends in the south with several superficial parallels to what took place in the 1920s; do these latest regionalist tendencies represent a real reawakening of the original bid for a Basra with a special political status?

Basra in global perspective

Failed separatist initiatives are legion in twentieth-century international history. A large number of such unsuccessful secessionist movements managed to survive after their demise, as underground opposition, in exile under the auspices of some regional power finding them useful, or in more distant metropolises receptive to their ideas. Many dormant separatisms woke to life during the 1990s as new communication technologies like the Internet facilitated the articulation of minority points of view.

A much smaller sub-group of failed separatisms are the schemes that disappeared entirely from the politics of the state against which they had been directed, with no signs of resurgence even during stages of extreme domestic turbulence. In these cases, the flames of separatism, often seen as an all-powerful tool in the hands of social elites ready to exploit them, receded without leaving even a smouldering ember. Visions of a separate political existence may not be extinct, but they have certainly been wiped out from the public arena. The interesting aspects of these instances are, firstly, what they can reveal about the constraints and barriers that face elites seeking to redraw the political landscape in a bid to erect new borders and identities, and, secondly, the insights they offer into the question of how ideological competitors with larger nationalist scopes came to triumph instead, often to the point of establishing a virtual monopoly.

The 1920s separatist movement in Basra belongs to this latter class of failed separatisms, and shares certain basic features with projects that emerged in other geographical areas. A high proportion of the secessionist attempts which failed and went on to disintegrate were unsuccessful pro-colonial undertakings. The Basra scheme was emphatically pro-British, yet it suffered the same fate as that of others who have pleaded the case for a special link with a colonial metropolis: rejection, incorporation into a larger unit more suitable to the colonial power's own needs, and, ultimately, abandonment. During the course of the twentieth century, people of Jazira (various pro-French movements in the decades prior to Syria's independence in 1945), Newfoundland (pro-British movement defeated by referendum in 1949 which led to federation with Canada), Ambon (pro-Dutch separatist republic suppressed by Indonesia in 1950), Goa (annexation by India in 1961 protested by pro-Portuguese elements), and Papua (pro-Australian secessionist movement failed when Papua New Guinea became independent in 1975) all saw their demands for a privileged imperial connection come to nought.[5] Today's inhabitants of Anjouan (an island within the Comoros federation with pro-French currents active from the mid 1990s onwards) and Gibraltar (under British rule but affected by the possibility of future concessions from London to the Spanish government) are worried that a similar destiny may be awaiting them. Many of these peoples have been allotted labels similar to the "more British than the British themselves" cliché associated with the Basrawis in the interwar period.

The apparent paradox of the willing collaborator ultimately being spurned by the colonial power is a central problem in the analysis of such examples. It is true that these movements were mostly latecomers, aspiring to a status as crown colonies in an age when such attempts were becoming increasingly unfashionable. Yet, throughout the twentieth century, there were also groups who successfully maintained their territorial exclusivity under imperial patronage in the face of nationalism with a wider territorial scope. Examples include Ceuta and Melilla (kept by Spain as colonial enclaves when Morocco became independent in 1956), the Cayman Islands (demanded autonomy from Jamaica in the 1959 West Indies Federation and stayed as a British colony when Jamaica became independent in 1962), Mayotte (remained French instead of being incorporated into the Comoros in 1975) and Anguilla (retained by Britain, separated from St. Kitts & Nevis in 1980).[6] Why then did the Basra separatists fail? Was it because their scheme was incongruent with British imperial interests? And was the separatist movement's sudden disappearance from the Iraqi political scene after the British mandate simply a result of its being inextricably linked to a colonial system and mode of thinking?

Another characteristic of many collapsed separatist undertakings is the failure to create a common identity for the area they target – often as attempts to defend a small-scale, civic sort of local patriotism succumb to pressures from nationalism defined in greater terms. That was the case in Basra, where the separatists aimed for a city-state with mercantile cosmopolitanism rather than lingual or religious exclusivity as the basis for a common identity. (Shi'i sectarianism had no role during the early years of the separatist effort.) Similar schemes to create city-states later in the twentieth century, notably in Penang (now in Malaysia) in the late 1940s and in Aden (in the south of Yemen) in the 1950s, also disintegrated soon after their inception and likewise gave way to nationalisms with a wider range.[7]

This is a special aspect of Basra's failure that relates to a wider problem in the politics of nationalism: the general impotence of micro-nationalisms based on civic ideals, and the ascendancy of ideologies favouring larger and perhaps simpler definitions of the nation. Also here, a few contrasting success stories are noteworthy: In the 1920s, local politicians in Fiume (the city of Rijeka in modern Croatia) did manage to create popular support for a small, independent polity despite strong pressure from Italian nationalism; Singaporeans, torn between competing Malay, Indian and Chinese identities, have tentatively managed to develop a mercantile conception of national identity for the cosmopolitan trading hub.[8] Why could not the Basra notables achieve something similar, when their political ideals had so much in common?

Disliked by imperialists and nationalists alike, failed separatisms have been confined to the margins of historiography. Many projects of this nature feature in historical narratives merely as "noise" – unworkable, utopian visions that temporarily halt the progression towards greater nationhood before they give in to centralising forces almost as a matter of course. Such tendencies can be found even in the works of authors entirely disassociated from the nationalist paradigms in question. What little is known about separatisms in, for instance, Aleppo and Aden is thus found as sideshow material in some of the best volumes focusing on the larger entities into which these regions became incorporated – Syria and South Yemen. Here there is information about "a Christian nationalist organisation called the White Badge... [aiming at] Aleppo's separation from Damascus" and the Aden Association, "[advocating] that an independent Aden should join the British Commonwealth".[9] But these projects have received scant attention as subjects worthy of examination in their own right, outside the straitjackets of national histories.

One way of avoiding a passive projection of today's political map on the past is to employ counterfactual thinking.[10] As soon as the existence of a multitude of competing visions at a given historical juncture is ascertained, it becomes not only legitimate but indeed imperative to ask about the roads *not* taken – however pathetic and abject their failures, and however obscured their trajectories. Such counterfactualism permits a more *prospective* approach and an assessment of the full range of options available to the political elites at the time (including those that pointed in other directions than to the contemporary states), not only by contemplating "what if" scenarios but also by identifying potentialities that actually existed – and on that basis generating plausible "why not" questions rarely found in accounts preoccupied with explaining the forces that prevailed. In this study, such an approach means that the more predictable questions about why and how the victorious Iraqi nationalists marched forward in the south are matched with questions that arise from the alternative scenario of a stronger separatist movement: If the separatists had been more enterprising, would there have been cultural and symbolic resources readily available to buttress their vision? If they had been more successful with organising their campaign, would forces in the British imperial machinery have been prepared to support an autonomous Basra? What if the shaykh of the tiny desert emirate of nearby Zubayr had succeeded in persuading the British to create another Kuwait on Basra's doorstep? If such external factors conducive to the realisation of the separatist ambitions existed, why then did the separatists not exploit them? Pursuing this kind of counterfactual problems is necessary to explain the tortuous ascent of Iraqi nationalism, because only then will there emerge a fuller picture that includes both the deeper factors that were on the side of the nationalist forces as well as the degree of contingency involved in their eventual triumph. This is not an attempt at the Sisyphean task of obliterating teleology. Rather, it is a much more modest proposal to throw into confusion the traditional storyline by simply adding an alternative *telos* that can make for a different perspective on the past. In fact, both those who are mainly interested in Iraqi nationalism as well as those who are fascinated by the lost cause of the Basra separatists stand to profit from such a re-reading of Iraqi history, for the suppression of the Basra separatist movement in standard Iraqi history works has also meant the quiet interment of a good deal of information about the rise of Iraqi nationalism itself.

That nationalism, and its meteoric advances in the region around Basra between 1920 and 1945, have global parallels of their own. What links the Iraqi experience to a wider family of political ventures is the attempt to build a nation in a particularly challenging terrain – where religious, linguistic and administrative traditions presented a confusing criss-cross instead of cultural homogeneity that could unequivocally point towards a particular configuration of people and territory. In this respect, there are several similarities between Iraqi nationalism and the projects of non-ethnic nation-building in the states of Spanish America in the nineteenth century, and also between Iraqi nationalism and two of its contemporary cousins in Libya and Transjordan. None of the lands courted by these ideological campaigns formed an obvious candidate for nationhood, and yet they all went on to survive as separate states in the era of nationalism. How do the achievements of Iraqi nationalists in the interwar years compare with what happened in these territories? By 1945, was an "Iraqi" identity as meaningful and as well entrenched as an "Argentine" one?

Basra and the emergence of the modern Middle Eastern state system

From a regional perspective, the significance of the political turbulence in Basra in the interwar period lay in its contribution to an atmosphere of volatility. At least until 1928, echoes of the 1921 Basra petition for a separate existence lingered on and had a strong impact on local politics. In this regard, the example of

Basra separatism challenges the conventional view that the modern state system of the Middle East stabilised soon after the end of the First World War in 1918, or at any rate after the Lausanne Treaty of 1923 between the Allies and the Turkish nationalists.

Several recent studies show how localist movements elsewhere in the region had similar disruptive effects throughout the 1920s. Apart from the well-documented Kurdish aspirations for autonomy in their areas of ethnic dominance, there was resentment throughout much of the Arabian Peninsula at being incorporated into Najd (and later into Saudi Arabia), and regionalist movements emerged in Ha'il, Hijaz and 'Asir.[11] In the districts around Mosul bordering on Syria, both Yazidis and Christians supported local movements rejecting the Iraqi and Syrian states that competed for their loyalties.[12] Other regions which have received less attention by historians exhibited similar localist inclinations in the interwar period as well: In south-western Persia, autonomist tendencies among the Arab population remained strong also after 1925 (when Tehran initiated its centralisation policy), and mandated Syria was a patchwork of mini-states, with separate identity projects emerging in Aleppo, Latakia and Jazira – in addition to the better-known demands for self-rule from Druze areas in the south-east.[13]

All this means that the 1920s can be seen as an experimental phase in the history of the modern Middle East. Territorial stability in any meaningful degree was not achieved until around 1930, at which point there was a rapid accumulation of decisive bilateral agreements and treaties between key states: Iraq and Persia (1929 provisional agreement), Iraq and Najd (1931 treaty of good neighbourly relations), Iraq and Syria (1933 border delimitation by the League of Nations) as well as Yemen and Saudi Arabia (1934 peace treaty). Before these settlements, many of the existing states in the region not only struggled with internal enemies of their own, but were also extensively involved in subversive initiatives in neighbouring areas.

With all this seditiousness going on simultaneously within the region, challenging the newborn, European-designed and League of Nations–sponsored state system must have been perfectly plausible to contemporary local politicians. And yet ultimately no synergy powerful enough to topple the new order came about. A comprehensive analysis of the failures of individual separatist movements and the victories of their ideological adversaries therefore also involves studying wider regional links that had a bearing on the domestic tugs-of-war. In the case of Basra, this implies analysing several transnational processes, including both those that undermined the status quo (such as the diffusion of ideas from autonomous Muhammara in south-western Persia, or Basra's flirtation with successful state-builders in the neighbouring Arabian Peninsula) as well as those that helped stiffen the fledgling regional state system (like intergovernmental collaboration between Baghdad and Tehran against rebellious elements in shared border zones).

Basra and studies of Iraqi nationalism

Two broad approaches to territoriality are notable in the vast body of literature dealing with Iraq's history as a modern state. The main differences between them concern the extent to which "Iraq" is seen as a product of modern politicians, and, among scholars inclining towards a constructivist interpretation, when and how the concept is seen to have been created.

In the classical, nationalist position, there is little question as to what Iraq has been at various times in history. In this perspective, Iraq is an almost timeless concept that can be applied meaningfully throughout the history of mankind. In the introduction to *Britain and Iraq: A Study in Foreign Affairs*, which focuses on British policy towards the eastern provinces of the Ottoman Empire in the nineteenth century, some recurrent features of this position can be seen:

> Mesopotamia is the name the Greeks used for the land of The Two Rivers, but the inhabitants of the land have always called it Iraq. As old as history itself, there was a flourishing civilized city on the Euphrates called "Uruk". In line with the Semitic custom of calling the whole by the name of its parts, the whole land came to be known as Iraq... During the latter part of the [Ottoman] period Iraq came to be constituted of three major Wilayet (governorates): Baghdad, Mousil and Basrah.[14]

An altogether different approach is taken by historians who view modern Iraq largely as a British creation, an entity that emerged from the contingencies of the First World War, and with British rather than indigenous agency as the driving force:

> Iraq was a consequence of what may be termed a series of logical accidents. Basra was required for prestige and the defence of India; Baghdad for prestige and the defence of Basra; and Mosul for prestige, the defence of Baghdad, and the viability of the whole.[15]

In recent decades, this latter interpretation has become popular among historians, and today dominates in histories of Iraq written by non-Iraqis. It is frequently accompanied by an almost complete annihilation of "Iraq" as a historical concept possessing any degree of continuity:

> After a lengthy period of deliberation and indecision the occupying British authorities decided to unite the three disparate Ottoman provinces of Basra, Baghdad and Mosul into one nation-state that would be called "Iraq", a name borrowed from the medieval past of the region.[16]

The idea of Iraq as a modern creation is today *de rigueur* to the extent that proof of the country's "artificiality" is seldom called for at all. Historians who do feel obliged to provide some sort of justification for this position frequently turn to one of the first chapters of Hanna Batatu's milestone *The Old Social Classes and the Revolutionary Movements of Iraq*, suggestively entitled "Of the Diversity of the Iraqis, the Incohesiveness of Their Society, and Their Progress in the Monarchic Period toward a Consolidated Structure". A favourite citation is Batatu's example of how weights, measures and currencies differed among the three cities that were later to form the building blocks of modern Iraq – Basra, Baghdad and Mosul.[17] Once the premise of artificiality is established, inferences about deep-seated Shi'i separatist proclivities in "the south" often follow without any further discussion.[18] Even the authors of some of the most recent and balanced interpretations of Iraqi history express a degree of scepticism at suggestions that an "Iraqi" identity might indeed have pre-dated the 1914 British occupation.[19]

Two efforts to mediate between these polarised positions stand out. In 1994, Yitzhak Nakash published *The Shi'is of Iraq*, which emphasised the Arab (as opposed to the Persian) identity of the Shi'is in the former Ottoman provinces of Basra and Baghdad. In Nakash's interpretation, the processes of conversion of Arab tribes to Shi'ism in the region culminated in an attempt at "Shi'i state formation" – covering a territory referred to as "Iraq" – during the 1920 revolt against the British.[20] In his analysis, the territorial framework of the modern state of Iraq is thus linked to local processes that antedated the coming of the British in the First World War. Still, Nakash's main concern is to explore the "Arab" Shi'i self-identification, and the question of how the radical Shi'i clerics as early as in 1920 came to adopt the specific geographical concept of "Iraq" as part of their rhetoric is more in the background.

Another proponent of a "continuity" approach in studies of territorial identity in Iraq is Hala Fattah. Although her studies on trade and religious networks in the old Ottoman provinces of Basra and Baghdad concentrate on smaller regions, she also traces the emergence of a greater Iraqi identity among local elites in the nineteenth century. In particular, she singles out religious Sunni scholars and their attempt "to affix an Ottoman-Iraqi-Sunni identity" on this part of the Ottoman Empire, rendered as a counter-strategy to the growth of Shi'ism and the concomitant fear among Sunni elites of becoming marginalised.[21] Fattah identifies the writings of the Sunni cleric Ibrahim al-Haydari from the late 1860s as the seminal contribution to an Iraqist trend that grew stronger towards the end of the century. The conclusions of her analysis pose another challenge to scholarship that dates the creation of modern Iraq to the aftermath of the First World War, even though the exact mechanisms that made an Iraqi identity eventually replace regional ones receive less attention.

Most studies dealing critically with territorial identity in twentieth-century Iraq grant to Basra only a shadowy existence. Authors writing from a constructivist position often take for granted the presence of a Basra particularism, resorting to the heuristic (but grossly incorrect) model of a "Shi'i" Basra, a

"Sunni" Baghdad and a "Kurdish" Mosul, and sometimes surmising entrenched regional antagonisms merely on the basis of this analytical tool.[22] (In fact, the Ottoman province of Baghdad included all the four holy cities of the Shi'is as well as most of the Shi'i tribes of the Middle Euphrates, leaving the notion of Basra as the principal fastness of Shi'ism in this period quite untenable.) On the other hand, the Basra separatist movement that did materialise in 1921 is notably absent from these analyses – in fact, it has been left largely unnoticed by authors with nationalist, constructivist and revisionist inclinations alike.[23] Given the tension between the differing interpretations of the emergence of "Iraq" as a concept of national identity, the neglect of an indigenous political movement with an anti-Iraq agenda comes across as a serious historiographical lacuna, in particular because this movement remained demonstrably hostile to unity with Baghdad throughout the 1920s, only to suddenly collapse and vanish almost unnoticeably. In this sense, Basra separatism – through the story of its own decline – casts light on one of the most stunning achievements of Iraqi nationalism.

Basra, Iraq and the craft of constructing nationalisms

My argument in this book is that the movement to create a separate political entity in the Basra area failed because a potential that existed was not exploited. The failure was not due to lack of material resources, for the supporters of the project belonged to the dominant social groups in Basra and commanded control of both the prospering commerce of the city as well as much of the arable lands in an area unique for its agricultural productivity. Nor was the failure ultimately caused by repression from the British side. Although leading British policy-makers were rather hostile to the visions of the Basra separatists, their opposition to the project was tempered by their recognition of its underlying pro-British attitude, and leading personalities within the British administration in Iraq as well as in London repeatedly considered a possible British withdrawal to the head of the Gulf, even after the separatist movement had faded away. Nor was the scheme for separation crushed by the new Iraqi regime which the British installed. On the contrary, this regime took a rather passive stand vis-à-vis the local political scene in Basra during the first half of the 1920s, and the social dominance of the instigators behind the separatist demands persisted for some time.

Instead, the main reason for the separatist failure had to do with to the strategical choices made by the social elite behind the project. After having launched their movement on a cosmopolitan and secular platform with a petition for a special political regime, the separatist leaders went idle. They did not develop their dreams into a scheme that could fit the nuts and bolts of practical politics; they failed to trigger public enthusiasm for their conceptualisation of Basra's ideal future; and they did little to expand the coalition behind the scheme. As a consequence of this passivity, advocates of competing visions were able to take control of the political stage. The political energy of the local inhabitants was subsequently channelled in many different directions: Some groups attempted to establish even narrower territorial frameworks subdividing the Basra region; others looked to patrons elsewhere in the region – including Tehran, Riyadh and the holy cities of the Shi'is (Najaf and Karbala' in particular); while a third category of challengers emphasised links with the new Iraqi capital in Baghdad. None of these projects, however, saw the port city and its immediate hinterland as the ideal focal point for a political community. Thus the political visions of the powerful magnates behind the separatist vision gradually became marginalised, despite all the material factors that worked to their advantage.

Not until 1927 did a purely sectarian Shi'i separatist project emerge in the south. It was to prove just as inefficient as the movement for autonomy that had been framed in cosmopolitan terms, but for different reasons. The Shi'i separatist leaders did not hesitate to take their ideas into the public domain, and were able to back up their demands with powerful symbolism. Their problem was instead their position as elites within the Shi'i community. Young and innovative they certainly were, but their standing in the Shi'i scholarly hierarchy was modest, at most. Higher up in the system, other ideals reigned, and the quietism and anti-sectarianism professed by the leading ulama were firmly anchored in long-standing traditions in Shi'i political thought. None of this was the stock of ideas from which sectarian separatisms could be easily constructed, and Shi'i political activism in the interwar period soon reverted to a non-territorial agenda, leaving it to others to define the geographical framework for local politics.

Eventually the most effective competitor to Basra separatism was Iraqi nationalism. This was not because it was predestined to achieve such a prominent position: Basra before the First World War was a hub that connected India, Arabia and Persia with the inland Ottoman provinces, and the networks of its citizens encompassed all these areas. Regional connections to Muhammara and Kuwait were as strong as those to Baghdad at the time. On the other hand, the frequent contention that "Iraq" did not exist at all in late Ottoman times is not tenable either. For it did so, at least in the minds of some Basrawis, who understood by it roughly the area stretching from the Gulf to the northern reaches of the Ottoman province of Baghdad. My study emphasises how this new generation of intellectuals – mostly of Sunni lower and middle class background – managed to impose their own Iraqist territorial vision on Basra in the crucial post-war years of transition. Already experienced as career climbers and administrators in areas north of the Gulf city, they energetically set to work in the 1920s to promote a larger political community congruous with their own geographical zone of activity during the late Ottoman era, linking Basra to Baghdad and areas beyond. The concept of a "unified Iraq" gradually filtered through – in classrooms, in newspapers, in the activities of voluntary organisations and in the first rudiments of political associations. The cumulative effect of these efforts, greatly assisted by separatist inertia in the public domain, was such that by the time Iraq became independent in 1932, most territorial alternatives had already been sidelined in the southern parts of the country. That was a remarkable achievement, given the open-ended character of the debate only a decade earlier and the limited economic means at the disposal of the young Iraqi nationalists. Where they had succeeded in overpowering the wealthy Basra notables – and later persuaded the Shi'i clergy to come over to their own side – was in the professional field of constructing new nationalisms. Their victory was to have an enduring impact on Iraqi politics for the rest of the twentieth century, and remains influential today, as Iraqis set about structuring a new democratic system for the future.

I have divided the rest of the book into eleven chapters. Chapter 2 outlines the basic natural, demographic and economic characteristics of Basra and its environs around 1908, when the autocratic Sultan Abdülhamid II still ruled the Ottoman Empire. Chapter 3 seeks to give an idea of what "the state" may have meant to people living in Ottoman Basra, and the categories of political identity in local use at the time. Chapter 4 traces developments in Basra after the Young Turk revolution of 1908, when far-reaching changes in the appearance of the state induced local elites to come up with a political vision of their own, seeking to reform the Ottoman state, but also threatening it with more radical action. Chapter 5 goes on to analyse the collapse of Ottoman power and its replacement by British military rule during the First World War. The chapter also examines the evolution of British strategic thinking on Basra, a dimension critical to understanding the controversy over the subsequent separatist movement in the Gulf city. Chapter 6 charts how Basrawis in 1921 reacted to the creation of a British-sponsored Iraqi monarchy by launching a secessionist scheme. It then surveys the slim historiography of this protest movement and discusses some of the main divergences between different interpretations. Particular attention is paid to the way in which Iraqi historians have effectively consigned the subject of southern separatism to the footnotes of their scholarship. This is followed in chapters 7 and 8 by analyses of the failed campaign to turn the autonomist political dreams into reality, focusing on the local and the centre–periphery levels respectively. These chapters also describe the first seeds of a competing anti-separatist project – a collection of heterogeneous factions who nevertheless agreed that maintenance of the link with Baghdad was crucial to a happy and prosperous future. Chapter 9 shows how, in the context of passivity among the traditional Basra elite, political life in the Gulf city flourished in many different directions in the late 1920s, leading to new micro-separatisms as well as to movements connecting to capitals in neighbouring countries. Territorial changes in the wider Gulf region and their impact on the politics of Basra are a central feature of this chapter. Chapter 10 explores how the competition over identity definitions was at last won by anti-separatists who by 1930 had coalesced into an Iraqist trend – a nationalist current which rapidly gained such recognition that both friend and foe of the government in Baghdad came to speak the same language with regard to the territorial integrity of the young state. Chapter 11 summarises the main features of the separatist failure, examines the constraints facing elites with political visions kindred to those of the Basra separatists, and discusses the nature of the nationalist logic that eventually came to prevail – a logic that went on to dominate politics in southern Iraq for almost seventy years. Finally, chapter 12 turns to the situation in the south after the 2003 Iraq War and provides a survey of recent developments related to ideas of territoriality. It shows how the well-established paradigm of a unitary state contributed to Shi'i scepticism towards federalism in the immediate post-war period, and traces the emergence of a new territorial alternative which compromises between centralist and separatist extremes: a regional vision for the south, with Basra once more the linchpin – not unlike the status it enjoyed in the final days of the Ottoman Empire.

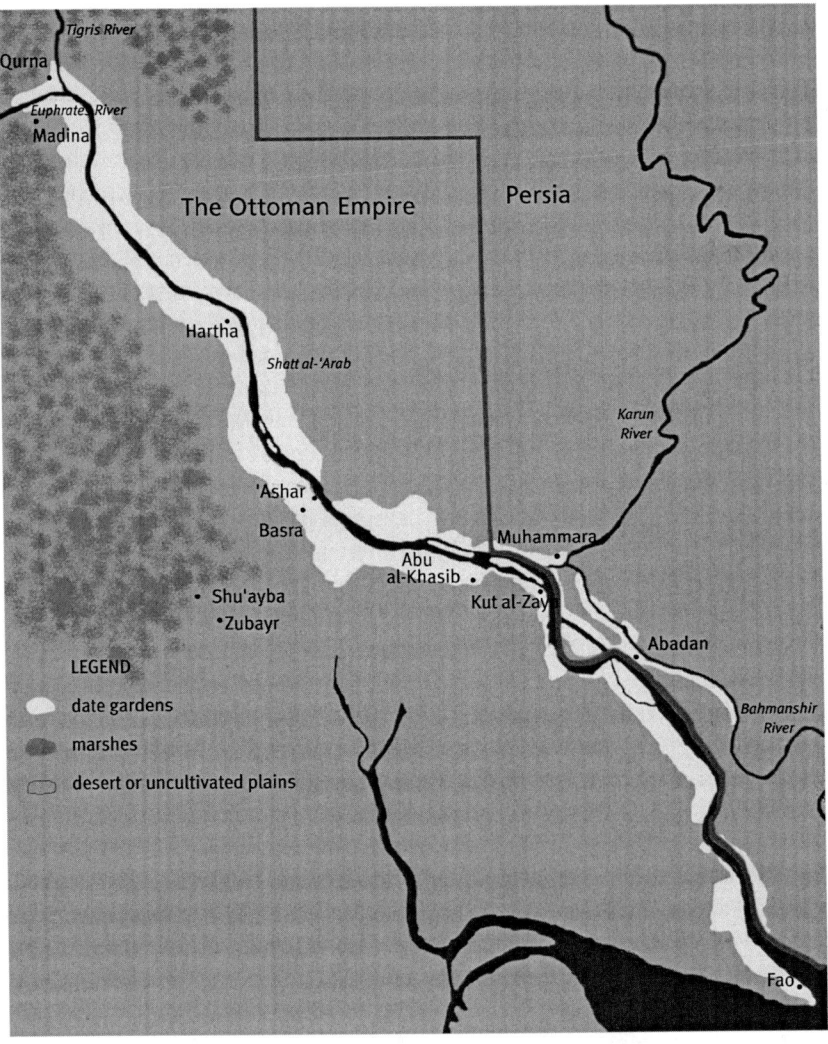

Map of the Shatt al-'Arab region around Basra in late Ottoman times (scale 1: 900,000).

2 The Land of the Date

The most prominent topographical feature of the region around Basra in 1908 must have been its date gardens – an almost continuous belt of palms on both sides of the Shatt al-'Arab, from the Persian Gulf to Madina on the Euphrates. At its widest, the cultivated zone extended for several kilometres on either side of the river. The area also included the Ottoman provincial capital of Basra with its suburb 'Ashar, situated approximately in the middle of the date belt, as well as the smaller centres of Abu al-Khasib south of Basra, Qurna at the junction of the Euphrates and the Tigris, and Madina on the Euphrates. Numerous hamlets dotted the riverbanks. The date belt continued on the Persian side of the river from the town of Muhammara down to the Gulf, constituting a region with common geographical features traversing the river.

Beyond this lush land, the physical environment was dramatically different. Flat desert – mostly barren wasteland, sandy in parts, stony elsewhere – adjoined the date gardens on both sides of the river all the way from the Gulf to Qurna. The only permanently inhabited site in this zone was the town of Zubayr, barely twenty kilometres west of Basra, but separated from it by salty desert soil unsuitable for cultivation. North of the city of Basra, the desert gradually gave way to marshes, encircling the cultivated belt to the west, the north and the east. Some of the marsh area was permanently flooded, consisting of lakes, rivers and swamps covered with reeds, while other parts were liable to annual inundations.[1]

Two environmental factors formed the basis of the agricultural wealth of the date-garden belt. The first was the Shatt al-'Arab, the river created by the confluence of the Euphrates and the Tigris at Qurna. It watered the date palms, served as the main source of drinking water for the population, and constituted the principal route of communication, as many overland paths could become impassable during periods of flooding. Indeed, the river was the sole possible approach to some outlying areas of the cultivated zone, such as Madina, a locality surrounded by marshes considered off-limits to the people of the riverbanks. The second main pillar for the rich agriculture of the area was the hot climate. Summer temperatures averaging more than 40 degrees Celsius and a high level of humidity created ideal conditions for the cultivation of date palms. Yet the life-giving nexus of water and high temperatures was also responsible for many problems. With late spring came the danger of inundation as the snow melted in the mountains and the water reached its highest levels around May. A serious flood could destroy entire date gardens. During the hottest summer months, the heat was so intense that those few who could afford it moved to locations with a more agreeable climate such as Zubayr or selected spots on the riverside, described by the Ottomans as oases in an otherwise insalubrious environment.[2] The combination of water and high temperatures also made Basra a breeding ground for flies and mosquitoes, which attacked both humans and livestock, and led to the proliferation of insect-borne diseases. Even sharks would sometimes migrate from the Gulf into the lower reaches of the river.

The date-garden belt was flanked by two eco-systems of a very different kind. North of Basra, the riverbanks could offer only narrow patches of terra firma. Beyond this land, great expanses of marshes opened up, providing a suitable environment for rice cultivation, a reservoir of reeds on which water buffaloes could feed, and home to a rich fauna which included wild pigs, migratory birds like geese and ducks, and a variety of fish. Constituting an enormous backwater to the great rivers, the area was less exposed to seasonal flooding as the waters would rise more slowly here. On the other hand, attacks from wild animals such as wolves and jackals, violent storms in places where the marshes were really seas, and diseases transmitted by snails were the principal threats to human life in this zone.

South of Basra, desert landscapes extended eastwards and westwards from the edges of the cultivated belt, in sharp contrast to the verdant riverside. Here, water was a scarce resource. Yet also this desolate space contained natural reserves exploitable to nomads with herds of camels, horses, sheep and donkeys. There were several wells and, in some places, good areas for grazing. For much of the year, however, large parts of the desert around Basra could be almost empty, as the nomads moved westwards to the vast steppe in the direction of Najd during the cooler months, when grass was plentiful in the higher areas.

Demography

Within this natural setting, the demography of Basra was intimately connected to environmental parameters capable of creating sudden natural disasters or outbreaks of serious communicable diseases. However, during the last decades before 1908, nature had been comparatively benign to the area. Heavy floods had become less frequent, and plague, which had ravaged the city during the late eighteenth and early nineteenth centuries, was now a rarity. Similarly, cholera had been declining during the late nineteenth century, although malaria remained a threat in the damp environment.[3]

These trends were reflected in demographic developments. After a fall in population during the early nineteenth century, the decades after 1850 were a period of recovery for the Basra region. However tentative and problematic estimates made by travellers are, they consistently indicate a city population dwindling from a high level (perhaps 50,000) in the late eighteenth century to a much lower figure (5,000 is suggested) around 1840, followed by a gradual rise.[4] More material indicators of the size of the population, like the existence of 500 to 600 houses abandoned in ruins during the mid 1840s, corroborate the descriptions of a temporary decline during the early nineteenth century.[5] In addition to a probable reduction in mortality levels, migrants from the immediate countryside, Najd, the Gulf and Persia, as well as African slaves added to the population growth after 1840.[6]

By the early twentieth century, the population of Basra had increased considerably. The Ottomans never had more than some 5,000 members of the urban population recorded in their registers, but Ottoman estimates of the total population were in line with most travellers' accounts, yielding a total of around 40,000 for the city and its environs.[7] The majority of the inhabitants of the date-garden belt, however, had their homes outside the city proper, in riverside hamlets. For this area as well, Ottoman registers included only a few thousand individuals, but government estimates gave totals closer to 100,000 people.[8] Apart from the population of Zubayr, which was said to be around 5,000, there exist no reliable estimates of the population of the desert and marsh zones bordering the cultivated area.[9]

Agriculture

Developments in Basra's main agricultural sector – the cultivation and trade of dates – provide another key to understanding the demographic recovery of the area in the nineteenth century. Date palms, which could live for some eighty to one hundred years, were planted during spring. They were watered by the tidal action of the river, so the most important task for the date-growers was to create and maintain a system of small channels to lead the water from the creeks and the main waterways up to the palms. The channels had to be kept free from silt to avoid disruptions to the water supply, and embankments were required to protect against the annual flooding. The date crop was usually harvested between September and November, a period characterised by intense activity and an influx of date-packers from peripheral areas with a more mixed economy. Some of the harvest was kept by the peasants (dates were a staple food for most inhabitants), while the surplus was shipped to Basra for export. The soil beneath the palms could be used to supplement the production: it supported the cultivation of fruits, vegetables and winter crops like barley and wheat. The area near Qurna had a more varied agricultural economy, with date crops complemented by the growing of rice and the keeping of buffaloes, cattle and sheep. Yet, even these most diversified agricultural districts relied on imports of cereals from outside the region.[10]

Apart from a damaging flood in 1896, which reportedly destroyed more than a million palms, the final decades of the nineteenth century were a period of strong growth for the date sector. Signs of increased production were evident by the 1870s, when much wasteland was developed to satisfy the demand from the export market.[11] A substantial rise in production took place during the late 1880s, when exports to North American and British markets gained pace. Within a few decades, these new outlets came to replace India and other regional markets as the principal buyers of Basra's dates.[12] Export statistics indicate that, with the exception of some years with failed crops, annual export volumes rose steadily from some 40,000 to 70,000 tons between 1887 and 1908, suggesting considerable economic growth in the period.[13]

Trade

Regional and international trade was the other main sector of employment in Basra. In addition to the export of dates, a commodity in which the region around the Shatt al-'Arab was one of the world's leading suppliers, chief export articles included grains and wool from the areas around Baghdad and Mosul, horses from the Arabian Peninsula and liquorice root from the 'Amara area. Imports consisted of goods like cotton, machinery, metals, tea, coffee, sugar, and rice. Until the end of the nineteenth century, African slaves also formed part of Basra's import trade, in contravention of international agreements to which the Ottoman Empire was a party. Much of the merchandise entering Basra was shipped on to Baghdad and smaller towns and cities on the Tigris and the Euphrates, with a substantial share in transit to western parts of Persia via Baghdad and Khaniqin.[14]

This voluminous trade had a profound impact on the daily life of many Basrawis, with distinct seasons for the major commodities. The trade in grains dominated the winter months, followed by wool, then horses and finally dates in two autumn months of intense activity. Most of the date-garden belt was to some extent involved: the city of Basra had an unrivalled position in trade with its two large bazaars and a steadily growing international business quarter in the suburb of 'Ashar, but smaller bazaars were also found in Abu al-Khasib, Qurna and Madina. Zubayr formed a separate emporium for trade with the large, nomadic tribal confederations living in the eastern parts of the Arabian Peninsula.

Basrawis of various callings had their daily jobs in this commercial environment. Professional merchants played an important role, but also many inhabitants with other main occupations would periodically seek to supplement their income by engaging in trade on a smaller scale. Other Basrawis became involved in trade more indirectly, as financiers, shipping agents, port labourers, packers or carriers. Moreover, international trade linked the urban areas to the countryside, where work related to the transportation of cargo was a major source of employment.[15]

With commerce such an important factor in the economic life of the region, the value of the total trade of the port of Basra is another key indicator of local development. Statistics for the years between 1887 and 1908 again show a general growth for the period as a whole, although figures for individual sectors reveal annual fluctuations much sharper than those that affected the date trade.[16] Commerce with India gained pace towards the middle of the nineteenth century; trade with Europe – Britain in particular – increased gradually after the opening of the Suez Canal in 1869, and then rose sharply after the turn of the century. As the annual tonnage figures for ships calling at the port of Basra increased,

Britain began to overtake India as Basra's principal trading partner also for merchandise other than dates.[17]

The processes of growth that exerted influence on Basra towards the close of the nineteenth century were thus linked with revolutionary developments in international shipping, trends in the world economy, and regional markets extending well beyond the limits of effective Ottoman influence. Dhows from as far away as India entered the Shatt al-'Arab, British steamers anchored outside the city of Basra and caravans from Arabia arrived in Zubayr, in a cycle repeated year after year. This is not to say that the Ottomans had no interest in these developments – indeed they had. Customs dues were collected, quarantine arrangements put in place and occasionally the export of certain items would be prohibited with reference to high domestic demand.[18] But, with a general policy of free trade, Ottoman attempts at directing and influencing these patterns could not substantially change the overall tendency towards British economic dominance.

Still, the demographic recovery and economic growth of Basra in the second half of the nineteenth century cannot be studied in isolation. It would not have been possible were it not for the fact that the state had made a comeback in Basra since the late 1860s. In fact, the Ottomans now controlled the Gulf city more firmly than at any point since the sixteenth century, as a look at some key aspects of social and political life in the area will reveal.

3   The Ottoman State in Basra, circa 1908

In 1908, Basra was a part of the vast Ottoman Empire, as it had nominally been for most of the preceding four centuries. Despite temporary interruptions caused by the emergence of semi-autonomous regimes as well as a brief Persian occupation, the Ottoman Empire had been the state power with the most direct impact on Basra ever since the 1530s.[1] Yet, the Gulf port was also clearly on the edge of the empire, some 2,400 kilometres from Istanbul, a distance even a swift rider would need more than 14 days to cover.[2] Baghdad, in Ottoman times, was considered so far away from the imperial capital that its marginality had become proverbial: "[Even] from Baghdad a false account will [eventually] return" (*yanlış hesap Bagdat'tan döner*). Basra lay further away than this.

Still, despite its peripheral location, Basra was also the Ottomans' point of access to areas of political and military significance. It was the central port of the "Gulf of Basra" (Basra *körfezi*), by which term they referred to the inner parts of the Persian Gulf. It was also a main centre of population along the disputed border with Persia, and the southernmost provincial headquarters before the Arabian Peninsula, which was under Ottoman suzerainty but had no government presence.

With this difficult combination of peripheral location and strategical importance, the Ottomans restricted their operations to prioritised tasks and geographical areas. The result was a legacy of "the state" quite different from that of provinces where government agencies could operate under more favourable conditions. In some areas of administration, it was the deliberate choice of the Ottomans to limit their role. In other fields, the state was forced, for lack of resources or in the face of unfamiliar challenges, to be less active than in more central parts of the empire. The consequence was that several non-governmental forces exercised influence in Basra alongside the state.

Ottoman administrative arrangements

Although the entire date-garden belt was in theory integrated into the Ottoman system of provincial administration as a *sancak* (district within a province), this small zone exhibited marked internal variations in terms of the state's involvement in local affairs.[3] In the urban area of Basra there was a fully-fledged Ottoman administration and daily encounters between the individual citizen and the state. Conversely, communities living on the margins of the district, such as the Dafir tribe in the desert west of Zubayr and the marsh tribes around Qurna, generally led their lives without reference to the state at all, with the tribe fulfilling central tasks of protection and mediation.[4] Most of the cultivated area around Basra lay somewhere between these extremes.

The fragmented nature of Ottoman involvement around Basra was reflected in the limited physical vestiges that reminded the inhabitants of the state and its

18

presence. Outside the urban neighbourhoods of Basra, any buildings associated with the state were few and chiefly linked with the military, like the small governmental complexes at Fao and Qurna, a barracks at Madina and a few police stations and army posts along the Shatt al-'Arab. Additionally, there were a handful of school buildings situated in the rural district south of Basra, as well as one in Zubayr. The Ottoman heritage was also meagre with respect to communications: although there was a carriage road within the built-up area of Basra, the creeks and inlets that ran through the city were the preferred routes of communication. Outside the urban area, the river was seen as the highway most firmly within the grip of the state, but Ottoman vessels accounted for only a fraction of the ships which plied the Shatt al-'Arab. There were practically no port facilities capable of accommodating steamers.[5]

Despite these superficial indications of passivity on the part of the state, there is much to suggest that the Ottoman role in the Basra area remained important. The very existence of large and valuable estates of date palms, a typical long-term investment, was one indication that this was an area fundamentally linked up with the doings of an organised state capable of offering the necessary stability.[6] And although the extent to which the Ottoman administration penetrated the districts around Basra varied from one locality to another, most people of the zone between Fao and Madina would encounter the state at several points in their lives.

Basra functioned as an Ottoman centre in several ways. It was the capital for the vilayet (province) of Basra, in theory comprising a vast polygon stretching from Qatar and Hufuf in the south to the Gharraf districts between Nasiriyya and 'Amara in the north, and often seen by the Ottomans as the nucleus for an even more grandiose sphere of influence extending into both Arabia and Oman.[7] Basra was also an important military centre, with a permanent garrison of some 400 to 500 men, and the headquarters of the Ottoman navy in the Persian Gulf region. Its naval base with around 200 to 300 marines served as the staging point for military expeditions and troop transports both upriver and to parts of the empire as far away as Yemen. Finally, Basra was an important customs collection point, the perfect location for overseeing the Shatt al-'Arab bottleneck through which maritime trade to upriver areas had to pass. Ottoman officials maintained a customs station in Basra's suburb of 'Ashar, where they levied duties on all seaborne cargo.[8]

This meant that Basra formed part of several distinct Ottoman administrative hierarchies. Historically, the area had been a province directly subject to Istanbul during the sixteenth and seventeenth centuries but was subsequently subordinated to Baghdad – which from 1747 to 1831 formed a semi-autonomous principality of the empire, ruled by freed Georgian slaves (*mamluks*). For the first decades after the Ottoman recovery in 1831, Basra remained attached to Baghdad, but later regained its status as an independent province directly under Istanbul between 1850 and 1862, 1875 and 1880, and finally from 1884 onwards.[9] However, the administrative separation from Baghdad was not total. Although the naval authorities in the Gulf answered directly to the Ottoman admiralty in the capital of the empire, the garrison in Basra received its orders from the headquarters of the sixth army corps in Baghdad. Similarly, the collection of customs was directed from offices in that city, and the jurisdiction of the Baghdad court of appeal extended to Basra as well.[10]

Officials on the Ottoman payroll in Basra were largely from outside the area. Many government officials had been recruited from parts of the empire closer to the power centre in Istanbul, but also the more immediate regions to the north of Basra, like Baghdad and Mosul, were well represented.[11] Similar patterns prevailed in the navy, with a majority of commissioned sailors originating from Istanbul, and smaller contingents from the Black Sea coast, Syria and Egypt.[12] With its stifling climate and peripheral location, Basra was not popular among professional officials, and turnover was high, particularly among army officers and bureaucrats.[13] Many of them were accused of exploiting their short periods of tenure in the city to maximise their personal profits rather than to advance the interests of the state and the public.[14] On the other hand, the naval base was seen as something more of a career opportunity, and its commanders tended to outlast several provincial governors.[15]

Only a small number of the persons employed by the Ottoman authorities were engaged in matters of local administration, and of these, few were stationed outside the urban area. Within the Basra *sancak*, the two *kazas* (subdistricts) of Qurna and Fao featured small permanent government administrations.[16] The next subunits within the administrative hierarchy, the *nahiyes*, of which there were eight, had a more improvised character. This administrative level was in many cases staffed solely by a *müdir* and his clerk, sometimes using their own dwellings as governmental offices. In some peripheral places, like Zubayr, there were frequent intervals when no Ottoman officials were present at all.[17] The expansion of the Ottoman administration beyond the city gates of Basra and the compound at Qurna was in itself a recent phenomenon: only since the 1860s had the state been able to assert itself in the Abu al-Khasib area to the immediate south of Basra; the fort at Fao was a structure dating from the 1880s; and the Ottomans were still busy regularising their presence in Zubayr as late as in 1895.[18]

Security and justice

In theory, all the lands of the empire were subject to the new Ottoman system of law which had gradually replaced the old Sharia-based courts in the decades of Ottoman reforms after 1839. In practice, the significance of the Ottoman state as an administrator of justice varied highly around Basra – with the city centre receiving the lion's share of official attention.

Basra was thoroughly pervaded by Ottoman laws and regulations. An issue such as the correct levying of fees in the local bazaars became the subject of detailed correspondence with the imperial capital; elaborate directives for government supervision of food prices were in place; and ambitious town-planning projects emerged, such as a scheme for eradicating mat huts (*sarifa*s, lower-class dwellings on the outskirts of the city susceptible to fire) to have them replaced by modern, brick-built housing.[19] Even some of the footbridges in Basra were subject to special tolls, leaving the poorest inhabitants with no alternative but to enter the water and swim to cross the river.[20]

There were, however, frequent complaints from the general public about the actual workings of the Ottoman system. Corruption and collusion with generous local forces was widespread, and serious crime, including burglaries and murders, went unpunished.[21] Harbour and river policing was ridiculed by British observers who grumbled about the impotence of a navy vessel that could "scarcely float".[22] Armed guards for the bazaars had to be bought by private capital; attempts to standardise measures and weights in local trade failed.[23] The periods of assertive and in some cases reform-minded governors were short-lived episodes, remembered by the population for the temporary respite from lawlessness and insecurity which they provided.[24] Despite all these shortcomings, the population definitely looked to the state for the provision of public safety in the urban areas, and made representations to Istanbul when they felt threatened by an increase in crime. The frequent conspiracy theories about local notables engineering sudden waves of crime in order to rid themselves of an unpopular governor are testimony that security was seen as a central aspect of what the state was expected to deliver.[25]

Beyond the city gates and the immediate confines of Ottoman outposts in the countryside, implementation of the legal system was sporadic. The sole policy not open to negotiation was the maintenance of telegraphic communications northwards, often under threat in the sparsely populated areas north of Qurna where semi-nomadic Marsh Arabs roamed.[26] Rather than being a permanent feature of rural life, Ottoman law came into practice whenever expeditions by the military or the gendarmes were successful in apprehending suspected criminals, who were subsequently taken to Basra for trial. The Ottomans were at times unable to enforce the law even at the centres of some of the *nahiye*s with designated military contingents, particularly in the peripheral parts of the *sancak*. Reinforcements from Basra were often required during quarrels between the Ottoman authorities and the local population in Zubayr, and special military expeditions sometimes had to be sent to Madina to address the most basic issues of criminal justice.[27] Finally, the desert was considered off-limits to Ottoman soldiers unable to match mounted camel warriors, while control of the marsh areas was limited to small garrisons posted along the adjacent main rivers, beyond which the Ottomans complained that the severe heat created impossible conditions for their troops.[28]

Where the state was unable to guarantee public security, other forces came into play. A distinct aspect of urban society in late Ottoman Basra was the prominence of criminal gangs. These were people who had been taken under the personal protection of their employers among the local notables and who lived from the booty of their raids, often having broken all links with the state. In 1904 one influential local resident managed to get sixty of his retainers employed as police constables, but they refused to take up their posts – because their names would then be entered in the Ottoman population registers.[29] Groups on the margins of urban society dominated these gangs. Africans (*zencis*), often slaves or former slaves, were frequently employed as assassins, and Arabs from the marshes were also recruited. Some ended their days in jail or were executed, but many managed to escape prosecution by hiding on the estates of their employers or their employers' protégés. Such was the power of these gangs that many Basra notables would dare to move about the city only when accompanied by personal armed guards.[30]

Outside the immediate urban area, tribal communities fulfilled many of the security functions which the state sought to undertake in areas more firmly under its control. Basra was frequently described as a "detribalised" area in the early twentieth century – a notion which makes sense to the extent that the entities claiming to constitute tribes in the area were much smaller and weaker in military terms than the large confederations to the north of Basra, such as Bani Asad on the Euphrates and Al Bu Muhammad on the Tigris.[31] However, also large zones within the date-garden belt continued to be ruled according to laws of tribal rather than Ottoman origin. Migrations during the past decades of agricultural expansion had created new villages populated by people of different tribal origins, but tribal units remained the primary point of reference for many inhabitants also in their new-found environments. This was particularly true of the *kaza*s of Qurna and Fao, but even within the urban hinterland of Abu al-Khasib and Hartha did segments of the population resort to tribal heads rather than Ottoman administrators for many fundamental concerns of daily life.[32]

The Ottomans spoke of the tribes in derogatory terms, emphasising their "wildness" (*vahşet*) and widespread illiteracy, and condemning their acts of plunder and robbery (*nehb ve garât*).[33] But to the local inhabitants, a tribal section – typically counting a few hundred armed men living with their families in a village society – could provide basic personal security as well as protection for dwellings, crops and livestock. Internal quarrels were settled by customary tribal laws, which offered solutions for crises threatening to disrupt village life. The organisation of agricultural production and distribution of income as well as other important questions affecting the future of the tribal section could be addressed through such tribal institutions as the guest house of the leading shaykh. Tribal ties and solidarities formed deterrents against troublesome outsiders by – theoretically at least – linking the section to a wider tribal confederation.[34] In sum, the tribal unit created a complete social framework where the state was in many senses superfluous, and, to some extent, could be seen as a rival.

Despite such conditions, the Ottomans did not do much to counter tribal fragments who preferred their own methods to those of the state. Within the date-garden belt, resident shaykhs with authority over several thousand armed men were limited to peripheral Qurna and Madina.[35] As long as basic security along the river could be maintained and the telegraphic communications system remained in place, the Ottomans made few attempts at breaking down what remained of tribal influence. Clearly, the state had different priorities when its officials ventured beyond the immediate urban area.

Taxation

A primary concern for the Ottomans was administration of agricultural lands. All lands in the empire were considered as state lands (*mirî*) unless specifically alienated as private property (*mülk*) or as religious endowments (*evkaf*). In theory, the state had the right to tax the *mirî* lands as landlord in addition to the tax on agricultural produce. However, in the nineteenth century, much of the state lands were actually held by tribes living outside the areas of effective government control, and these often paid no tax at all. In the second half of the century, the Ottomans encouraged those in possession of state lands to register their plots in *tapu* – a process which created private and hereditary leases and a form of landholding whereby the lands in question remained state lands, but the actual occupant received personal privileges guaranteeing his right to remain on the land. At the same time, the government waived its demands for rent, allowing the registrant to increase his share of the produce or to sublease the lands with himself as a landlord entitled to rent.[36]

Around Basra, as in many other areas in the proximity of governmental centres, the introduction of these changes from the early 1870s meant that almost all the cultivated lands were eventually affected by contractual relationships between their occupants and the state, as *mülk* (especially on the outskirts of the city itself), *evkaf*, or as *mirî* lands held in *tapu*. On the other hand, unregistered state land (held by occupants either through leases from the government or by usurpation) was a residual category of landholding found only in certain distant areas around Qurna.[37] Another consequence of the land registration was the emergence of a segment of absentee landlords. There was widespread fear among cultivators that the process was nothing but a prelude to conscription and many were reluctant to enter their names in the official registers. Instead, industrious townsmen made much of the new arrangements and the favourable terms, often through advancing dubious claims to areas in the rural hinterland. The importance of urban investors was enhanced in Basra because much of the land along the Shatt al-'Arab was still undeveloped when the new legislation was introduced, so capital investment was needed to turn these lands into cultivated areas.[38]

Another tendency particularly prominent around Basra was the initiative of some tribal leaders living outside the area to register as their own property lands occupied by cultivators over whom they made shadowy claims for tribal leadership. The outcome of this process varied from place to place. Individual members of the Sa'dun clan of the upriver Muntafiq area (along the Euphrates, north of the *sancak*) became nominal holders of large estates along the Shatt al-'Arab, even though their tribal connection with these areas was frequently questioned by the cultivators themselves. Often, the Sa'duns had to rely on influential nota-

bles of Basra in order to assert their new-won rights. Shaykh Khaz'al of Muhammara (in Persia), on the other hand, managed to centralise ownership of
several properties around Basra in his own name, and, from his base across the
river and outside Ottoman jurisdiction, exercised effective leadership for a tribal
community that spanned the Shatt al-'Arab.[39] Only in Qurna and in Abu al-
Khasib was the pattern of absentee landlordism broken, as some residents in
these areas did register their lands in *tapu*.[40]

As for the principles underlying the collection of revenue from these rich
agricultural lands, the system in use was a local peculiarity, based on age-old
traditions and subsequently adopted by the Ottomans. Tax was calculated on
basis of a fixed rate per *jarib*, a unit for measuring area roughly corresponding
to an acre – hence the size of the estate rather than the size of the crops governed the amounts due to the state. The original registration of lands according
to this system took place in the late 1860s; after a revision around the turn of the
century, no further changes in the rates were made. Accordingly, the extensive
regeneration of land during this period resulted in greatly outdated rates and a
very light burden of taxation, much lower than the fifth of the production that
was levied in other parts of the empire.[41]

The practical significance of the intricate systems of ownership varied. Correspondence between local and central authorities often concerned efforts to
settle land affairs and elucidate legal disputes. Yet, "snatching" (*nez'*) of land
was a frequent complaint, and some petitioners hinted that the local authorities
would occasionally condone such activities.[42] More systematic was the state's
approach in questions of revenue. Whereas Ottoman authority was weak in
many parts of the *sancak*, the state undertook revenue collection from a remarkably extensive area at the beginning of the twentieth century, covering
places far beyond the zones of permanent Ottoman presence.[43] Non-collection
in Zubayr and parts of Qurna was described as an exception to the prevailing
patterns, and the tiny strip from Fao to the junction of the two rivers produced
as much revenue as did the geographically much larger Hasa' (the south-
western part of Basra vilayet along the coastline of the Arabian Peninsula) and
Muntafiq together.[44] For tax on livestock, the institution of tax collectors
(*mültezims*) was widely used, often with sureties provided in landed property.
Income from animal tax was particularly important in the peripheral zones
around Zubayr and Qurna.[45] In this manner, taxation maintained a certain Ottoman influence in many districts where few other signs of the state were visible.

The state had a less direct role when it came to the relationship between the
nominal landholder and the actual cultivators. Although most date-growers
worked for absentee landlords from Basra, there were important differences of
status between them. In some areas, tenancies were hereditary; they entitled the
tenant to half the produce after government tax, but also implied responsibilities
in terms of bearing the expenses of cultivation. Known as *ta'ab*, this system was
another oddity of the Basra area not of Ottoman origin. In other localities
around Basra, often at places closer to the city, the position of the agricultural
workers was more similar to that of tenants elsewhere in the empire. The peas-

ants (*fallahun*) worked on contracts for a year or more; while they had fewer tasks than those working under the *ta'ab* system, they also enjoyed less protection against eviction and were given less of the produce, usually between 10 to 25 per cent after taxes. In some cases, the use of a tribal middleman (*sirkal*) would reduce the tenant's share by a further 5 to 10 per cent. A third category of agricultural workers had a much looser connection with the land and stayed only for seasonal activities, such as the planting of new date palms, or the packing of dates. Many of them were nomads from upriver areas or semi-nomads from the country around Muhammara. They worked for wages, were often paid in cash, and departed again when the work was finished.[46]

The Ottomans were not the originators of these arrangements, and their attempts at intervening in the relationship between tenant and landlord were far less methodical than their collection of taxes. There were instances where the state offered police support to landlords wishing to evict their peasants, as well as attempts on the part of the local authorities to reinstate tenants who had been unlawfully ejected. But many landlords complained that, despite large sums paid in tax every year, the state was unable to protect them against crimes committed by their tenants. The cultivators enjoyed tribal support and could seek refuge in territories where governmental forces were reluctant to enter.[47]

Conscription

Next after taxation, military conscription – introduced in Basra around 1870 – was the most intrusive feature of Ottoman rule. Christians and Jews paid a military tax instead of serving; otherwise recruits were to be selected from the entire male Muslim population by allotment.[48] However, exemptions could be bought by those who could afford it, and some groups in Basra had also managed to obtain collective dispensation after special agreement with the government. This included the people of Zubayr, who had acquired en bloc exemption under an agreement that instead bound them to act as auxiliaries against any attack directed against the Basra area from Najd.[49] Recognised descendants of the Prophet, including a few hundred Basrawis who claimed to have the medieval Sufi leader Ahmad al-Rifa'i as their ancestor, were also sheltered from the draft.[50]

Once recruited at the age of twenty, the conscript was liable for three years of service in the regular army, six years in the reserve, and eleven years in a locally based territorial army, before his service ended at the age of forty. In practice, the periods of duty were frequently and arbitrarily extended, and service in the army was associated with poor conditions and the likelihood of a premature death as a soldier of a badly equipped force. Recruits from Mosul, Baghdad and Basra (who formed the sixth corps of the Ottoman army) tended to be kept within the area of these three provinces, but military expeditions frequently took the soldiers to unfamiliar territory, as armed guards for tax collectors in remote tribal areas such as Muntafiq, or to outposts of the empire in the

Gulf like Hasa' or Qatar. Outside the region, service in Yemen was not un-usual.[51]

In the context of conscription, the Ottomans' distinction between people en-tered into the population registers (*muharrir*) and those that were not (*gayr-i muharrir*) was important. At the beginning of the twentieth century, the ratio was some 6,000 males actually featuring in the Ottoman population register in the *sancak* of Basra as against an (Ottoman) estimate for the entire male popula-tion at about 100,000. The process of registering the rural population had made substantial progress only in the districts immediately south of the city, and the inhabitants of this area probably felt the pressure of conscription in a much more material way than the 95 per cent of the *sancak*'s population not included in the state lists.[52] Still, the Ottomans found compromise solutions for areas not covered by their rolls, for instance by recording the names of the *mukhtars* (vil-lage headmen) only, and then leaving to the local population the internal scram-ble over who should serve.[53]

In this way, both city dwellers and villagers were affected by the threat of conscription. In 1890, an expedition was sent to Qurna to recruit local men to the army; at about the same time, a great many inhabitants of the west bank of the Shatt al-'Arab fled to Muhammara to avoid being drafted in.[54] For the re-gion as a whole, the state's actions yielded measurable results: In 1888, naval authorities said that the "required numbers" of conscripts had been obtained locally, and after the turn of the century the Basra area counted about 1,100 members of the reservist territorial army whereas the Fao area had about 950 men of the same category.[55] In one instance, a Bahraini resident at his own property in Abu al-Khasib was taken as a recruit and sent to 'Uqayr in Hasa' for service, which shows that even men of some means could get into trouble at the hands of the recruitment officials.[56]

Education and religion

If the Ottoman state was relatively effective in collecting taxes, customs duties and conscripts in the Basra area, it was underperforming in education and mat-ters relating to religion. Sunni Islam was the religion of the state, and was repre-sented officially by the government-appointed *kazi* (judge), *müfti* (legal author-ity) and through the government schools, where religion formed an important component of the instruction. But official statistics of the early twentieth cen-tury counted only around ten primary schools (each usually run by one or two teachers) in the *sancak* of Basra. For most of the late Ottoman period, there were only two secondary (*ruşdiye*) schools of the civilian category (for boys between 12 and 15 years of age) in the area, and, with the exception of a small college for the recruitment of teachers, no local educational options beyond this.[57] Private religious schools organised by Sunni Muslims had existed both in Basra and Abu al-Khasib, but many of these had declined and disappeared dur-ing the 1880s.[58] By 1904, the number of mosques with government personnel in the entire *sancak* was less than 30, half of which were situated in the city it-self.[59] In short, only a minority of the population of Basra was touched by the institutions meant to defend the religion of the state – a marked contrast to other parts of the empire which experienced strong growth in state education in the same period.[60]

During the nineteenth century, a formidable challenger to the state had appeared: Shi'ism. Until the 1820s, Basra had been described as basically a Sunni city, with a minority of Shi'is of mainly Persian origin.[61] Around 1830, however, a shift must have occurred. A Persian visitor in the late 1840s asserted that the majority of the population was now Shi'i.[62] Similarly, in the 1860s, a Sunni from Baghdad, Ibrahim al-Haydari, complained about the increasing influence of Shi'ism in Basra, whose inhabitants he described as "originally Sunnis". He portrayed the Shi'is as migrants from Persia, Bahrain and the Shatt al-'Arab region.[63] British consular sources from the 1880s point to the existence of Shi'i communities numbering tens of thousands, and a description of Basra published in an Ottoman calendar in 1890 gave figures of 50 per cent Shi'is among the inhabitants of the city, almost 80 per cent Shi'is in Abu al-Khasib and virtually 100 per cent Shi'is in Qurna.[64] From the early twentieth century onwards, a strong Shi'i majority was consistently reported in the city of Basra as well.[65]

The causes of this remarkable development in the region around a city which was after all an Ottoman provincial capital were complex. At the time, Haydari pointed to the absence of Sunni ulama in Basra, the consequent intellectual decay of the city, as well as immigration.[66] Population movements seem particularly relevant: Basra had experienced a dramatic decline of its population in the late eighteenth and early nineteenth century, and the subsequent recovery and population growth may have contributed to the change in its sectarian composition. An interesting testament to the buzzing migratory population movements in Basra towards the end of the nineteenth century is the distinction drawn in Ottoman population estimates between "natives" (*ehil-i asliye*) and "foreigners" (*gureba*), and the sizeable proportion formed by the latter in some villages.[67]

The influx of Persians was considerable, estimated at a quarter of the population by one traveller in the 1820s, and now encompassing all social classes in the city instead of being a small, mercantile elite only.[68] Still around 1900, various sources indicate a fairly large minority of Persians in Basra, in the region of an eighth of the population.[69] Anecdotal evidence also supports Haydari's contention that some of the Shi'i influence came from the Gulf, which contributed substantially to the stream of immigrants to Basra during the second half of the nineteenth century.[70] Sayyid Nasir, the leading Shi'i *'alim* (religious scholar) of Basra during the 1880s, was from Bahrain.[71] The existence of a community of Akhbaris in Basra also indicates links with that island, which was the main centre for the Akhbari sub-current within Shi'i Islam at the time. Shaykhism, a more unorthodox Shi'i trend which had been founded by Shaykh Ahmad al-Ahsa'i from the Hasa' area in the eastern Arabian Peninsula, was represented in large numbers, whereas a French visitor during the 1880s mentioned the existence of a community of Babis, an offshoot from Shaykhism.[72]

A second key to understanding the changes in the religious composition of the area during the nineteenth century is found in Haydari's remarks about immigrants from the areas around the Shatt al-'Arab (*ahl al-badiya min shatt al-'arab*) who had become Shi'is – the term *badiya* here referring to either the desert on the west bank of the river (inhabited by nomads) or the "open country" beyond the date gardens on the Persian side (home to a semi-nomadic population).[73] For these groups of converts to Shi'ism, parallels can be drawn to what took place north of the *sancak*, in districts closer to the holy cities – where tribal shaykhs in search of ways to retain their tribal prestige in a non-nomadic environment found suitable alliance partners in Shi'i sayyids (recognised descendants of the Prophet) looking to broaden their congregation.[74] The sayyids became important local figures in Basra as well; some were even given lands by Sunni landowners who were in the process of developing lands and in need of tenants ready to embrace a settled lifestyle.[75] Yet, the sayyids did not start from scratch, for in the rural areas around Basra – in contrast to the city itself – Shi'ism had enjoyed a certain popular base for centuries, as the many eminent Shi'i ulama recruited from the region bear witness to.[76] And the fragmented nature of Shi'i society in Basra, with subdivisions between 'Usulis, Akhbaris, Shaykhis and possibly Babis, supports a theory about diverse origins rather than a uniform process of conversion of nomadic tribes.

What was the significance of this rapid change in Basra's sectarian make-up? Basically, it meant that a growing number of the citizenry became members of congregations whose elites considered Ottoman rule illegitimate. In contradistinction to the Sunnis, Shi'i clerics held that a succession of imams of the Prophet's family had followed in his footsteps to form a unique link between God and mankind, offering guidance to the believers and carrying on the project of communicating God's will to man. The twelfth of these imams disappeared in AD 874 under mysterious circumstances, leading his adherents to believe that he had entered a state of occultation (*ghayba*) from which he would one day return as a Mahdi to restore justice in the world before its final destruction. In the absence of the Twelfth Imam, Shi'i clerics maintained, any human government would be problematic – and a government claiming to represent the succession to the Prophet but lacking a credible family connection to him (such as the Ottoman regime) would constitute blatant usurpation. Although sections of the Shi'i clergy by the early twentieth century had moved quite far in acquiescing with temporal state structures (seen most conspicuously in Persia, where in this period a clerical movement was afoot to actively reform and remodel the system of government), most scholars maintained the traditional ideal of keeping a distance from the modern state, in quiet protest.[77]

In this manner, the Shi'i ulama deprived the Ottomans of the recognition and support of a steadily increasing proportion of the population. In mainstream 'Usuli Shi'ism, the *mujtahids* (jurists qualified to interpret Islamic law) formed the alternative focus of authority, as every lay Shi'i was required to choose a *mujtahid* as a spiritual guide and source of emulation (*marja' al-taqlid*) for social and religious conduct. In Akhbarism, a more egalitarian view of the community of believers (and a more orthodox view of Islamic law) was the rule, but the ulama nevertheless had a leading role as narrators (*muhaddiths*) of the traditions of the Prophet. Shaykhism and Babism had strong eschatological elements, and had fostered leading figures believed by some of their devout followers to be the very Mahdi whose return all Shi'is were yearning for. The controversial views of the Babis had already made them into a persecuted group in neighbouring Persia, where they had been involved in political militancy and an outright assassination attempt on the shah.[78]

Ottoman efforts to arrest these mass defections to potentially subversive milieus were negligible, even though they had been concerned about the "day by day" spread of Shi'ism since the late 1880s.[79] The state had strengthened links with the local Sunni community and its leader, the *naqib*, had renovated several Sunni mosques, and viewed Naqshbandi Sufi brotherhoods in Basra and Abu al-Khasib as bulwarks against the influence of Shi'ism.[80] However, Istanbul did little to initiate a counter-policy within such key areas as culture and education, constrained as it was both by financial pressures and a limited ability to win over the Shi'is when an active policy was occasionally embarked upon. The schooling of the majority of children in the Basra area was in practice left to private Koranic schools where patterns of conversion to Shi'ism were reproduced, and nothing in the way of effective counter-propaganda against the Shi'i preachers was devised.[81] Even attempts at removing selected Shi'i students to surroundings more attuned to the ideology of the state failed. Special priority had been given to recruiting Shi'i pupils to a new school in Istanbul for children of tribal origin, specifically designed to shape the loyalties of an emerging generation of leaders from the peripheries of the empire. But for the year 1896 the authorities reported that only a single student for the tribal school had been found locally, and the recruits for 1897 turned out to be members of leading families of the Sunni minority.[82]

Whereas formal recognition of the Shi'is as a communal body was impossible for the Sunni state, their existence and indeed their growth was in practice tolerated. A Shi'i notable was even allowed to finance a small mosque within the barracks area in 'Ashar.[83] A telling indication of the difficult position of the Ottomans was the fact that Ottoman soldiers stood guard on ships carrying Shi'i pilgrims to Karbala' and Najaf.[84] The revenues deriving from the expenditures of these pilgrims were such that the treasury could not risk losing them.

The result of all this was a sectarian geography in the Basra area around 1908 dramatically different from the situation one hundred years earlier. Sunni strongholds could still be found within the old town of Basra, in the central neighbourhoods near the *saray* (government compound) as well as in the southeastern Mishraq quarter.[85] In these areas, many of the traditional elites of Basra society had their homes, with Sunnis of old and noble families living in close proximity to the most prominent Christian and Jewish notables. The mosques of the town remained mostly Sunni by denomination, thus contributing to an environment in which traditional patterns of Sunni dominance were more easily perpetuated. Outside of Basra, Sunni influence was limited to Abu al-Khasib, where there was a wealthy community of landowners and merchants, as well as Zubayr, whose inhabitants were mostly of Najdi origin and adhered to the Hanbali school of Islamic jurisprudence – reckoned as the most conservative branch within Sunnism.[86] In fact, Zubayr had acquired a certain character of being the last bastion of Sunni Islam in the area; it was to this desert town, named after a Sunni hero of the classical Islamic age, that wealthy Sunnis from urban Basra – whether Hanbalis or not – would transfer the bodies of deceased relatives for burial.

By now, the Shi'is had made inroads almost everywhere. The countryside had been profoundly affected by the processes of conversion, and the date-garden belt from Madina to Fao had become solidly Shi'i.[87] In the old town of Basra, the neighbourhoods around the Simar bazaar had been the traditional home of affluent Persian merchants, and during the nineteenth century nearby Farsi became a centre of Shaykhism.[88] Gradually, also many of the neighbouring quarters were influenced by a growing Shi'i population, but it was the suburb of 'Ashar which exhibited the most dramatic manifestations of the new trend. Whereas the Ottoman state itself had started an initiative for a gradual relocation from old Basra towards then-vacant areas along the riverside during the late nineteenth century, what developed here was hardly a model Ottoman urban space. Many immigrants from the Shi'i countryside settled in 'Ashar, and privately built Shi'i mosques proliferated.[89] Indian Shi'is also maintained a large guest house by the riverfront.[90] Moreover, foreign merchants were quicker than many of their Basra counterparts to appreciate 'Ashar's proximity to the river, and the suburb soon acquired a cosmopolitan atmosphere, with Indian, Persian and European traders prospering alongside Shi'i immigrants from the Gulf or the more immediate countryside. By sponsoring the development of 'Ashar as a competitor to Basra, the Ottomans in fact accelerated the advance of social groups who – in theory at least – were viewed as heretical enemies of the state.

With respect to non-Muslim communities, Basra was more similar to an ordinary Ottoman *sancak*, and the existence of small minorities of the other monotheistic religions was seen as an integral feature of Islamic society rather than any threat to the government of the kind posed by sectarian divisions among the Muslims. There were small communities of Jews and Christians, mainly concentrated in the old town of Basra. Armenians had first dominated among the Christians but gradually Catholic Chaldeans immigrating from Baghdad and Aleppo surpassed them in the nineteenth century, assisted by a steady influx of co-religionists from Tall Kayf in Mosul who took up work as crew for steamers on the Tigris.[91] There was also a community of Syrian Catholics, in addition to a lesser number of Syrian Orthodox Christians.[92] In line with official Ottoman policy, these non-Muslims were granted a degree of autonomy in religious and educational affairs. Many ran schools of their own, where subjects such as European languages featured more prominently in the curriculum than was the case in the state schools.[93]

A distinctly un-Ottoman aspect of Basra was the presence of a community of Mandaeans, a gnostic sect whose members described themselves as "belonging to the religion of John the Baptist". This sect was concentrated in rural areas further north, around Madina and 'Amara, but some members of the community had also settled in the city of Basra. The Ottomans treated the Mandaeans much as they treated the recognised non-Muslim communities of Jews and Christians, and accorded them exemption from military service on the payment of a fee.[94] There is no record of any outright conflict between them and the state, but their occasional requests for the good offices of British consular officials suggest that the lack of formal inclusion in the Ottoman system may have been a source of strain in periods. This happened for instance in 1896, when a Mandaean silversmith was accused of supplying bullets to (Muslim) tribal sections which had taken up arms against the government. His arrest in a context when all the tribesmen escaped justice suggests a certain scapegoat dimension to the affair.[95]

Other areas of government

During the early twentieth century, the Ottomans made several attempts at improving the efficiency of their administration and expanding the scope of the state's activity beyond its traditional minimalist level. But whereas other provinces saw novelties such as pharmacies, hospitals and in a few cases even state museums, the fruits of these reform policies were few in remote Basra.[96] Here, public health care was practically confined to a small dispensary as well as quarantine arrangements for long-distance travellers, and the most conspicuous public works initiative was a wave of road-straightening projects – many of which were subsequently abandoned.[97] Government projects were frequently sold to contractors rather than being carried out by the state itself.[98] The provision of drinking water and a public tramway were examples of projects where private initiative was expected; both failed to reach the implementation stage during the Ottoman era even though they had been under discussion for several decades.[99]

It could be tempting to use the customs house and the six guns placed directly outside it – representing the best of Ottoman firepower in the area – as a caricature of the Ottoman minimum strategy in Basra: accumulation of revenue, and military defence of the imperial periphery.[100] But this would be to ignore the more comprehensive vision of the state often discernable in Istanbul's correspondence with the local authorities, albeit infrequently translated into practical politics. One example of the more enterprising Ottoman state materialised in 1889, in Zubayr. Due to the lack of water and irrigation at the small desert town, large areas nearby had remained unproductive wasteland. To improve conditions, local authorities designed a canal project to connect Zubayr with Basra. The state allocated the necessary funds, implemented the scheme, and explicitly emphasised agricultural development (*ziraat ve i'mar*) as an important feature of its policy.[101] Similarly, at an earlier stage, the state had given dis-

pensation from customs duties on silkworms in order to encourage silk production in Basra – again indicating that it was not for lack of good intentions that
the role of the state was so circumscribed in the region.[102]

Where the state was absent, others stepped in – also forces from outside the
empire. Despite periodical efforts to reduce the dominance of foreign companies in the commerce and shipping of Basra, trading figures for the late Ottoman period show an increasingly strengthened British position. The commercial
involvement of foreign merchants was accompanied by further fragmentation of
the Ottoman role, for instance in the monetary sphere, where silver rupees and
krans featuring the portraits of British and Persian monarchs had largely replaced the Ottoman liras.[103] The trade of Basra also involved other states or
their agencies more directly: The first large financial institution to be established in the city was a branch of the Imperial Bank of Persia; the first limited
lighting and buoying carried out on the Shatt al-'Arab was of British Indian and
not Ottoman origin; and it was usual for citizenry of Basra to have their mail
delivered through the Indian postal service.[104] In this manner, Basrawis would
encounter representatives of several different states operating in the area where
they lived, to some extent competing with the nominal state power.

Political institutions

Despite government weaknesses, prior to 1908 Basra notables focused more on
getting a maximum out of the Ottoman system, and less on trying to replace it
with something different. Although the urban population resented oppressive
Ottoman officials, they were equally fearful of the potential excesses of
neighbouring tribal forces.[105] Accordingly, if an Ottoman governor proved too
troublesome, the local elites made attempts to get him replaced by someone
more amenable.[106] Landowners pursued influence at the central political level
through presents to the sultan or voluntary donations for charitable purposes and
relief funds.[107] Local merchants competed for concessions, monopolies and tax
farms for various consumables, and some Persians took out Ottoman citizenship
in order to facilitate their work within the empire.[108] Even from outlying Qurna,
where it was generally acknowledged that the writ of the state had limited impact, petitions would routinely arrive in Istanbul.[109]

The state also took steps to incorporate local elites into the imperial system.
They encouraged notables of the city to compete for titles and decorations from
Istanbul, and promoted participation by Basrawis in local administrative or-
gans.[110] A municipal council with a native mayor was instituted in Basra in
1870 and later at Qurna as well, and from the 1870s onwards the Ottoman governors and, later, subdistrict governors (*kaim-makams*) had administrative councils on which local notables were represented.[111] Although they were appointed
and dismissed by the authorities, these representatives of local society did have
some say in matters of local administration.[112] Also the Shi'is participated to
some extent within the system: In one case, a local Shi'i was able to rise to the

rank of a pasha and become head of the municipality of 'Ashar;[113] another member of the sect with a strong position in river steamship transport managed to acquire the support of the local authorities in his request for advancement to a higher grade in the Ottoman system of civilian promotions.[114] But with the Ottoman constitution and parliament in suspension since the late 1870s, the basis for much of this interaction between state and individual was clientelism – with few options for participation without resort to a culture of patronage and cronyism.

In the years before 1908, there was one notable exception to the picture of relative amicability between state and local population. Since the 1890s, the Ottomans had felt a challenge from members of an aristocratic family of Basra, the Naqibs. The name of this family reflected their role in supplying candidates to the position as *naqib*, leader of the *ashraf* (descendants of the Prophet) in the city – an honorary position which in practice remained hereditary for long periods, and for centuries had in Basra been associated with families claiming descent from the medieval Sunni Sufi saint Ahmad al-Rifa'i.[115] The Naqibs controlled sizeable agricultural estates in the area – properties theoretically set apart for charitable purposes and the upkeep of the Rifa'i shrine in the marshes north of 'Amara, but in the nineteenth century successfully registered by the Naqibs as their personal property.[116] Their material wealth enabled the family to act as patrons for the criminal gangs of Basra, and thereby to acquire a dominant position in local urban society.[117]

The problem for the Ottomans was not the strong position of the Naqibs as such – after all, they tolerated many infringements on their own theoretical monopoly of violence – but what the family did with it. Many believed that the Naqibs through their clients were capable of orchestrating disruptions to the security of the city, such as sudden upsurges in armed robberies or piratical activities on the Shatt al-'Arab. This was used as an effective tool vis-à-vis the imperial centre, as nothing was more damaging for an Ottoman governor than a stream of telegrams from his province to Istanbul complaining about security issues and accusing local authorities. As a result, several Ottoman officials came to blame their dismissals on the deeds of the Naqibs, whereas others capitulated and became pawns of the family, giving the local dynasty a free hand for instance in matters relating to their agricultural estates.

The Naqibs also had powerful allies in the region. Based across the river, Shaykh Khaz'al – the ruler of Muhammara and its environs as a semi-independent Persian principality since 1897 – was a power broker in Basra as well: much of the population on the Ottoman side of the river south of the city claimed to belong to his tribe and looked to him as their tribal chief.[118] This was a reciprocal sort of relationship, enabling individuals threatened by Ottoman authorities to seek refuge in areas controlled by Khaz'al, whereas the shaykh, for his part, could muster the tribesmen for seasonal agricultural work on his grain estates on the Persian side, as well as for military expeditions against contenders among the tribes of 'Arabistan. From the late 1890s, the Naqibs had increasingly collaborated with Khaz'al in seeking to oust bothersome Ottoman

governors in Basra, and the international dimension to their relationship made it
easy for the criminals they hired to escape across the river to the Persian side,
where the Ottomans had limited redress.[119]

The ruling family of Kuwait constituted the final element in what one observer described as a triumvirate directed against Ottoman interests in the
area.[120] The Ottomans had gradually given up exercising direct influence over
Kuwait proper – whose theoretical status as a *kaza* within the *sancak* of Basra
had been rendered next to meaningless when the British effectively established
a protectorate over the town in 1899.[121] But Shaykh Mubarak also became a
source of trouble in his capacity as a landowner along the Shatt al-'Arab on
good terms with the Naqibs. Here he possessed large estates over which he exercised effective jurisdiction, and many of the cultivators were of Kuwaiti origin and belonged to families over whom the shaykh had substantial influence.[122]
Occasionally, Mubarak even despatched large armed contingents to the area to
settle affairs connected with his properties, clearly encroaching on Ottoman
sovereignty and demonstrating the existence of another security gap uncom-
fortably close to the governor's premises in Basra.[123] After the turn of the century, the shaykh of Kuwait was less involved in organising outright banditry of
the kind pursued by the Naqibs and Khaz'al, but his continued friendship with
the Basra family added to the worries of the local authorities as it gave them
another field in which to put pressure on the Ottomans: the anomalous situation
in Kuwait, with no Ottoman officials and with clandestine British undertakings.
Repeatedly, the Naqibs exploited the "Kuwait issue" to bolster their reputation
as an indispensable force in local politics and a broker through whom a restoration of Ottoman influence in Kuwait might one day be accomplished – a prospect that in reality became increasingly improbable each time the Ottomans
made a new concession to the Basra dynasty.[124]

On the surface, this trio acted in accordance with the status quo, with the
Naqibs and the shaykh of Kuwait at least formally taking up positions in the
Ottoman administrative structure, and the shaykh of Muhammara resorting to
Ottoman courts to settle his land affairs in Basra. The Naqibs had, moreover,
built strong links to the sultan and his entourage, in particular the Aleppo-based
cleric Abu al-Huda al-Sayyadi, who was a Rifa'i Sufi like themselves.[125] One of
the younger members of the family, Sayyid Talib, served as governor for the
sancak of Najd from 1902 to 1904, although the Ottomans also kept a watchful
eye on him and monitored with concern his contacts with the Persian government and his travels to India.[126] Ambitions somewhat beyond those of an ordinary Ottoman notable did become apparent in 1904, as Talib arranged for a collection of poems honouring himself to be published in Cairo. Though rhetorically this publication stayed within the confines of accepted language (Talib's
accomplishments were described as acts of "devotion to the Ottoman sultan"
and his family's relation with Istanbul rendered as "bonds of servitude") the
presence of contributions from subjects of Khaz'al of Muhammara reminded
the reader of Talib's allies outside the Ottoman borders, and may even have
been seen as flirtation with Shi'ism.[127] The Ottomans found a typical compro-

mise solution for this ambitious young man by appointing him to a seat on the council of state in Istanbul – a fate that frequently befell notables in the Ottoman peripheries whose local influence was becoming too strong. Ultimately, also the Naqibs refrained from transgressing Ottoman red lines in the period before 1908, using their influence to maximise their own power within the system rather than devising alternatives to the existing regime.

Identity issues

Basra's contacts with the wider world pulled its inhabitants in several different directions. A limited number of local men chose careers within the state bureaucracy and were given jobs in the Basra countryside or in other parts of the empire, and a few became Ottoman servicemen through employment at the local naval base.[128] Both Shi'is and Sunnis travelled on pilgrimage to the holy cities of Hijaz and the symbolic pinnacle of Ottoman power, and a few Basrawis would even make the long journey to the capital of the empire at some stage in their lives.[129] An exclusive set of notables became fully integrated into the imperial elite, to the point where they, sons of the periphery, eventually adopted the discourse of the centralising state: in the 1890s, Ahmad al-Zuhayr, of a family of notables from Zubayr, presented proposals both for the administration of the Arabian Peninsula and for the pacification of the Dayr al-Zur district in Syria, emphasising such policies as bringing nomadic Arabs into permanent settlement (*masakin-i sabita*) and evoking the possibility of British designs and intrigues (*desais*) on the region.[130]

On the other hand, Basra's position as a port of trade as well as its religious complexity created links between its inhabitants and areas where the Ottoman position was even weaker, as well as areas outside Ottoman jurisdiction altogether. The immediate neighbours in Kuwait and Muhammara had managed to wrestle de facto independence from the Ottoman and Persian regimes respectively, and frequently received visits from Basra notables. Traders in Zubayr and Basra maintained contact with Najd and other parts of the Gulf (where Ottoman rule was only nominal), and cultivated links with Egypt, an area of Ottoman suzerainty but under British control.[131] Many merchant families of Basra had extensive overseas networks with branches in Indian cities such as Bombay, and some had travelled widely in Asia, even beyond India.[132] According to a common saying, Bombay and Baghdad had become equidistant from Basra after the introduction of steamships.[133]

Also the Shi'is had liaisons with multiple centres outside Basra. They went on pilgrimage to the holy cities of Najaf, Karbala', Kazimayn and Samarra' and followed the rulings of jurists (*mujtahids*) based in these centres of Shi'i orthodoxy.[134] But contacts within the Shi'i world at the time went in many directions and transcended imperial borders: Some Shi'is of Basra looked to Isfahan for guidance; many Shaykhis saw Kirman, also in Persia, as the spiritual centre of their faith; while Akhbari ulama (who had traditionally opposed the very concept of emulating a *mujtahid*) nurtured links with co-religionists elsewhere in the Gulf and around Suq al-Shuyukh, a desert town to the north-west of the *sancak* of Basra.[135]

Sources on the language situation, identity symbols and lifestyles suggest that the impact of this complex set of links was considerable and that Ottoman culture had several serious contenders. Knowledge of the Turkish language was very limited: Apart from a minority of locally recruited civil servants, Basra had not seen the emergence of a segment of Turkish-speaking Arab notables comparable in scale to that found in other large Ottoman cities, and the Ottomans often experienced difficulties in finding bilingual intermediaries.[136] Although some young men had adopted the clothing style associated with the Ottoman regime (fez and European-style dress), many Basra notables favoured attire of the kind in vogue in Najd and the Arabian Peninsula, consisting of woollen cloaks (*'aba'a*s) and head cloth held in place by elaborate head ropes.[137] Wealthy Basrawis had falconry, an activity mainly cultivated by Arabs elsewhere in the Gulf, as a favourite leisure pursuit.[138] But the situation in Basra was not a simple bipolar struggle between Turkish and Arab culture. English had made significant inroads as a foreign language.[139] Turbans similar to those used in Persia and India were in widespread use.[140] The music scene was dominated by the community of freed African slaves as well as the Jews, whose orchestras were in great demand for weddings and other local festivities.[141] In short, Basra's position as a mercantile centre on the edge of the empire made it into a breakwater where impulses from areas outside were constantly being thrust against those emanating from Istanbul.

During the rule of Sultan Abdülhamid, there were few vehicles for the articulation of political aspirations challenging Ottoman supremacy – if any such ideas should exist. Basra had only one printing press and one newspaper, both under governmental control.[142] Of the semi-public forums in the city, the traditional *diwan*s (informal gatherings maintained with a certain level of hospitality), which had fostered local literary talents in the first half of the nineteenth century, were now less flourishing.[143] A new trend among the Shi'is, the establishment of *ma'tam*s (assemblies with a similar social function but a more pronounced religious character) was still in its infancy.[144]

All the same, there is little doubt that the links between Basra and neighbouring regions helped to make Basrawis aware that, outside the effective rule of the Ottomans, there were alternative ways of political organisation, as well as larger cultural communities with whom they could feel affinity. Basra poets had rhapsodised over chiefs of the Gulf and the Arabian interior already in the early nineteenth century.[145] Later, many Basra notables functioned as local agents of forces enjoying an independent or semi-autonomous position within the empire, such as the amirs of Najd and Ha'il, the shaykh of Kuwait, and tribal chiefs in areas north of Basra like Chubayish and Muntafiq.[146] Some Basrawis were even accused of having spied for Ibn Sa'ud and sent in exile to Konya in Anatolia as punishment.[147]

Other stimuli came from areas outside the empire altogether. Local Persian merchants made requests for copies of a Persian opposition newspaper which monitored the debate over constitutionalism in their home country.[148] A number of locals regularly read foreign publications with a distinctly pro-Arab profile, including the London-based *al-Khalifa* – leading to imprisonment and forced exile in Diyarbakir in one case.[149] A tribal uprising north of Qurna in the 1890s became intertwined with wider sectarian and international questions when Ottoman soldiers shot dead a Persian trader visiting the area, and later explained the episode with a reference to his belonging to the same sect as the (Shi'i) insurgents (*eşkıya'*).[150] The Ottomans also worried about persistent rumours of growing British influence among the inhabitants of Basra, a tendency they speculated might be supported by the Egyptian khedive.[151] Yet no decisive initiative was made in Basra for changing the area's connection with the empire before 1908. Then, in July that year, the mammoth imperial machinery of the Ottomans was struck by a political earthquake. The convulsions were to be felt even in the peripheral Gulf.

4   Basra and the Young Turks

On 23 July 1908, under pressure from pro-reform officers and bureaucrats in the imperial capital affiliated with the underground Committee of Union and Progress (CUP), Sultan Abdülhamid was forced to restore the constitution that he had set aside in 1878. This marked the start of a period of unprecedented political openness in the Ottoman Empire.

An eyewitness to Basra reactions to the "revolution", the American missionary John Van Ess, described the Gulf city on the day of the regime change with these words:

> It was a sight for the gods to see Basra on that day when the constitutional regime began. Moslems hugged Christians and both hugged Jews. All called each other brothers. The Committee of Union and Progress then raised their heads. With a tray on which was the Quran and a revolver they clattered through the streets demanding allegiance to the new regime at the point of the gun.[1]

This snapshot captured several elements later to become prominent in the Young Turk regime: Public euphoria over a vision of a more egalitarian society that could replace the old order, attachment to religious symbolism despite flirtation with secularism, and continued use of violence in politics, new democratic ideals notwithstanding – all were to have some impact on Basra over the next years. On the other hand, the already existing CUP caucus interestingly alluded to by Van Ess (and presumably made up of government officials) was to prove less influential. In fact, for the first year and a half of the revolutionary era, very little changed in Basra.

Status quo preserved, 1908–1909

Initially, the Young Turks were more concerned with exploiting their new-found position in the capital than with attending to reform in the provinces. The extreme periphery of the empire was also the last place where anyone eager to benefit from the change of guard would like to be stranded during this crucial transition period. Basra experienced no less than four different governors during the first year of the new regime, none of whom managed to assert himself locally.

Instead, the traditional notables continued to dominate the interface between the imperial capital and the Gulf city, in much the same way as under weak governors in the past. The Naqibs remained in league with Shaykh Khaz'al, and their scion Sayyid Talib soon managed to get key officials in the local government on his own side. There was, however, a new facet to their sway over local affairs. A central demand from the Young Turks had been the reconvention of the Ottoman parliament, defunct since 1878. Parliamentary elections were held in early December 1908 for Basra's two seats on the assembly, with Sayyid Talib topping the list along with another figure from a well-established notable family, Ahmad al-Zuhayr – both now officially aligned with a local branch of the CUP. The two other candidates to garner substantial shares of the vote also belonged to the old elite of landed Sunnis, indicating that for now the local elite was coping with the changing times.[2]

If old structures of political power remained intact in Basra beyond the start of the Young Turk revolution, certain changes to local society were nevertheless evident. Education and freedom of the press were central items on the CUP's reform agenda, and the empire-wide proliferation of new schools and newspapers in the immediate aftermath of the events of July 1908 came to affect Basra as well. At the initiative of Sulayman Faydi, a young Mosuli who had moved to Basra a few years earlier, a private school was set up in December, patterned on a Beirut institution of learning where Arabic was the main language of instruction.[3] Turkish was also taught, emphasising the idea of Arab-Turkish brotherhood, and the project had the blessing of the local authorities in its initial year. It was a pioneering effort in a much-neglected sphere, and the school managed to recruit pupils from leading families across the sectarian divides in Basra, including Persians and Arab Shi'is.[4] Whereas the government also in the post-revolutionary period remained concerned about the strong position of Shi'ism around Basra, its own attempts at strengthening educational institutions by rehabilitating some old institutions of learning in the city failed to yield results comparable to the success of the new private school.[5]

Faydi was also influential in the second main new development to hit Basra in this period, the establishment of private, local newspapers.[6] His bilingual publication *İkaz* (in Turkish and Arabic), launched in May 1909, was to become a regular feature of Basra's intellectual life over the next year and a half – and the most enduring one of a total of four new broadsheets set afloat in the first year after the revolution. Throughout 1909, *İkaz* maintained a relatively neutral position vis-à-vis the CUP government. There was some mild criticism of the performance of the local administration, for instance complaints on muddy conditions in the 'Ashar River and the services of the local telegram office.[7] But there were also poems praising the new sultan, Mehmed V (installed by the CUP in May 1909 after they had deposed Abdülhamid), and casual reports on the activities of the local CUP branch – of which the newspaper's editor remained a member.[8] *İkaz* was briefly suppressed in the early autumn of 1909 after a quarrel with the local governor, but Faydi quickly challenged the decision by petitioning Istanbul, claiming the whole affair was a miscarriage of justice from which he expected redress once a proper investigation was carried out.[9] A few months later, the paper resumed publication.

A formally pro-government approach also characterised the first steps of the Basra notables selected to represent the area in the main new political arena of the post-revolutionary period – the Ottoman parliament.[10] Sayyid Talib's early contributions to debates in the assembly featured a demand for "more of the state" rather than less of it, with proposals for making the government's collection of taxes in the Gulf region more effective and for improving communications in order to challenge Britain's dominance in steamship traffic.[11] Similarly, Ahmad al-Zuhayr took petitions from Basra which were critical of the state of insecurity around the city and turned them into a parliamentary speech emphasising the dangers of foreign intervention if the Ottoman position were further weakened – thereby bringing the peripheral protest into a rhetorical form more acceptable in the imperial capital.[12] Zuhayr also voted in favour of the government's budget (Talib was absent at this vote), and participated in a parliamentary visit to Britain in the summer of 1909.[13]

Young Turk rule in Basra, 1909–1912

Süleyman Nazif Bey's assumption of the Basra governorship in October 1909 initiated a new phase in the Gulf city's relationship with the Ottoman state. Nazif, originally from Diyarbakir and formerly a government official in Bursa near the Ottoman capital, was the first post-1908 governor to make a sustained effort to implement Young Turk policies in Basra. Unlike his immediate predecessors, he remained in office long enough to make a difference, and was succeeded by two other strong-minded and long-lasting administrators, Hüseyin Celal Bey from December 1910 to August 1911, and then Hasan Riza Pasha until July 1912.

"Reform" was a watchword for the CUP. One of its first manifestations in Basra was decidedly physical, and reflected the trend among many pro-CUP governors of seeking to alter the spatial characteristics of Ottoman cities to bring them more in line with new ideals. Soon after his arrival in Basra, Nazif set about unprecedented demolition activities in 'Ashar aimed at improving the road linking the suburb to the old town. He hoped eventually to establish a tramway to facilitate communications between the two disconnected urban centres. The project met with resistance from several circles, including mercantile elites whose ramshackle warehouses and outlets stood in the way of progress, as well as Shi'i Indians who owned an 'Ashar pilgrims' hostel facing the same predicament. But in contrast to earlier governors, under whom such disagreements had invariably resulted in compromise with local forces and the effective dilution of government policy, Nazif stayed the course – and pressed ahead with the clearance work during the winter.[14] Other initiatives by the local authorities in this period, such as the expansion of telegraph services to Abu al-Khasib and an upgrade of police equipment (including new telephone lines), were improvements as far as security was concerned, but also implied that the state was consolidating its presence in the area to entirely new standards.[15]

In spring came a second indication that more profound change was on its way. For more than a decade, neighbouring Shaykh Khaz'al had, in cahoots with the Naqib family of Basra, abetted organised crime in the date-garden belt

by offering safe refuge for gangs of robbers, either at his seat of power in Muhammara on the Persian side of the river, or at his estates in Ottoman territory
south of Basra. In April 1910, after a new bout of trans-river marauding and
general lawlessness in Khaz'al's area of influence on the Ottoman side, Basra
police issued orders for the arrest of some of his followers, forcing them to seek
refuge at nearby Kut al-Zayn, where a key tribal ally of Khaz'al resided. Earlier
such incidents had usually resulted in the state meekly giving in to local forces,
but this time the government branded the villagers' refusal to comply as a rebellion (*isyan*). Failing to apprehend the men, the local authorities proceeded to
bombard the place from a naval vessel, inflicting extensive structural damage
both on the mud huts and some of Khaz'al's brick buildings, and causing such
terror that one of the wives of the shaykh allegedly died of fright.[16] The tribesmen managed to escape to the Persian side, but another indication of the new
determination to challenge local strongmen had been displayed. Moreover, Nazif's action was clearly part of a wider policy to improve the standing of the
government in the region – in this period the idea of upgrading Zubayr to *kaza*
status due to its "strategical importance" was being seriously considered in Istanbul.[17]

Even more threatening changes lurked in the background. Up until this point,
Basra notables had generally been able to secure for themselves seats in local
administrative institutions, if necessary by liberal bribes to the governor of the
day. But again, Nazif introduced new procedures. In early 1910, he snubbed
local notables in favour of a young and talented outsider in the competition for a
vacant seat in the local court of first instance, thereby signalling a meritocratic
intent that held the potential to upset existing relations between state and society
in Basra.[18] Even more worryingly, rumours emerged that the CUP planned to
convert private *mülk* lands to ordinary state lands of the *mirî* category. This
would increase the tax burden for many Basra landowners, and there was additional speculation that a more profound revision of the favourable terms of the
jarib tax assessment system was on its way. Stories of this kind remained current well into 1911.[19]

At the same time, CUP policies were beginning to contradict the liberal principles that initially had accompanied their revolutionary project. In particular,
some of the recently emancipated intellectuals who had found work in schools
and newspapers came up against new restrictions and constraints. Only one year
after its inception, the private school founded by Sulayman Faydi saw a takeover attempt by the local CUP branch, who intended to change its name and
make Turkish the main language of instruction.[20] Limits to freedom of expression in the press also became apparent when *İkaz* was shut down for a second
time in June 1910, after it had criticised the conduct of the Basra police.[21]

The Young Turk governors complemented their zealous implementation of
government policies with efforts to create greater public enthusiasm for the activities of the state. Before the revolution, any ventures of this kind had been
minimal in peripheral Basra, limited to the refurbishing of a few holy sites associated with important personalities in Sunni history such as the mausoleum of

Ahmad al-Rifaʻi in the marshlands north of the date-garden belt.[22] Heralding a change in approach, Nazif in 1910 sponsored a municipal project to erect a statue in Basra of the nineteenth-century reformer Midhat Pasha – in order to preserve the public memory of this great statesman.[23] Nazif's successor, Celal Bey, lent support to individual journalists sympathetic to CUP policies, and relied on them to buttress his local actions such as denying foreigners the right to buy land around Basra.[24] And in October 1911, in the context of Italian attacks on Ottoman lands in Tripoli, the last of the strong Basra governors loyal to the CUP, Hasan Riza Pasha, organised a large public demonstration, joining local groups under a pro-government umbrella. African drummers, horsemen from Zubayr and even some Jews came together in a united show of support.[25]

Gradually, the CUP managed to attract partners from local society. Some were individuals of relatively humble social origins or persons with a background as civil servants, fitting the description of the Young Turks' core electorate in the imperial capital and standing out in local society first and foremost because of their status as *effendis* – literate men with an education from the modern Ottoman schools. But also certain Basra notables started to interact more closely with the new regime, going beyond formal membership in the local CUP branch – in which almost everyone had enrolled immediately following the revolution. A prominent example was Ahmad al-Zuhayr, one of Basra's two parliamentary deputies. A local notable of high standing and one of the few Basrawis who had moved to Istanbul to serve the government under the regime of Sultan Abdülhamid, Zuhayr quickly metamorphosed into an eager supporter of the CUP. One of the most emblematic signs of his new party affiliation appeared in September 1910, when he presented the Ottoman state with a boat to patrol the Shatt al-ʻArab.[26] This was the perfect antithesis to the old order in Basra, in which the Naqibs in partnership with Khazʻal had used the Shatt as the main instrument in their Mafia-like activities. More notables followed suit, including ʻAbd al-Wahhab al-Qirtas, who succeeded Zuhayr as Basra's second deputy after Zuhayr died in late 1910.[27]

Other Basra notables found themselves less impressed by the new regime as its features grew more distinctive. In the days of Süleyman Nazif and Celal Bey, Sayyid Talib of the Naqib family twice adopted the old tactic of showering Istanbul with angry telegrams accusing local authorities of misconduct, in the hope of bringing about the incumbent governor's dismissal.[28] But also Talib's strategies of protest developed in this period and became more sophisticated, ultimately linking discontented Basrawis to citizens elsewhere in the empire who experienced similar problems with the government. The parliamentary arena proved particularly useful, where Talib began developing ties with other deputies critical of the government.

In late 1909 Talib made an impassioned parliamentary speech against the poverty-stricken government's plan to sell a river navigation monopoly for the Tigris and the Euphrates to a British firm.[29] In his Basra constituency, opinion on the scheme was divided: many prominent Jewish and Christian merchants were opposed to it because they feared a rise in transport duties, whereas other notables in fact owned shares in the British company in question.[30] In parliament, Talib added ideological force to the more utilitarian arguments, portraying the planned concession as a dangerous sell-out to foreign forces and reminding his audience of how British influence had crept into Egypt and the Gulf. Most other deputies from the regions affected by the monopoly also protested – some with pragmatic and protectionist arguments, others echoing Talib's focus on the direction of foreign policy and his implicit criticism of pro-British tendencies within the CUP. Although the government won the vote, the grand vizier resigned and the scheme was subsequently cancelled due to the strong opposition. Moreover, Talib's fierce anti-British rhetoric patterned on a public discourse in vogue under Sultan Abdülhamid connected him to a wider group of politicians also critical of the government. Many of them were sympathetic to the old regime, and in subsequent parliamentary sessions, both Talib and his new allies continued to use their votes actively against the Young Turks.[31]

In other areas of government, broad discontent was generated *because* of the new freedoms introduced by the Young Turks. With the sizeable post-1908 growth in education and media, language almost automatically became a contentious issue wherever an alternative to Turkish existed. In Basra, in 1910, one notable enquired why public announcements of the naval authorities were given in several foreign languages, including French and Greek – but not in Arabic; a journalist discussed the role of Arabic in the law courts (where the use of Turkish had recently been made mandatory); and another writer insinuated that the authorities might do well to study the British practice of respecting the local languages in the areas they colonised.[32] Again there were links to the larger Ottoman debate, where language was a hotly contested issue in many Arab, Armenian and European provinces, and deputies from these regions often found themselves in a common position vis-à-vis the government.

Basra and Ottoman opposition forces

By 1911, the list of contentious questions on which the CUP and local elites in Basra had differing views was growing in size. Certain concerns were purely local ones, especially the Naqib faction's worries that their dominance of local society through crime and bribery was coming under attack. Other issues, like the general nostalgia for the old regime and its more lenient practices, as well as specific questions like the status of the Arabic language, were connected to empire-wide agendas. On this level, the Moderate Liberal Party (established in November 1909) already represented an alternative to the CUP, and in September 1911, Sayyid Talib exploited growing local dissent to sponsor the formation of a Basra branch of this organisation. Combining his pre-1908 role as an affluent, charismatic boss for the criminal gangs of Basra with a new mantle as patron of talented journalists and intellectuals in the local press, he managed to persuade many local notables – mostly Sunni landowners and including several CUP members – to join his project.[33]

Although the Moderate Liberal Party (all its various branches considered as a whole) did have a majority of Arab members, it was first and foremost an Ottoman opposition party. Its concern for the Arabic language, Islam and resistance to foreign infiltration appeared more like a longing back to the previous regime than an attack on the concept of multi-ethnic empire as such. Defence of the empire's territorial integrity was certainly the gist of the ideological message disseminated at the local level in Basra, where one newspaper close to the party published a demand for improving the fortification of Fao, to prevent the lands from falling into the hands of "the West".[34] Similarly, protests against the closure of a law school in Baghdad were framed in terms quintessentially Ottomanist: the school should be kept open in order to maintain brotherly relations between Arabs and Turks.[35]

In early 1912, the Moderate Liberal Party merged with other oppositional forces across the empire to form a more substantial political organisation, the Party of Liberty and Entente. The Entente became the main challenger to the CUP in the ensuing parliamentary elections, and carried on much of the ideological heritage of the old Moderate Liberal Party. In Basra, the tug-of-war between Talib's faction and local CUP loyalists was now becoming more pronounced. CUP partisans were still able to secure victory for their candidate in municipal elections in March, but the parliamentary contest in April ended with a tie and two representatives to each party – following a campaign marred by irregularities and accusations of government violence towards the opposition.[36] Even more indicative of the CUP's waning position was the fact that they soon lost control of the municipality due to infighting among representatives, with friends of Sayyid Talib taking up vacant seats in the assembly as CUP men resigned one after another.[37]

Although local governors continued to promote CUP policies, there was in 1912 a reversal to old standards with regard to their length of tenure – few remained in office more than a half year. Local government activity also fell back to the minimal level seen before the Young Turk reformists. In June 1912, local authorities cited taxation and conscription as first priorities in a debate about administrative reorganisation within the *sancak* of Basra, issues that had been the preoccupation of the Ottomans in Basra for decades.[38] They were less effective in handling the counter-challenge in the ideological sphere from the Entente, and more and more Basrawis – now also including government officials – defected to the opposition as Sayyid Talib consolidated his recent gains.[39]

In July 1912, developments in the Ottoman capital further strengthened Talib's position, as anti-CUP forces in the military ousted the government and installed a new cabinet aligned with the Party of Liberty and Entente. A purge of CUP loyalists in the provincial administration followed, and extended to other bastions of Young Turk influence as well. In Basra, a local newspaper loyal to the CUP was closed down in this period.[40] During the autumn, several individuals in favour of the counter-revolutionary trend rose to positions of power in Basra, including an Arab vice governor who soon became aligned with Talib. People close to the Basra strongman also emerged victorious when parliamentary elections were re-run in the autumn; notables who had held on to their CUP memberships, such as 'Abd al-Wahhab al-Qirtas, now formally changed sides; and a period of unprecedented stability in municipal administration began as another pro-Talib personality, Salih 'Abd al-Wahid, assumed office in August 1912.[41] Local newspapers backed up Talib's political current with articles emphasising the centrality of Islam in the project of reforming the state.[42] Symptomatically, when rumours of an imminent attack by Muntafiq tribes were heard in November, the large number of armed men who were loyal to Talib were considered the city's key asset for self-defence – and a more significant force than the 300 Ottoman soldiers in the area.[43] Within less than a year, and by using traditional tactics in combination with new ideology, Talib had effectively turned state–society relations in Basra back to pre-revolutionary patterns.

Radicalisation and decentralisation, 1913–1914

Barely had the conservative turn in Istanbul steadied before a counter-coup by the CUP in January 1913 brought the Young Turks back to power, even more determined than before to monopolise power. Among their first priorities was to deal with growing discontent in multiple provincial centres.

Once more, the counter-strategy adopted by Basra notables wary of more Young Turk rule consisted of creative borrowings from other parts of the empire. In Beirut, Damascus and Aleppo, fresh reform initiatives had come to light during the brief counter-revolutionary period in 1912, and for the first time the instrument of territorial decentralisation (*lamarkaziyya*) had acquired widespread currency as a core demand in the Ottoman political process. In February 1913, Talib used these precedents as a blueprint for a new project – the Basra Reform Society (Jam'iyyat al-Islah al-Basriyya). In a petition presented to the government, the central demand was the immediate convocation of a council for the province to deal with local dissatisfaction.[44] In March, a meeting held with the shaykhs of Muhammara and Kuwait to amplify the new demands exposed the full regional and international dimensions that linked Basra to high politics.[45] Even at this stage, however, the reformists maintained conciliatory language. They framed their demands for a provincial assembly in the most general terms possible, and in carefully couched language described "the fundamental cause" of Basra's misery as "the utter destruction of science and education and all they mean in our environment" (*muhitmizde ilm ve maarif'in bütün manasiyle indirasi*).[46] Talib also continued to support the central government with substantial voluntary financial contributions to the ongoing war effort in the Balkans.[47]

The Committee of Union and Progress had a less sympathetic attitude to decentralisation than its predecessors, but did go some way to meeting the old demands for language reform in spring 1913. Along with a new policy of emphasising Islamic, Arab-Turkish brotherhood in the empire (now stripped of its

Balkan possessions), this helped to silence the calls for decentralisation in Syria. In Basra, on the other hand, the new law for the provinces provoked strong criticism in newspapers loyal to Talib and the aggressive attitude against the government showed no signs of abating. It was expected that the majority of the population "between Fao and Qurna" would support Talib if called to arms.[48] Feeling themselves threatened by the local political movement, the Ottomans conceived a plot to kill Sayyid Talib, and in June tried to implement it in alliance with 'Ujaymi al-Sa'dun, a leading shaykh of the Muntafiq tribal confederation. Characteristically, however, Talib had already been alerted to the scheme by one of his informants, and managed to have the plotters murdered.[49]

With this overt assassination attempt the gap between the CUP and Talib appeared unbridgeable. Although elections for a vilayet council were completed in July with Talib's supporters winning the highest number of seats, the Basra Reform Society now entered a phase of radicalisation – setting it apart from the other Ottoman provinces (where the tendency was towards compromise), and therefore requiring more creativity on the part of the Basrawis.[50] In August 1913, the party published a political programme that called for general administrative decentralisation for Basra province with local control of revenue, leaving to the central government only such matters as foreign policy, defence and imperial communications. Several specific demands were also listed: the official language of the province should be Arabic, knowledge of Arabic should be a prerequisite for holding government office, and concessions to foreigners should be outlawed.[51] Many of the points relating to general principles for decentralisation were clearly inspired by earlier demands for reform from Beirut, but the negative attitude to foreign intervention was specific to the Basra scheme and a continuation of a theme Talib had used rhetorically both before and after the Young Turk revolution.

Even more distinctive for Basra was a political pamphlet attributed to the Reform Society and circulated both in Baghdad and Basra in the autumn of 1913. The text fiercely attacked the CUP, warning of the secularism of the party, the government's intention to make Sunday the official holiday as per the European pattern, and its plot to sell the country to foreigners and Jews – the holy cities of Najaf and Karbala' inclusive. The tenor of the message was decidedly subversive, pro-religious and filled with pan-Islamic references calculated to unite Sunnis and Shi'is against a government described as "illegitimate" (*ghayr mashru'a*) and even "infidel". The remedy prescribed was still the "decentralisation" programme, but the seditious language was unprecedented.[52]

However, whereas his political movement retained an outwardly anti-foreigner outlook, Talib simultaneously turned to the British with private advances of a quite different nature. Between 1912 and 1914, he repeatedly approached British representatives with requests for assistance in transforming Basra into a special administrative unit whose status would be guaranteed by outside sponsorship, along the lines of Mount Lebanon or Egypt.[53] British officials maintained that Talib envisaged himself as the future ruler of such an entity, possibly in league with other autonomous Arab rulers on the Arabian periphery of the Ottoman Empire. In the inner circle of Talib's supporters among Basra's landowners, also others were said to favour the idea of some sort of Arab liberation under British aegis.[54] The pro-British theme, however, was not cultivated in the public addresses of the movement, suggesting that whatever preferences some moneyed affiliates of Sayyid Talib may have had for the British, they were deeply unsure about how such proposals would go down with a wider audience. In this way, the reform movement exhibited an uneasy dualism: in the public domain, the anti-foreigner rhetoric of the young, often lower middle class intelligentsia dominated; in daily business dealings, the wealthy landowning core supporters of the movement depended on British shipping and access to foreign markets – through which the annual date crops could shelter them from the economic turbulence of trade with other commodities.[55]

Developments in the autumn of 1913 and 1914 demonstrated the extent to which Talib's personal influence had been decisive in making developments in Basra exceptional in comparison with other provinces. For some time, the radical trend remained manifest: telegrams to Istanbul in December 1913 cited the fates of Albania and Yemen as relevant examples of what could happen to Basra if local demands were not heeded; despatches from the local authorities about "no developments of any political nature" throughout the autumn only signalled the extent of collusion with local forces now prevailing; and the new deputies returned to the Ottoman parliament in early 1914 were all loyal to the reform movement.[56] But then, Talib made yet another turn. He agreed to act as Ottoman mediator vis-à-vis Ibn Sa'ud (who in 1913 had occupied Hasa' in the Arabian Peninsula and thus stood on Basra's south-western doorstep) and reestablished peaceful relations with the government in early spring 1914. Instantly, the movement for decentralisation disappeared from the political scene in Basra.[57] A new Ottoman governor was sent to the Gulf city, and plans for reform projects, including enhanced postal services, electricity and a tramway, were again unfolded on the drawing board of the local government.[58] Yet, beneath the facade, the hard facts of Basra politics remained the same. Talib had full control of the process of appointment when a vacancy in the shaykhship of Zubayr emerged in June, and Basra was still seen as an area of refuge where individuals at odds with the CUP in other regions of the empire might seek shelter.[59]

Only in the extraordinary circumstances of preparations for war in the autumn of 1914 did the Ottomans decide on a showdown to eradicate the influence of Talib, and despatched a large special force to arrest him. Faced with this threat, the Basra leader chose exile rather than to try to mobilise for a confrontation. He departed for Najd and then Kuwait, leaving to his compatriots to deal with the Ottoman government in the increasingly apocalyptical political climate. The Basra reform movement found no new role without Talib – another indication of the personalism that had been so central to its success. By October, for the first time since 1912, the Ottomans were back in full force in the Gulf city, determined to guard the eastern approaches to their exposed empire in a time of escalating international crisis.

Territory and identity

Many of the demands put forward by the reform movement in Basra reflected ideas more firmly rooted in intellectual circles in other Arab cities of the empire, such as Cairo and Beirut, with which Basra had close contact.[60] There was, however, also some significant local input to the demands for decentralisation for Basra, in particular related to the concepts of identity used in the discourse of the new political movement.

Several newspaper articles in the press supportive of the reform movement employed the notion of "our country" (*baladuna*) or "our city" (*baldatuna*) as a basic frame of reference. For instance, in a complaint about soaring prices, a journalist wrote: "There is probably not a single *balda* in the world which equals the *balda* of Basra with respect to the increase in prices."[61] Or, as one of the first newspapers wrote in a leading article: "Basra, in contrast to the other Ottoman *bilad* [plural used with both *balad* and *balda*] is devoid of newspapers."[62]

The reform movement and its supporters also referred to larger communities of which Basra was considered to form a part. Local newspapers carried many articles on developments in the wider region of the Gulf and Oman as well as Najd, signalling an interest on the part of the Basrawis in events in the Arabian region beyond the imperial frontiers.[63] Indications of shared communities extending in a northerly direction were also apparent – as during the meeting between Sayyid Talib and the shaykhs of Muhammara and Kuwait in March 1913 in support of the reform movement, when those gathered emphasised the need to communicate with the holy cities of the Shi'is in a common bid for decentralisation.[64] In 1909, a Basrawi writing from Bombay referred to "the Arab world" as he enumerated ulama from both Egypt and Syria.[65]

The 1913 petition for decentralisation, which focused on the province of Basra as the framework for its demands, incorporated explicit concepts of identity with a wider range. Whereas all officials in a reformed provincial administration should have knowledge of the Arabic language, the requirements for the governor were more specific. He should be an "Iraqi", so that he would have "a complete knowledge of local tribal conditions".[66] Similar ideas were evident in articles in the press. The penetration of British influence into "the Iraqi region" (*al-qutr al-'iraqi*) by the strengthening of their position in the area around Basra, particularly at Abadan, was noted with concern by journalists in both Baghdad and Basra.[67] Another local newspaper article demanded Arabic as the official language and referred to "the Iraqis, and especially the Basrawis", who mostly could only speak their native language.[68]

As a geographical expression, "Iraq", in use since the classical Islamic age, had remained fairly common. For instance, in 1896 a group of Mandaeans, a marginal community in the Madina area just north of Basra, described themselves as inhabiting "Ottoman Iraq".[69] Similarly, in 1892, a Shi'i author born in

Basra wrote a treatise on the weights in use in "Iraq", where he included the standards peculiar to both Basra and Karbala'.[70] What was meant by "Iraq" was more disputed: Authorities on geography took it to refer to the triangular lowland area along the rivers from the mouth of the Shatt al-'Arab to Ramadi on the Euphrates and Takrit on the Tigris (in distinction to the higher lands to the north-west of this area known as al-Jazira), whereas the Ottomans sometimes referred to all the three provinces of Basra, Baghdad and Mosul as "Iraq", the Young Turks at one point even appointing a (Baghdad-based) "reformer" charged with improvements in this entire area, if only for a brief period.[71] However, the inclusion of Mosul broke with the standard geographical connotations, and this usage of the name was often accompanied by a clarification of the term.[72] Still, Haydari had written about "the Kurdish tribes among the people of Iraq" in the 1860s with reference to tribes and areas far north of Takrit.[73] The concept was clearly an elastic one.

Also the idea of "Iraq" as something more than descriptive geography antedated the efforts of the intelligentsia of the Young Turk period. As early as in the 1830s, the poet 'Abd al-Jalil al-Tabataba'i had paid tribute to the Ottomans for (temporarily) "retaking" Muhammara, conceptualising their victory as a restoration to Basra of one of its lands, as well as a triumph affecting "all of Iraq" (*arja' al-'iraq*).[74] This was a usage more impassioned than that of the geographers and administrators, and a sign of a wider sense of identity that appealed to certain segments of the population at least.

To what extent "Iraq" was meaningful as an identity label to the population at large is a more difficult question. There was certainly no shortage of alternative foci. Although the dynamics of life in hectic, cosmopolitan Basra tended to erode traditional loyalties to family and tribe, certain general categories denoting a shared geographical origin, like "Najdis", "Bahrainis" and "Hasawis", persisted.[75] The town quarter (*mahalla*) was an alternative frame of social reference in the urban environment, but *nisba*s (adjectives denoting descent or origin) based on the names of distinct town quarters were gradually disappearing, probably signalling a weakening of neighbourhood social ties.[76] Sturdier frameworks for a communal spirit were rooted in religion: Shi'i solidarities were at work when edicts from the holy cities induced Basrawis to support specific factions in local power struggles; the Jews had links with wider international societies such as the Alliance Israélite Universelle in Paris; and Christians maintained relations with representatives of the Roman Catholic Church and in some cases had taken out French citizenship.[77] Among the Sunnis, religion was also being utilised by movements with a political edge; this could be seen for instance in Zubayr, where a pamphlet appeared shortly before the First World War chastising Muslim parents for sending their children to private schools staffed by Christian teachers.[78] And on Basra's periphery there were further cases of religious mobilisation on a wider scale: In the autumn of 1913, the Basra newspaper *Sada al-Dustur* reported the formation of an aggressive Islamic association at Artawiyya in Najd, whose members called themselves al-Ikhwan (The Brethren) and demanded that others should join their movement or else be reckoned as polytheists (*mushrikun*) – an ominous forewarning of a wave of puritan Islamic campaigning from the Arabian interior.[79] Other movements were afoot in neighbouring Kuwait, where the Salafi teachings of the Egyptian modernist Rashid Rida attracted some young men of Zubayr.[80]

In the countryside, the village formed the most important social framework, but in the more transparent setting of the rural community, groups based on common descent could be maintained and nurtured more easily. Although several hamlets along the Shatt al-'Arab had a mixed population with various myths of descent, many households did perceive themselves as "satellites" of larger tribes with core territories further away from Basra. One such tribal confederation on the periphery of the Basra area, consisting of tribesmen from Bani Asad and Madina, had used the name *ahl al-jaza'ir* ("people of the islands") in the late nineteenth century, indicating a sense of territorial attachment to the area north of Qurna, where thousands of small "islands" formed the basis of settlement in the marshlands. During a rebellion among these people in 1895, one of their standards was captured, but its language or symbolism is unknown.[81] Similarly, tribes on both banks of the Shatt al-'Arab professing loyalty to Khaz'al were part of a larger tribal community with its centre in Muhammara, covering much of the geographical area of Persia known as 'Arabistan. Some of these tribesmen resisted Ottoman interference on the pretext that their shaykh was Khaz'al, but little is known beyond this about their conceptualisation of the community they belonged to, or their sense of identification, if any, with the territory inhabited by the rest of Khaz'al's tribesmen.[82]

These communities generally had little to do with the reform movement of late Ottoman Basra, whose elite was drawn from a particular social and sectarian background. The majority of Sayyid Talib's supporters were affluent Sunni landowners of the old town of Basra, and the intellectuals attracted to his project were also largely Sunnis, many originating outside Basra.[83] Both the local elites as well as the outsiders participating in the movement were further distinguished by the fact that most of them were already familiar with and had participated actively within the Ottoman system. On the other hand, the rural areas from Fao to Madina were not represented (except through their absentee landlords); the suburb of 'Ashar was peripheral to the new party (which had its headquarters in the old centre of Basra); and Shi'is and non-Muslims were grossly under-represented. Thus only a limited selection of the multiple concepts of identity in Basra found expression in Talib's political organisations between 1911 and 1914. But over the next years identity questions in Basra were to become complicated by the emergence of a new power in local politics. In November 1914, British warships were steaming towards the shores of Fao, with instructions to land.

5   British Occupation

In November 1914, the Ottoman presence in Basra and the surrounding countryside came to an abrupt end. Faced with an invading British military force, the Ottomans withdrew from an area that had formed part of their empire for most of the preceding four centuries. The local inhabitants woke up to a political vacuum where profound uncertainty about the future was the key feature. Was Basra now to become a British colony? What about the neighbouring areas – would they too be incorporated into the British Empire? And who would be in charge of the day-to-day conduct of local government – British officials or the Basrawis themselves?

For most of the war, these central questions were to be left dangling in the air. An important result of the worldwide conflict was the emergence of the concept of self-determination as a central principle for the post-war settlement. In theory, then, the Basrawis along with others "liberated" from the Ottomans were from now on to have a decisive influence on their own future. As this came so soon after the appearance of a local reform movement with a distinctive political agenda, the Basrawis could be expected to have views of their own on the issue. But, despite the fanfare as a new discourse of democracy and nationalism became established in international politics, self-determination in this age was not to become synonymous with the unshackled articulation of local opinion.

In Basra, Britain had interests of its own to safeguard. For more than a century, London had treated Basra primarily as an important commercial market within the Ottoman Empire, not as potential territorial acquisition. In line with this policy, free trade and blue waters had been Britain's main priorities in questions affecting the Gulf port. But, after the Ottomans entered the First World War on the German side in late 1914, such an approach became untenable. Imperial priorities were cast in a new light when the former policemen of the region, the Ottomans, were finally declared a spent force. Over the next years, Britain was to completely reverse its traditional policy on Basra – but the new line would prove directly related to tendencies discernible during the final decades prior to the war.

Basra in British policy before the First World War

Until the outbreak of the First World War, British policy towards the Basra area had been guided by an overarching commitment to preserving Ottoman territorial integrity wherever possible. In the nineteenth century, this policy had initially been pursued with optimism and hopes for Ottoman reform. During the 1870s, the positive view of the Ottoman Empire was shattered by increasing conflict between the regime and Christian subjects in the Balkans, yet the original policy was largely maintained. The perpetuation of the Ottoman Empire was perhaps no longer the objective of this exercise – but it was a useful way of averting the disequilibrium in European politics which would inevitably accompany a scramble for Ottoman territory, and of enhancing stability in an area strategically important as a key stretch of the highway to India. To approach Basra as a gateway for British capitalism, not a bridgehead for political expansion, was consonant with this policy.[1]

The nineteenth-century British practice of establishing treaties with selected local rulers in the Gulf along what became known as the Trucial Coast (modern-day United Arab Emirates, Qatar and Bahrain) was not essentially a contradiction of the government's basic policy, even though the Ottomans sometimes claimed the affected areas as their own. These moves were justified with reference to the need for complementing the Ottomans in peripheral zones where their authority seemed weak and where near-anarchic conditions threatened British maritime interests. The policy was comparable to other seemingly acquisitive measures taken ostensibly to safeguard the Ottoman Empire, such as the establishment of British administrations in Aden (1839), Cyprus (1878) and Egypt (1882). But in the Gulf, Britain chose to rely on local rulers whose main task was to combat piracies and, later, not to allow anyone else to control their lands. Anglo-Ottoman disagreements concerning the Trucial Coast were thus translated into a process which took the form of a traditional border dispute, where Britain claimed that areas controlled by the ruling families who had signed the original treaty arrangements were outside the Ottoman Empire. This process of demarcation culminated with an Anglo-Ottoman convention in 1913, which defined the Trucial Coast (and, further afield, Aden with Hadramawt) as areas beyond Ottoman jurisdiction.[2]

More complex was the background to British policy towards Kuwait, Basra's immediate neighbour and in Ottoman administrative terminology a *kaza* within this *sancak*. In the early 1890s, British policy-makers had not even contemplated challenging the Ottoman position north of Bahrain.[3] Yet, in 1899 the British and the shaykh of Kuwait concluded a secret treaty designed to protect the Gulf town against Ottoman encroachments. This has traditionally been explained as an effort to guard against any Russian or German threats in the shape of grand railway projects that might connect Europe with the Gulf by a terminus in Kuwait. Equally significant for understanding long-term trends in British policy, however, are some early suggestions for guarantees to the shaykh of Kuwait that antedated the discussion about Russians, Germans and railways. As early as 1896, officials at British diplomatic missions in the Gulf with a background in the Indian civil service had argued that in itself the autonomy of the shaykh of Kuwait represented something worth defending.[4] They saw the possibility of expanding the trucial system to include Kuwait – something that would represent a far more aggressive approach than the original policy, which merely involved stepping in wherever Ottoman failures created dangerous power vacuums. Here the idea was that a local shaykh was preferable to the Ottomans. Still, this special policy for the Gulf was allowed expression within an area like Kuwait, long considered as undisputedly Ottoman, only because it eventually came to dovetail with traditional British interests related to European power struggles – in which Russian and German expansionism were perceived as possible threats and constituted a legitimate basis for taking action.

The territory of the *sancak* of Basra north of Kuwait was not challenged by this current within British policy-making. Eventually it became clear that areas under direct Ottoman influence around Basra might also serve as a possible end-point for a railway line, but Britain never seriously contemplated annexation of Basra for the sake of a rail terminus. In 1906, a British report described such alternative termini as being "outside the limits of any possible extension of British protection".[5] Instead, Britain sought to obtain arrangements that would minimise the possibility of German influence at the head of the Gulf if the railway should indeed become a reality, and treaties in line with this policy (including a British veto on any railway construction between the Basra terminus and the Gulf coastline) were concluded in 1913 and 1914. And whereas Basra on two occasions received attention in military schemes for offensive action in the Gulf, the area was merely discussed as a spot at which British power could be easily demonstrated. During crises in Anglo-Ottoman relations in 1906 and 1911, British and Indian military authorities were asked to analyse the possibilities of a temporary occupation of Basra, but no decisive support for even such limited measures materialised.[6]

British representatives in Basra generally adhered to the policy of preserving the territorial integrity of the Ottoman Empire. One exponent of this attitude was Francis Crow, British consul in Basra from 1903 to 1914. Crow's chief aim was to create a secure environment for British trade. He criticised corrupt governors and praised honest ones, congratulated those who made efforts to pacify the tribes threatening river communications, and even made suggestions as to the best land policy for checking tribal influence.[7] Requests for British protection from tribes north of the Basra area, and later from Sayyid Talib, were routinely declined, often without prior consultation with his superiors.[8] Offers to the British from local landowners for purchases of vast estates on the Shatt al-'Arab failed to arouse his interest.[9] One official described him as "rather hostile to the Government of India".[10]

An expression of the British consul's pro-Ottoman attitude may be seen from an episode in 1910. The Young Turk governor in Basra had decided to do something about Shaykh Khaz'al's strong influence on the west bank of the Shatt al-'Arab, and his tribesmen's constant evasion of Ottoman authority. He launched a punitive expedition against one of the strongholds of Khaz'al's supporters, Kut al-Zayn. At first, Crow lauded the governor's action and commended him for doing something about Khaz'al, who for years had been a "thorn in the flesh" and a threat to public security in the Basra area. Later, however, he was reprimanded by his embassy in Istanbul, who made him aware that Khaz'al's autonomous position within Persia was supported by secret undertakings on the part of Britain. Crow subsequently found himself forced to acquiesce in Khaz'al's activities, even when they ran counter to his own vision of an improved Ottoman administration.[11] This incident illustrates the growing friction in diplomatic circles as to how to guarantee British maritime control in the Gulf, an issue that was to become much more pronounced after 1914.

Basra in war

After the outbreak of the First World War in August 1914, the scenario of an Ottoman alliance with Germany became more likely, and British policy on the Persian Gulf had to be adjusted. The map of the Gulf would look starkly different if Basra were transformed into a hostile base from which German naval forces could operate freely. The despatch of an expeditionary force to the head of the Gulf was conceived as the appropriate means to curb any such development.

Two concrete objectives influenced the decision-making process leading up to the campaign. The first of these referred to the long-standing British Indian aim of pacifying the Gulf through the "trucial" system of treaties with local rulers. The arrival of a military force would have a stabilising and reassuring effect on this system, and might also encourage a wider split between Arabs and Turks. In this respect, the motive of the Indian Expeditionary Force "D" (IEFD) was of a demonstrative rather than a possessive nature. A second objective was of more recent origin. After the discovery of oil in the area north of Ahwaz in Persia in 1908, the Anglo-Persian Oil Company had established a refinery at Abadan, on the east bank of the Shatt al-'Arab south of Basra. In January 1914 the Admiralty had voiced interest in the refinery for the process of converting the navy from coal to oil, and the protection of the refinery and the oil fields was added to the tasks of the expeditionary force.[12] By the autumn, it was clear that rapprochement between Istanbul and Berlin was changing the international landscape. On 29 October 1914, the Ottomans entered the war on Germany's side. Britain declared war on the Ottomans on 5 November, bringing to an end a century of non-intervention policy. British forces landed at Fao on the following day.

The Basrawis now faced a quandary. A regime with which most of the populace had been but vaguely acquainted suddenly expected their full loyalty, and many thought the Ottomans would pass death penalties against traitors.[13] The invading forces, though technologically superior to the Ottomans, were unable to offer unambiguous guarantees for the future. Sayyid Talib had estranged both the Ottomans and the British by his contradictory schemes for local autonomy, and was now in exile in Kuwait. In this context, what prevailed was the logic described by British soldiers as "upstream of us, hostile; downstream, friendly".[14]

Several leading shaykhs on the Shatt al-'Arab participated with the Ottomans in one of the few major exchanges of fire during this leg of the campaign. The battle of Kut al-Zayn, a village south of Basra, took place on 17 November, with some 1,000 Arab irregulars taking part in addition to the 4,000 Ottoman soldiers.[15] British sources claim that the Ottoman authorities had "ordered" local notables to participate as irregular soldiers.[16] Iraqi accounts, on the other hand, emphasise links to more fundamental ideological questions. One of the participants, a tribal shaykh of Sharish who died in the action, had according to his sons amassed an armed force as a response to the "arrival of a special messenger from the great *mujtahid* Sayyid Kazim al-Yazdi who brought the fatwa about the jihad" – a reference to the holy war declared by the Ottomans with the backing of the Shiʻi clergy.[17] Religious propaganda from the Shiʻi holy cities may have influenced other volunteers as well, as tribal leaders from Madina, Dayr and Hartha fought alongside a few pro-Ottoman Sunnis from the city of Basra and inhabitants of Hamdan village.[18] The British won a decisive victory and the Ottomans subsequently decided to evacuate Basra and to withdraw to Qurna. The invading forces entered the Gulf city without any resistance on 22 November, and managed to drive the Ottomans out of Qurna on 9 December. Thus fell the whole date-garden belt to a non-Muslim power within less than a month.

Local resistance to the British after the occupation was sporadic. A major confrontation between the British and the combined forces of the Ottomans and Arab paramilitaries at Shuʻayba in April 1915 did not involve local tribes to any significant extent.[19] Shaykh Ibrahim of Zubayr refused to join either side in the fighting, but was already providing the British with intelligence on Ottoman troop movements.[20] Soon after the fall of Qurna, the principal shaykhs of that area also transferred their loyalties to the British.[21] From then on, active resistance was limited to isolated localities and the fringes of the marshes.

British sources offer some glimpses of the scant opposition that did materialise. Throughout the spring of 1915, tribesmen around the Qurna marshes created trouble by engaging in sniping, theft of army stocks, and attempts to destroy telegraphic communications. Large groups of Arabs, often numbering thousands of men, gathered in villages, "dancing and singing", "shouting, stamping and gesticulating". British soldiers spoke of "Salvation Army meetings" that culminated in "flag-hoisting ceremonies", featuring green, red, orange and brown standards. Later followed attacks on British positions, accompanied by shouts of *la ilah illa allah* (there is no god but Allah).[22]

The slogans and some of the colours in the flags used (green was a colour associated with the caliphate, red was the colour of the Ottoman flag) point to the religious dimensions to these acts of resistance, and support for the jihad against the infidels.[23] But the presence of brown and orange flags suggests additional local – and tribal – connections. Among the most prominent participants in the anti-British resistance were tribesmen from Bani Mansur, Halaf and Sharish, all of whom had experienced recent attempts by their neighbours to assert tribal authority over them.[24] Making a stand in the struggle between British and Ottoman forces could be a vehicle for these tribes to establish themselves in local rivalries. Indeed, one of their adversaries, the shaykh of Madina, was quick to inform the British that his people were prepared to assist in punishing the pro-Ottoman Halaf.[25] The occupation authorities agreed to this "experiment", which reduced their security problems, but also had a marked effect on a local power struggle.[26]

Similar rivalries in the Basra area were brought to an end by Britain's selection of "friendly" shaykhs, whom they subsequently supported against challenges from other tribesmen. This was the case in rural districts south of Basra, where the influence of Muhammara-based Shaykh Khaz'al was tolerated and indeed encouraged; in Zubayr, where Shaykh Ibrahim ibn 'Abdallah was given a free hand; and among the Dafir of the desert west of Zubayr, whose shaykh's influence over client tribes was bolstered by Britain's insistence that the subordinate tribal sections use him as the sole point of contact with the occupying forces.[27] British authorities could perhaps not issue guarantees for the future, but they threatened with sequestrations, rewarded loyal shaykhs with confiscated lands, afforded leniency in fiscal questions, and distributed arms and monthly subsidies.[28]

Within the city of Basra, doubts about the future persisted for some time. Almost all administrative officials, as well as some local notables, fled with the Ottoman troops north to Qurna and later to 'Amara. At least one leading Shi'i notable continued to support the jihad propaganda also after the British occupation, by conveying messages from the holy cities to the shaykh of Muhammara in December 1914, trying to induce him to take part in the war against the infidels.[29] Until the battle of Shu'ayba, many inhabitants were anticipating the return of the Ottomans.[30] However, no organised resistance surfaced, and gradually the distance between Basra and the battlefront increased as British forces advanced northwards, pursuing an uneasy mix of military and political objectives.

Early wartime schemes and strategies

The main objective behind despatching the IEFD to Basra had been to prevent anyone else from using the area to threaten British interests in the Gulf. But the idea of a permanent British presence in Basra soon gained ground. In particular, the creation of the IEFD brought about a volte-face in India's attitude to Basra. Initially, its support for the campaign had been wavering, with the fear of provoking domestic opinion through a conflict with the Ottomans. Now that the war was an inescapable fact and India had been assigned a leading role in conducting the campaign in the Gulf, the viceroy, Charles Hardinge, became the foremost spokesperson for Indian annexation of Basra.[31]

Such annexation could serve several objectives. It would eliminate any restrictions on India's relationship with the shaykhs in the Gulf, which had been the subject of long-winded and cumbersome negotiations with the Ottomans for decades. It would fill the loopholes in Britain's security system for the Gulf by transforming Ottoman territory into British havens. Beyond the question of maritime supremacy, Basra was also seen as possessing intrinsic value: grand schemes which had emerged over the last decade for irrigating the land between the Euphrates and the Tigris were now linked to the question of finding an out-let for emigration from India.[32] After a visit to Basra in February 1915, Baghdad was also added to the viceroy's list of desiderata, but he maintained a distinc-tion between Basra, considered as a potential area of annexation, and Baghdad, over which he thought a looser form of protectorate should be established.[33]

In London, initial reactions to India's new-found enthusiasm for Basra were cool. The foreign secretary, Edward Grey, was anxious to avoid offending the other allies by further annexations and protectorates after Egypt and Cyprus had been joined to the territories of the British Empire in late 1914. But Hardinge's identification of Baghdad as a forward objective for the campaign gained sup-port among officers of the IEFD, who deemed it strategically sound. The mili-tary campaign soon developed a logic of its own, according to which it would always be desirable to control the tribes north of the occupied territory to pre-vent collusion between these tribes and the Ottomans. In this manner, a domino theory pertaining to the entire alluvial plain from the Gulf to north of Baghdad was established. Influenced by such views among IEFD commanders, India is-sued orders to secure the entire province of Basra in April 1915. By the autumn, this objective had been accomplished.[34]

A controversial aspect of the initial phase of the campaign is the extent to which Britain became bound by various declarations issued by officials of the IEFD to the population of Basra. Two statements in particular have been the focus of debate: the address by the chief political officer, Percy Cox, to inhabi-tants of Basra on 22 November 1914, and the speech by Hardinge delivered on 4 February 1915 during his visit to the area. In the former statement, Cox said, "no remnant of Turkish Administration now remains in this region. In place thereof the British flag has been established – under which you will enjoy the benefits of liberty and justice both in regard to your religious and your secular affairs."[35] In February, Hardinge stated, "we may be permitted to indulge in the confident assurance that henceforth a more benign administration will bring back to Iraq that prosperity to which her rich potentialities give her so clear a title."[36]

Highly diverging interpretations of these statements emerged. In London, many officials considered that a binding assurance had been given that the Ot-tomans would not be allowed to return.[37] On the other hand, IEFD personnel who hoped to allay local fears of a return of the former regime repeatedly ap-pealed for a clarification of British intentions – which indicates that the state-ments issued were seen as insufficient guarantee for a continued British com-mitment.[38] Perhaps the most unequivocal expression of British intentions is cap-tured in the secret letters issued on the outbreak of the war to the shaykhs of Kuwait and Muhammara. These documents contained promises to the shaykhs in return for their military co-operation with the IEFD, and asserted that their date gardens situated in Ottoman territory "between Fao and Qurna" should re-main in their possession, exempt from taxation, "for ever", if they entered the conflict on the side of Britain.[39] Such a promise implicitly envisaged British annexation, and the commitment to the shaykhs would continue to haunt Britain for several decades.

India's appetite for new territory in combination with the lure of Baghdad as a military prize of great symbolic significance had an impact on London's first attempts to study Britain's war priorities in the Middle East more systematically. In 1915, an interdepartmental committee under Maurice de Bunsen reached conclusions that were basically in line with Grey's cautious policy, and signalled a preference for a devolution of the Ottoman Empire rather than its wholesale partition. Nevertheless, India's wish for the annexation of Basra was incorporated into even the most conservative of the solutions proposed. The committee's report concluded that Britain's primary objective in the region should be to "straighten ragged edges" rather than acquire new territory.[40] The incorporation of Basra into the trucial system would, it was felt, accomplish this end.

Notions of a special position for Britain in Basra and perhaps also Baghdad were thus beginning to take root in London, although the recommendations of the de Bunsen committee were never adopted as official policy. Again other circles, particularly within the Foreign Office, held a view of the Arab provinces of the Ottoman Empire considerably different from that of the Indian government, envisaging a far more active role for the local population in bringing about liberation from the Ottomans. When the British later in 1915 decided to support a revolt against the Ottomans led by the sharif of Mecca and some form of Arab semi-independence after the war, this dualism caused them to expressly except Basra and Baghdad from the general plan of Arab self-rule. Their reservations were embodied both in the correspondence with the sharif as well as in the Sykes-Picot agreement with France – the two famous British commitments to future political arrangements in the Middle East that were later to have a profound impact on London's ideas about the post-war settlement in the region.

The inclusion of Baghdad along with Basra in these documents had resulted from a sudden optimism over the possibilities for a quick British military triumph. Instead, a severe setback followed, with collapse on the Tigris front and a humiliating retreat southwards. A full withdrawal to a coastal enclave around Basra received serious attention in Whitehall in the summer of 1916.[41] But the eyes of many politicians had by now become fixed on Baghdad as a natural focus for a British advance, at least as an effort to inflict a symbolically important defeat on the Ottomans. Offensive operations were restarted in the autumn, and in March 1917, British forces finally reached the coveted city.

Discussions over more long-term political objectives could now resume. The conclusions of an interdepartmental committee for the administration of the areas controlled by the British forces emphasised a compromise between the supporters of annexation and those who favoured semi-independence for the Arabs. This was achieved by a policy of administrative differentiation between the vilayet of Basra, which was to be annexed (but by Britain rather than by India, which had been stripped of its supervisory role after the 1916 military defeats), and Baghdad, where a British protectorate with an "Arab facade" was to be established.[42] To London, a two-state solution seemed the ideal way forward.

The British officials then in Baghdad had misgivings about the idea of Arab self-rule as well as the prospects of administrative differentiation. Cox asserted that it would be "much more satisfactory" to have a uniform administration for the two provinces – a solution he considered compatible with a distinction in terms of political status, which "need not make itself felt on the spot".[43] However, he also disclosed a fundamental dislike of the whole project of political differentiation, describing the two provinces as "from every point of view inseparable" and using terms such as "united Mesopotamia". Cox's hostility to the introduction of special regimes was further expressed by his criticism of a proposal for an independent Shi'i enclave around the holy cities. But London's policy remained unchanged for the rest of 1917, and the option of handing back Baghdad to the Ottomans while keeping Basra as a British colony surfaced repeatedly during discussions over policy.[44]

Basra under British rule

Meanwhile, at the local level in Basra, British officials made much of the assumed difference between their own rule of occupation and the regime of their predecessors.[45] In some spheres of government, changes were indeed evident. A new police force (partly made up by Persians and Indians) brought a sense of improved security to the urban areas.[46] The Ottoman legal system was replaced by a code based largely on an Indian model, except for personal status law where the existing regime was maintained – with the important modification of Shi'i judges for the first time receiving official recognition along with their Sunni and non-Muslim counterparts.[47] There was a clear expansion of government activity in the health sector, with the creation of new hospitals and dispensaries in Basra, Fao, Qurna and Zubayr.[48] The military campaign demanded an upgrade of infrastructure in the area, resulting in a hyper-modern port terminal, a railway gradually expanding northwards, improvements to the local road network, and a piping system for drinking water for the troops.[49] Conscription was abolished, although forced labour for wages at government rates was imposed on some rural communities.[50]

Still, many spheres of Basra society remained untouched by the new regime. British authorities refrained from policing the countryside, and came to rely on trusted tribal shaykhs and headmen.[51] The actual workings of the "tribal equilibrium" were without interest as long as no serious threat was posed against British interests. Consequently, violence threatening the stability of this system was punished, while violence within the units of the system was ignored and sometimes even encouraged, especially in cases where it could be seen as helping to keep existing arrangements in place. British reports approved of "slight extortions" on the part of shaykhs against tribal subjects and attempts to "bring to heel" groups which had "assumed an independent attitude".[52] Similarly, they reported that the tribal influence of Khaz'al provided "freedom of crime in the Fao district where no police is required and no crime is taking place" – a statement which was either naive, or meant that the autocratic behaviour of selected strongmen had a green light from the occupation authorities.[53] The most notable difference from the Ottoman regime was that the practice of non-involvement was now made official and codified – through the "Tribal Criminal and Civil Disputes Regulations", which gave customary tribal law a central position in the legal system for the countryside.[54]

In other areas of administration, much of the Ottoman arrangements were maintained, or legacies of inaction perpetuated. The revenue system was left largely unchanged, and Ottoman documents were used as the basis for settling land disputes. In localities near the British military camps there were investments and construction projects related to the war effort, but infrastructure other than that directly related to the well-being of the occupation forces was neglected. Where there were no troops, little expansion of the state's activities took place beyond basic upgrading of healthcare.[55]

Another similarity to the Ottoman era was passivity in education. The British closed the few existing schools and were slow in opening new ones, in particular at the secondary level, where they feared political activity.[56] As a result, only a handful of schools, all at the primary level, were in operation during the war – and due to the lack of British staff, wide-ranging autonomy was granted to the American missionary and pre-war resident of Basra, John Van Ess, in organising the first official schools.[57] Also the participation of the native population in the administration of local affairs remained limited; in the urban areas it actually declined during the early war years. Selected notables were summoned to local councils in the city of Basra, but these forums accomplished little beyond abstract discussions of projects for which financial backing was not forthcoming.[58] In the rural areas, the Ottoman administrative entities were largely maintained, but in some places, local shaykhs were now given jobs as *mudir*s (local governors), positions which had formerly been the preserve of Ottoman career officials. A small municipal council for Qurna was re-established as early as 1916.[59]

British rule affected local society more indirectly as well, particularly in relation to billeting and requisitioning. Owners of large houses were asked to evacuate their premises in order to accommodate troops, date gardens became encampments or were damaged during military operations, valuable palms were felled for construction purposes and river craft were requisitioned by the military authorities. Additionally, the arrival of refugees from areas under Ottoman control created congestion in the city, and a blockade affecting all traffic of goods and people to upriver areas remained in force for most of the war.[60]

But the British presence also brought welcome spin-offs. Large-scale operations, such as railway building and the construction of an embankment from Ma'qil to Zubayr, demanded manpower – an opportunity eagerly grasped by unskilled workers as well as by migrants from farther afield, particularly Persians.[61] Similarly, to commercial circles, the occupation brought new possibilities. The foreign forces needed supplies and provisions of all kinds, and entrepreneurs and contractors earned easy money during the first years of the campaign when confusion reigned in the British camp.[62] Clerks were in such a high demand that the British failed to get hold of many of the men they wanted, who preferred the booming mercantile sector instead.[63] As more and more money was pumped into the local economy, prices of foodstuffs went up, and rents quadrupled. Yet, towards the end of the war, British officials maintained that the only Basrawis not to have benefited materially from the occupation were families whose investments were tied up in real estate rather than in commerce.[64] Inhabitants of the countryside experienced similar positive economic developments: workers in river transport did well, and the British demand for reed mats from the marsh areas was such that there was hardly anything left for civilian purposes.[65]

During most of the war, British authorities had only vague ideas of how the people of the occupied territories viewed the new regime, usually interpreting the absence of trouble to mean satisfaction with the departure of the Ottomans. After having been entertained at various receptions during a visit to Basra in 1917, a leading British official reported that "no underlying political hostility was perceptible".[66] In early 1918, Cox found "sheikhs and leaders of town communities" to be "thoroughly appreciative" of the British regime.[67] The generous subscriptions to a hospital in Basra in memory of a British general – in the excess of 100,000 rupees and no doubt an expression also of Basra's blooming wartime economy – were highlighted in reports to London.[68]

In a context of war and censorship, the political life of Basra was effectively reversed to pre-1908 conditions. No newspapers appeared other than an officially sponsored English-language daily which was mostly concerned with international developments, and political parties were now non-existent. Ironically, in this period, it was in Istanbul that the idea of the political unity of the areas now under British occupation was publicly promoted – through a booklet that lamented the "separation of Iraq" (*firak-i Irak*), combining romantic poems on Basra and Baghdad and celebrating their Islamic heritage.[69] In the occupied areas themselves, on the other hand, there was little open debate about political arrangements for the future, reflecting the upper hand of the "Indian school" of administrators in the Basra area and their traditionalist style of imperialism. But in 1918, new impulses were to hit British policy-makers.

1918: The year of self-determination

A radical change in Britain's policy on Basra took place during 1918, in relation to global developments. In April 1917, the United States had entered the war on the side of the Allies, and President Woodrow Wilson soon came to express a desire for a post-war settlement along lines quite different from those followed by Britain and France until then. The new focus on concepts such as "democracy" and "national self-determination" gave impetus to liberal-minded forces

close to the British prime minister, David Lloyd George, who set about harmo-
nising London's and Washington's war aims during the autumn of 1917. The
process culminated with Lloyd George's speech at Caxton Hall on 5 January
1918, into which several ideas for a post-war settlement now popular in American circles had been incorporated. This included a reference to "Mesopotamia,
Arabia, Syria and Palestine" as areas entitled to "recognition of their separate
national conditions".[70] If taken literally, this would have profound implications
for the people in British-occupied areas such as Basra.

With respect to the areas held by the expeditionary force in the Gulf, the
chief question sparked off by Lloyd George's speech was whether Basra could
still be annexed or not. Staff at the India Office thought the idea would now
have to be ruled out.[71] Interestingly, however, both Cox and George Curzon, the
influential chairman of several successive interdepartmental committees for
Middle Eastern affairs during the war, were convinced that annexation of a limited area along the coast was still feasible. Cox justified this position with reference to "our assurances to the inhabitants and the millions of money we have
sunk in making the port"; Curzon suggested that if annexation should prove
"too inauspicious", then "a terminological variant", such as "perpetual lease" or
"enclave" could be employed.[72] A memorandum by Cox along these lines was
in fact approved by the interdepartmental committee responsible for policy for
the occupied territories.[73]

But the concept of self-determination was seized upon by other figures in
London's policy-making circles. Some were genuine liberals, others were attracted to the idea because insisting on it could help Britain get rid of undesir-
able zones of French influence in Syria laid down in the Sykes-Picot agreement.[74] After sessions specifically devoted to "the question of Basra" in the
context of the new priorities, Curzon was by the autumn of 1918 left as one of
the few key officials who voiced concern about relinquishing a British stronghold in Basra through a commitment to "no annexations".[75] His efforts were to
no avail: an Anglo-French declaration emphasising the intention of France and
Britain to support the principle of self-determination in "Syria and Mesopotamia" was agreed upon in principle. It fell short of explicitly ruling out annexation, but supporters of permanent British protectorates in the Middle East
thought the concord dealt a decisive blow to their ambitions.[76]

The question of administrative differentiation between Baghdad and Basra
remained open. There was nothing in the concept of self-determination that tied
Britain's hands as to the number of states to be recognised in a post-war settlement. But in London, this aspect came in the background of grander discussions
about traditional imperialism versus a peace based on liberal principles, and
British administrators in Baghdad were left to take initiatives of their own. Cox,
who had previously criticised the administrative distinction between Basra and
Baghdad, had accompanied his criticism with an assertion that political differentiation (which he understood to be Whitehall's ultimate motive) could be retained even without administrative separation. However, his deputy, Arnold
Wilson, who temporarily took his place from the summer of 1918, set aside this

provision. Wilson moved ahead with an administrative amalgamation of Basra and Baghdad in September 1918, and thereupon reported the fait accompli to London, arguing that the move was "in conformity with general instructions given by [the] Eastern Committee".[77]

Wilson justified the change of administrative status with arguments clearly revealing that a differentiation of political status was unthinkable to him. He claimed that "Turkish division of Iraq into separate Vilayets was neither dictated by topographical necessity nor based on political or racial divergences, nor did the boundary follow any natural line of cleavage", and, showing a fundamental aversion to the 1917 policy, added that "there is now, to be hoped, no longer any intention of applying to Southern districts of Iraq preferential treatment, which was, even in 1917, hard to justify from standpoint of local requirements."[78] And in the final days of the war – German leaders had since October made repeated overtures for an armistice and their Ottoman allies were facing heavy losses on the eastern front – Wilson played a decisive role in bringing about a British advance further north to Mosul. In his view, this brought political unity to a region that was an organic entity in economic and geographical terms – and created the minimum of contiguous territory required for a viable new state.[79]

In London, staff at the India Office acknowledged that Wilson's interpretation of his "general instructions" as to Basra's administrative status was farfetched, but refrained from protesting – choosing instead to rely on Cox's earlier assurances that an ultimate differentiation of status would always be possible.[80] Subsequent notes by the India Office in relation to anticipated peace negotiations indicated that control of Basra in fact remained a pivotal interest of the Indian government, but this view was not accompanied by policy measures to secure special treatment for the coastal enclave.[81] After the armistice on 11 November, also participants in the Eastern Committee emphasised that the question of the eventual number of states in the area remained unsettled. It was suggested that there might be "two lieutenants", one in Baghdad and one in Mosul.[82] Others hinted that each of the three provinces might favour a separate ruler. The secretary of state for India later asked, "What does an Arab facade mean? One Arab ruler? Why not three or four?" However, no one specifically picked up the "question of Basra".

In a remarkable about-face, the chairman of the Eastern Committee, Curzon, hitherto the strongest proponent of differentiating between Baghdad and Basra, adopted Wilson's argument about the need for administrative unity as his own view at a meeting on 27 November. In a retrospect of the development of British policy, he applauded Wilson's abrogation of the two separate administrations, an arrangement he characterised as an "impossibility", and asserted that this was something "we all have realised for long". The meeting concluded with a decision to carry out an enquiry about the views of the inhabitants. Crucially, the committee reiterated Wilson's view of the ideal territorial configuration of the new state by asking the respondents to say "yes" or "no" to the acting civil commissioner's preferred vision, "a single Arab state from Mosul down to the Gulf".[83]

In late November, when orders came from London for a sounding of local views on the future, Wilson had thus already managed to get the home government to adopt a suggestive framing of the question about the territorial composition of a future state. Yet he went even further. He attached detailed instructions to the political officers who were to carry out the enquiry, stating that the question about territorial unity from the Gulf to Mosul "only arises in Kurdistan, Mosul Wilayat and Dair uz-Zor", and demanding that the alternative be portrayed as "establishment of separate state, roughly Mosul Wilayat not under British protection".[84]

In Basra, the enquiry was implemented through a series of interviews with sixteen notables of the city and its surrounding countryside.[85] The selection of representatives indicates that sectarian biases from Ottoman days were preserved: among the interviewees, there were nine Sunnis, three Shi'is, two Christians and one Jew.[86] Two of the Shi'is (a man from Qurna and a Persian) were employed by the British local administration as *mudirs*, while the third was an *'alim* from Karbala' now in receipt of a British subsidy.[87] Thus, in practice, the urban Shi'i Arab majority of Basra was excluded during this first British attempt at analysing popular opinion, and landowners and merchants based in the old town of Basra or at landed estates in Abu al-Khasib continued to dominate.

Given Wilson's efforts to engineer results compatible with his personal visions, it is difficult to evaluate the results from this consultation (or "plebiscite", as it was unfittingly labelled). The territorial composition of a future state was evidently discussed, but only as a debate over Mosul's attachment to the core area of Baghdad and Basra, whose internal relationship was not on the British agenda. Most of the respondents who addressed the issue agreed that Mosul was "part of Iraq"; two claimed that Mosul had more in common with Aleppo or Kurdish areas further north; one stated that the interests of Basra's inhabitants were confined to the area south of 'Amara. Two interviewees called for the three Ottoman provinces to become united within a British-controlled framework, but with wide-ranging local autonomy for each of them.

Questions about the ruler for the new political entity and Britain's role were also tackled, and local candidates to the position as an "Arab amir" subjected to scrutiny. Shaykh Khaz'al of Muhammara received a solid share of criticism from the respondents, as did Sayyid Talib, now in exile in India, where he had temporarily taken up residence after his failed pre-war attempts at playing the Ottomans and the British off against each other. The interviewees reportedly concluded that they preferred British rule to any local potentate. Whatever the truth of that analysis, a "section of educated Muhammadans" had views that evidently stretched the interpretative skills of the occupation officials: the support expressed in this camp for an Arab amir became rendered as a view held "partly as a matter of religious duty, and without enthusiasm", and their inability to agree on a particular candidate was highlighted. This was remarkably reminiscent of Wilson's own summary of the plebiscite for all the occupied territories: no one could agree on a local nominee, so British rule was left as the sole option.[88] Even supposedly loyal officials in London were unable to hide their dislike of how the enquiry had been conducted.[89]

The concept of self-determination was thus off to an uneasy start in Basra. Throughout 1919 and for much of 1920, a huge gap remained between the liberal ideas expressed in London and the traditional imperialist approach of the administration on the ground, where little was done to expand the process of consultation among the local population. A council covering the former *sancak* of Basra (now referred to as a "division") was added to the municipal institutions in November 1919, but its scope remained limited to giving advice on local affairs. Recruitment patterns confirmed the practice of the plebiscite, with over-representation of Sunnis and non-Muslim minorities, and under-representation of the Shi'is.[90] In April 1920, one member of the council felt compelled to remark that none of its decisions had been acted upon.[91]

While London spent much of 1919 waiting for an outcome from the peace talks at Versailles, Wilson used the time to entrench his own vision of a large, single state. He plagued the imperial metropolis with requests for public statements that might solidify Britain's hold over all the territory from the Gulf to Mosul, and further ingrained the idea about administrative unity by circulating a constitutional scheme for a single state.[92] In Whitehall, any request potentially prejudicial to Mosul's status was rejected, with reference to the ongoing negotiations with the French. (Mosul had been allocated to France in the wartime Sykes-Picot agreement and was still claimed by Paris.) Yet, during the course of this exercise, concepts such as "United Mesopotamia" and "Iraq proper" emerged.[93] Originally, they were merely linguistic simplifications to express the distinction between "Basra plus Baghdad" on the one hand and Mosul on the other, but the consequence of their increased use may have been a deeper conceptual merger between Basra and Baghdad in the minds of London officials. Even though Curzon maintained that all options remained open for configuring the occupied territory into one or several future states, London's failure to support any particular territorial alternative left room for manoeuvre to the industrious Wilson in Baghdad.[94]

The absence of protests from Whitehall against Wilson's one-state policy is even more remarkable given the appearance in the British press of a "Back to Basra" scheme. During the mounting post-war economic crisis in the country, alternative scenarios for a more limited, cheaper British presence in the Arab world emerged. Members of the military elite had already identified a smaller enclave around Basra as a strategic core area; the press used the huge costs of the military presence in territory further north as a point of attack against the government; and in August 1919, *The Times* asserted that Britain's "correct scientific border" in the region was at Qurna.[95] In early 1920 the question became a matter of parliamentary debate, as the opposition suggested that Britain limit its presence to the old province of Basra.[96] But during all these challenges, members of the cabinet remained loyal to Wilson's vision of a single state, particularly after the French territorial claims to Mosul petered out in the second

half of 1919. The melange of arguments marshalled by the government to defend its policy included several points stemming directly from Wilson, among
them conclusions derived from the self-determination antics of the previous
winter. Thus, in March 1920, Curzon advised that "the mandated territory must
include Mosul, since there is no suitable physical boundary between Mosul and
the Persian Gulf, since the inhabitants object to the partition of their country,
and since the oil-bearing regions of Mosul are essential to the revenues on
which the future development of the whole country will depend."[97]

Within the Foreign Office, only Hubert Young consistently advocated an
alternative solution. In January 1919, and again in April and July 1920, he
called for a concentration of British interests in Basra, French control in "Beirut
and the Lebanon", and a United States mandate for the vast inland territory in-
between.[98] In this manner, pivotal European interests would be preserved, and
the concept of self-determination might be developed more vigorously outside
these zones of traditional imperialism. Young, at least, was aware that London's
hands-off approach in territorial questions did not mean the absence of policy:
"Ever since Sir Arnold Wilson was translated from his post . . . he has done his
utmost to stereotype and unify the three vilayets and Southern Kurdistan.
Events have proved the unsoundness of this policy, but it will be exceedingly
difficult to undo."[99] Yet, despite positive remarks from his colleagues, this challenge to Wilson's vision was never brought to the cabinet table.[100] Instead, further strengthening of the one-state scheme came with the San Remo conference
in April 1920. The Versailles peace conference had agreed in principle on
"mandates" as the best instrument for making nation-states of former German
and Ottoman lands but had not completed the distribution of territory to the "tutelary powers"; at San Remo it was formally agreed that Britain would undertake the mandate for "Mesopotamia" with a view to setting up "an independent
state of Iraq".

To the limited extent that the British administration held a dialogue with the
local population on political questions, it was Wilson's particular vision that
was propagated. Already in 1918, a pattern of centralisation had been established in education, as boys wishing to proceed beyond the primary level
schools of Basra were advised to travel to Baghdad.[101] And in early 1920, the
British arranged an excursion along the new railway to Baghdad for Basra notables, again leaving little doubt about their preference for greater territorial unity.
Comments by the British military governor reveal the message conveyed: "The
journey much impressed them and they felt the truth of what Col. Wilson told
them at an interview, namely that Basrah was no longer an isolated unit but an
integral portion of Mesopotamia."[102]

The 1920 uprising

After the plebiscite of December 1918, the political elite of Basra stayed aloof
from the political debate emerging elsewhere in British-occupied territory in the

Middle East about the future of the region. More active in this mounting discussion were ex-Ottoman officers from Baghdad and Mosul who had participated in the Arab revolt and the campaign for Damascus, and now worked in the temporary administration in Syria under the leadership of Faysal ibn Husayn, son of the sharif of Mecca. Their political party, al-'Ahd (The Covenant), had split into "Syrian" and "Iraqi" branches after a disagreement in December 1918.[103] Early in 1919, members of the latter branch published a political manifesto urging the establishment of an independent state of Iraq, within a triangular territory stretching from the Gulf to Dayr al-Zur on the Euphrates (in modern-day Syria) and Diyarbakir (in south-eastern Turkey).[104] In March 1920, they proclaimed Faysal's brother, 'Abdallah ibn Husayn, as king of Iraq (Faysal's Damascus administration became the kingdom of Syria during the same month), and also attempted to instigate an anti-British revolt in their home regions from bases in Syria. No persons from Basra became directly involved in this movement: hardly any Basrawis had ever made it to officer rank in the Ottoman army.

The most significant event on the political scene in Basra in this period occurred in February 1920, when Sayyid Talib returned from exile in India.[105] This was the pre-war iron ruler of Basra against whom several leading notables had warned during the plebiscite a little more than one year earlier, and British observers described his homecoming as a "bombshell". The occupation authorities were themselves apprehensive because of Talib's reputation for brutality and intrigue, but at the same time attracted to his ability to command large-scale political support. Talib, for his part, had made up his mind as to which horse to back, and after having reactivated some of his "friendships" with local elites (British sources say many notables renewed "their submission" to him), travelled to Baghdad in order to investigate the possibilities of associating himself with the scheme for a mandated regime.[106]

During the same period, Basra's increasingly peripheral position vis-à-vis the new centre in Baghdad did not arouse any strong protests. The local councils were designed to be non-political, and there was little discussion of Basra's status in relation to the other British-held territories. Some were disappointed by the failure to establish an agricultural school like that in Baghdad, and others complained about the charges levied by Baghdad health authorities for services in the Basra area.[107] On the other hand, two influential merchants won support when they asserted that British measures and weight systems should be standardised in "the whole of Iraq", so that the entire area would conform to the "rest of the British Empire".[108] Members of the council also welcomed the restoration of Ottoman law codes which had started in 1919 to conform with the practice in Baghdad, in place of the Indian-inspired system introduced by the British in Basra during the war. The desire for a uniform system of law in "all of Mesopotamia" was expressed, suggesting that within the British imperial framework, Baghdad did not appear as a threat to these Basra elites.[109]

The first major signs of uneasiness about future relations with areas further north came in the summer of 1920, during a large uprising against the British in some of the occupied territories. The nascent nationalist movement of the

Baghdad and Mosul officers in Syria had inspired urban inhabitants of Baghdad to present similar demands for Iraqi independence, a propaganda which intensified when the news of a British mandate was announced in May. This coincided with increased anti-British agitation by Shi'i ulama of the holy cities and dissatisfaction in several tribal areas. All this rebellious energy set off an uncoordinated yet highly effective revolt against the British which lasted well into the autumn of 1920.

The Basra area remained almost entirely unaffected by the revolt. As political agitation against the British was on the rise in Baghdad, the divisional council in Basra passed a resolution expressing satisfaction with the British regime and distancing themselves from the nationalists in Baghdad.[110] Many believed that Sayyid Talib had instigated the declaration through his adherents, but the support of some of his enemies was interpreted as a sign of wider support for the British among the "educated classes" of Basra.[111] This view was echoed by Cox, who had visited the city en route to London. However, Cox's report provided additional information that yielded a more complex picture of Basra opinion than that conveyed to London by Wilson. Some Basrawis expressed concern about the "extremist agitation" of Baghdad, and concluded that "if concession is made to it, they will ask to be separated from Baghdad".[112] The prospects of an Arab amir provoked similar separatist threats. According to this group of notables, isolating Basra from Baghdad could be justified with the "great commercial, strategical and political interests and importance vested in port of Basra".

Meanwhile, other Basrawis took a less alarmist view. Wilson had decided that co-operation with Sayyid Talib might be the best way to stem the mounting opposition to the British, and in late July summoned him to Baghdad. The goal was to establish a committee of ex-deputies (of the Ottoman parliament) from the vilayets of Basra, Baghdad and Mosul, to work out a framework for elections to a constituent assembly for a new state under British mandate. With pre-war structures of power the point of departure for the new committee, Basra came to be represented by people who were Talib's old friends from the pre-war reform movement: most were Sunni landowners, but the contingent from the Gulf city also included one Jewish representative as well as two Sunni lawyers originally from Baghdad and Mosul.[113]

The business of the committee was to create a draft for an electoral law as a first step towards a constituent assembly. In line with Wilson's wishes, and evidently in conformity with many committee members' own ideas of a greater "Iraqi" political entity, the delegates discussed procedures for selecting representatives from the three old provinces of Basra, Baghdad and Mosul and the creation of a "centralised, national government" (*hukuma markaziyya watani-yya*).[114] The committee's report was later overtaken by events, but the proceedings were an important exercise for promoting political interaction among notables from the three vilayets.

Basra was not devoid of the sort of anti-British activity seen in Baghdad, but it failed to arouse public support on a similar scale. Attempts were made to mobilise popular opinion for demonstrations through the dissemination of propaganda in coffee shops (such as translations from the *Times of India* about British policy in the region) and by way of speeches in mosques followed by private meetings after prayers. One "unauthorised procession" came about in June, but was quickly dispersed by the police. During Ramadan, some Basrawis travelled to Baghdad to meet with leaders of the popular movement there, who criticised the British and had adopted the word "independence" as a recurrent item of their vocabulary.[115]

In Basra, backing for these politicians was limited. The agitators soon abandoned the old town of Basra, unable to muster support for their cause in its conservative environment. The suburb of 'Ashar appeared to offer more promising territory – as well as spaces where they could operate, such as the coffee shops and the Khudayri Mosque. In terms of social background, these activists were quite different from the body of men who had passed the resolution of Basra's divisional council condemning the activities of the Baghdad nationalists. The group counted several Shi'is, while the Sunnis who took part were largely men of non-Basra origin, from places such as Samarra', Kirkuk and Erzurum. They came from more modest backgrounds than the traditional elite of the divisional council, and included teachers, imams, and a headman of workers in the port – although two sons of Basra landowners had also joined the circle.[116] Despite their lack of success, the unanimity about Basra's attitude to the British had clearly become broken.

Towards an Arab kingdom, 1920–1921

In London, the revolt ignited further calls for a withdrawal to Basra, seen as being untouched by the "extremist" agitation.[117] Yet, the government remained firm in its defence of the vision of a unitary state, backing up its case with a curious blend of arguments which epitomised an ongoing rupture in the discourse of international politics. To speeches focused on traditional imperial and strategic interests, points related to the aspirations of the local population were eclectically added. Within one and the same passage of a speech in defence of the policy of a single, unified state, Lloyd George alluded to the demands for territorial unity ostensibly put forth by the local people in the plebiscite, before proceeding to defend a British presence in Mosul by referring to the envy expressed by the French opposition over Britain's attainment of that valuable area.[118] Similarly, in the House of Lords, Curzon talked of strategy and the importance of not turning the lands north of Basra into a second Transvaal or Khartoum (the core territories of the 1880 anti-British Boer republic and the 1885 Mahdist uprising in Sudan respectively), but added that the process of consulting the population about the most desirable form of state was still ongoing.[119] And in a lengthy speech, J.D. Rees claimed that the story of Sinbad the Sailor contained decisive proof for the necessity of administrative unity from Basra to Mosul – without specifying the precise basis of this baffling thesis.[120]

This exercise of defending a British presence from the Gulf to Mosul further cemented the vision of a single state among cabinet members. Although Curzon demonstrated sentimentality upon a renewed effort by Young to promote a separate solution for Basra in October, he once more refrained from putting forward that scheme as an alternative.[121] Similarly, at various junctures during the autumn of 1920, the silence of opponents of a single state was decisive in strengthening precisely the scheme to which they were so sceptical. First, Britain entered a peace treaty with the Ottomans at Sèvres in August where "Mesopotamia" was mentioned as a separate entity and the sole clauses for possible subdivision of this territory related to the Kurdish-speaking parts of Mosul. When the French later presented a draft for their mandate for "Syria and Lebanon", British officials remarked that this apparent act of splitting up the area might not be in accordance with the Treaty of Sèvres (where only "Syria" was mentioned) but took no action and presented no counter-proposal for Basra.[122] Finally, when the draft for a British mandate for "Mesopotamia" was worked out during the autumn, only Kurdish areas were specifically mentioned as territory where an autonomy scheme might be implemented.[123]

The revolt in the occupied territories was finally brought under control during the autumn of 1920, and British policy-makers could turn to questions affecting the future. It became clear that Britain would undertake a mandate for the occupied territories, still referred to as "Mesopotamia", and this would be done under the leadership of Percy Cox as British high commissioner. The question of an Arab ruler or figurehead remained unresolved, as did, in theory, the ultimate combination of territory into a state or states. By October 1920, Cox was ready to depart for Baghdad, and the India Office hoped that his personal skills would help sort out the confusion about administrative principles which had arisen during Wilson's regime, as well as the several political issues still outstanding.

One of these remaining political issues concerned Basra's status within the new state. Shortly after his arrival, Cox reported on the lack of "enthusiasm for a national government" in Basra and Qurna.[124] But the establishment of a provisional Arab government necessitated a provincial administration in all British-held territory, so the question of a governor (*mutasarrif*) for Basra came up for discussion. Cox recalled earlier schemes of administrative differentiation as well as the huge British investments in the port installations, and wrote to London outlining the consequences of centralisation and incorporation that would inevitably accompany any such appointment. He concluded by asking about "what our policy may be in regard to Basra".[125] In London, that was not entirely clear. John Shuckburgh of the India Office came up with a draft answer, consenting to a governor appointment on the assumption that British policy was to assume the mandate for "the whole of Mesopotamia". He went on to add: "If this premise is incorrect, the draft is, of course, wholly inappropriate."[126] Kinahan Cornwallis in the Foreign Office concurred with Shuckburgh, while Young, who had persistently advocated the policy to which Cox's suggestion would deal a decisive blow, refrained from intervening.[127]

While London hesitated and failed to produce a clear answer, Cox made up his mind: he proceeded with the appointment, evidently viewing the very execution of the mandate as linked up with the territorial vision of a single, large state.[128] When the War Office suddenly proposed a withdrawal of troops to Basra, Cox threatened to resign and claimed that in order to undertake the mandate, Britain would need to maintain military control over the entire territory from Basra to Mosul.[129] His increasingly influential colleague, Gertrude Bell, elaborated on the arguments against a withdrawal of army units. She noted the difficulty of pulling back troops to Basra and then attempting to execute the mandate over the whole area from that base.[130] She also pointed out that the scheme would create a northerly, possibly pro-Ottoman "Moslem state behind us clamouring for their one port" – something that would eventually make the British hold on Basra untenable as well.[131]

Back in London, the cabinet supported Cox with respect to the question of withdrawal, but acknowledged that his methods for settling the issue of Basra's incorporation into the provisional Arab government were not in conformity with normal bureaucratic procedure. All the same, Basra's status was not deemed worthy of a rupture with Cox at this stage. One official commented: "The moment is most inopportune for a controversy with Sir P. Cox on a (comparatively) minor question of administration. I submit that we must acquiesce in what he has done".[132] The absorption of Basra into the new administrative system was thus sanctioned.

Britain's policy became much clearer during the early months of 1921 when it was decided that the newly established Middle Eastern Department at the Colonial Office, under Winston Churchill, would assume main responsibility for much of the Middle Eastern region, including all mandated territories. An interdepartmental conference held in Cairo in March 1921 took up many of the unsettled questions relating to the administration of the occupied territories.[133] The delegates agreed that Britain should support the establishment of a state with an Arab ruler, Prince Faysal ibn Husayn of the sharifian family of Mecca (who had lost his throne in Syria in the summer of 1920 when the French mandate administration was initiated). A central demand on the part of British public opinion – the reduction of military expenditure – would be met through a scheme for air control by the Royal Air Force (RAF), which was to replace most of the ground battalions. Territorial questions, on the other hand, received only limited attention, which indicated that the disintegration of a policy on Basra had in fact created the policy of a unitary state. The sole dispute concerned the Kurdish-speaking parts of Mosul, over whose status special provisions relating to Kurdish national aspirations had been laid down in the Treaty of Sèvres. On the advice of Young, and against the wishes of Cox, the conference decided to maintain the Kurdish areas of Mosul separate from the Arab government for the time being. This was done in order to keep different models for the future afloat simultaneously: the creation of an independent Kurdish entity embracing Kurdish areas beyond the borders of Mosul would remain a viable option, while Cox hoped that a representative body of Kurds eventually would opt for a merger with the new Arab government.[134]

Finally, agreement was reached in Cairo on a rough plan for promoting the candidature of Faysal. The pretender to the throne would travel to the occupied territories, and Britain would try to work up enthusiasm for him without destroying the fiction about a process of self-determination. Then, some further and as yet unspecified theatrical acts would be devised in order to seal the inauguration of a new regime, the kingdom of Iraq. Just one small problem still remained: no one had really asked the inhabitants of the occupied territories what they themselves wanted. In 1921, Basra was to come up with an answer of its own – an answer openly in conflict with British policy.

6   The 1921 Basra Separatist Project

During the spring of 1921, rumours about the imminent establishment of an Arab kingdom – a single entity that would extend from the Gulf to Mosul, ruled by an amir – gained ground in Basra.[1] At the same time, despite a cloak of on-going "consultation" with the inhabitants and promises of an upcoming "referendum", the British made abundantly clear their intentions of installing Faysal ibn Husayn as ruler. In April, on the basis of a rather contrived package of evidence of alleged incitement to public violence, they expelled Sayyid Talib, one of Faysal's chief contenders to the Iraqi throne, to Ceylon. In June, officials in Baghdad announced that Faysal had boarded a ship from Jeddah and was on his way to Basra. But in Basra, the leading notables had other things on their minds than an Iraqi kingdom.

The emergence of the separatist movement

The first signs of a new political movement in Basra appeared during a meeting between Percy Cox and two leading landowning merchants of the city, Ahmad al-Sani' and 'Abd al-Latif al-Mandil, on 7 April 1921.[2] In the interview, the two Basrawis asked for a separate administration for Basra under direct British rule, arguing that Basra was a merchant city with interests different from those of Baghdad. They now feared that rule from Baghdad could prove to be "a worse affliction" than the Ottoman regime. At the same time, rumours started to reach the British intelligence network that a petition was in preparation, demanding an end to Arab influence in the local administration and the re-establishment of a purely British regime from Fao to Qurna.[3] In May, a petition from Mandil and Sani' requesting British rule was addressed to the high commissioner, and there came further rumours of growing support for such a scheme.[4] By now, British officials had realised that a more elaborate petition was on its way, and on 14 June, the local divisional adviser in Basra could report its contents in detail.[5] British officials formally acknowledged the existence of a separatist movement at the same time as they authorised local newspapers to reproduce a pro-Faysal speech given by Churchill in the House of Commons, in which schemes challenging the vision of a unitary kingdom were discouraged, and the Basra movement specifically mentioned.[6] On 20 June, the petition was formally presented to the high commissioner by a delegation of six men who had travelled up to Baghdad from Basra.[7]

One of the few things almost all sources on the separatist petition agree upon is the text of the document. The appeal from Basra, with some 4,500 signatures altogether, consisted of "a sheaf" of printed copies of a text in Arabic, which in turn was a translation of a master document framed in English.[8] Iraqi researchers who had access to files of the Iraqi Ministry of Interior in the 1970s reported no trace of the original, signed petition there, but multiple copies exist of the printed version in English, as well as several transcriptions purporting to reproduce the original Arabic translation. All these documents are almost identical to the letter, and no controversy about the actual demands of the petition has ever appeared.[9]

The petition consisted of two elements. First, arguments were given in support of Basra's claim to separate treatment. These included the pro-British atmosphere in Basra since the occupation in 1914, the undisturbed state of the area during the 1920 revolt, the special position of Basra as a cosmopolitan port with a strong mercantile character, and the belief that Basra's progress would be "different in kind and in speed from that of Iraq". These circumstances meant that the citizens of Basra were to be seen as a "minority" (*fi'at al-aqalliyya*) among the inhabitants of the areas under British control. There were no references to any special historical, religious or ethnic heritage apart from the general cosmopolitanism of the Basra area.

Secondly, a scheme was presented for establishing a separate political existence for Basra (*istiqlal siyasi munfasil*). This was essentially a confederative formula: The "United Provinces of Iraq and Basra" (*wilayata al-'iraq wa-al-basra al-muttahidan*) were to be put under British "tutelage" (*wisaya*) and governed by an "amir" or some other "ruler" (*hakim*) to be selected by the people according to procedures not further specified. However, most of the petition dealt with areas of government to be separated from this confederal authority and instead vested in the local government: the choice of a local ruler (to be nominated by a local assembly), defence and internal security (Basra would have its own army and police force), as well as legislation and revenue matters (a separate legislative assembly for Basra would control all revenue generated locally). Governmental functions under the confederal authorities were to be limited to common systems for post and telegraphs, currency and weights, railways and inland waterways, a foreign diplomatic service, as well as responsibilities for defence co-ordination in the event of external aggression. The petition contained no demands for a special status for the Arabic language or for the role of Arabs in the administration. The borders of the projected statelet of Basra were not defined, although the zone from Fao to Qurna inclusive was understood to be the area targeted for special rule.[10]

In sum, the proposed system of government stressed the separation between Iraq and Basra rather than their unity. It went much further towards radical decentralisation than the scheme for local government put forward by Sayyid Talib before the war. Also his petition had contained a demand for control of revenue, but the provisions concerning a separate army and security apparatus were entirely new features. One of the final paragraphs of the petition even hinted at the possible termination of the confederation if Iraq should prefer an end to British guardianship at a time when Basra wished to preserve the link to the British Empire. By emphasising checks vis-à-vis Baghdad rather than the development of common institutions, the scheme was more reminiscent of the relationship between the princely states of British India than of a politically united entity. British officials saw it as a modification of the demands for direct

British rule presented in April and May, altered by necessity as London's support for Faysal had crystallised.[11]

Competing historical interpretations

Contemporary British observers unanimously claimed that the majority of the "leading citizens" of Basra were in favour of the petition. From May onwards, the separatist movement was consistently described as the most popular local political current.[12] In June, the local British divisional adviser could mention only two significant personalities who had not signed the document calling for separation.[13] Cox informed London that, despite the existence of a counter-petition carrying 1,500 signatures, "practically all individuals who carry weight" were on the side of the separatists.[14] Bell thought the petition had the support of "practically all the solid merchants and landowners", and when a dinner in favour of Faysal's candidature for the Iraqi throne was arranged in Baghdad a few weeks later, she complained about the composition of the delegation from Basra: "The Basra deputation isn't very good, because the leading people there want to be separated from the rest of Iraq."[15]

Historians focusing on British policy in Iraq have not devoted much space to the Basra petition movement. It was mentioned in a footnote by Philip Ireland in 1937, in a subordinate clause by Stephen Longrigg in 1953, in one sentence by Elie Kedourie in 1959, in a series of footnotes and passing references by Peter Sluglett in 1976, and was again briefly touched on in a footnote by Toby Dodge in 2003. Yet, to the extent that the petition has received any attention in these works, the emphasis has been on the separatists, not their opponents, and the movement has been seen as a genuinely local one emerging in opposition to the prevailing British policy.[16]

Interpretations of the separatist petition concentrating on the indigenous input to the affair (most of them happen to be written by Iraqis) are dramatically different.[17] Only one year after the Basra demands had been presented, the nationalist press in Baghdad published several articles on the circumstances surrounding the project, purporting to represent the views of "eyewitnesses". In the *Rafidan*, the petition was described as essentially a piece of fraud: only seven people knew about the real purpose of the separatist appeal, and only two were intimately acquainted with its exact contents.[18] These seven men were from the traditional elite of the city and included *chalabi*s (merchants) and notables with titles from the Ottoman era: agas, beys and pashas. Illiterate townsmen, for instance vendors of fruit, vegetable and ice cream, were tricked or forced into signing the petition, which had been initiated by a British official bent on seeking revenge for the dismissal of his protégé (an obvious allusion to the expelled Sayyid Talib and his British adviser). This figure found the means to do so in the separatist petition, which was designed to find support among those who had prospered during the pre-war "Talibian state" (*al-dawla al-talibiyya*) and would pave the way for the comeback of Sayyid Talib as ruler of the new state-

let. The article portrayed a strong social contrast between Talib's sly and powerful supporters and the people who signed the petition, describing how the signatories humbly had to take off their shoes as they entered the palace of one of the
seven magnates in order to put their names on the separatist document. By contrast, opponents of the project were described as the *ahrar* ("freeborn individuals" or "free thinkers") of the city.

A second newspaper article gave a slightly different and somewhat less sen-
sational account, but reiterated the theme of a small economic elite exploiting
ignorant and innocent popular masses.[19] This report stated that some of the
landowners in Basra feared for their fortunes in case an Arab government were
installed in Baghdad. To prevent this, they organised the separatist petition, and
through their "hangers-on" (*adhnab*) managed to obtain the signatures of peasants and townsmen on the pretext that the petition merely involved a demand
for exemption from taxation and conscription.

The first book to mention the petition was published in 1924, entitled
Ta'rikh al-qadiyya al-'iraqiyya (The History of the Iraqi Question) and written
by Muhammad Mahdi al-Basir, an anti-British nationalist politician from
Hilla.[20] Basir reproduced none of the claims put forward in the nationalist press
about the fabrication of the petition, but stated that a "group of Basra notables"
(*nafar min wujaha' al-basra*) were behind it, and mentioned Mandil and Sani'
specifically. He then asserted that they were opposed by counter-petitions,
whose promoters travelled to Baghdad and received assurances from the British
authorities that Basra would "remain Iraqi". Basir himself had been in prison in
June 1921, and his account was apparently based on information from friends,
in addition to the 1922 newspaper articles on the subject.[21]

In 1933, adding to a wave of biographies which appeared in the wake of the
death of King Faysal, Muhammad 'Abd al-Husayn included his version of what
happened in Basra in the spring of 1921 in *Dhikra al-faysal al-awwal* (Memoirs
of Faysal I). The author, originally from Kazimayn just outside Baghdad, had
been working as a journalist in Basra at the time, and in his book mentioned the
existence of a conflict between separatists and anti-separatists. The supporters
of the separatist scheme were characterised as a "small group" (*nafar qalil*),
with only weak convictions: as soon as they had listened to the eloquent speech
given by Faysal upon his arrival, they changed their minds and discarded their
original plan. The separatist project dissolved spontaneously, "like salt in the
sea".[22]

A further account of the separatist petition appeared in 1952, written by another contemporary observer. In his memoirs, Sulayman Faydi, the prominent
pro-reform politician of late Ottoman Basra, wrote about the 1921 events in
some detail.[23] Faydi, who had been in Baghdad when the petition came about
and must have based his information on what others could tell him, did not re-
peat the accusations of fraud put forward in the nationalist press in 1922. Nevertheless, he maintained a sharp distinction between the separatists and the anti-
separatists in terms of their social backgrounds. The separatists were portrayed
as a small, greedy and immoral segment of rich people (*al-mutrafun*), trapped in

the "noose of colonialism" (*riqbat al-isti'mar*) and bent on protecting their wealth from any reckless future Arab government. They were opposed by a party of Basra's youth (*shabab al-basra*) who rose against the "slaves of the power" (*'abid al-quwa*) behind the petition. No names of separatists were given, but those of a few anti-separatists did appear. Whereas Sulayman Faydi clearly singled out a segment of the local elite for their role in bringing about the petition, he also directed accusations against British officials employed in Basra, particularly one of the judges, who allegedly threatened to arrest opponents of the project for separation. On the other hand, according to this account, Cox did not act upon the petition, but kept it in order to use it as a bargaining card in negotiations with Faysal.

No new perspectives on the Basra separatist movement emerged until 'Abd al-Razzaq al-Hasani in 1974 published a new edition of his work on the history of Iraqi cabinets. The previous version from 1953 had made brief mention of the separatist movement, but seemed to be based entirely on the accounts of Basir and Faydi.[24] The 1974 edition offered more details.[25] Again, the separatists were presented as a small elite (several names were given, the first such list to appear), whereas their opponents (the "[Iraqi] nationalists", *al-wataniyyun*) were said to be strong enough to defeat the project and consign it to its "deep grave" (*lahd 'amiq*). In Hasani's view, Britain could not be persuaded to support the scheme, but he still ascribed to external forces a role in the drama: he quoted from Sulayman Faydi the story of the British official who threatened the anti-separatists with arrests – but, without informing the reader that he was departing from the original text, he inserted the words "the Jew" in front of the name of the British official.

A more controversial British role was outlined in 1978 by the Palestinian historian Hanna Batatu, whose study combined Iraqi and British sources.[26] He mentioned the separatist project and its repercussions throughout the 1920s, and clearly associated the movement with one particular segment of Basra society, the big landowners (*mallaks*). However, he also alleged that Britain stimulated the movement, at least in periods: "Of course the British did not create the separatist proclivities of Basrah's mallaks . . . But it looks as if there were gentle British pushes with the elbow somewhere along the line."[27] Yet, the exact nature of these "gentle pushes" was not revealed by Batatu.

Finally, a 1979 Iraqi study of Basra under the early years of British rule discussed in unprecedented detail the emergence of the separatist petition.[28] Hamid Ahmad Hamdan al-Tamimi differed from previous authors by hinting that also the anti-separatists lacked popular support in Basra. He mentioned, for instance, how British authorities had no qualms about using Basra as a place of deportation for troublesome Iraqi nationalists after the 1920 revolt – a clear indication that they hardly saw Basra as a place seething with the thoughts and ideas of the rebels from the northern cities.[29] But a marked ambiguity as to the support for the separatist petition remained in Tamimi's work, with a tendency to externalise or marginalise the supporters of the project. He described the proponents of the separatist appeal as an "aristocratic, financial clique" (*fi'a aristuqratiyya maliyya*), and noted that support for British rule was particularly strong among merchants of foreign origins – Jews, Armenians, Indians and Persians. He also implied that certain individual members of the British administration opposed to the new policy of an Arab kingdom and in favour of the old scheme for Indian annexation of Basra could have engineered the project. Sidney Solomon Abrahams, mentioned first by Sulayman Faydi as a British "judge", then by Hasani as a "Jew", had now become "a fanatic Jew" (*yahudi muta'assib*). Tamimi added that popular opinion in Basra had been very "confused" (*mushawwash*) because Khaz'al of Muhammara and Sayyid Talib had maintained their candidatures for the Iraqi throne well into 1921. All in all, Tamimi's view of the movement was not so unlike earlier interpretations: the separatist petition basically lacked popular backing, although it did receive the support of a few well-to-do Basrawis.

Reactions to Tamimi's book from other Iraqi historians suggest that even the limited significance he ascribed to the petition was a step too far. One reviewer pointed out that the original documents of the separatist appeal had never been identified; the writer went on to quote from informants close to leading Basra personalities of the early 1920s who maintained that there had merely been a brief discussion of the idea of separation and no local support for it at all.[30] In 1980, leading Iraqi interpretations of the events thus seemed remarkably similar to those given in Baghdad newspapers as early as 1922.

The extent to which the legacy of the Basra question had become a vexed issue also for Iraqi politicians became evident with a book by a Baghdad notable of the mandate era, Tawfiq al-Suwaydi, published posthumously in 1987. In an attack on Muzahim al-Pachachi (one of his political adversaries and also a Baghdadi), Suwaydi accused him among other things of having authored the Basra petition for separation, which was subsequently signed by "simple souls and demagogues" (*al-busata' wa-al-ghawgha'iyyun*).[31] The reply came in 1989 in the shape of a book on Pachachi authored by his son 'Adnan, refuting these allegations and placing the blame for the separatist movement squarely in the British camp, with allegations that the British high commissioner had been involved.[32]

For the rest of the period of Ba'th rule in Iraq, the historiography of the Basra separatist movement remained at a standstill. A brief account by Jihad Salih al-'Umar in 1989 essentially reproduced the views of existing secondary sources.[33] Then, in 2003, the US-led occupation of Iraq brought a sea change which also altered the climate for writing history. No longer subject to the dictates of an official, nationalist trend and with US censors focusing on matters with more immediate political ramifications, alternative interpretations of Iraqi history now stood a better chance of finding expression. It is therefore remarkable that several historical articles published in Basra newspapers in 2004 described Faysal's 1921 arrival in the Gulf city without making the slightest mention of the separation movement.[34]

British policy and the calls for separation

On the whole, British reactions to the Basra separatist project in 1921 were negative. Cox openly discouraged the idea of separation during his interview in April with Mandil and Sani', and wrote to London that such a scheme would be "detrimental to the interests of Iraq as a whole".[35] Similarly, as the Basra petition began to take shape, the high commissioner stated that this was one of the projects that threatened to jeopardise the policy agreed on during the Cairo conference, and that it therefore ought to be "discouraged".[36] Other key officials in Cox's administration expressed similar views. Bell told some supporters of the petition that "an Arab state in Baghdad would never leave in peace a Basrah under British rule and that their sons and their sons' sons would be on the side of the Arab state", and when the Basra separatist delegation consulted her, she again strongly discouraged the project.[37]

London reactions were almost identical. Staff at the Colonial Office echoed Cox's views, commenting that the scheme "would be highly inconvenient both upon political and financial grounds".[38] The paradoxical situation whereby the cold shoulder was given to the most pro-British elements in the occupied territories was not seen as a major problem. A leading official wrote, "we may sympathise with their apprehensions, but it is obvious that we cannot be deflected from our general policy."[39] Others ridiculed the very idea of a small political unit based on Basra, claiming that "the suggestion of a separate army, legislative assembly etc. might be suitable for medieval times, but would be unworkable today."[40] General aversion to an upsurge of small and expensive protectorates in the region was evident also in the way the increasingly cost-conscious Colonial Office handled other requests for autonomy during this period, among them a scheme for an autonomous "Assyro-Chaldean state" for Christian minorities in parts of the old Ottoman vilayet of Mosul. In London, this met with a sarcastic remark: "If having taken up this scheme His Majesty's Government found time hang heavy on their hands, they might set about establishing an effective protectorate of the Desert of Gobi."[41]

Even Hubert Young, who at the Foreign Office less than a year earlier had signalled a preference for British consolidation in the Basra area, was unenthusiastic about the separatist demands. Now in a new environment at the Colonial Office, he contributed arguments to counter his former pet scheme by minuting, "sub-division of mandated territory is the great complaint which is brought against the French in Syria".[42] Still, Young clung to some of his earlier ideas, and proposed that limited decentralisation in economic affairs might be included in a future organic law, along with a clause allowing for individual provinces (with the Kurdish areas as another potentially independent unit) to remain under British mandate, in the event that it was terminated for the new state as a whole.[43]

The secretary of state, Churchill, was new to Middle Eastern affairs. On the question of the territorial composition of the projected state, he commented that he had "a perfectly open mind" with regard to Basra, and that his sole axiom in relation to the Kurdish areas was that Britain should "not put Kurds under Arabs". But he also stated his preference for relying upon Cox ("who alone knows the local situation"), and did not want to impose too elaborate instructions on him.[44] In his speech in the House of Commons on 14 June, Churchill effectively reproduced the high commissioner's arguments against the Basra separatist project.[45] Although some of Young's second thoughts could be seen in subsequent telegrams to Cox, the primary focus at this stage was to get Faysal on the throne; any remaining questions about the precise territorial configuration of the state should be resolved by a constituent assembly to be formed after his accession.[46]

Given such attitudes among key officials in Baghdad and London, the idea that the Basra separatist project had somehow been orchestrated from British centres of power can safely be laid aside. A different matter, however, is the attitude of subordinate British officials, for this is the level of administration against which most of the accusations from Iraqi historians have been directed. The British administration included individuals from various social backgrounds and with conflicting ideological outlooks, and there was no guarantee that Cox's views would be automatically reproduced by staff seconded to outlying areas.

Yet, Iraqi claims about the "Indian school" within British policy-making milieus as an instigator of the separatist project are clearly at odds with the historical record of this particular circle within the British imperial machinery. After all, it was Arnold Wilson, the spiritual guru of the "Indianists", who had championed the idea of territorial contiguity from the Gulf all the way to Mosul. In 1921, Wilson, now in graceful exile as director of the Anglo-Persian Oil Company in neighbouring Abadan, explicitly stated his support for Faysal, despite earlier reservations. This view was communicated in private letters to former subordinates whom he evidently considered trustworthy, in a correspondence where the ongoing separation movement in Basra was mentioned only casually and not represented as anything but indigenous enterprise.[47]

The British judge who assisted the separatists in converting their ideas into a document in English, Sidney Solomon Abrahams, has also been accused of misdeeds by various Iraqi authors, and his influence on the process of drafting the petition has been questioned. However, in London the petition text was described as a "modification" and a "great improvement" on previous demands, presumably those raised during Cox's interview with Mandil and Sani' in April.[48] That meeting had been a direct talk between the three men, most likely conducted in Arabic, and there is nothing to suggest that Abrahams was present.[49] Moreover, Abrahams's tenure at Basra had lasted less than five months by the time the petition came about.[50] It seems doubtful that, in the course of this short period, he should have succeeded in winning over much of the local elite and getting them to agree to a project which was purely his own private stratagem.

Perhaps the most intriguing of the charges directed against British officials in relation to the separatist petition are those concerning John Philby, because his dislike of official British policy was openly admitted by himself at the time. Relations between Philby (who was adviser to the Ministry of Interior of the provisional government) and the rest of the British administrative apparatus in Baghdad remained smooth well into 1921, but disagreements about the head of state for the emerging political unit and the degree to which the concept of self-determination was to be given real content brought about a rupture during the course of the spring.[51] Philby held that the occupied areas should be trans-formed into a republic under a president, and believed that his protégé and min-ister, Sayyid Talib, would prevail in a democratic contest.[52] But the Cairo con-ference and rumours of Britain's decision to support Faysal made Philby suspi-cious about Cox's intentions with respect to the forthcoming "election" of a ruler, and his misgivings were only strengthened in April when the high com-missioner deported Sayyid Talib to Ceylon on charges of sedition (related to Baghdad politics rather than to Talib's southern connection).[53] In an attempt at reconciliation, Cox gave Philby the task of travelling down to Basra to meet Faysal for his June arrival, but the move backfired: throughout the journey, Philby maintained a cool attitude towards the pretender to the Iraqi throne.[54] In early July Philby was forced to give up his post, as Cox could no longer tolerate a subordinate who actively sought to undermine his policy.[55]

Philby made no secrets of his antipathy to the process whereby Britain's in-stallation of Faysal was to be masked as a democratic exercise in self-determination. In June 1921 he openly advocated the establishment of a repub-lic, and during the journey with Faysal up to Baghdad repeatedly stressed that the people had the right to choose whomever they liked as head of state.[56] Some of the petitions for a republic addressed to the British during early July (from tribal areas along the Middle Euphrates) were inspired by officials loyal to Philby, and through his position as acting minister of interior (to which he had been appointed after Talib's expulsion), he successfully delayed efforts by the central British secretariat to establish moderate pro-sharifian newspapers.[57] All these aspects of his activities were well known among his colleagues, and are frankly portrayed in Philby's writings.[58]

The big question is whether Philby had a second, hidden agenda, related to Basra and Sayyid Talib, as the *Rafidan* alleged. The chief problem of this theory is chronology. The gist of the separatist demands was communicated to Cox in early April, prior to the dismissal of Sayyid Talib, and at a stage when Philby was still working within the system in the hope that a real election would be held.[59] The demands presented at that time were in turn echoes of ideas dis-cussed by Sani' with Bell late in 1920, and largely in harmony with views communicated to Cox as early as June 1920, when Philby was still in London.[60] In the period after Sayyid Talib's deportation, Philby did not visit Basra until 22 June, when he went there to receive Faysal.[61] By then, the petition had been cir-culating for several weeks, and had already been delivered to Cox in Baghdad. The question of timing aside, there is nothing to suggest that the establishment of tiny British protectorates was an activity particularly close to Philby's heart. He was quick to identify Ibn Sa'ud's expanding Arabian kingdom as the most viable political entity in the region, wrote critically of the partition of Syria, and mocked the "petty commercialism" he thought the Basra notables (with the express exception of Sayyid Talib) represented.[62] If Sayyid Talib had a hand in the Basra petition, it was more likely his own personal enterprise than that of Philby. This raises the question of the local leadership of the separatist movement.

Local elites and the separatist project

Two men repeatedly approached British officials with demands for separation and were seen by the mandatary as the main movers behind the scheme: Ahmad al-Saniʿ and ʿAbd al-Latif al-Mandil.

The pair had remarkably similar backgrounds. Born in Zubayr to Najdi immigrant parents, they belonged to Sunni families who had managed to establish themselves as landowners and traders despite relatively humble origins.[63] Their fathers had dealt cleverly with the Ottomans, but the sons had cultivated relations with more than one centre of power in the early twentieth century – Mandil as agent in Basra for Ibn Saʿud; Saniʿ as arbiter in an internal feud among the ruling family of Kuwait.[64] Towards the end of the Ottoman era, by which time both men had established themselves as developers of agricultural lands in the Basra countryside, they went on to align themselves with the reform movement of Sayyid Talib. It was only after the British occupation that they began interacting with Baghdad, and then only cautiously: Saniʿ (who visited the new capital for the first time in his life in 1920) was reportedly dissatisfied with conditions in Baghdad and made few contributions as minister without portfolio in the provisional government, whereas Mandil never actually took up his position as minister of commerce and instead made a visit to Najd in the winter of 1920–1921.[65] At the local level, they were more successful in handling the new political realities, and Saniʿ was appointed governor of Basra by Cox in early 1921.[66]

Saniʿ and Mandil were joined in their efforts by a larger delegation put together for the presentation of the separatist petition. This body was diverse in ethnic and religious composition, probably by design in order to demonstrate a broad local consensus about Basra's demands. Yet several other delegates shared the occupational, if not the ethnic and religious, background of the two landed merchants who headed the project. Aga Jaʿfar ibn ʿAbd al-Nabi, of a Shiʿi family from Kazerun in Persia settled in Basra for a few generations, was a naturalised Ottoman with success in river shipping, commerce and land-developing activities.[67] Yaʿqub Nuh, of a Jewish merchant family with links to both India and Britain and to areas upriver, had invested business profits in landed property and had served as a communal representative in local councils in the late Ottoman period.[68] And Yusuf ʿAbd al-Ahad, a Syrian Catholic of Mosul, had come to Basra as a clerk, worked his way to the top by engaging in date trade and buying up land, and had established links to both the Ottomans (by representing his community in the governor's council) and the French (by maintaining close links with the Carmelite mission in Basra and enjoying status as a French protected subject).[69]

The two other members of the separatist delegation had different backgrounds. 'Abd al-Karim al-Sa'dun, of the Sunni ruling clan of the great Muntafiq tribal confederation based along the Euphrates well to the north of the date-garden belt, had been raised in a section of his tribe with a tradition of co-operating with the state. He had received an Ottoman education in Istanbul and served under the old regime until the Young Turks demoted him and made him join forces with Sayyid Talib back home in Basra.[70] Sayyid 'Abd 'Ali ibn Fakhir was also something of an outsider: although he was a merchant like most of the other petitioners, he was a Shi'i Arab resident of rural Qurna, on the northern periphery of the old *sancak* of Basra.[71]

Anti-separatists

The original petition carrying the 1,500 signatures *against* separation has not been identified in Iraqi archives either, but its contents are known from a British translation that incorporates a few key terms from the Arabic original.[72] This supplication was basically framed as an antithesis to the separatist document, to which it explicitly related. Instead of focusing on the city's economic position, as the separatists did, the petitioners evoked Basra's historical attachment, "from the times of the Chaldeans down to the times of the Persians, the Arabs, the Turks and the British" to "al-'Iraq al-'Arabi, which extends from Fao to the north of Mosul". The "renaissance" of this territory could be achieved only if complete unity were preserved. A particular "shape" (*sigha*) for the "territory" (*muqata'a*) of Basra would destroy this prospect.

No names of the delegation of twelve men who formally presented the petition have been preserved in British reports, where the endeavours of a Baghdad lawyer settled in Basra since the final years of Ottoman rule, Muzahim al-Pachachi, are highlighted in analyses of the forces against separation.[73] But Iraqi sources identify individuals with stronger local connections associated with the anti-separation effort. Several newspaper accounts from 1922 linked the counter-petitions against separation to two Basrawis, and Sulayman Faydi's account added the names of four other local men.

The most senior advocate of unity with Baghdad was Muhammad Amin 'Ali ibn 'Abdallah Basha'yan. His Sunni family had enjoyed high status in the nineteenth century when they owned vast properties, but after a period of declining fortunes many of the Basha'yans in late Ottoman times combined work for the government with trading activities.[74] Drawing on the rich heritage of a family which had produced manuscripts on Basra's history and government-sponsored travelogues on the Hijaz area, Amin 'Ali distinguished himself as a newspaper publisher in the Young Turk era, and was one of the few Basrawis with a background from a landowning family to remain a member of the CUP beyond

1911, instead of joining the fast-growing reform movement.[75] During the war, he was exiled to Kuwait on suspicion of harbouring pro-Ottoman views and did not return to Basra until the end of the decade.[76]

The background of the other leading anti-separatist, 'Abd al-Kazim ibn Haji Khalaf al-Shamkhani, posed a sharp contrast. A Shi'i, of the Katarna tribe domiciled on both sides of the river north of Basra, he had started his career as a headman (*dubash*) for the coolies in the port, worked his way up as the local representative of the British steamship company Mesopotamia Persia Corporation, and by the early 1920s had become a merchant and a landowner himself.[77] He won acclaim as a great benefactor, showed an early interest in politics, and during the 1920 uprising was among the few Basrawis to travel to Baghdad to join the anti-British agitation.[78]

The other four known anti-separatists came from social circumstances more similar to Basha'yan's than to Shamkhani's. 'Umar Fawzi, of a Sunni family of bureaucrats from Kirkuk, had been educated at Ottoman schools in Baghdad and worked as a government official in Hasa' before starting as a lawyer and a journalist in Basra in the period of the Young Turks and finally aligning himself with Sayyid Talib.[79] Ahmad Hamdi ibn Mullah Husayn, belonging to a family of Sunni clerics and with education from schools in Basra and Hijaz, had similarly worked as a journalist and a teacher before the war.[80] 'Abd al-'Aziz al-Mutayr, of a Sunni family of Najdi origin, had studied in the new Ottoman law school at Konya and had subsequently been appointed assistant public prosecutor in Najaf and 'Amara during the final years of Ottoman rule.[81] Finally, Muhammad Zaki, of a Sunni family of modest means from a village south of Basra, had studied law in Baghdad, served in the Ottoman army during the First World War, and after being wounded had spent several years in the Ottoman capital before returning to Basra as a lawyer.[82]

Motives and intentions

Any discussion of the local input to the separatist movement must ask whether there was continuity with Sayyid Talib's pre-war movement, perhaps with anti-foreigner rhetoric and decentralisation demands now conveniently replaced by a more fashionable pro-British discourse. Some of the retrospects on the movement published in Baghdad newspapers in 1922 hinted at precisely such a connection, involving Philby and his protégé, Sayyid Talib. Evidence of a link to Philby may be lacking, but there are interesting traces of a special relationship between Talib and the two leading separatists.

Sani' and Mandil had been among Sayyid Talib's closest collaborators during the late Ottoman era, and Sani' had stayed in touch during his wartime exile in India. Talib and Sani' resumed their dialogue in early 1920, and the pro-British statement of the Basra divisional council during the 1920 revolt was partly attributed to Talib's influence. Sani's subsequent appointment as governor during Talib's reign as minister of interior in the provisional government also suggested the continuation of a working relationship between the two.[83] Relations between Mandil and Talib, on the other hand, were more strained after the war. Mandil never actually took up his position in the provisional government, and British observers suggested that this was due to personal animosity between him and Talib.[84]

Beyond these links, Talib had at times expressed ideas converging with the separatist vision. Before the war, he had sounded out the British about the possibilities of establishing an emirate based in Basra with London's support. In these overtures, Basra had been depicted as a potential unit in a string of British-protected principalities in Arabia and the Gulf. And during the 1920 revolt Talib had suggested that it might be necessary to keep Basra separate from Baghdad and Mosul in the future, should it prove impossible to impose a uniform administration on the entire territory under British occupation.[85]

Despite such affinities, there are several problems attached to a theory of Talib as the architect of the 1921 separatist demands. For most of 1920, he worked energetically in Baghdad to secure influence within the framework of the developing system. Talib was disappointed when the aging *naqib* of Baghdad, 'Abd al-Rahman al-Gaylani, and not himself was made head of the provisional government, and despaired at not being allowed to travel to Cairo for the conference in March 1921, when rumours about Faysal's candidature had started to spread.[86] Yet, he camouflaged his own personal ambitions by outwardly endorsing the *naqib* as the best candidate for the crown, and during the subsequent weeks visited several centres in the areas south of Baghdad (including Basra) in a campaign in favour of Gaylani, with the slogan "Iraq for the Iraqis".[87] Upon Cox's return to Baghdad (when the first demands for separation had already been communicated), Talib appeared to be still working towards his goal of establishing the *naqib* (and in the *naqib*'s shadow, himself) on the Iraqi throne, and declared to Cox that he was against importing a "foreign" (i.e. Arabian) ruler.[88] Eventually, his ambitions brought him into direct conflict with the British authorities whose preferences with respect to a future king were becoming increasingly manifest. During a dinner party in Baghdad in April, Talib made a speech warning about disastrous consequences if Britain interfered with the process of electing a new ruler, and went on to allude to the military capabilities of some of the Middle Euphrates and Tigris tribes.[89] These remarks were later used by British authorities as a pretext for deporting him on accusations of fomenting civil unrest.

It is not inconceivable that the Basra separatist scheme could have been exploited by Talib in a similar manner, as a threat designed to assist him in his own struggle for power. But he did not use it then, at the height of his desperation, and British observers claimed that the demands of Sani' and Mandil were made as a reaction against Sayyid Talib's agitation during his tour in March, not in response to it.[90] The main point here is that the notables of Basra continued to advocate separation long after Talib had left the scene. By the time the work with the petition intensified, Talib was already on remote Ceylon, forced into exile for the second time in his life.[91]

This strongly suggests the existence of motives for separation unconnected with Sayyid Talib and his political games. As early as in 1918, Ahmad al-Sani' had explained why he did not want an Arab administration, by showing a British officer a new brick in his house. That brick replaced what had been a loophole, where, prior to British rule, his armed guard had been positioned day and night. He foresaw that Arab self-government would make it necessary for him to remove the brick again.[92] Later, during an interview with Bell in the autumn of 1920, he criticised the attitude of the Baghdadis and their growing agitation for independence. Why couldn't they realise the advantages of British rule? Sani' justified his own view with a variation of the theme mentioned in 1918: Before the occupation, he had been unable to inspect his date gardens unless accompanied by "twenty armed men". But now, Basra was a safe place. Baghdad, with its foolish attitude, might well be left "to stew in its own juices", as long as Britain would hold on to Basra.[93]

Bell later added more information about separatist leitmotifs in paraphrases of their arguments. In an account of how Mandil defended his separatist vision during a dinner party in Baghdad in August 1921, she summarised the Basra notable's position in brief: "He's a great merchant and he wants to fish in the quietest waters he can find – quieter than those that flow through Arab kingdoms."[94] This echoed the mood of the April 1921 meeting of Sani', Mandil and Cox, where the Basra notables had expressed their aim of escaping the "jealousies and disturbances which would inevitably accompany the setting up of an Arab state".[95]

This emphasis on security for persons and property, as well as the desire for political calm, may have been relevant also for other leading supporters of the separatist petition – many of whom had experienced trouble during chaotic phases of Basra's Ottoman past. Aga Ja'far had seen a whole bazaar of his demolished when the Young Turks set about improving the road system of Basra in 1910;[96] Nuh and 'Abd al-Ahad had lived through a decade before the war when several Armenian and Jewish colleagues had been murdered during armed robberies;[97] and a known supporter of the separatist project, Taha al-Salman, belonged to a family whose leading personality had been killed in 1904 at the hands of local strongmen resentful of the family's powerful economic position.[98] More recently, the merits of political stability had been demonstrated to the entire local mercantile community when Basra's commercial environment continued to function normally during the 1920 revolt, whereas business was brought to a standstill in Baghdad.[99]

In the absence of more specific evidence about the motives of separatists and anti-separatists, a comparison of their social background may offer contextual clues. While the separatists were generally in their fifties or sixties, the opponents of separation tended to be younger, some barely in their thirties. In sectarian terms, the separatist delegation represented a broader spectrum than the leading anti-separatists (who with one exception were Sunnis), but it is noteworthy that the two Shi'is of the delegation were representatives of the small and affluent Persian community of Basra, as well as the peripheral town of Qurna. The large, urban, Shi'i Arab population of Basra was not represented,

Qurna. The large, urban, Shi'i Arab population of Basra was not represented, and the Shi'i tribesmen along the river who looked to Shaykh Khaz'al of Muhammara for leadership had no deputy among the separatists. Geographically, the old town of Basra was over-represented in both camps; only one of the anti-separatists (Shamkhani) was based in 'Ashar. A few of the anti-separatists had family ties to the local Sunni clergy, while the separatists were not intimately connected with any religious leaders. Most of the separatists belonged to families who had settled in Basra within the past generation or two, but also their adversaries included individuals whose parents or grandparents had migrated to Basra relatively recently, and people originating from north of Baghdad as well as Najd figured on both sides of the political divide.

With respect to education and professional background, there was a clear distinction. The separatists were dominated by landowning merchants, whereas those in favour of closer ties with Baghdad and the north were largely men who had spent most of their lives as civil servants or in liberal professions, after having completed at least some of their education within the Ottoman system. However, this dichotomy should not be pushed too far. Few in the group of ex-Ottoman officials had devoted their time exclusively to administrative tasks. As was usual in the mercantile atmosphere of Basra, many had business activities going on at the same time. Similarly, the separatists had never shunned the Ottoman state, and many of them had been members of its local councils. What can be said is that the anti-separatists, to a larger degree than those who favoured a special status for Basra, had looked to the Ottoman state for a living.

The geographical spheres of activity of the two contending groups were also different, but here the lines of division were more blurred. Some of the separatist leaders, especially Mandil and Sani', had in the past been more oriented towards their ancestral lands in Najd as well as towards the Gulf, where their diplomatic activities had given them prestige, and where they must have gained insight into alternative ways of political organisation outside the Ottoman system. But at least three of the separatist leaders (Nuh, Aga Ja'far and Sa'dun) held extensive agricultural properties along the Gharraf River in Muntafiq, an area which they now sought to detach; another member of their party ('Abd al-Ahad) had recently migrated from Mosul, where his sect (the Syrian Catholics) enjoyed a stronger position than in Basra; and the secessionist with a tribal background from Muntafiq (Sa'dun) had spent considerable time in the Ottoman capital during his earlier career. Nor is it possible to claim that the desire among the anti-separatists to unite with Baghdad had been formed in a context void of alternative influences: Basha'yan had travelled extensively in India, including Bombay (with which Basra's mercantile elites were well connected); 'Umar Fawzi had been an official in Hasa' in Arabia for some years; Ahmad Hamdi ibn Mullah Husayn had received his education in Hijaz.

The most prominent contrasts between the separatists and the anti-separatists were thus related to age and profession. Why, then, did young ex-Ottoman officials have such a passion for closer links with Baghdad? A possible lead may be found in events during the final months before the separatist dispute erupted.

After the 1918 administrative unification of Basra and Baghdad, Ottoman legal codes had been reintroduced to Basra, bringing about a return to the system with which the anti-separatists were familiar. In the first months of 1921, three of them had received licences to practise law before the courts of the occupied territories, while a fourth had seen his brother appointed governor of 'Amara (north of the proposed border between Basra and Iraq).[100] To these career advances, the separatist scheme doubtless presented a threat – because a special administrative system for Basra might resurrect old ideas about direct British administration, and a reversion to an Indian-inspired judicial framework. The three newly authorised lawyers had received their education in Baghdad, Konya and Istanbul, and their former classmates were dispersed all over the old Ottoman territories. Instead of forming part of a vast network of ex-Ottoman graduates, they now risked becoming jobless and isolated in a British colony and in a city whose main fame lay in its dates and its trade, not its contributions to state bureaucracy.

The text of the anti-separatist petition includes some passages that support this interpretation of motives for greater unity. In summing up their appeal, the anti-separatists highlighted two issues: Firstly, that there should in the future not be any difference of status between the district (*liwa'*) of Basra and any other district (in Iraq); secondly, that the laws of Basra should be identical with the laws of the other districts.[101] The second demand was implicit in the first, but the point about a uniform legal system from Basra to Mosul was clearly of special significance for the petitioners and merited express mention. This kind of anti-separation stand could appeal also to those who were quite unenthusiastic about Faysal, or indeed Iraq: the separatist alternative would almost certainly preclude the return of the Ottomans to Basra, and adherents of the old Istanbul-based regime may have looked to the anti-separatist camp simply to avoid turning the Gulf city into a British citadel.

The popular masses and the separatist petition

How representative of the popular masses of Basra were the separatist demands? That question must remain largely unanswered. What can be concluded is that the foremost local elite of Ottoman times now dominated the separatist delegation. Mandil and Sani' had risen to prominence in the years before the war; Aga Ja'far was one of the Persian merchants who had been most successful in dealing with the Ottomans; Nuh and 'Abd al-Ahad had represented Jews and Christians on many occasions under the old regime. This in itself suffices to negate any speculation that some of the separatists had hijacked the other members of the delegation and were parading them as figureheads for a broadly based coalition which had no real existence. On the elite level, there was indeed such a coalition, and the leaders of the separatist delegation were as representative, or rather as unrepresentative, as councils of notables had been during Ottoman days.

The arithmetic of the numbers of separatist and anti-separatist signatures (4,500 pros, 1,500 antis) probably does not say a lot about popular support or resistance to the schemes. If anything, the figures say something about the social power of those who initiated the petitions, for all-pervasive social and economic ties had made the large masses of Basra's population subservient to an elite of landowners. Townsmen living in sumptuous palaces controlled both rural date-gardens and urban real estate, and proper accommodation was hard to find for the poor. Many urban notables of Basra became patrons for the impoverished, feeding and protecting people who came to their houses and social gatherings (such as the *diwan*s and *ma'tam*s), and expecting loyalty in return.[102] The social power behind these relationships had been amply demonstrated during the late Ottoman period, when Basra notables were able to recruit hundreds of men from their properties whenever they needed a workforce in the city.[103] Obtaining a few hundred petition signatures each must have been a comparatively simple task.

For estimations of popular opinion it is necessary to look to other periods, when less was at stake for the elites given a hearing by the British. Interestingly, during the carefully stage-managed plebiscite in late 1918, some information about popular resistance trickled through in official reports. Sani' stated in his interview that "since the armistice, 30 per cent of the population has crossed over to you [i.e. become pro-British]." Others claimed that 60 per cent of the population would not want British rule "at any price". A former Ottoman deputy said that there was "a good deal of talk about 'kafir' rule [i.e. rule by the infidel]".[104] What is important here is not the percentages, but the clear perception among elites (who may well have been largely pro-British themselves) about a popular opinion that was hostile to British rule.

Any expressions of anti-British feeling in Basra during the 1920 revolt had been concentrated in mosques and coffee shops in the suburb of 'Ashar, where people of more diverse social backgrounds than those represented on the local councils participated. Some of these circles remained active in 1921.[105] But there were also political groupings without strong links to either of the two main camps in the dispute over separatism. Much of their activity took place at the house of Shaykh 'Abd al-Mahdi ibn Ibrahim al-Muzaffar, an 'Ashar cleric who had emerged as a popular figure in Shi'i circles. In contrast to other Shi'i ulama of Basra, he did not cultivate close links with the British. Instead, he invited visitors from Najaf, as well as local mullahs who delivered speeches about the calamities expected to befall anyone abandoning the Ottomans in favour of infidel rulers.[106] Reports of these meetings mention some Shi'i merchants, but also give the names of unknown people who never reappear in the sources, such as Mullah Khalaf, Mahmud Effendi Shallal and Hamid Tutunchi. These individuals may have been of scant interest to the British, as their social influence was insignificant in comparison with that of the elites of the two contending camps in the separatist dispute. Nevertheless, that these meetings took place at all suggests the presence of active political elements in Basra who stayed aloof from separatists and anti-separatists alike.

What was in the minds of most of the some 6,000 people who put their
names on petitions for or against the inclusion of Basra in a future kingdom of
Iraq in June 1921 will forever remain a secret of history, as will the question of
whether they had any clear understanding of the documents they signed. What
is known is that on 23 June 1921, the popular masses of Basra took part in an
event that was probably just as important to them as vague documents about
states which did not exist. On that day, they had the first opportunity to form an
impression of the man who was about to take up the role as "Arab amir". Faysal
ibn Husayn had arrived by boat one day earlier, in the late afternoon. Crowds
said to number thousands of persons had lined the narrow streets when Faysal
disembarked and was transferred by car to the house of Ahmad al-Sani' – one
of the leading separatists, but in his capacity as governor of Basra also charged
with providing a minimum of courtesy for the throne pretender.[107] On the following day, after closed receptions with groups of notables, Faysal appeared to
the crowds who had collected in adjacent streets and on roofs and balconies and
wherever it was possible to catch a glimpse of the courtyard of the governor's
house. Some elements of the subsequent ceremony were familiar to the onlookers, such as music and parades of Boy Scouts, which had been common features
of public festivities in the late Ottoman period. Other ingredients were entirely
new, however. In place of the Ottoman standard, there was now a flag associated with the sharifian family of Mecca. Instead of speeches in a foreign Turkish tongue, there were talks and declamations in Arabic by young men from
Basra and Baghdad. And not least, there was a man in the centre of the spotlight
who was himself an Arab: Faysal, a Hijazi, who finally addressed the masses in
an eloquent speech which drew a massive round of applause.

Importantly, the vocabulary of the speeches delivered staked out a new political discourse with a direct bearing on the row over Basra's political status.
Slogans such as "Arab unity", "Iraqi unity", and "complete independence" began to fill the air, and Faysal was welcomed to "the Iraqi lands, the residence of
the caliphs and the cradle of science". A banner with the text "Long Live Basra,
Part of Iraq"(*li-tahya al-basra juz'an min al-'iraq*) was seen as the work of the
anti-separatists, whereas not a word of separatist propaganda was reported from
either British or Iraqi sources.[108] In short, everything visible in the public spaces
of Basra on that day seemed designed to remind the masses that they were part
of a larger community, not an isolated enclave.

A local movement with a limited audience

British and Iraqi interpretations of the separatist movement are contradictory,
but there is little doubt that the conspiratorial aspects of the Iraqi accounts can
be discounted. The separatist petition of 1921 was not a British-engineered plot
to harm Arab nationalist interests – on the contrary, it had local roots in Basra.
Furthermore, in light of the outspoken British hostility towards the petition,
some credibility must be ascribed to their analyses as regards the composition

of the group which instigated it – whose social importance British officials had no motive for exaggerating. A significant part of Basra's social and economic elite in Basra, particularly the landed merchants, did have strong aversions to uniting with Baghdad and Mosul in an Arab kingdom in 1921. There were important exceptions to this general tendency, particularly with respect to men who had worked as civil servants during the Ottoman regime. But on the whole, the notables of the late Ottoman era were heavily represented in the group which British sources described as "separatist" after the war. This interpretation is supported by statements from observers unconnected with either the British or the contending local factions at the time. John Van Ess, the representative of the mission of the Reformed Church of America and a Basra resident since the turn of the century, claimed that during the 1920s, "Basrah and all of South Iraq were not at all enthusiastic about Feisal, or indeed about the whole idea of independence, and remained strongly separatist until the entry of Iraq into the League of Nations in 1932."[109] Similarly, French officials reported the scheme as an elite movement that had emerged in opposition to British policy.[110]

But the validity of the British analysis of local support for the petition stops at the elite level – which was, after all, as far as London was interested in going towards "self-determination". Scattered evidence suggests that the pro-British attitude underlying the petition was not shared by the population at large, and whatever traces remain of political involvement from the lower social classes point in other directions than that of separation. Some of these activities were carried out in co-operation with visiting Baghdadis and indicate a community of interest linking certain groups in the two cities in the anti-separation campaign. Equally important, however, is that many Basrawis opted to keep their distance to both main parties. Therefore, although the Iraqi historians' focus on a social divide between anti-separatists and separatists probably is a sound one (albeit vastly exaggerated and externalised so as to give to foreigners an aggrandised role), it seems far more dubious to assume that everyone who was not a separatist necessarily gave wholehearted support to the leading opponents of the petition.

The British later expressed disappointment with the ceremonies for Faysal in Basra, and complained of the lack of public enthusiasm.[111] But whatever the quality of his reception, it is significant that the anti-separatists managed to capture the public spaces of Basra during the festivities. No publicity for the separatist programme flowed through the roads and alleyways of Basra during Faysal's procession; the separatist leaders merely communicated their views to the amir in private. On the contrary, new slogans of Arab and Iraqi unity dominated the public domains. Although the separatists remained more favourably positioned than their contenders, and the kingdom of Iraq had not yet become a reality, their failure to make a stand on the symbolic battleground on the day of Faysal's arrival was an ominous sign. And it would soon emerge that the separatists also lacked a unified agenda. Even among the social elite of the Basra region, some wanted to go their own ways.

1. The Shatt al-'Arab, the busy but under-developed shipping lane to the eastern parts of the Ottoman Empire. Photograph from circa 1900.

2. 'Ashar River, the main thoroughfare from the old town of Basra to the riverside suburb of 'Ashar in late Ottoman times.

العراق العراق

3. More than mere geography: Detail from political pamphlet claiming to speak on behalf of "the people of Iraq" and circulated in Basra and Baghdad, 1910.

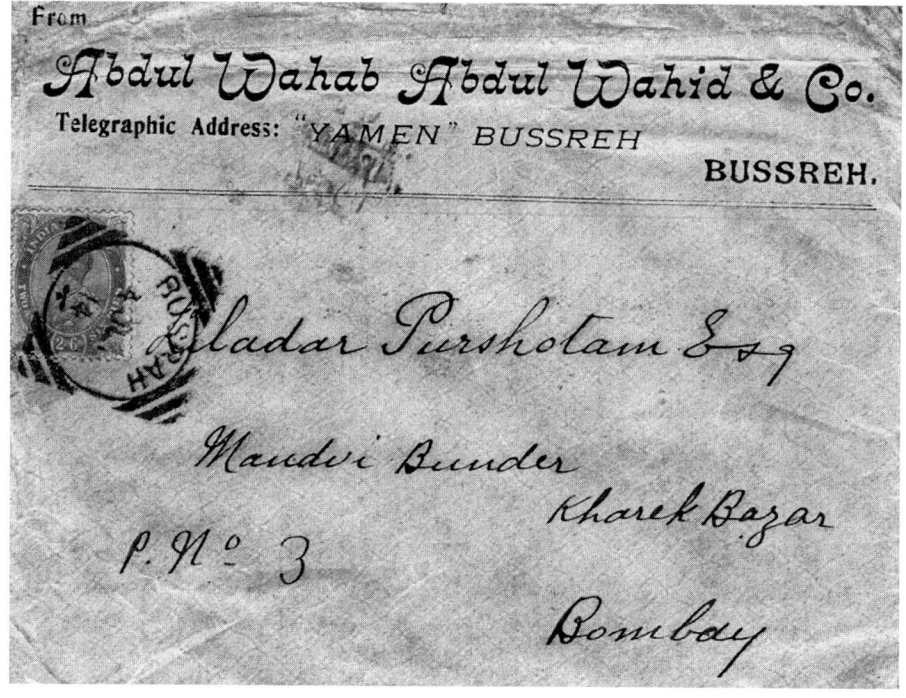

4. Fragmented state power: Letter from Basra merchant sent to India in July 1914 via the British mail, one of the several foreign agencies involved in late Ottoman Basra.

5. Indian infantry sepoys examining booty in Basra during the First World War.

6. Natives of Basra with their donkeys at races organised by the British occupation authorities, circa 1917.

7. Separatist leaders 'Abd al-Latif al-Mandil (left) and Ahmad al-Sani', considered enfants terribles by the British but here momentarily brought to order to pose for the camera of Gertrude Bell – one of the centralisers of early modern Iraq and a chief political antagonist. (Reproduced with permission from Newcastle University Library.)

8. Shi'i self-flagellants during Muharram procession in Basra. The displays of the parade revolved around Imam Husayn's death as a martyr at Karbala' in AD 680.

9. No passion for Sumer: The ziggurat at Ur, one of the mysterious structures unearthed near Basra that failed to stir the imagination of the local separatists. (Reproduced with permission from the University of Pennsylvania Museum of Archaeology and Anthropology.)

10. No synergy: The hypermodern Abadan oil refinery next door to Basra on the Persian side of the river – kingpin of the British imperial system, but never a powerhouse for pro-colonial and regionalist ambitions.

11. Cosmopolitan 'Ashar, centre of the new Basra and the battleground where Iraqi nationalism scored many of its victories in the south.

12. Patrons at a Basra coffee shop. Coffee shops were the points of entry – in the eyes of many traditional notables, the crevices – where new political ideologies found local audiences.

13. British fighter plane in action in the Kurdish mountains in the late 1920s. Through its operational activities, the RAF became a key supporter for the vision of a large Iraqi state extending beyond the strategic coastline around Basra.

14. The Iraq Museum in Baghdad in the late 1930s, the central depository of archaeological finds from Basra in the south to the Kurdish areas in the north.

15. Shi'i universalism: Demonstrations against a federal Iraq in Kirkuk, February 2005, with posters and sayings of Imam Husayn conjoined to banners with a "no" to federalism. (Photo by Khalil al-A'ani, EPA, reproduced with permission from Scanpix.)

16. Pro-federal Basra politician Wa'il 'Abd al-Latif photographed during a federalism conference in March 2005. (Photo by Ali Haider, EPA, reproduced with permission from Scanpix.)

7   Struggles over Political Space

The Basra separatist petition of 1921 failed to produce immediate political concessions from the British authorities. On the other hand, several developments
during the early 1920s meant that the social elite behind the petition could still
nourish hope. With respect to British policy-making, the lack of official support
for the separatist demands was counterbalanced by internal policy quarrels and
calls for withdrawal to the Basra area from the increasingly outspoken opponents of Lloyd George's coalition government. The conflict with Turkey over
Mosul, and the general unsettledness of Middle Eastern territorial questions in
the period (with border alterations and autonomist initiatives continuing in
neighbouring Syria, Arabia and Persia) contributed to an unstable situation
where things could be expected to change quickly. Moreover, the British-
sponsored administration in Baghdad was not overly aggressive in the Basra
area during its early years, and the separatist elites managed to retain many key
positions locally, for the time being at least. All this helped to provide a window
of opportunity for the separatist elite – a situation that was to last for the next
five years.

Ambiguities in British policy

The initial negative reactions to the Basra separatist movement continued to
dominate the policy of the British residency in Baghdad in the early 1920s. In
1922, Cox was central in framing a document that effectively refuted the
separatist petition, and in the course of this process he also managed to get
Young, originally the most ardent Whitehall supporter for a smaller state based
in Basra, over to his own side.[1] For the remainder of his period as high commissioner, Cox continued to speak and act as a centraliser on behalf of the Baghdad
government, overruling London's plans for Kurdish autonomy (and possibly
independence), as well as taking an assertive stance on Iraq's behalf in border
negotiations with Ibn Sa'ud – these ended with a 1922 agreement on a common
border and a neutral zone north-west of Basra where tribes of the two states
shared grazing rights.[2] After 1923, the policy of a unified state was maintained
during the first years of Cox's successor, Henry Dobbs, who shortly after arriving in Baghdad telegraphed to London about "separatist tendencies" in the north
among Kurds and Yazidis which he was making "every effort to minimise".[3]

In London, the overall tendency was also in the direction of support for a
centralised state. A committee on Iraq under the new Conservative government
of Andrew Bonar Law (whose supporters in the press had made loud calls for
withdrawal to Basra during the election campaign in late 1922) in fact came to
exactly the same conclusion regarding a separate Basra as had the previous administration, although the committee did advocate early termination of British
responsibility for the mandated territory as a whole.[4] This was followed up in

1923 by plans for drastically accelerating Britain's tutelary mission in Iraq (the anticipated time span was reduced from twenty to four years), making the prospects for elaborate autonomy arrangements less realistic.[5] Later, the northern Mosul vilayet became a source of dispute with Turkish nationalists who had turned the Anatolian rump of the Ottoman territory into a formidable regional military power and now wished to get rid of the humiliating Treaty of Sèvres. But despite concessions to the Turks on several issues during negotiations at Lausanne, the new British government defended the vision of Iraq as an integral entity stretching from the Gulf to the Kurdish mountains – a stand spearheaded by Curzon, a survivor from the previous cabinet.[6]

A further cabinet change and eight months of Labour rule in 1924 brought no change in the official British position, despite that party's earlier support for complete or partial evacuation.[7] After the Conservative comeback late in 1924, also Leo Amery at the Colonial Office and Austen Chamberlain at the Foreign Office defended the territorial integrity of Iraq on the lines that had been advocated by British officials at the Baghdad residency ever since the days of Arnold Wilson. This policy was highlighted by the success in securing a League of Nations ruling on the Mosul question in Iraq's favour in 1925.[8]

In Basra, the leading British official (known as an "administrative inspector"), Major W.C.F.A. Wilson, remained loyal to this policy. On the one hand, he had no sympathy for those he described as "watani" officials – young nationalists supportive of King Faysal, often of northern origins.[9] He preferred the personal qualities of separatist leaders such as Sani', whom he complimented for his "energy, tact and sound common sense".[10] Yet, Wilson did not embrace the political project of the separatists. Rather than focusing on the radical demands of the petition, he portrayed it as "a request for a measure of Local Self Government" compatible with a unitary state model.[11] (This was possibly an attempt at moderation between the local notables and Baghdad, for Cox and Young had certainly seen no such common ground.) The fact that Wilson continued in the same position in Basra throughout the first half of the 1920s suggests that relations with the residency in Baghdad must have been relatively harmonious, and that the high commissioner did not perceive Wilson as a threat to the ongoing process of state-building.

Despite this facade of a coherent policy, ambiguities in the official line soon came to the fore. The clearest example was the inclination of British high officials, Cox in particular, to treat the scheme for a British withdrawal to Basra as a potential bargaining card vis-à-vis Faysal as soon as London's euphoria over the king's successful accession in 1921 had abated. Before long, Faysal joined Iraqi nationalists in rejecting the very concept of the "mandate", and as the British tried to alleviate the criticism by negotiating an Anglo-Iraqi treaty (which could more easily be construed as a partnership of sorts), the high commissioner came quite close to exploiting the sensitivities surrounding Basra. Apparently on his instigation, questions were raised in the House of Commons in May 1922 about what Britain would do to meet the wishes of the population of Basra (whose separatist petition of the previous year was mentioned) in case negotiations for a bilateral treaty should collapse and Britain decided to withdraw.[12] However, staff at the Colonial Office were worried that contradictions in British policy might be detected if Cox's games were pursued in the public domain. Despite several requests from the high commissioner for statements guaranteeing British consolidation around Basra in the case of withdrawal, no such public announcement was made, and no complaints from Faysal's camp about foul play related to Basra during the negotiations ever emerged.[13] Moreover, it is evident that Cox was at heart a firm opponent of any such withdrawal; he was interested in the issue only to the extent that it could be used to bring pressure to bear on the Iraqi king.[14] The Anglo-Iraqi treaty was eventually signed in October 1922.

Subordinate British staff also occasionally gave consolatory messages contradicting official policy to the promoters of a separate Basra. For instance, in 1923, after the plans for a shortened, four-years British presence had been announced (and the Anglo-Iraqi treaty amended accordingly), Bell reported apprehensive reactions in Basra before adding that "more responsible Basra opinion" was aware of "loopholes" in the treaty which would enable Britain to "exert pressure on the Iraq government when necessary". On expiry of the treaty, fresh consideration would be given to "the question of a guarantee of the rights of Basrah".[15] Although far from being an incitement to further separatist activities, the statement does reveal the existence of a dialogue between British officials and Basra separatist leaders and a hint from the mandatary that separatist demands would be given a hearing at any critical juncture in Anglo-Iraqi relations.

Additionally, influential circles in Britain continued to consider a mandate covering all the territory from the Gulf to Mosul as too expensive an undertaking, a view shared by advocates of moderation in imperial expenditure and military experts who maintained that a base around Basra would provide everything required by British interests.[16] These ideas had been forcefully expressed in the opposition press during the 1922 election campaign, and within the various governments officially supportive of the territorial integrity of the new state, key personalities were repeatedly on the brink of reverting to the scheme for consolidation around Basra – a phenomenon seen during crises of financial pressure as well as during tension with the Turkish nationalists.[17] Some British official circles still felt that Basra belonged to the British Empire in a different manner than the rest of the mandated territory, notably the War Office, whose viewpoint as late as in 1925 was summarised as "Basra must be British" by worried staff at the Colonial Office.[18]

Cox's successor in Baghdad, Henry Dobbs, took a more complex stand on the issue of Basra. In public, he continued to support the centralised state and, unlike Cox, did not ask London for veiled threats of British withdrawal to the head of the Gulf to bluff Faysal into submission.[19] On the other hand, he, to a greater extent than Cox, considered precisely such a withdrawal to be a realistic exit strategy at critical junctures. In 1924, when the revised Anglo-Iraqi treaty was due to be discussed in the first session of the constituent assembly for Iraq,

Dobbs anticipated trouble from Iraqi nationalists opposed to the strong position the document would grant to Britain. Consulting London on arrangements for a non-ratification scenario, he exhibited sentimentality for the original plan of a British-controlled enclave along the coast and proposed that Basra might become "like one of the old free cities of the Hanseatic League, administering herself and the territory immediately adjoining and leaning on us for external defence".[20]

Dobbs's despatch on the subject of Basra did not change London's policy.[21] The fact that three successive governments of different political colouring between 1922 and 1924 had all decided to ignore the press campaign for withdrawal to Basra, along with the firm British support for Iraq in the Mosul question, must have given the whole idea of an evacuation to the Gulf an aura of retrogression. Nevertheless, Dobbs had indicated, and would continue to do so later, that he could see some positive aspects in the Basra separatist scheme. While he kept these views confidential, it seems likely that he could have been receptive to indigenous demands for isolating the south under British protection. However, no such representations were forthcoming during the early years of Dobbs's period in office, for the Basra separatists were fully occupied holding their fragile coalition together.

Zubayr as a separate emirate

In the middle of the secessionist quarrel in Basra in 1921 came a demand that the small desert town of Zubayr west of the Gulf city be granted a separate political existence. This was a development that attacked the very core of the Basra separatist movement, whose two most prominent representatives were of Najdi origin and Zubayris by birth. It demonstrated that even though the Basra notables were able to engineer petitions carrying thousands of signatures, there were people who shared their social background as well as their aversion to rule from Baghdad who nevertheless could come up with different and competing ideas.

The scheme for an independent emirate in Zubayr was headed by Shaykh Ibrahim ibn ʿAbdallah. His forefathers, originally from Haraymla in Najd, had vied with other Najdi families for the shaykhship of Zubayr in the nineteenth century. Ibrahim's father was shaykh of Zubayr in the 1880s and the 1890s, but was deposed when a competing faction associated with a different place of origin in Najd (Hirma) joined forces with the Ottoman governor in Basra. After some time in exile in Kuwait, a comeback attempt on the part of Ibrahim's family failed in 1907, and Ibrahim was sent to jail in Mosul after having been implicated in the murder of the new shaykh of Zubayr. Another pro-Ottoman figure was then installed as shaykh. However, when Sayyid Talib successfully attained local control in Basra during the closing years of Ottoman rule, he also decided to bring a change to Zubayr, and Ibrahim, now back in Basra, became a useful card in these plans. In 1914, Talib, supported by armed forces under his control, arranged for Ibrahim to be recognised as shaykh of the desert town.[22]

Ibrahim adopted a pro-British attitude in the early days of the war. He acted as a courteous host for British official visitors to Zubayr, all the while maintaining an autonomous position in the town, unchallenged by overburdened occupation administrators.[23] The shaykh of Zubayr was in many ways the perfect answer to British administrative requirements in an isolated area, and as long as he was able to deliver political stability on his own turf, no one worried particularly about the rules, taxes or customs charges he applied to his own subjects.[24] Ibrahim, on his part, expressed gratitude for the businesslike and predictable conduct of the new regime: Whichever British official was in charge in Basra, Ibrahim was consistently treated in the same friendly manner; whereas under the Ottomans, "sometimes I was prosperous and sometimes not, for everything depended on the whim of the wali [i.e. governor] for the time being – and the walis were changed very frequently."[25]

While the introduction of a new regime had been gradual elsewhere around Basra, practically nothing had been done in Zubayr. When Ibrahim was asked in early 1921 to conform to the new, Baghdad-based system by formally accepting the position as a *qa'im-maqam* (local governor) and discontinuing the practice of collecting his own taxes on merchant goods passing through the town, he reacted with anger and refused to change the current arrangements. The subsequent exchange of letters with British authorities coincided with the emergence of the scheme for a separate Basra, but in these documents, Ibrahim furnished arguments to support the view that Zubayr should have an administration of its own, entirely separate from that of Basra.

In his letters, Ibrahim discussed the factors he saw as the legitimate basis for Zubayr as an independent political entity. He argued that Zubayr shared the characteristics of certain other small districts in the region (Kuwait and Qatar, as well as Khamisiyya, in the desert to the north-west of the Basra division) in having preserved "the legitimate customary shaykhdom"(*al-mashyakha al-'urfiyya al-shar'iyya)* throughout the Ottoman period and the war years.[26] Historically, Zubayr had served as a "fort" (*istihkam*) to Basra, autonomous but friendly to it, prepared to provide armed assistance when necessary. Moreover, Zubayr was distinct from the adjacent areas in terms of culture and religion. It had its own traditional heritage and customs (*'adat wataniyya*) and its inhabitants were strict followers of the Hanbali school of Islamic jurisprudence. This set the Zubayris apart from "Basra and Iraq", making them more similar to the people of Najd.

In order to preserve this state of affairs, Ibrahim suggested a form of administration in which interference from the outside would be minimal. The ruler of the shaykhdom should maintain control over internal matters by collecting taxes and enforcing law and order through his own police force. He should also be responsible for external relations with Basra as well as with "the rulers of Najd". Further, he should ensure that no impulses foreign to the traditional way of life in Zubayr could make their way into the town. According to Ibrahim, a separate customs regime for Zubayr would enable him to maintain the estimated 200 men such a system of administration required. A large majority of the inhabitants, he alleged, would accept no other form of government; failure to provide him with the authority to maintain this kind of regime would result in their despising him (*haqara*) and prevent him from keeping the peace in the town. The limited powers of a *mudir* or *qa'im-maqam* bound by the regulations of the state would not suffice to fulfil these tasks in a satisfactory manner.

Just like the Basra separatists, Ibrahim faced counter-petitions. But the names of the signatories show that the battle over Zubayr's political future was a more even contest than that underway in Basra. In the port city, almost all the prominent notables had signed the separatist petition, whereas in Zubayr, several leading merchants and landowners stood up against Ibrahim and his demands for greater autonomy. Families traditionally loyal to the Hirma faction against the Haraymla emigrants formed one element of the coalition that challenged the incumbent shaykh, but the presence of figures not connected with either of these camps signified that the question went beyond factional conflicts of the past.[27] Some adversaries focused on Ibrahim's alleged misrule and tyranny as well as his personality – in one instance describing him as "a commoner" (*shakhs 'adi*). Others emphasised the administrative links with Basra during the past half-century, portraying Ibrahim's assumption of power as an act of separation (*infisal*) from Basra, and expressing a clear wish for formal reunification and the reinstitution of a regular *mudir*.[28] A newspaper article attacked both his practice of heavy taxation as well as his rigorous enforcement of a religious ban on night-time gatherings, music and cinema, and there were demands that Ibrahim be placed on trial and expelled from Zubayr.[29]

The multifaceted nature of the propaganda against Ibrahim illustrates the wide range of aspirations within this small desert town. One group within the anti-Ibrahim front attacked the local strongman personally rather than the institution of the shaykhdom or the basic idea of Zubayr as a separate polity – after all many of the families involved had themselves held the shaykhship in recent decades and may not have been particularly keen to see their local autonomy summarily abolished.[30] Although most of these families owned land closer to Basra, the years of Ottoman rule had demonstrated that such absentee landlordism was not incompatible with residence in a semi-independent town enjoying special privileges – a kind of arrangement which their neighbours in Kuwait and Muhammara had tenaciously held on to after the war.[31] Also other factors spoke for the viability of an independent emirate based in the town. Its merchants had a clientele of traders and nomads from Najd who preferred Zubayr to the riverine Basra, and the arid country immediately outside the town was thought to have a potential for agriculture if an adequate system of irrigation could be devised.[32] Even access to the sea was a possibility: to the south of the town stood the ruins of a castle of a Zubayr merchant who in the nineteenth century had considered establishing a port at Umm Qasr.[33]

On the other hand, several Najdi families who had arrived in Zubayr in the previous century had merely used the town as a base for establishing themselves as merchants in Basra. To them the prospect of isolation may have appeared as a threat, with Ibrahim's self-devised customs regime a manifest warning about the dangers inherent in the traditional shaykhdom as a model of government. The emphasis in some counter-petitions on the common, Ottoman legal framework that had formerly united Basra and Zubayr was a challenge to Ibrahim's capricious handling of judicial and fiscal affairs. Such tones indicated that the shaykhdom, if it were to persist, would have to adopt mechanisms that could rein in any wayward future rulers.[34]

Others again were looking beyond Basra. In Zubayr there were families with traditions of serving the state during Ottoman rule, who had produced pashas and beys accustomed to participating in the institutions of government. Some had attended schools in Istanbul and later held Ottoman official positions in the vilayet of Basra; others had contributed to the formation of a local CUP branch in Zubayr.[35] Just like the Basra notables, these Zubayris had sent petitions for promotions and Ottoman titles to the authorities in Istanbul.[36] Many of the considerations that shaped the stand of the Basra anti-separatists may have applied to this group as well, and indeed one among them, Sulayman al-Zuhayr, took an active part in the struggle against the Basra separatist petition. He had been in Istanbul early in the First World War and remained in Ottoman territory for several years before returning to his home region. Soon thereafter, he became an active politician and authored newspaper letters in support of Faysal, maintained contact with Baghdad nationalists and provided some of the Basra anti-separatist groups with a venue for political meetings, the Hariri Library.[37]

All this shows that the Basra separatist project came under direct pressure from the upsurge of political activity in Zubayr. The separatists of the Gulf city managed to attract some Zubayris to their own vision of a separate Basra (inclusive of Zubayr), but Ibrahim's exchange with the British authorities and the general public debate about the future that it sparked off demonstrated dissension at the very heart of the separatist initiative. And the scheme for a separate emirate of Zubayr was only the first of several local challenges that were to confront the separatist leaders in the 1920s.

Separatist control of the local administration

With the separatist petition still unanswered, British officials who supported a centralised kingdom under Faysal in the late summer of 1921 asked the Basra separatists to take part in the administration of the new Iraqi regime on an equal basis with the inhabitants of the areas further north. At first, this was a relatively gentle process of centralisation in which the Basra notables could retain some control of local affairs; more critical events affecting centre–periphery relations – such as the convocation of a general assembly for the new state and the framing of an organic law – had been postponed indefinitely.

The installation of Faysal as king of Iraq was the first in a series of steps inaugurating the new regime. The new king was "elected" in a "referendum" only marginally more democratic than Arnold Wilson's plebiscite of 1918, with signatures being collected on printed standard proclamations in support of the sole remaining candidate in the race. In Basra, it fell to the separatist governor, Ahmad al-Sani', to arrange the acclamation; he reported that the people would sign the proclamations only on condition that their secessionist petition of June be taken into consideration.[38] The enthronement then took place in Baghdad on 23 August 1921. A large delegation of Basra notables was invited to the capital, and representatives of both separatists and anti-separatists attended the festivities.[39]

At the local level, things looked promising for the separatists, for Ahmad al-Sani' remained in control as local governor under the new regime. The make-up of his administrative team also put him in a good position to control local developments. Sani' was "assisted" by the British administrative inspector, W.C.F.A. Wilson, who was a mere thirty years old, and who often came to adopt the views of the Basra magnate. Sani' also had considerable influence on the composition of his council (*majlis idara*), a key institution of local government.[40] After a process of nomination and selection, three prominent notables who had already worked together with him in framing the separatist petition – Taha al-Salman, Yusuf 'Abd al-Ahad and Ya'qub Nuh – became members of the council.[41] A fourth member, a Meccan trader, 'Abdallah al-Khalil, who had come to Basra with more or less empty hands and worked his way up to an influential position in the mercantile community, also favoured separation from Baghdad.[42] In this manner, leading Sunnis in coalition with non-Muslim elites dominated, just as in Ottoman times – and the governor had managed to surround himself with people who shared his particular vision for the future.[43]

Relative stability prevailed also within the sphere of rural administration during this transition period. Key posts such as the district governorships of Abu al-Khasib and Qurna as well as several of the subdistrict governorships remained in the hands of locals appointed early in 1921; many of these officials kept their jobs for the first half of the 1920s. Several of them were members of rich, Sunni landowning families from the prosperous and fertile Abu al-Khasib area, and some belonged to families closely associated with the separatist movement.[44]

As governor, Sani' quickly set about trying to subdue local signs of opposition to his own plans. In Zubayr he had led the endeavour to curtail Ibrahim's powers from early in 1921, to such an extent that British authorities in Baghdad had warned local officials to take care lest the "friendly" Shaykh Ibrahim receive unfair treatment at the hands of Sani', who was known to harbour a personal grievance against him.[45] It was Sani' who suggested that the local newspaper publish an announcement to the effect that Zubayr formed part of the Basra division and that only the authorities in Basra were authorised to collect taxes.[46] Even the high commissioner, the highest ranking civil British official in the country, got a taste of the strong will of Sani' in this matter: When Cox asked what conditions would have to be met for his old friend and ally, Ibrahim, to be able to remain in his position in Zubayr, he received a curt reply from

Basra, demanding the desert town's complete submission to the governorate of the Gulf city.[47]

In April 1921, Ibrahim was made to travel to Baghdad for further discussions. Due to his intransigence, these ended in a formal dismissal; he was detained as a "guest of the government" and eventually forbidden to return to Zubayr.[48] Again, in this process, Sani' played a significant role. In June, Cox was anxious that the dismissed shaykh should at least be able to live peacefully in Basra, but the answer from the local authorities was stern: public security would be threatened by his presence anywhere around Basra, and the only suitable place would be exile in Kuwait.[49] Soon after Ibrahim had been dismissed, a member of a landowning family of Abu al-Khasib was appointed as *mudir*, and Sulayman al-Ghamlas, of an old Zubayr family of Najdi origin and reportedly a friend of the governor, was installed as mayor.[50] Ibrahim made repeated pleas for permission to return to his native land as a common person, but to no avail. Although Cox expressed sympathy and felt that Britain was indebted to the shaykh for his staunch attitude during the war, the local authorities in Basra had the final say. Ibrahim was to remain in Baghdad under government supervision until 1925.[51]

Whilst the activities of Shaykh Ibrahim of Zubayr presented the most tangible challenge to the separatists in the early 1920s, also sporadic incidents elsewhere on Basra's periphery hinted at alternative ideas for how local society should be restructured in the wake of the Ottoman collapse. Early in 1922, some villages around Madina refused to pay taxes and rent to their landlords despite instructions from the governor to come to Basra to settle their case. At the heart of the matter was an internal tribal dispute, but the sections who refused to pay also demonstrated a more basic hostility to the concept of central authority, by dismissing offers of negotiation and withdrawing with their animals and other movable property into the marshes.[52]

To Sani' and the British inspector, the episode threatened the stability of the whole of Qurna (where many Basra landowners held valuable estates) and was in their view a test case for the government's ability to act.[53] Again, the governor and the inspector took the initiative and, after having first expressed reservations against King Faysal's proposal to intervene personally, recommended to Baghdad that the recalcitrant villages be bombed.[54] Cox quickly approved of their plans for a military operation involving airplanes, gunboats, police forces from Qurna as well as auxiliaries from neighbouring tribes.[55] In a series of air attacks on 16 January 1922, the RAF dropped 158 Cooper bombs on the rebellious villages "with excellent effect" (which included the killing of at least twelve tribesmen), before groups of local men loyal to the shaykh of Madina moved in to burn what remained of the dwellings.[56] Later, in March 1922, Sani' travelled to Qurna to preside over a meeting of the Madina tribes where all their village headmen agreed to share collective responsibility for the good behaviour of the inhabitants – the Basra governor once more defeating his own periphery.[57]

New political venues

Despite all the energy spent in controlling potentially subversive local forces, certain venues and events escaped the efforts of the separatist governor. One of these was the election for a municipal council, which must have been quite difficult to manipulate – there were more than 900 electors, who all cast their votes in a single round. The governor still had the option of choosing the head of the twelve-man council, but in January 1922 Sani' was faced with a result list dominated by the Basha'yan family (prominent in the anti-separation agitation) as well as several Shi'is, all with more votes than for instance his own son, or separatist allies such as Yusuf 'Abd al-Ahad, Ya'qub Nuh, and 'Abd al-Razzaq al-Na'ma. Eventually, Sani' appointed one of the Basha'yans, Ahmad Nuri, as mayor.[58] In this manner, the institutions of local government opened up avenues for politicians who had been marginalised during the first years of British rule. Even though British officials frequently labelled them as "pro-Turkish" and "anti-British", some managed to retain their seats on the municipal council throughout the first half of the 1920s.[59]

More challenges to the separatists soon appeared, as new events took the political life of Basra into unfamiliar territory where the landowning notables were reluctant to set foot. In March 1922, Ahmad al-Sani' was absent when General Jibra'il Haddad Pasha arrived at Basra for a formal reception.[60] (The general was a Syrian who had served with King Faysal in Damascus and now had come to Iraq to assist in the formation of an Iraqi army.) In April, the anniversary (according to the Islamic calendar) of the 1916 Arab revolt was celebrated throughout Iraq for the first time, but also on this occasion, Sani' left it to his assistant, Jad Ghawi (a Palestinian who had served the British administration in Sudan) to attend, leading to murmurs in the local press about the low-profile commemoration of this event.[61] And then, in November 1922, Sani' failed to turn up at a reception for Amin al-Rihani, a Lebanese intellectual who had spent much of his life in the United States.[62] In some cases, the local press attributed the non-appearance of Sani' to his being "indisposed", his age, and the fact that some of the arrangements took place at a late hour. Nevertheless, there were other events were those same factors constituted no hindrance for the Basra governor – the fund-raising party for a new Chaldean school in February 1922 is but one example.[63] Moreover, it was not just Sani' who was absent on important occasions, but rather the whole separatist elite. In their place, other voices with different agendas reigned.

The detailed reports of Rihani's visit in November 1922 and of the speeches given in his honour provide some clues as to what ideas and rhetoric entered the symbolic space left open by the separatists.[64] At a large tea party, Amin 'Ali Basha'yan spoke of the glory of the Arabs in their golden age, their subsequent sufferings in history, their reawakening and finally the need for the Arabs to become united in a "single entity" (*kutla wahida*). In his view, "the Hijazi, the Yemeni, the Egyptian, the Syrian, the Iraqi, the Marrakechi and the Tunisian" were all sons of the same Arab nation, so the people should celebrate Rihani not as a "Lebanese" or a "Syrian", but as an "Arab". By the same token, Muhammad Zaki drew attention to the Arabic language as the common bond that had saved the Arab nation during its years of decline, and commended Rihani for his services to this sacred language. Others again were more concerned with "the East" (*al-sharq*) and its relationship with "the West", in particular Ahmad Hamdi Mullah Husayn, who pointed out how civilisation, architecture and science had first appeared around the Nile and the Euphrates –areas he spoke of not as the Arab homeland, but as "the East".[65] Similarly, to Khalaf Shawqi Amin al-Dawudi, editor of the local newspaper *al-Awqat al-ʿIraqiyya*, Rihani was important as an intermediary between "Eastern" and "Western" culture. Dawudi, who frequently published portraits of the Turkish nationalist leader Mustafa Kemal in his own paper, praised the way Rihani represented "the eminence of the East" (*al-nubugh al-sharqi*).[66] Finally, ʿAbd al-Hamid Effendi, an employee at the law courts, also discussed the "revival of the East", but observed that the Turks had now become united, and it was time for the Arabs to bring about their own reunification, "as it had been in the past". The message to the around 200 guests who attended the gathering at the Hotel Iraq Palace clearly stressed Basra's connection with wider communities – not its parochial interests.

Other elements within Basra's diverse social environment may have been less interested in Rihani and such ideas about larger "Arab" or "Eastern" communities. To many Shiʿis, the central political issue during much of 1922 and 1923 involved participation in the forthcoming elections to a constituent assembly for Iraq. Taking part in these elections would constitute a definitive step towards recognising Iraq as a state, and the debate was intense. Yet, the separatist elite did nothing to intervene in this exchange of views. Instead, it was the religious authorities of the holy cities who influenced large segments of Basra society by predicting dire consequences for those who might choose to take part in the elections.[67] Later, in the summer of 1923, meetings were arranged in the city in support of Mahdi al-Khalisi, an *ʿalim* of Kazimayn who had been expelled from Iraq to Persia because of his leading role in the election boycott.[68]

The Shiʿis boosted their activities with powerful symbolism to a much larger extent than other communities in Basra. The annual celebrations of Muharram, the holy month of the Shiʿis, featured dramatic re-enactments of the martyrdom of Husayn, with scenes emphasising the suffering of his party as their brutal opponents burnt their tents, took women captive and left others to die from thirst.[69] One of the processions marched behind the Persian tricolour and congregated at the Persian consulate for the performance of their passion play.[70] In 1925, imams in Basra offered prayers for the success of the Rif Republic against Spanish forces in North Africa, presenting the struggle as a decisive battle between Christianity and Islam.[71] Evidently, here were universalistic themes that could command much larger audiences than the separatist credo. Questions relating to the territorial subdivision of the Islamic lands, on the other hand, received scant attention in Shi'i discourse at the time; in fact many Shi'i fatwas faithfully reproduced the territorial component of the new British-sponsored order by referring to the "Iraqi community" (*al-umma al-'iraqiyya*) – however much the texts protested against the particular regime in control of this territory.[72] This tendency, along with the emphasis on a fundamental conflict between religions and civilisations, put the Shi'is on a collision course with the cosmopolitan, secular and localist framework outlined in the separatist petition.

Alternative educational institutions

The silence of the separatist elite in the new political venues was paralleled with inaction in the field of education. Educational affairs had been centralised from Baghdad already during Wilson's regime, and for much of the 1920s, Basra had neither a secondary school of its own nor facilities for training new teachers.[73] Naturally enough, the local state schools adopted the national Iraqi curriculum devised by British authorities in Baghdad; if they were to challenge the message of Iraqi unity propagated through these institutions, the separatist elite would have to find other channels.

A possibility for an alternative educational structure appeared early in the 1920s. Subscriptions for a private school (*madrasa ahliyya*) had been gathering pace after the war, and by May 1921, a sum of 40,000 rupees had been collected and deposited in a bank account. A committee dominated by supporters of the separatist project controlled the finances. However, during 1921 and 1922, these men were unable to make any progress on the project, despite impatient reminders in the local newspaper.[74]

Instead, individuals with other agendas seized the initiative. In 1921 some teachers in Basra arranged a theatre play to raise more money for the school, but the theme chosen for the performance suggested that the young regisseurs were not content with a narrow focus on Basra. What they staged was *The Conquest of Andalusia* (*fath al-andalus*), with a theme from the golden age of Arab history when Basra was merely one component of a much wider empire.[75] By June 1922, the central government had acquired an interest in the school project, and it was later decided that it should be controlled by the Ministry of Awqaf. Not until the summer of 1923 was the scheme actually implemented – and then with the local authority for religious endowments in charge. Its director was a Sunni *'alim* of Baghdad origin, and the new school, Rahmaniyya, subsequently came to be dominated by Sunni teachers, many of whom were connected with the Naqshbandi Sufi order and thus linked up with wider religious circles.[76] One of these teachers, Ahmad Hamdi Mullah Husayn, had already featured in the vanguard of the anti-separatist camp.[77] Once again, the separatists had failed to maintain the initiative – and this even though they had been entrusted with a large sum of money which could have been utilised to their own advantage.

Another educational enterprise to develop outside the governmental structures in the early 1920s was based in Zubayr. During the First World War, Muhammad Amin al-Shinqiti, a Mauritanian scholar educated at al-Azhar, had arrived in the desert town.[78] He had been expelled from Kuwait because the ruler
feared his anti-British propaganda, but Shaykh Ibrahim had welcomed him, allowed him to teach and provided some limited financial support.[79] Shinqiti applied to the authorities in Baghdad for permission to open a school in 1920, but
did not receive an official permit until January 1923.[80] One of the leading separatists, 'Abd al-Latif al-Mandil, in fact supported the school financially.[81]

However, although the institutional framework was thus prepared, the Najah
School never became a centre for separatist propaganda. It provided a course in
basic accounting which may have suited the requirements of Basra's commercial establishment, but its fields of specialisation were religion and Arabic language, and its teachers largely men with a religious education.[82] And even
though Shinqiti himself was sympathetic to Islamic modernist Salafi teachings
that stressed the ideal of transcending denominational and sectarian differences
of all kinds, an image of insularity stuck to the new project: many Basrawis associated Salafism with the strict Hanbali branch of Islamic jurisprudence, and
this, as well as a location in a town reputed for its orthodox Sunnism, may be
why the new centre of learning never appealed to broader strata of Basra's
population – the universalistic approach of its headmaster notwithstanding.[83]
The Najah School did not develop beyond the primary level, so its pupils had to
move on to Basra for intermediate and to Baghdad for a full secondary education.[84]

A more centrally located institution which did succeed in appealing to a wide
spectrum of Basra's public was the school of the Reformed Church of America,
known as The School of High Hope, situated between Basra and 'Ashar.
Founded in 1912 with permission from the Ottoman authorities, it had since its
early days managed to attract pupils from across the ethnic and sectarian divides
of Basra.[85] Both Shi'is and Sunnis, from urban as well as rural backgrounds,
sent their sons to this school in the early 1920s, while a separate establishment
for girls was pioneering female education in the region.[86] The school was supported financially by the local elite, and it did have a secondary level.[87]

Despite such qualities, the American school became no separatist hotbed.
The director, John Van Ess, was familiar with the separatist current, and in fact
related it to his own interpretation of ancient Mesopotamian history – in which
Assyria and Babylonia competed for hegemony and created a historical legacy
of north-south antagonism that constituted a real challenge for modern-day British state-builders in Iraq.[88] But Van Ess had priorities of his own. First and
foremost he was a missionary, whose school organised daily Bible classes and
had a chapel on the school campus. Among the accomplishments highlighted in
his annual reports was the recruitment of some graduates to Hope College in
Michigan, another institution affiliated with the Reformed Church.[89] Moreover,
Van Ess was on foreign territory, a US citizen dependent on the goodwill of the
Iraqi authorities, and his frequent social intercourse with British officials may

have provided him with insights into British policy that were more realistic than the separatists' assessments.[90] He had close friends among prominent Iraqi nationalists and took pride in fostering candidates for Iraqi government service.[91]

As for the citizenry of Basra, the school's focus on Christian values may have prevented them from any closer association with it beyond what their sons could acquire in terms of education. The annual reports of the mission school stated that although some boys showed a degree of interest in Christianity, with a few even "near entering the Kingdom", most pupils had not yet "gathered courage enough to confess Christ as their saviour".[92] Such language revealed the prime concerns of the authors: here was yet another group of people operating in Basra whose gaze was directed at things rather larger than the port city.

History and the definition of new political communities

The scheme for separation of Basra had not been preceded by any vibrant cultural movement specific to the Gulf city. Hence, the ideological mythology required to sustain it would have to be created from scratch, patched together from the symbolic resources available. And although the separatist demands of 1921 did include a sketchy vision of a cosmopolitan, mercantilist and pro-British mini-state, there was a striking dearth of references to historical precedents that might have strengthened the movement – as a model for inspiration and as a reservoir of glorious myths and paragons.

There was no shortage of adventure with a localist edge in the history of Basra. Since its foundation in the early Islamic period, the Gulf city had formed part of several political entities that had emerged in opposition to the regimes prevailing further upriver. In the ninth century, it was the centre of the great Zanj revolt which challenged the Baghdad-based Abbasid caliphate and created its own government for fourteen years. In the first half of the tenth century, another revolt against the Abbasids was led by the Qarmatis, who came to control much of the Gulf littoral from Basra south to Qatar. Again, for much of the seventeenth century, Basra was governed by rulers from the Afrasiyab dynasty who enjoyed a virtually independent position vis-à-vis the Ottomans. Basra could also boast of an ancient past prior to the Islamic era that was distinct from the history of areas further north: In Parthian times, a Hellenistic kingdom known as Characene maintained local autonomy from around 130 BC to AD 220, and before the emergence of the great Babylonian civilisations, the Basra area – the parts of it not submerged at the time – was dominated by the Sumerians (circa 3800–2000 BC), a people of obscure origins who were at war with the Semitic population to the north and were eventually conquered by them.

Not all these epochs were equally suitable material for legends designed to emphasise Basra's separate status. The Zanj revolt had been carried out by a group of African slaves against their Basra landlords. They had rallied around an alleged descendant of 'Ali in order to legitimise their revolt against the Abbasids.[93] Eventually, this Shi'i-coloured uprising was brought to an end when

Abbasid forces from Baghdad came to the rescue of the Basra landlords. Similarly, the Qarmati regime was associated with Isma'ilism, and its history of frequent attacks on caravans of pilgrims and eventually the theft of the Black
Stone of the Kaaba in Mecca made it an unlikely focus if sectarian controversies
were to be overcome.[94] Even inventive historians would find it difficult to re-
clothe these episodes of Basra's history in acceptable garb. On the other hand,
the period of Afrasiyab rule in the seventeenth century was not encumbered
with such heavy connotations of sectarianism or heresy.[95] During the reign of
this family, itself of Turkish descent, Basra enjoyed a golden age when trade
prospered, relations with European mercantile powers were good, and Shi'is as
well as Sunnis held prominent positions in the city government. Similarly, the
various pre-Islamic civilisations of the region's ancient history were untainted
by doctrinal differences, and held a potential as a point in the past from which
all Basra might gather inspiration.

When the separatist movement emerged in 1921, both the Afrasiyab emirate
as well as the old Sumerian civilisation were known to the elites of Basra,
whereas the history of Characene remained obscure.[96] Yet, knowledge as well
as the tangible relics of these historical epochs were unevenly distributed. This
could be seen for example in the writings of Anastas Mari al-Karmali, a Baghdad Christian who had been entrusted by the British with writing the first official textbook of Iraqi history.[97] He was one of the few contemporary historians
of the region to even touch on the Sumerians, but apart from portraying them as
a non-Semitic people who had contributed to the early Mesopotamian civilisations before being swallowed up (*ibtal'a*) by Semitic groups from farther north,
he offered little in the way of detail about their culture or politics.[98] At the time,
knowledge about the Sumerians and other ancient Mesopotamian civilisations
was the preserve of outsiders.

During the nineteenth century, British, American, French and German excavations in the areas north of Basra had created the basis for a whole science of
Sumerology, but many important artefacts had already been taken away to
European museums, and scholarly publications on the subject were almost exclusively in European languages. After the British occupation, Baghdad became
the centre for all matters archaeological, and Percy Cox's close associate,
Gertrude Bell, dominated this sector of the administration until her death in
1926. In order to gain access to materials that might amplify and sustain a mythology linking Basra up with the Sumerians, the separatists would have needed
the collaboration of Western archaeologists or, preferably, Bell herself. She had,
however, militated against the separatist scheme from its very beginning and
was an unlikely partner in such an enterprise, while the academics who were
digging at Ur (north-west of Basra) in the mid 1920s – who did try to collect
much-needed financial assistance locally – failed to receive substantial backing
from the Basra notables.[99]

As for the Afrasiyabs, their existence and conflicts with the Ottomans were
well known, but mainly from Ottoman accounts where this dynasty was depicted as destructive rebels.[100] A key Ottoman history of the region, first pub-

lished in 1730 and used extensively by subsequent writers, mentioned only in passing that the reason for punitive expeditions sent from Baghdad in the 1660s was the ruler of Basra's revolt against the Ottoman state, and then proceeded to detail the restoration of the central authority's power.[101] A similar bias could be seen in later works by Basra historians on the Ottoman era, as well as in the account included in the official Ottoman yearbooks for the vilayet in the early twentieth century. In both cases, the whole first half of the seventeenth century was summarised in two sentences, mentioning the name of the local "governors" (thus preserving a semblance of normalcy), but without any details about the nature of their rule.[102] Later, in the setting of post-war Baghdad and with pro-Arab sentiments on the rise, Karmali employed the sources available to him to write the Afrasiyab emirate into a larger context of continuous "Arab revolts" against the Ottomans led mainly from the Basra area. However, he seemed unable to offer a more thorough description of local developments beyond mentioning that the "banner of revolt" (*liwa' al-'isyan*) had been raised by a succession of personalities within the Afrasiyab family.[103]

Sources which could have provided a more inspiring backdrop for the history of the Afrasiyab state did exist, but were not easily accessible to the separatists. European libraries possessed rare copies of books by seventeenth-century French and Portuguese travellers to Basra, with comprehensive descriptions of a regime that favoured trade with Europeans, hosted Christian missionaries, protected a multi-religious community including a large number of Mandaeans, and was so effective from Qurna to the Gulf that no one "dared to touch a date" before having paid the appropriate tax to the ruler.[104] Collections of Shi'i biographies printed in Tehran and Lucknow in the late nineteenth century contained details about Shi'i scholars who had worked in Basra under the Afrasiyab family – another indication of a regime altogether different from that of the Ottomans.[105] Finally, some important source material had been deposited in the Basra area itself, but it was well guarded. The family library of the Basha'yans, an aristocratic family settled in Basra for centuries, included substantial texts from both Sunni and Shi'i authors who had served the short-lived Afrasiyab state.[106] This material existed only in manuscript form and was not immediately available to the separatists, who came mostly from families whose presence in Basra dated back only a few generations. If the separatists dominated Basra in material terms, it was the anti-separatists who continued to control some of the major wellsprings from which a separatist legend could derive inspiration.

In 1924, this situation was to change dramatically – in a rather astonishing manner. The anti-separatist Amin 'Ali Basha'yan, whose family had been loyal to the Ottomans for centuries, then took the initiative to publish a manuscript by a seventeenth-century Shi'i *'alim*, Fath Allah ibn 'Alwan al-Ka'bi. This work, *Zad al-musafir* (Provisions for the Traveller), was written by a contemporary of the Afrasiyab rulers who described the downfall of their dynasty at the hands of the Ottomans. But before the narrative reached the point at which the local principality collapsed during the rule of one of its less benevolent sovereigns, the author had elaborated on the virtues of the earlier leading figures of the Afrasi-

yab emirate. Suddenly, the secrets of Basra's separate existence during this period entered the public domain in unprecedented detail.[107]

At first glance, Basha'yan's publication of this book, in the midst of an ongoing struggle between supporters of different identity projects in Basra at the
time, could come across as self-destructive. Here was the story of a local principality ruled by a Sunni where a Shi'i *'alim* could become an official judge.[108]
Here were words of praise from the Shi'i author for the wise Sunni ruler in
Basra who fostered an atmosphere of learning and science.[109] Here were vivid
descriptions of the sorrow and fears of a population fleeing for their lives when
forces from Baghdad eventually managed to restore Ottoman rule.[110] In short,
here were the elements of a romantic tale of an autonomous Gulf state whose
geographical extension matched almost perfectly with the territory targeted by
the Basra separatists three hundred years later. Admittedly, the decay of the
Afrasiyab regime during the final years of its existence was also an element of
the story (and the ancestors of the Basha'yans appeared briefly as a pro-
Ottoman force in the drama), but during the editorial process, which involved
creating a book of fifty-six pages from an original manuscript of several hundred folios, the publishers appear to have been guided by academic rather than
manipulative or strongly nationalistic principles: they faithfully followed a
scheme in which the original *maqama* (a genre of rhymed prose) was given in
its entirety, while the much longer commentary (*sharh*) was omitted where it
treated more general philological themes, but preserved wherever it touched on
matters of local significance – even when this meant dwelling on the brilliance
of the early Afrasiyab period.[111]

Interestingly, the publication of this book was not the only instance where
anti-separatists contributed to public awareness of themes from Basra's past
antithetical to their own political visions. Karmali's government-sponsored
textbook had called attention to the frequent conflicts between north and south
in ancient Mesopotamia, which the author contrasted with the experience of
Egypt.[112] Khalaf Shawqi Amin al-Dawudi, the local newspaper editor who had
hailed Rihani and was close to many of the anti-separatists, had apparently no
qualms about publishing an article discussing the old antagonisms between Ak-
kad and Sumer.[113] And even leading British officials refrained from enforcing
unity in Iraq's complicated past. The first publication issued by the Iraq Museum, which appeared in 1926 and was authored by Gertrude Bell, spoke of the
Sumerians as a people who had arrived from the outside (possibly from Persia
or India), were "superior" to the local Semitic population and had brought with
them the art of writing and the use of copper.[114] In 1925 Bell specifically suggested to an American archaeological team that they concentrate their initial
survey of ancient Mesopotamian sites right in middle of the Sumerian core area
north of Basra, and later issued them with a permit to excavate there.[115]

The absence of censorship and the apparent enthusiasm for publishing historical accounts on the basis of their intrinsic interest rather than their suitability
for this or that nationalist vision, suggest strong self-confidence on the part of
the supporters of a unitary Iraqi state. The fact that adversaries of the vision of a

separate Basra made significant contributions to the publicly available literature precisely on the subject of the area's historical ruptures with Baghdad indicates that the separatists were simply not seen as credible opponents in the battle over nationalist symbols, and that the risk of the newly released materials ending up as secessionist propaganda was considered negligible. Apparently, it was the separatists' lack of initiative, rather than the initially uneven distribution of symbolic resources, which led to their paralysis in the symbolic domain – rendering them incapable of rushing in to fill the ample political space available in post-war Basra. This passivity was to have serious consequences for the fate of their interaction with the new centre – Baghdad, now the capital of Iraq.

8   Interaction with a New Capital

There was a new regime in Baghdad, but many aspects of Basra's relationship with institutions of central government remained unchanged in the early 1920s. The special system of taxation on date gardens, considered a lighter burden than the revenue regime in areas further north, was still in place.[1] The new state borders were not directly injurious to Basra's commerce, with transit trade to Persia and Arabia continuing along pre-war routes. And although income from date production and trade dwindled somewhat from the record-high levels of the immediate post-war years, so did prices in general.[2] An exception to the rule was the 1923 reform of the municipality tax system, whereby property tax – a significant portion of the total municipality budget – was transferred to the central government. This did represent a painful step towards centralisation in the eyes of the municipal authorities, whose progress reports throughout the 1920s remained slim.[3] But on the whole, the tax burden did not increase, and the freedom from conscription continued.

In many ways, what the centre gave back did not present any great change at first either. The key project of the Public Works Department, Maude Memorial Hospital, was finished in 1923, but had been financed entirely from subscription among the local population.[4] The 'Ashar River remained in desperate need of dredging and cleaning.[5] And in education, Basra still had no proper governmental institution beyond the "intermediate secondary" school for boys between 13 and 15 years of age.[6] More indirectly, the emergence of Baghdad as a capital did bring about a change in the level of government activity locally: part of the customs administration was removed to Baghdad, and this added to the loss suffered when the high levels of expenditure associated with the British war effort disappeared.[7] But then again, the Basrawis were not accustomed to a particularly enterprising state.

A more important change related to communications. In 1922, travel time between Basra and the Iraqi capital on the new railway was down to 22½ hours, compared to steamship travel of earlier times which could easily take four to six days.[8] This opened up for more rapid communication and exchange of ideas, for example by making Baghdad newspapers available for sale in Basra as well.[9] No corresponding revolution in communications with other areas in the Gulf or with Najd took place. A taxi service with motor cars to Kuwait was not opened until the mid 1920s, and as interference from tribes in the border area remained a problem, the maritime route between the two neighbouring areas was still the preferred way to travel.[10] The Najdi highland remained as distant as it had been in the past.[11] With these developments as a backdrop, the Basra separatist leaders started a process of reluctant interaction with the capital city which they had tried so hard to escape by their 1921 petition.

Resignations and silent protests

One of the foremost separatist leaders, 'Abd al-Latif al-Mandil, was given two ministerial jobs in the new regime between 1921 and 1923 – an experience that ended in frustration. First appointed to the Ministry of Commerce in the new cabinet formed after Faysal's accession, he was faced with the difficult issue of the Port of Basra.[12] Britain had invested heavily in the port during the war, but now, with moderation in imperial expenditure the new watchword, wanted a takeover by Iraqi authorities and a return on British investments. The key decision to prepare for Iraqi ownership of the port was made by the British adviser to the Ministry of Commerce at a meeting in London in August 1921; it was subsequently approved by several ministers, all prior to Mandil's assumption of his new role later in September. The incoming minister was then charged with exploring the possibilities of raising the necessary funds, a process which culminated in a scheme for purchase of the port by the Iraqi government. Mandil thus dutifully acted as a centraliser on behalf of the state by promoting a policy that would cement ties between his own city and the new Iraqi capital.[13] In so doing, Mandil not only put his own separatist scheme at risk. He also became estranged from powerful circles in Basra who advocated a dismantling of the new facilities altogether and reversion to pre-war methods of midstream discharge and loading – a trade in which they had specialised for decades.[14]

In March 1922, only days after the ministry had delivered its report on the port question, Mandil clashed with the new regime on a different issue. He was among five ministers forced by Faysal to resign after a disagreement over defence arrangements and policy towards Iraq's neighbour to the west, Ibn Sa'ud.[15] The king had already singled out the formation of an army as a matter on which he could placate Iraqi nationalists, and, after an episode of frontier raiding from Najdi areas, wanted to take firm action. But the cabinet had been lukewarm, and the tenor of its debate showed a disinclination to become embroiled in a serious conflict as a result of the king's personal enmity towards Ibn Sa'ud.[16] Now Faysal's policy was clearly veering towards the costly and dangerous nationalism-induced brinkmanship against which the Basra separatists had specifically warned.

In an interview with a Baghdad newspaper soon after resigning, Mandil announced that he would have nothing more to do with politics, and returned to Basra.[17] He was not to remain idle for long, however. In the autumn of 1922, he travelled to Hasa' to assist Ibn Sa'ud in developing the commercial potential of the area and to organise its revenues.[18] Later that year, he participated in the Najdi delegation in trilateral negotiations with Iraq and Kuwait, and took an assertive role on Ibn Sa'ud's behalf in questions concerning the border zone between Najd and Kuwait – where it was thought oil could be found.[19] Although the trip had been arranged with the concurrence of Cox, British representatives were worried that Mandil was up to something "deeper", perhaps involving "oil" and "the French".[20] Despite these Najdi adventures, Mandil was again invited to take part in the new Iraqi government formed in December

1922, as minister for religious endowments.[21] This time he completed his tenure, but the personal relationship with Faysal remained strained. The Basra minister was absent during Faysal's first visit to the southern Gulf city as king in June 1923, and in September that year, the Iraqi monarch personally intervened in a land settlement case in Mandil's disfavour.[22]

In Iraq's first nationwide elections in 1924, Mandil and other separatists had no problems in getting elected as Basra representatives to the constituent assembly, whose task was to discuss the new organic law for Iraq as well as to ratify the amended Anglo-Iraqi treaty of 1923.[23] Mandil was chosen to represent Basra in the committee charged with examining the draft for the constitution, a process which in theory constituted a fresh possibility to customise the new political system to accommodate some of Basra's concerns about over-centralisation. And yet, Mandil absented himself from several committee meetings and apparently never brought the separatist demands to the negotiating table.[24] As for the treaty, reports at the time suggested that prominent Basra leaders were against it because they would have preferred a more direct system of British rule.[25] Dobbs reproached them for this attitude, as he by now had decided to push the treaty through and was already having enough trouble defending it against Iraqi nationalists in the assembly who opposed it from an anti-British platform. But Mandil's absence on the day of voting on the treaty suggests that he was uncomfortable with both alternatives – the nationalist "no" and the moderate "yes".[26] He had silently left the Iraqi capital and spent the subsequent summer in Syria.[27]

Two further members of the Basra separatist delegation chose to stay away from the assembly after having first been elected as members. Yusuf 'Abd al-Ahad, Basra's Christian representative, received threatening letters soon after the elections. These were attributed to a larger campaign against pro-British representatives, which also resulted in a murder attempt on two tribal shaykhs in the streets of Baghdad. 'Abd al-Ahad promptly departed for Bombay and never took up his seat in the assembly.[28] Similarly, Sayyid 'Abd 'Ali of Qurna was elected only to resign shortly afterwards, citing the threats carried out by anti-British nationalists in Baghdad.[29] Finally, three of the remaining representatives of Basra followed Mandil's example and stayed away when the treaty came up for voting.[30] Once again, the separatists demonstrated their dissent through acts of silent withdrawal.

Ironically, while the Basra separatists had been unsuccessful in promoting their ideas on the local scene, the spectre of "Basra separatism" did become established currency on the emerging market of Iraqi politics in the early 1920s. People from outside the Gulf city operating within the framework of Iraqi politics discovered the usefulness of the Basra scheme as a bargaining card in their own power games within the system, and contributed to utilitarian reincarnations of the project with little connection to the original movement. One example was Naji al-Suwaydi, a young Sunni Baghdadi with administrative experience from the Ottoman regime, who shortly after having been dismissed as minister of justice in 1922 was allegedly involved in a revival of the Basra movement.[31] Some six months later, however, he was back as a minister, and went on to hold several ministerial appointments during Faysal's reign as well as becoming prime minister on one occasion – all indicating the existence of other, ulterior motives behind his brief career as a "Basra separatist".

Another instance of outsiders employing the idea of Basra separatism to further their own interests occurred in the Muntafiq area, north of the zone delineated by the separatists in 1921. Here, tribal leaders of Bani Asad and 'Abbuda joined a Sa'dun shaykh and ex-governor of Muntafiq in calling for a larger project of separation, involving the whole former vilayet of Basra, and aiming for British support.[32] There is, however, no evidence of co-operation between the promoters of this scheme and the notables behind the 1921 separatist petition. One year later, the Bani Asad shaykh proclaimed a general revolt against the Iraqi government in the Jaza'ir marsh area, perhaps an indication of motives more to do with finding a framework to preserve his tribal leadership in a period of tumultuous upheaval.[33] Nevertheless, the Muntafiq shaykhs undertook something from which the Basra notables refrained: through several public meetings, they made a serious attempt at broadening popular support for their project.

The bitter experiences of leading Basra separatists in the new capital were paralleled by the ordeals of the separatist scheme as a collective political movement. The current in favour of cutting ties with Baghdad continued to manifest itself during the 1920s, but had lost much of its original momentum. Instead of developing into a full-scale political movement, it now appeared only in the shape of rumours and unverified reports. In early 1922, the British administrative inspector in the city claimed that the separatist demands continued to be "universally expressed", and later in that year, Cox pointed out that he expected disappointment if his negative answer to the separatist petition were communicated locally.[34] French observers maintained that the Basrawis favoured the mandate, but would push for separation should the relationship with Baghdad develop unpleasantly.[35] Baghdad nationalist newspaper reports in May 1922 suggested that the movement was being "revived", whereas the minister of interior published a letter refuting such claims, demanding an end to public discussion of the matter.[36] In 1923, "apprehension" was expressed in Basra when the Anglo-Iraqi treaty was reduced from twenty-five to four years, although hopes lingered on that Basra's special demands could be met in a future treaty.[37] In January 1924 it was even rumoured that some Shi'i notables of Basra were beginning to take an interest in separatism. However, when these reports reached the Iraqi police, no substantial evidence could be found.[38] As a political movement, Basra separatism remained as thin on the ground as earlier.

Although the separatists suffered from obvious organisational problems, it was equally clear that some of the sentiment behind the original petition persisted. In May 1925, Mirza Muhammad Khan Bahadur, a Persian inhabitant of Basra employed by Shaykh Khaz'al of Muhammara as his local representative, was attacked by a Baghdad nationalist newspaper, the *Mufid*, for having plotted against his Arab employer.[39] This provoked angry reactions in the local Basra newspaper, where it was asserted that the allegations were wrong, and that

pouring scorn on one of the most prominent citizens of Basra was a major mis-
take.[40] This in turn roused a more general assault in the *Mufid* on Basra, its inhabitants and their alleged lack of nationalist attitude.[41] How could they defend
Mirza Muhammad in this manner, presenting him as one of the *ashraf* (descendants of the Prophet) of the city, when everyone knew he was a Persian? The
writer also castigated Basra for the prominence of foreign merchants in its affairs and politics, and asserted that only a handful of its youth had any interest
whatsoever in the Iraqi nationalist cause. He even advocated the despatch of a
nationalist delegation from the capital to rectify matters, and announced a forthcoming remonstrance about the activities of the American mission – an article
which, however, failed to materialise.

The responses to these accusations in the shape of newspaper letters written
by local residents are interesting as many of them reflect a spirit reminiscent of
the proud, mercantile cosmopolitanism detectable in the 1921 separatist petition. One writer stated that there was nothing anomalous in the presence of a
large number of foreigners in the city: on the contrary, these immigrants inter-
acted amicably with the inhabitants and contributed to the prosperity of Basra.[42]
This state of affairs should be seen as perfectly normal, and the experiences of
more advanced countries elsewhere demonstrated amply the useful role played
by talented immigrants in the progress of civilisation. Another writer enquired
rhetorically: How could Mirza Muhammad's Iranianness (*iraniyyatuhu*) prevent
him from being one of Basra's *ashraf*? And surely the inhabitants of cities like
Alexandria, Paris and London were known by the name of their city and not
their place of origin? The letter went on to mock the *Mufid*'s emphasis on Arab
racial purity (*qahtaniyya*) and hinted that the author who had criticised Basra
was in fact in sympathy with the Turks, the only "foreigners" this writer wished
to get rid of.[43] Yet another contributor pointed out that the population of "southern Iraq" (*al-'iraq al-janubi*) had mixed with the people of Persia for centuries,
and claimed that the focus on racial purity was misguided, as very few "pure"
Arabs in fact lived in the region.[44] In sum, the letters from Basra showed that its
inhabitants continued to disagree with the Baghdadis on fundamental issues
about nationalism and citizenship – but these indignant protests were also testament to the past failure in communicating Basra feelings to intellectuals in the
new Iraqi capital.

The anti-separatists and the wider Iraqi community

The phenomenon of anti-separatists stepping in wherever separatists stayed passive was repeated in the political arenas of the capital. The Basha'yan family
had already asserted themselves firmly on the side of the anti-separatists, and
during 1922 continued to cultivate links with areas further north. Baghdad
newspapers commended Amin 'Ali for the position he had taken against separatism, and the family's office in Basra received many guests considered by British intelligence officials as "extremists".[45] As a consequence, the Basha'yans

were suspected of harbouring sympathies for the Turks, but, as their public speeches and actual patterns of interaction with the new regime demonstrate, they made an effort to establish ties with Faysal as well as some officers close to him from the beginning.[46] When Ja'far al-'Askari in November 1923 became the first prime minister to be recruited from Faysal's entourage, Salih Basha'yan was rewarded with the post of minister for religious endowments, a position previously held by Mandil, the leading separatist spokesman. In this capacity, he made a tour of the Tigris districts in 1924 to encourage participation in the forthcoming elections.[47] At one point he acted as minister of interior, and both he and his brother secured seats in the constituent assembly, where they voted in favour of the Anglo-Iraqi treaty. To the British, the Basha'yans had by now become perfect, "moderate" politicians: they did not engage in subversive, "extremist" nationalist politics that could threaten the Anglo-Iraqi accord, and they also distanced themselves from backward separatist schemes that would interest the British only if all else should fail.[48]

Many other anti-separatists followed the path of the Basha'yans to the new capital, although they aligned themselves with forces in Baghdad more critical of the British and the treaty. Shamkhani supported Iraqi nationalist circles in Baghdad financially, hosted 'Abd al-Ghafur al-Badri (the Sunni editor of the Baghdad-based *Istiqlal* newspaper and an outspoken critic of the British mandate), and in 1925 arranged a large banquet for Yasin al-Hashimi (then co-opted as prime minister, but a well-known antagonist of British policy in Iraq).[49] Shamkhani also maintained links with Shi'is elsewhere in Iraq, visited the holy cities, and contributed 16,000 rupees to the upkeep of a Shi'i shrine in Kufa, near Najaf.[50] Similarly, Muhammad Zaki managed to get elected as a Basra representative to the constituent assembly by posing as a pro-treaty candidate during the elections – only to become one of the treaty's most vocal opponents upon arriving in Baghdad.[51] He contributed to a report strongly critical of the proposed accord, and together with Iraqi nationalist representatives, voted against the final treaty later on. His activities in the assembly exposed him to a wider circle of nationalists, and in August 1924, he joined with other lawyers in the capital in an application for permission to establish a political organisation named Hizb al-Istiqlal (The Independence Party).[52]

Also Basrawis less involved in politics experienced the emergence of Baghdad as the new metropolis. In the summer of 1922, directors of local schools throughout Iraq were summoned to a general meeting in the capital. In addition to lectures and debates on educational affairs, they were taken on a sightseeing trip of Baghdad that covered all the governmental institutions, including many new ones, like the electrical power plant, the airbase, and specialist units for X-rays and bacteriological analyses.[53] Several teachers from Basra attended, and were thus able to meet with counterparts from other regions of the new kingdom.[54] In subsequent years, a number of young Basrawis were also taken to Baghdad for longer stays as recruits to the national teachers' college.[55]

Alternative strategies for dealing with the new centre

As their own separatist movement became increasingly impotent and the British continued to insist on dealing with Iraq through one central authority in Baghdad, various alternative options for securing at least their most essential objectives emerged for the Basra notables during the early 1920s. Gradually, some of the energy from the separatist enterprise became redirected to such projects.

One possibility was to work within the system and support the pro-British current in the country. This would contribute to secure commercial relations with Britain and minimise the influence of unpredictable radicals in Baghdad, who had already demonstrated their ability to bring business to a standstill in pursuit of nationalist objectives. Such an approach became embodied in ʿAbd al-Muhsin al-Saʿdun, a brother of the Saʿdun delegate in the 1921 pro-separation caucus who was now finally back after several decades in Istanbul. In contrast to most of the separatist leaders, he had years of experience at the central level of the Ottoman regime behind him, both as an officer and as a parliamentary deputy for his native Muntafiq.[56]

Saʿdun entered government as minister of justice in 1922, took up residence in Baghdad and soon became a favourite of British administrators, serving as prime minister for much of 1923.[57] Although he had spent most of his life in other parts of the Middle East, he was put up as a candidate for Basra in the 1924 elections for the constituent assembly and obtained the highest number of votes of all the local contestants.[58] He apparently worked in harmony with separatist leaders such as Saniʿ and Mandil (the latter served as his minister for one year), but, unlike them, was able to use the new system of government to his own advantage. By doing so, Saʿdun provided people of his constituency with a more constructive model for approaching Baghdad. And while leading members of the separatist elite continued to sidestep the emerging challenges, there are signs that they may have started realising the predicament in which they found themselves: although they personally refrained from entering close relationships with the new regime, many made sure that their sons and other near relatives of the younger generation were given governmental positions in its administration, also outside of Basra.[59]

However, some of the actions of Mandil and Saniʿ make it difficult to discount another alternative strategy. Mandil resigned his seat in the first Iraqi cabinet under Faysal's reign after a row over policy towards Ibn Saʿud, before travelling to Hasaʾ to assist the Najdi ruler with developing its commerce and to take part in the 1922 ʿUqayr negotiations as member of the Najdi delegation. He maintained a residence in Zubayr, where the population was overwhelmingly of Najdi origin, and supported its religious school, dominated by a teacher of Salafi persuasions. Later in the 1920s, Mandil was considered as a "Najdi ambassador to Basra and Baghdad" by one observer.[60] Similarly, Saniʿ used his local power to placate Ibn Saʿud in issues involving Zubayr or the desert west of Basra, for instance by recovering loot belonging to Najdi tribes.[61]

All this took place in the context of continued Najdi expansionism during the first half of the 1920s. Ibn Rashid, who had been the dominating force in the desert area west of Basra and the ruler of an independent emirate based in Ha'il, was finally defeated in December 1921. In 1924, Hijaz disappeared as a political entity without intervention by Britain, its wartime ally, followed by the veiled incorporation of 'Asir into Najd as a "protectorate" in 1926. And during previous negotiations with Iraq, Ibn Sa'ud had indicated the Euphrates as the ideal eastern border of his domain.[62] These developments were covered by the local press in Basra, where Ibn Sa'ud's flirtation with the desert tribes living west of Basra was reported and where violent raids on shepherds in the desert (even near Zubayr) committed by ultra-orthodox bands of pro-Saudi Ikhwan (a Wahhabi brotherhood) from Najd created big headlines, reminding the Basrawis of the military power that the Najdis were capable of mobilising.[63] Persons of Najdi origin in Basra must have followed this development with particular interest. After 1922, Mandil and Sani' in fact did more to cultivate relations with Najd than to press their separatist demands vis-à-vis Baghdad.

Finally, one other external force remained influential in Basra in the early 1920s. The British had established good relations with Shaykh Khaz'al of Muhammara before the war, and although there had been certain criticisms and mild attempts at reform, little was done to curb his influence on the Iraqi bank of the Shatt al-'Arab after Faysal's accession in 1921.[64] People continued to traverse the international border between Iraq and Persia with little hindrance, and each year, large numbers of Khaz'al's tribesmen and peasants crossed the river for seasonal work on the Persian side.[65]

In this manner, the shaykh of Muhammara (who despite his independent behaviour was technically still a provincial Persian vassal) remained an influential figure on both sides of the river. When the Shi'i inhabitants on his estates south of Basra signed declarations referring to "our amir", they meant Khaz'al, not Faysal.[66] Sani', the governor and the highest-ranking Iraqi official in the region, continued to sign letters to the shaykh with a deferential *'abdukum* (your servant) in 1921.[67] In October that year, Khaz'al was even represented by a delegate at the ceremony celebrating the appointment of Hashim al-Naqib as the new *naqib* of Basra, a function at which all the other guests were of old Sunni families.[68] With his ability to appeal to several sections of Basra society, the Muhammara-based shaykh represented another concrete alternative to the abstract separatist vision. But in 1925, Khaz'al disappeared from the local political scene when the Persian government moved to consolidate its grip on the southwestern periphery. This was only the first of several developments that year which were all to become fateful for the Basra separatists.

Separatist setbacks

Khaz'al's arrest and removal to Tehran in April 1925 signified a comeback for the centralising state in the inner Gulf region. It was followed by another act of incorporation on the Iraqi side of the Shatt al-'Arab in May, when the government in Baghdad arranged elections to the first Iraqi parliament and asked Basra to vote for its representatives.

The separatist elite chose to ally itself with 'Abd al-Muhsin al-Sa'dun during the election campaign.[69] The results of the elections were described by the British as "satisfactory", meaning that they thought the deputies would generally support Sa'dun.[70] Yet the election of the "extremist" 'Abd al-Kazim al-Shamkhani came as an unpleasant surprise to British observers, and, along with the success of another politician with strong ties to Baghdad, was a clear indication to the separatist elites that their efforts to control the local political scene were running aground.[71] After the election, 'Abd al-Latif al-Mandil once more demonstrated his uneasy relationship with Baghdad, by first obtaining leave of absence and later resigning when attempts at extension proved unsuccessful.[72] Others who had previously employed similar exit strategies now chose to co-operate with Sa'dun in following a pro-British course within the bounds of the established political framework.[73]

During the course of the summer, the disappearance of Khaz'al was also beginning to make its mark on Basra. A substantial portion of the mainly Shi'i population living between Abu al-Khasib and Fao had hitherto stayed aloof from the new Iraqi regime, boycotting elections and evading Iraqi officials on the pretext that they were Khaz'al's tribesmen.[74] Now that Khaz'al was gone they had to reorientate themselves politically. Some saw in Khaz'al's demise the disappearance of a protective shield and the emergence of a new threat: the Iraqi state, whose registrations of primary voters for the forthcoming elections were perceived as a prelude to conscription. They declared that, given their status as Khaz'al's tribal subjects, they must be considered Persian citizens with the right to sidestep Iraqi electoral registration and with immunity against any future attempt at conscription.[75] Others were just as worried about the new Persian masters. During the summer of 1925 an alliance was forged that joined tribesmen on both sides of the river in a rebellion against the new authorities in Muhammara.[76] The revolt was accompanied by much looting as there was a food crisis on the Persian side of the river at the time, but many observers thought the aim of the revolt was to restore the semi-autonomous principality of Khaz'al and emphasised the prominent role played by members of Khaz'al's private army (*ghulams*).[77]

As on previous occasions, the Basra governor, Ahmad al-Sani', lost no time in responding to turbulence on the outskirts of his fiefdom. The demands for Persian citizenship were confronted with threats of expulsion to the other side of the river, and the local authorities made unprecedented efforts to seal the porous border during the rebellion in July – to prevent tribesmen from the Iraqi side from joining their allies against the Persian soldiers.[78] The uprising was soon brought under control. But while Sani' achieved his objectives, it was increasingly unclear whose interests he was really serving. In 1921 he had subjugated Zubayr so that it would form part of "the government of Basra". But as Sani' continued to quell local political initiatives without converting their proponents to his own vision, it was the Iraqi (and now also the Persian) government which reaped the profits of policies that increasingly seemed to be raison d'état on the behalf of others, the separatist acting as a centraliser for Baghdad.

Finally, the return in May 1925 of Sayyid Talib, virtual ruler of Basra during the last years before the war, could not fail to make an impact on the local political landscape – despite Talib's assurances about future disengagement from politics and the ascendancy of his cousin Hashim to the hereditary position as formal *naqib* of Basra. But no close links between Talib and the separatist leaders evolved after his homecoming. Saniʿ chose the occasion of Talib's arrival to make a rare visit to Baghdad, and his prolonged absence became the subject of much local speculation. Mandil was present at the quay, but it was the Bashaʿyan family who hosted Talib on the day of his return and subsequently developed links with him.[79] In December 1925, Salih Bashaʿyan accompanied Talib on his first visit to Baghdad since his 1921 deportation, and it was Baghdad friends of the Bashaʿyan family who received the lion's share of the patronage distributed by the former strongman of Basra.[80]

Another recipient of Sayyid Talib's money during his stay in the Iraqi capital was Yasin al-Hashimi. Described by Gertrude Bell as a "local Saʿd Zaghlul" (a reference to the nationalist leader who had been central in pressurising Britain to abolish the protectorate in Egypt in 1922), and supported by individuals who admired Mustafa Kemal for what he had achieved in Turkey, Hashimi had formed the nucleus for the first party-based opposition to Saʿdun's pro-British policies. Muhammad Zaki, one of the Basra delegates to the constituent assembly and an ardent anti-separatist, had joined him in 1924 in criticising the treaty arrangements.[81] And as the Anglo-Iraqi treaty again became a matter of dispute in early 1926, more Basra anti-separatists came to support Hashimi in his struggle against the government.[82] The 1925 League of Nations award of Mosul to Iraq had been made on the condition that treaty relations with Britain should revert to the original twenty-five year period, and Hashimi's supporters felt that the prospects of independence were now being severely hampered. Sayyid Talib's active support for this current could only be limited, given his promise of non-involvement in politics. But his financial contributions to anti-British circles were another indication that Basra's resources were increasingly being diverted away from the separatist option.

1926: National party politics reaches Basra

The first anti-British opposition to the treaty in 1926 was effectively sidelined, as a large majority in the parliament remained loyal to Saʿdun. However, during the course of the year, Hashimi along with another politician critical of Saʿdun's pro-British approach, Rashid ʿAli al-Gaylani, managed to attract more sympathisers among the Iraqi deputies, aided by Faysal's support for them as a means to check the progression of Saʿdun's political career.[83] In November 1926, members of the parliament loyal to Hashimi and Gaylani, including some Basra anti-separatists, successfully challenged Sa'dun's nominee to the post as speaker of parliament, and the premier resigned.[84] The new ministry under Ja'far al-'Askari included both Hashimi and Gaylani as well as others who shared their political outlook, and also featured the ministerial debut of a leading Basra anti-separatist of 1921, Amin 'Ali Basha'yan.

The Basha'yans had held ministerial posts earlier, but this particular appointment was to have repercussions on the local political scene in Basra as well. One month after the change of government, Ahmad al-Sani' relinquished his post as governor. On the surface, the whole process appeared peaceful enough: the Basra separatist leader was given a seat in the Iraqi senate; his son continued to serve as governor of 'Amara before being transferred to an identical post in Baghdad.[85] Yet, there were mutterings that the motives behind the "promotion" of Sani' were insincere, and far-reaching local-level consequences became apparent as soon as the new ministry went on to appoint a successor. Several local candidates voiced an interest in the job, but to no avail. This time, Basra was brought into conformity with the bureaucratic system which by now had become firmly established in other parts of Iraq. A career official, someone unconnected with the area, was to have the job, and 'Ali Jawdat Bey al-Ayyubi assumed power in Basra in January 1927.[86]

Ayyubi later claimed that the first thing he did was to reduce the influence of the British administrative inspector. British officials, on their part, maintained that Sani' himself had wielded considerable influence as a "tribal sort of head of administration".[87] What was clear, at any rate, was that the Iraqi government was now beginning to assert itself more forcefully in the Basra area, at the expense of local autonomy. More career officials from other parts of Iraq were subsequently given jobs in the local administration, and, in contrast to their mightier counterparts in areas further north, the shaykhs of Basra's small tribes were not sheltered by the British against this new trend when it started to affect the rural areas as well.[88]

By 1927, Baghdad had achieved a much stronger position in Basra than only six years earlier. It was finally becoming the capital also for the Gulf city in the south. The separatist project was weakened, and the central government was in a position to consolidate its conquest. But in tandem with the expansion of the Iraqi state came a change in appearance. Faysal's second visit to Basra, in May 1926, had focused on inspections of Maude Memorial Hospital (which the inhabitants had paid for themselves) and Ruka Canal (which made it easier for ocean-going steamers to cross the silt-prone and shallow bar of the Shatt al-'Arab but was not something ordinary Basrawis would take much notice of).[89] However, high on the agenda of the 'Askari ministry was the creation of a viable Iraqi army, and plans to introduce conscription were under consideration. This policy, which emerged in the shape of census operations and a parliamentary vote on conscription, was to create a political explosion in Basra in 1927. But the energy behind it had little to do with the leading notables and the old separatist project.

Prior to 1927, political mobilisation among the Shiʿis of Basra had been limited. To some extent, this reflected developments within wider Shiʿi circles in Iraq. The harsh measures enacted by British authorities against the leading ulama of the holy cities after their boycott of the first Iraqi elections led many clerics to abandon politics. The religious leadership was further fragmented because none of the *mujtahid*s vying for support among the Shiʿi believers had managed to achieve paramountcy after the death in 1920 of Shaykh al-Shariʿa al-Isfahani, by then reckoned as the cleric with the greatest number of followers. This created a vacuum, and it took some time before a new group of Shiʿi politicians started to emerge outside the traditional religious hierarchy.

In April 1925, a small branch of the Hizb al-Nahda (The Party of the Awakening), a Shiʿi party based in Baghdad and emphasising sectarian demands, was opened in Basra.[1] The party urged Shiʿis to vote only for candidates of their own sect during the parliamentary elections, but failed to win any Basra representatives in 1925. Several members resigned; in May 1926 the organisation was described as "moribund".[2] Later that year, one of the leading Shiʿi ulama in Basra warned against participation in the annual Muharram processions, a practice which he labelled as sectarian and detrimental to Muslim unity.[3] From such quarters, little support could be expected for an exclusive Shiʿi political party.

However, in 1927, there was a marked upsurge in the activities of the Nahda, both in Basra and elsewhere in Iraq. The small Basra branch swelled to a substantial political organisation with more than one hundred members – the first political party to achieve such organisational success in the city since the prewar reform movement of Sayyid Talib. The local leadership was dominated by Shiʿi landowners and merchants of Basra originating from Qurna and Madina tribes, many of them residents of the suburb of ʿAshar, where the party's headquarters was also located.[4] The party had branches in Qurna and Madina, and the leaders corresponded with and visited these places frequently.[5] Also members of the local clergy supported the movement, and ʿAshar-based ʿAbd al-Mahdi al-Muzaffar (one of the two leading Shiʿi ulama of Basra and another immigrant from Madina) became a particularly close associate.[6]

The Shiʿis and Iraq's territorial integrity

The Nahda party focused on issues considered especially relevant for the Shiʿi community of Iraq. Conscription was particularly important, for earlier experience during Ottoman rule had shown that the members of the lower classes, the majority of whom were Shiʿis, were most vulnerable when officials came to pick their recruits. The king's announcement in 1926 of a forthcoming conscription bill, and the subsequent formation of a cabinet supportive of such a measure, made conscription a realistic threat to the ordinary citizen – something that would bring an end to the relative freedom from state intrusion that had followed the collapse of Ottoman rule. In Basra, bazaars and coffee shops soon became rife with gossip about imminent conscription.[7]

Several incidents during 1927 contributed to a growth in sectarian agitation in Iraq and led many Shi'is to engage in discussions about the future direction of the state. In January, a Syrian teacher in Baghdad published a history textbook on the Umayyad dynasty (AD 661–750) containing derogatory remarks about the family of 'Ali, which caused offence among Shi'is. The authorities eventually withdrew the book, but there were subsequent demonstrations in favour of its author by Sunni students and teachers from the secondary school in Baghdad as well as from the teachers' college, two key institutions in the country's tightly centralised system of education.[8] Moreover, some copies of the book had come into circulation, and exposed to the Shi'is the sort of attitudes that could be found at the core of the state educational apparatus. In a second incident, Iraqi police and army clashed with Shi'i mourners during 'Ashura (the tenth day of the holy month of Muharram) celebrations in Kazimayn in July 1927, leaving three civilians dead. Feelings of sectarian discrimination quickly became widespread among Shi'is in Iraq, and Basra was no exception.[9]

Anticipated parliamentary opposition from the Shi'is made the cabinet abort its plans for pushing through a conscription bill in June 1927. But the battle was merely postponed, and Shi'i schemes demanding radical change in the form of government in Iraq soon began to emerge. Proposals included a strong increase in the number of Shi'i ministers as well as a temporary return to direct British administration – a measure it was hoped would halt the marginalisation of the Shi'is until their young men had acquired modern education and were better prepared to serve in government positions. However, in an entirely new development, Shi'is now gave to their protests a territorial dimension, by making proposals for a decentralised (*lamarkaziyya*) form of government. An even more radical alternative, dividing the country along sectarian lines, was mentioned for the first time as a possible way forward.[10]

Despite its separatist traditions, Basra did not contribute much to the Shi'i rethinking of Iraq and its territorial make-up. At no point during the discussion of partition scenarios did the notion of Basra as a potential capital for the southern part of a divided Iraq take root, and all the main exchanges of views on the subject took place in Baghdad and the holy cities, where only a small number of Basra Shi'is participated. To begin with, the dominant forces were tribal leaders from the Middle Euphrates, who had earlier adopted a variety of means to weaken the Iraqi government in their areas – ranging from the destruction of railway tracks to pro-Turkish propaganda. Their new "decentralisation" demands may well have been a variation of the basic aim of obliterating government authority, rather than a project to create a new (Shi'i) central power by breaking up Iraq into ethnic and religious statelets.[11] Later, the tribal leaders were joined by lower and middle clergy of the holy cities, who approached the scheme from a different angle.[12] Religious scholars of this category had a less secure financial foundation than the leading *mujtahid*s (who now tended to favour non-participation in politics), and the emergence of entirely new state structures and new departments of government would imply fresh possibilities with remunerative prospects for disadvantaged ulama like themselves. More basic disagreements about attitudes to the British only added to the internal tensions within the Nahda: in many tribal areas along the Euphrates there were bitter memories of the 1920 revolt and continued scepticism to the British, but the urban leaders tried to present the party as a pro-British one.[13] The new territorial dimension to the Shi'i protest, in itself a radical development, consisted therefore of a variety of vague and partially incompatible threats rather than a coherent scheme for the devolution of Iraq.

The academic circles supporting the Shi'i movement conceptualised territory and identity in new visions. 'Ali al-Sharqi, a Najaf-educated *'alim* in his thirties living in Baghdad, was a prominent contributor to the Nahda newspaper as well as a poet; British intelligence officers described him as a member of the "inner circle" of the Nahda and "composer of their literature".[14] Starting in 1927, during the heightened sectarian agitation, he wrote a series of historical articles on the Shi'i areas of Iraq, published as instalments in the Nahda newspaper and the journal *Lughat al-'Arab*. This was, however, not the history of a unified Shi'i territory. Several articles dealt instead with the history of separate regions. The past of the Basra area was here narrated as the history of "the marshes" (*al-bata'ih*) and "the islands" (*al-jaza'ir*).[15]

'Ali al-Sharqi presented the history of Basra and its environs within a new framework. To him, all the towns and cities between the Gulf, Nasiriyya and 'Amara belonged to the sphere of the marshes. Over time, the capitals of the area had shifted between the various "islands" in this aquatic setting: medieval Wasit (north of present-day 'Amara) had been substituted by Basra, then Huwayza (across the Persian border) and finally Madina, to the west of Qurna. During recent decades, political leadership of the marshes had been taken over by the shaykh of the Khayyun clan of Chubayish (immediately north of the Basra division), "the leader of Bani Asad in particular and the shaykh of Jaza'ir more generally" – a chief who in 1924 had been deposed by the Iraqi authorities and exiled to Mosul.

Historically, Sharqi pointed out, the inhabitants of the marshes had often risen against outsiders who sought to dominate them politically, be they Ottomans or Persians. This had led them into alliances with small, local emirates, such as the regime of the Musha'sha' rulers based in Huwayza as well as the Afrasiyab dynasty of Basra. Even the desert town of Zubayr could be fitted into this historical vision as a "town of the marshes", as the usually dominant theme of an orthodox Sunni population of Najdi emigrants was balanced with references to the area's medieval African slave population – well known for their support of the Shi'i-inspired Zanj rebellion.

Sharqi's focus on the marshes made for a systematic revision of Basra's history. No longer was the point of departure the Ottoman or indeed any caliphate tradition, according to which the main feature of Basra's history was the continuous succession of provincial governors sent from the centre of the empire, interrupted only by sporadic rebellions. On the contrary, these rebellions, and the intellectual as well as topographical conditions that made them possible, were celebrated in a new framework with an emphasis on the anti-imperial heritage and a geographical focus limited to Basra and the extreme south. But all this was the brainchild of an outsider (Sharqi was based in Baghdad and originally from 'Amara, well north of Basra), who at the outset of 1927 had no particular support in the heartland of the area chosen as subject of his exercise in historical re-examination.

Even though Sharqi was to remain on the sidelines, the political activity of the Nahda in Basra in 1927 did show that local politicians were fully capable of creating both an organisational platform as well as public enthusiasm for a radical political project. A key factor in Nahda's success was its focus on a core issue that affected large sections of the Shi'i community – conscription. By presenting their struggle as one carried out by "the oppressed" (*al-mazlumun*), the Shi'i leadership also added a social dimension to their message.[16] Over and above that, they had a wider symbolic framework through which they could amplify and lend force to their arguments. Local notables had for some years paid large sums to attract preachers from the holy cities to the annual Muharram celebrations, when readings were given in the *ma'tam*s or *husayniyya*s (informal places of religious congregation) maintained by many leading families.[17] These preachers now incorporated the theme of resistance to conscription in their sermons. During Muharram, large processions of people carrying black banners roamed the streets of 'Ashar, and at night, the sound of drums and religious lamentations filled the air.[18] Another more low-key tool in political mobilisation was a Shi'i newspaper published in Baghdad and supported financially by the Basra community.[19]

The sudden success of the Shi'i propaganda was an equally clear indication of the past failure of the Basra separatists. For six years, the separatist elites of Basra had largely ignored the area's sizeable Shi'i constituency. Now this force was finally being mobilised politically in response to the challenge of an aggressive state that threatened with conscription. But to face this challenge, the Basra Shi'is chose a response devised by co-religionists in other parts of Iraq rather than the old separatist scheme. Ironically, in 1927 the separatist leaders were at last beginning to understand the necessity of establishing inter-sectarian co-operation in order to be politically successful in Basra. In February, Ahmad al-Sani' embraced the cause of Haji 'Adhar, one of the Shi'i leaders of the Nahda, in a by-election for a vacant parliamentary seat. But by then, the promoters of the 1921 petition had lost control of what was once their home turf. The winner of the electoral contest – which was supervised by the new nationalist governor – belonged to the Basha'yan family and enjoyed the backing of Sayyid Talib.[20]

In the autumn of 1927, Nahda leaders made appeals to Sani' and Mandil for financial support, thereby demonstrating that they still thought an inter-sectarian partnership an option.[21] At the same time, 'Ali al-Sharqi, the Shi'i historian, was on good terms with the former (Sunni) prime minister, 'Abd al-Muhsin al-

Sa'dun, whose family for centuries had played a special role in the marsh region that Sharqi had written about.[22] Two notables of the Nahda movement even claimed that Sa'dun would have supported a revival of the Basra separation movement at the time.[23] However, nothing radical was to come out of these new constellations of people and ideas. Schemes for dividing the country along sectarian lines did not achieve the same prominence in Basra as in areas further north, and 'Ali al-Sharqi was not taken up as the great intellectual figure who could guide the region towards independence. Instead, the symbolic dimension of the local Nahda campaign focused on well-established themes from classical Shi'i history as recounted by traditional preachers from the holy cities – sagas where Basra was merely one of many localities involved in a far greater struggle.[24] Another force counteracting a more pronounced sectarian campaign was the conservative rival of 'Abd al-Mahdi al-Muzaffar, Mahdi al-Qazwini, who was influential in the old town of Basra. Qazwini was a follower of the grand *mujtahid* Abu al-Hasan al-Isfahani of Najaf and shared his spiritual mentor's quietist approach to politics. The Basra cleric had earlier denounced as too unorthodox the practice of self-flagellation during the Shi'i 'Ashura commemoration, and had spoken out against all forms of *'asabiyya* (zealous partisanship) in religion, strongly condemning the Shaykhis, the Babis and others he saw as innovators within Shi'ism.[25] In Qazwini's own writings on history there was no insularism; instead he wrote on a canvas broad enough to cover the entire classical Islamic world: the protagonists of his stories would often emerge in places far away from Iraq like Damascus or Cairo, and the leading motive seemed to be to assert the righteousness of the Shi'is within the Muslim world as a whole.[26]

In the spring 1928 parliamentary elections, Sani' and other promoters of the 1921 petition did use their influence to persuade Shi'is to vote for 'Abd al-Muhsin al-Sa'dun. But Sa'dun, having been appointed prime minister early in the year, was now clearly working within the system again.[27] His subsequent machinations led to the marginalisation of the Nahda candidates in the elections (despite his initial flirtation with their leaders), and by making no reference to the sensitive issue of conscription in the programme of his cabinet, he also dampened public agitation.[28] In reality, however, this was nothing but another deferment of the problem, and as such a familiar feature of the Sa'dun strategy now followed by an increasing number of Basra notables. It was characterised by clinging to a pro-British attitude without ensuring institutional changes that could guarantee against future excesses on the part of the Iraqi nationalist government which they feared so much: heavy-handed centralisation, expensive (and probably dangerous) militarisation and ambitious foreign policies guided by ideologies for which they had no sympathy. The Basra separatist leadership in 1928 ended up employing what remained of their local influence to dilute the Shi'i protest movement, rather than co-opting it as much-needed fresh input to their own schemes.

Najdi citizenships in Zubayr

The Shi'is were not the only Basrawis to fear conscription. The population of Zubayr, who had enjoyed dispensation from military service in Ottoman times, were now on a par with all other Iraqi citizens. But instead of mobilising on a sectarian platform to protest the very concept of general conscription (as the Shi'is had done) the Sunni Zubayris used their international links to brace themselves for the encounter with the expanding state. During the pilgrimage to Mecca in the summer of 1927, at a time when agitation about conscription had been running high in Basra for a while, some men from Zubayr met with Ibn Sa'ud and asked for papers of Najdi nationality as a means to avoid the draft.[29]

In the autumn of 1927, census operations – widely viewed as an unmistakeable step towards conscription – were initiated in Basra and its districts. In Zubayr, taking out Najdi citizenship soon turned into something of a mass movement. Several thousand forms for the registration of individuals as Najdi citizens were procured by Ibn Sa'ud's agent in Kuwait as well as by a prominent Basra merchant of Najdi origin. Zubayr traders who favoured naturalisation held meetings and went from door to door in the desert town, advising that anyone interested should travel to Kuwait to complete the necessary formalities. The poorer sectors of the population were reportedly attracted to becoming "Najdis", but some landowners opposed the move, fearing it might jeopardise their landholdings along the Shatt al-'Arab, and suggesting they should rather try to pay their way around the threat of conscription. Members of the commercial elite later proposed mass emigration to an area of vacant land within Kuwait as a radical alternative.[30]

The idea of turning to Najd in a critical period was not accidental. Most inhabitants of Zubayr belonged to families who had migrated from Najd, often within the span of one generation. During Faysal's visit to the town in 1926, his reception ceremony focused on sword dance to the beat of drums, described as a "Najdi" tradition.[31] The population of Najd, on their part, reckoned Zubayr as part of the Arabian world, and many prominent men of Ibn Sa'ud's early administration had been born in Zubayr or had received their education at its religious schools.[32] On top of this, there were rumours of further Najdi expansionism (this affected other locations in the Gulf as well, including Bahrain, Qatar and even parts of Oman), and Ibn Sa'ud's officials made representations to the British in support of those Zubayris who wished to take out Najdi nationality papers.[33] The largest desert tribe living in the vicinity of Zubayr, the Dafir, had even begun to pay taxes to Riyadh, in contravention of the earlier British-brokered border arrangements that formally assigned their traditional *dira* (core territory of a Bedouin tribe) and allegiance to Iraq.[34] All these links and affinities notwithstanding, some 600 kilometres of barren desert set Zubayr apart from the Najdi capital, and the Zubayris' decision to turn in this direction was a glaring testament to the failure of local attempts to confront the challenges posed by new state formation. In 1921, several Zubayris had rallied to support the Basra separatist petition, but in 1928, the original separatist scheme for secession was no longer seen as credible defence against the expanding state.

The exact number of people from Zubayr who eventually took out Najdi nationality papers is not known. The Iraqi government despatched high officials to the town and warned that those opting for Najdi nationality would have to leave Iraq. It is evident that a considerable number of Zubayris were in the end registered in the census as Iraqis, but the first count of the population was not implemented stringently: agitation for Najdi citizenship resumed in 1928 as a "detailed census return" was then feared, suggesting that vital information had been withheld the previous year. As late as in December 1928, a supporter of Faysal pleaded with the Zubayris to comply with the country's census regulations during a royal visit, signalling that the issue remained on the agenda.[35]

More than anything, the nature of the Zubayr protests of 1927 and 1928 demonstrated the new limits of the political horizon – and in particular the extent to which the Iraqi state, with its territorial borders, was turning into a reality increasingly difficult to challenge. The state had begun establishing a physical presence in the desert by setting up police posts as well as passport controls at selected spots, signalling that Cox's arbitrary boundary lines of 1922 were starting to acquire meaning to state-builders in Baghdad.[36] Ikhwan raiders from Najd who violated the borders were now pursued by British planes as long as they were on Iraqi territory, if not always successfully. And absentee landowners on the Shatt al-ʿArab with residency outside Iraq (in particular the shaykhs of Kuwait and Muhammara) were beginning to experience trouble at the hands of Iraqi nationalist politicians – a pointer to wealthy Zubayris that any attempt to sever the connection between the desert town and the port might be accompanied by harsh measures against the riverside estates that formed the basis of their fortunes.[37]

The nature of the new exit strategies proposed by the Zubayris reflected this growing significance of the Iraqi state borders. Despite all the links between Najd and Zubayr, propaganda in the late 1920s did not call for Zubayr to be annexed by Ibn Saʿud. No one tried to except the whole territory of Zubayr from the Iraqi regime, as had been the case in 1921. Instead, the options under consideration related to individual escape from the expanding state, by taking out passports or, more radically, migrating to new territory outside Iraq. In a similar vein, the nomadic Dafir tribesmen responded to increased interference from Iraqi tax officials (coupled with the inability of the Iraqi regime to provide adequate protection against raiders from across the border) by seceding to Najd in the summer of 1927. This was a mobile form of separatism – involving the relocation of entire sections of the tribe across the border with Najd – and not a challenge to the boundary lines as such.[38]

The reactions of Basra separatists to the Zubayr agitation in this period also indicate that their situation had changed greatly since 1921. In the early 1920s, they had tried to subdue Shaykh Ibrahim's project because it threatened their own separatist dream. Now, ʿAbd al-Latif al-Mandil advised that those who wanted to take out Najdi nationality papers could do so, but should travel to

Kuwait to complete the process in order to avoid trouble with Iraqi authorities.[39] He personally refrained from registering as a Najdi, and had recently resigned as Ibn Sa'ud's official representative in Iraq.[40]

There were also signs that Ibn Sa'ud himself was beginning to accept status quo in the region instead of aiming for more expansion. This was particularly true with respect to the British-controlled areas, where he was discovering that London took quite literally the borders drawn in the sand during the 1920s – an attitude made possible by new aircraft technology. This was a stark contrast to the late Ottoman period, when administrative borders in the peripheral desert region had been purely fictitious. The policy initiated by Ibn Sa'ud in 1927 of forcefully preventing Najdi tribes from trading with Iraq (including Zubayr) and Kuwait was one indication that he was starting to round off his desert empire, at least in this direction.[41] His subsequent activities in the border area with Iraq focused on quelling an internal rebellion among Ikhwan tribes on the Najdi side, rather than engaging in brinkmanship across the boundary line towards the irredenta claimed during the 1922 negotiations.

Rebellious tribesmen and Persia

A third, distinctive response to the problems created by an expanding Iraqi state materialised south of Basra, in the area inhabited by tribes who in the past had professed loyalty to Shaykh Khaz'al of Muhammara. To these people, the combined Iraqi and Persian crackdown on the 1925 rebellion in Muhammara had indicated that their trans-river community was being bisected by the consolidation of new state forces on both sides of the river. In early 1928, they also faced the threat of conscription.

Their tactic for dealing with the new challenge emerged literally as Iraqi census officials entered their villages in January 1928. Most males in Kut al-Zayn refused to register and fled from the village, some heading for the Persian side of the river. This was a method also used in the past, as when the Ottomans had attempted to enforce conscription, or when the authorities had searched the villages for suspected criminals. This time, however, the villagers' response incorporated new elements. Upon arriving on the Persian side, they contacted local officials, tribal heads and ulama in order to obtain certificates of Persian nationality. Documents carrying five signatures were issued against a fee; the villagers could then return to the Iraqi side and proceed to the Persian consul in Basra to get Persian nationality papers (*tazkara*s) at a cost of between 10 to 20 rupees per individual.[42]

The Iraqi authorities attempted to arrest some of the villagers for having violated passport regulations, but the quest for Persian nationality papers only became more widespread during the spring and summer of 1928. Several thousand villagers took out Persian passports, principally in the area around Khaz'al's Kut al-Zayn properties, but also on neighbouring lands owned by the state or by Basra landlords, and even in areas closer to Basra. The campaign primarily affected agricultural workers who were the *ta'ab* tenants of absentee landlords, in addition to a smaller number of workers at the Anglo-Persian Oil Company at Abadan who commuted from homes on the Iraqi side of the river. Among the foremost agitators were leaders of the small Akhbari Shi'i community (which had adherents on both banks of the river) and Muhaysin shaykhs who had fled from the Persian side after Khaz'al's downfall in 1925, but also persons of more modest social backgrounds were active.

At the time, Persia had still not recognised Iraq as a political entity and consistently dealt with British officials only, creating an atmosphere where the local campaign against the census enumeration came to be intertwined with larger questions of identity and foreign policy.[43] Village mullahs and the ulama of Muhammara preached that it was a religious duty for Shi'is to take out Persian nationality papers, and the higher-ranking ulama of Basra did not object to the campaign.[44] Persian authorities in Muhammara and agents sent to the villages on the Iraqi side boasted of Persian plans to control both banks of the Shatt al-'Arab from Qurna to Fao, and there were rumours about designs on the holy cities of Iraq, "which formerly belonged to Persia".[45] The administration of the Persian Pahlavi School in Basra was upgraded, Shi'i merchants of Basra signalled their support for the movement, and the involvement of workers at Abadan – an environment seen as a possible bridgehead for communism – added to the apprehensions of local British authorities.[46] In the Persian capital, the parliament voted in favour of a grant to those from the Iraqi side who had fled to Muhammara.[47] And as a backdrop to all this, certain Persian journalists continued to cherish ideas of Ctesiphon (in Iraq, south of Baghdad) as a legitimate objective of Persian expansion, in a scheme to resurrect the old Sassanian kingdom.[48]

Gradually, the people who had taken out Persian passports started to act more boldly. Their original aim of avoiding registration in the census rolls as "Iraqis" was achieved, as the Iraqi authorities suspended census activities south of Basra altogether.[49] But the pro-Persian campaign was beginning to assume new dimensions beyond the question of an individual's status in the census register: soon the idea spread that the naturalised Persians were immune against the orders of any Iraqi government official, leading villagers to settle scores with their landlords.[50] In July, the agent of a Basra landowner was refused entry to his employer's estate and witnessed how newly installed and more compliant tenants were abducted by the villagers to the Persian side of the river, all with Iraqi police as passive onlookers.[51] In another instance, a police car was wrecked when local authorities tried to arrest some of the "Persians".[52] One of the villagers stated that, since they could hope for no sympathy from the Basra authorities who would listen only to the rich landlords, they had put themselves under Persian authority in order to improve their lot.[53]

The pro-Persian movement subsided in the autumn of 1928, parallel to a shift in official Persian policy on formal international recognition of Iraq. Negotiations with Britain were making headway, and Tehran saw a possibility for achieving two important aims: the cancellation of a judicial agreement dis-

criminating against Persian citizens in Iraq, as well as adjustments to the Shatt
al-'Arab boundary – the primary Persian demand being not land but water and
navigation rights. To ease matters with respect to the tribes around Basra, a senior official of the Persian foreign ministry was sent to Iraq; in a short time he
reached an agreement with the British that gave to people who had ended up in
Iraqi jails or had fled the right to an unconditional return to their lands.[54] In
April 1929, Persia granted diplomatic recognition to Iraq, in return for abrogation of the discriminatory judicial agreement as well as a promise of British
good offices in negotiations about the river. The Tehran patrons of the Basra
tribesmen now had incentives to normalise their behaviour in the region.

Separatist swansong

The threat of conscription was not the only change to the appearance of the
Iraqi state in Basra in the second half of the 1920s. A highly centralistic law for
the administration of the divisions (promulgated in April 1927) put an end to
any remaining hopes of a special status for Basra within the constitutional
framework of Iraq.[55] The increased use of outside career officials occasioned
local concern, as economic decline and deflation meant that having a government job was now more attractive than during the wartime boom.[56] During the
1928 elections, supporters of Sa'dun addressed Ahmad al-Sani' and deplored
the dominance of nationalist government officials, whose manipulations, it was
said, had brought about a situation whereby almost all the secondary electors
were anti-Sa'dun.[57] And finally, the state also expanded its field of activity. In
the early summer of 1928, Basra's date producers were confronted with detailed
regulations from the Ministry of Health concerning hygiene arrangements for
the packing of dates.[58] Only certified date-packing stations were to be used, and
these would be issued with annual licenses. Matters to be controlled by the state
included the number of workers, their dwellings, sanitary arrangements at the
packing stations and provisions for water. Officials and paperwork unheard of
earlier were about to enter the industry that was Basra's main artery.

At the same time, many felt that the state was not paying dividends. Basra's
canal system was still in poor condition, and pledges of money for improvement
had so far not yielded any results.[59] The "new government school" at Qurna had
in fact been built from voluntary donations.[60] Security was another sector where
the state failed to deliver, as raids by bands of Ikhwan from Najd continued to
pose a real threat to areas in the immediate vicinity of Basra at a time when the
central government had yet to establish good relations with its mighty
neighbour to the west.[61] Parliamentary deputies felt that the northern areas of
Iraq were receiving a disproportionate share of public funds, and the local English-language newspaper increasingly tended to blame "the central authorities"
whenever problems arose related to the finances of local governmental services.[62] All these tensions with Baghdad came in a context when Basra's economic potential for standing alone remained strong: none of the grandiose

communications projects for providing Baghdad with an effective western trade route had materialised (hence, its trade would have to pass through Basra, whatever its political status), and Basra's main markets in Europe and India continued to show a healthy demand for dates, despite the general decline in the economy.[63]

Occasionally, grievances about the actions of the central government turned into nostalgic talk about the days of British administration, when things had been so much better.[64] But some of the complaints about the new regime in fact related to technological changes introduced during the period of British military rule. In 1928, there were still mutterings about the railway, which had hurt sections of the Basra community involved in river transport. Similarly, local companies engaged in cargo handling had lost customers as a result of the upgrading of the port, which in 1928 was perceived as a costly institution for the Basrawis, draining municipal budgets with expenses for activities that actually served outside interests.[65] The British-built dike north of Zubayr was creating dust storms and arid conditions at several estates.[66] It was as if not only the new monarchical regime, but the very process of modernisation itself, worried segments of Basra.

The separatist elite of 1921 held on to many of their original ideas during this period. But although they were still among the richest and most influential men in Basra, they increasingly refrained from linking up their visions with practical politics. In the autumn of 1925, a British special service officer continued to refer to "people who are anti-Arab government" in the city.[67] In 1927, 'Abdallah al-Khalil threatened to resign from the governor's council when Ahmad al-Sani' had to leave his post as governor for a seat in the senate.[68] As late as March 1928, the British administrative inspector enumerated Mandil, Khalil and Sani' as well as a member of the 'Abd al-Wahid family among those who thought "Basra should not be part of Iraq".[69] But their ideas on the subject were mostly a matter confined to confidential reports. There are indications that even within the landowning segment of the population, support was declining, for in late 1927, the anti-separatist 'Abd al-Kazim al-Shamkhani was able to obtain the backing of 77 out of 130 landowners gathered to elect a committee to improve the date trade.[70] Also Basra's fragmented response to the challenge of conscription in 1928 made clear that the separatist project now carried little weight. Instead of receiving fresh separatist recruits from a population feverishly on the outlook for countermeasures against an intrusive state, the Basra notables saw their own Shi'i tenants rise against them under an ideological label connected with neither Basra nor Baghdad. Suddenly, after having been described as an almost docile community, the rural population of Basra had showed that they were indeed a political force to be reckoned with. The separatists had simply not pulled the right strings.

A further weakening of the project for separation was brought about by another ideological competitor. The forces of anti-separation from the early 1920s continued to make significant progress in the struggle for the political minds of the Basrawis, by maintaining political clubs like Nadi al-Shabiba (The Youth

Club) and Nadi al-Fayha' (The Fayha' Club), and by controlling the only Arabic-language local newspaper, *al-Awqat al-'Iraqiyya*.[71] The schools of Basra were filled with Baghdad-educated teachers who frequented these clubs, wrote articles in the local newspaper, and taught their pupils about the Arab conquests of Andalusia and about the sharifian family of Mecca as the saviour of the Arabs.[72] Young Basrawis wishing to emulate their teachers had no choice but to travel to Baghdad (or abroad), as there were still no facilities for higher education available in the southern region.[73] It was also the anti-separatists who appropriated Basra's local historical heritage: they dominated the Basra contingent in a 1926 joint British-Iraqi excursion to the Sumer excavations at Ur, and in subsequent newspaper articles about the event left out the mysterious Sumerians and wrote instead about the "city of Abraham" (*madinat ibrahim, 'alayhi al-salam*), a universalistic concept which was relevant for Muslims, Christians and Jews alike and would resonate far beyond southern Iraq.[74] (By way of contrast, none of the separatists established ties with the Yale scholar Raymond Dougherty who worked in the region in the mid-1920s on the basis of a theory about links between the ancient Sumerians and the modern population of southern Iraq.[75]) Even though the anti-separatist camp was far from constituting a coherent political movement, its various subdivisions were extraordinarily active in the intellectual life of Basra in this period. By the late 1920s, there was simply much less room for the separatist initiative than a decade earlier.

During Faysal's visit to Basra in late 1928, the only protest that the pro-separation notables took part in concerned a general reduction of taxes and more hiring of local people in the administration.[76] Some months later, they complained about the new date trade regulations, maintaining that these were unnecessary, threatened free trade, and could lead to the establishment of monopolies (*fath bab al-ihtikar*).[77] The original separatist petition, with its broad vision for a cosmopolitan port community under British protection, had degenerated into a blatant demand that Basra be allowed to dump its dates on to the world market without interference from health or revenue officials.

Pseudo-separatism

In these circumstances, a new group seized on the scheme for separation and used it for a different purpose. Rumours of Basra demands for separation did reappear during the summer and autumn of 1928, but some of the most prominent supporters turned out to be people who had spent most of the 1920s cooperating with Baghdad politicians, and would continue to do so later on.[78] 'Abbud al-Mallak and 'Abd al-Kazim al-Shamkhani had both been marginalised during the second stage of the 1928 elections, and their sudden embrace of the separatist project was interpreted as a protest strategy which could serve as a warning for the future.[79] Close associates expressed shock when the two were abruptly recast as pro-British politicians, and misgivings about their real intentions seemed confirmed when 'Abbud al-Mallak went on to spearhead yet another "separatist" project – that of creating 'Ashar as an independent municipality separate from Basra. It was widely thought that his underlying goal was to get a government job to make up for his lost seat in the Iraqi parliament. Some months later, the separatist rumours abated, and in early 1929 'Abbud found it more useful to revert to the anti-British rhetoric which he had used in the past.[80]

'Abbud al-Mallak was not the only one to take an opportunistic approach to the separatist scheme. The Indian population of Basra, still counting more than 1,000 persons, had hitherto attracted public attention mainly in relation to internal disputes. But in the autumn of 1928, they were faced with threats from a Baghdad government that sought to remove all non-Iraqis from the civil service. At the same time, local newspapers published letters in favour of having an indigenous workforce in the port. During the next months, several Indians of Basra rallied to the new call for separation.[81]

To rumours in Baghdad newspapers about a revival of the separatist scheme, the Basra governor responded to his ministry that such a scheme had no support locally. Significantly, he added that the original supporters of the project would have nothing to do with its second incarnation.[82] In short, it looked as if the label of Basra separatism had been hijacked, and was now serving entirely new objectives.

Between these two different versions of the Basra separatist project, a third one could be discerned in the second half of the 1920s. It was similar to the opportunistic variant inasmuch as it was associated with a person who was working mainly *within* the framework of the monarchy. The main difference was that the figure in question was immensely powerful, to the extent that Faysal feared he might prove a real challenge to the very system of government which had been introduced in 1921.

This third brand of separatism was connected with 'Abd al-Muhsin al-Sa'dun. Some Basra notables had gradually turned to his pro-British policy as an alternative, failing the realisation of their own separatist scheme. However, as early as in 1925, there had been rumours that Sa'dun, now newly appointed prime minister, was himself involved in plots aimed at doing something radical about the form of government in Iraq. Plans for a decentralised Iraqi republic had reportedly been discussed at a meeting in Basra in August, attended by an unusual cross-party gathering which included Sayyid Talib, members of the Sa'dun and Basha'yan families and 'Abd al-Kazim al-Shamkhani. According to this secret scheme, Sayyid Talib was to govern Basra, 'Abd al-Muhsin would control Baghdad, and a local candidate "who had the support of the ashraf" could take care of Mosul. Similar stories had circulated in Baghdad and Mosul, suggesting that the main idea was not to separate Basra, but rather to bring the old notables of all these cities back to power at the expense of Faysal and his officers.[83] No one who had participated in the presentation of the 1921 petition had taken part except 'Abd al-Karim al-Sa'dun (the brother of 'Abd al-Muhsin), and the scheme never resurfaced.

But also the separatist elite looked to Sa'dun for more radical alternatives to Faysal. In an intelligence report of a trip undertaken by Sayyid Talib and Salih

Basha'yan to Baghdad in late 1925, there is a reference to "the anti-King party in Basra", which it was thought would deprecate Sayyid Talib's attempt to in- gratiate himself with the king.[84] It is likely that this reference was meant to ap- ply to Mandil, Sani' and their supporters – apart from the Basha'yans (who were on good terms with Faysal) the only faction of enough local prestige that a report could have referred to them casually without further explanation. They remained staunch supporters of Sa'dun during parliamentary elections, and, at the same time, their dislike of the king's personality was well known.[85] Behind their support for the seemingly straightforward, pro-British shaykh, there may have been ulterior hopes for radical change – and after December 1926, when Sa'dun was turned out of office, radical politics may have held a special attrac- tion for him.

Sa'dun had himself hinted at ambitions of a republican tendency earlier, and Faysal, for his part, alleged that the southern magnate was secretly in league with Ibn Sa'ud.[86] But after January 1928, when he was once more appointed prime minister, Sa'dun seemed increasingly drawn towards compromise with the Iraqi nationalist forces around the king, and, importantly, came to change his views on conscription. In the summer of 1928, Nuri al-Sa'id, a proponent of compulsory military service, was included in his cabinet as defence minister, and during the subsequent Anglo-Iraqi negotiations over defence arrangements, Sa'dun went over to the nationalist side and eventually resigned when negotia- tions broke down. In the same period, he failed to kill off other ministers' pen- chant for imposing regulations on the Basra date trade.[87] At the end of 1928, a Sa'dun cabinet was for the first time reported to be unpopular among the sepa- ratist elite of Basra.[88]

The British administration and Basra's new political landscape

The British stance against Basra separatism continued to harden during the lat- ter part of the 1920s. London showed no appetite for the succession of new po- litical projects mushrooming in the Gulf city and instead added to the strength of the central government in dealing with remnants of dissent.

At the level of high politics, Britain's successful defence of Iraqi territorial interests in the Mosul dispute was followed by the conclusion of a tripartite agreement between Britain, Iraq and Turkey during the summer of 1926 – a clear signal of continued British commitment to the territorial integrity of the state carved out after the war. This policy was sustained in 1928 and 1929 by a drive to get Persia to recognise Iraq without sacrificing any mandated territory. The Colonial Office made preparations for the admission of Iraq as an inde- pendent member of the League of Nations within 1932, and, accelerated by the accession to power of a Labour government in London, issued a pledge to this effect in September 1929. By now, British policy on Iraq had acquired support across the political spectrum at home.[89]

Key officials within the British administration in Iraq supported London's line. On three occasions between 1925 and 1927, during critical phases of the Mosul settlement and the subsequent Anglo-Iraqi negotiations, Dobbs reverted to his emergency scenario involving Basra.[90] But in the autumn of 1927 he claimed that promising discoveries of oil in the north had decisively changed his view.[91] Again, in the context of the sectarian crisis that year, leading British officials remained critical of the Shi'is, despite their (admittedly sudden) conversion to a pro-British attitude. In June, Dobbs characterised the Shi'is as "recalcitrants", and still argued against having to rely on this "unstable and retrograde" community as late as November.[92] The Shi'i demand for a change in form of government was on one occasion characterised as "foolish".[93] Leading British officials in Baghdad repeatedly warned Shi'i leaders that any attempts to challenge Faysal by creating the impression of an alliance between the Shi'is and Britain would be counterproductive and would be seen by the British as an "embarrassment".[94] Similarly, when Baghdad newspapers in 1928 printed reports of a renewal of the Basra separatist movement, the high commissioner, far from trying to exploit the issue, sent a letter to the Iraqi prime minister stating that no petition on the matter had reached the British residency since 1921.[95]

Such attitudes also prevailed among British staff in Basra, where the administrative inspector in 1928 explicitly criticised the separatist attitude he sensed. He spoke of the need for "furbishing up the facade of the Iraqi government" in Basra, criticised Basra public opinion for not appreciating the contributions of the central government to the infrastructure of the city, and, in discussing the local politicians, singled out the young Iraqi nationalist Muhammad Zaki for praise. By contrast, he described supporters of the separatist scheme as representing "reactionary interests".[96] In this way, much of the centralistic spirit of the Baghdad residency was reproduced.

Also Dobbs's successor from 1929, Gilbert Clayton, was staunchly supportive of the central government during his brief six-month tenure in Baghdad, and was instrumental in negotiating the deal that ended the long-standing treaty stalemate between Iraq and Britain. This paved the way for the promise of independence given in 1929 and the subsequent Anglo-Iraqi treaty of 1930. At the heart of the new accord was the understanding that, in the future, Britain's strategic interests in Iraq would be looked after through permanent, low-key military installations maintained within a formally independent state. Instead of expressing British strategic interests through territorial control of a designated core area such as Basra, the new treaty implied an arrangement that would preserve Iraq's territorial integrity while Britain would be accorded a limited military presence through bilateral arrangements.[97] In the 1930s, Clayton's successor, Francis Humphrys, went on to throw his weight behind the proponents of a strong, centralised Iraqi state more unequivocally than any of the former British high commissioners in Baghdad.[98]

The greatest threat against a coherent British policy was not individual political officers committed to any particular ethnic or religious group among the Iraqis, but rather an entire institution imperilled by the direction of British policy. The Royal Air Force, a recent addition to the British military forces, had found in Iraq an opportunity for employment and reasons to justify its existence.[99] RAF reluctance towards early British evacuation was pronounced, and in June 1927, when the Colonial Office were discussing Iraqi membership in the League of Nations as a question of timing only (1928 versus 1932), a leading RAF official countered that the very idea of early Iraqi independence was mistaken, maintaining that the revised Anglo-Iraqi treaty prepared the ground for an unchanged British presence for a much longer period.[100] As late as in January 1929, air officials made similar comments, and staff at the Colonial Office later criticised the RAF for having deliberately checked the emergence of a strong Iraqi army in order to make British planes indispensable for the government of the country.[101]

Whereas the development of British policy has the appearance of a linear process when studied through Colonial Office lenses, the obvious failure of the RAF to grasp or accept its essence may help explain much of the confusion surrounding this policy locally in Iraq. Old-school imperialist ideas among airmen did not directly trigger any separatism, but the conception of Basra as an area "more British than the British" was integral to the RAF argument for a prolonged presence in the country.[102] Such attitudes blurred the picture of London's policy conveyed in Iraq, and those who favoured long-term British control may have been lulled into believing that the mandatary's commitment to the country would remain essentially unchanged for a considerable time to come – an impression perhaps assisted by the tendency of Iraqi nationalists to constantly raise critical theories about British intentions to stay despite the promise of independence.[103]

In addition to the policy dualism resulting from the existence of a separate agenda in the RAF, it is noteworthy that the old alternative of safeguarding traditional strategic British interests through a stronghold around Basra continued to attract attention at the highest levels of policy-making. While Dobbs had apparently abandoned his ideas for an exit strategy involving Basra in 1927, two years later the colonial secretary, Leo Amery, remained convinced that the alternative of withdrawing to the Gulf constituted Britain's "ultimate trump card".[104] Later still, during the 1929 negotiations for a new Anglo-Iraqi treaty, the official with most experience on Iraq at the Colonial Office, John Hathorn Hall, revived Young's old scheme for a British-protected enclave in Basra during discussions of the location of future RAF bases in Iraq. The Iraqi government objected to having any base in the vicinity of their capital, and Hall thought that a concentration at Shu'ayba outside Basra might offer an alternative.[105] But to him, this was not merely a question of the location of aircraft. He noted Basra's pro-British attitude, and while admitting that the withdrawal of the RAF from areas further north might bring about "oriental despotism" in those parts, he maintained that British interests could be adequately safeguarded through a presence in the politically stable and friendly port city, under some kind of separate regime.[106] Hall's views on the issue were reinforced by newly released information that effectively deconstructed the myth developed during the 1920s of Britain's need to hold Baghdad as an interchange for the new air route from Europe to India: For years, it had been maintained that flying from Cairo directly to Basra was unsafe because of the great distance involved and the "unsettled country" traversed, but during an interdepartmental conference in 1929 a high-ranking air official conceded that an air centre in Basra might indeed suffice to preserve British interests.[107]

Although Hall's remarkable resurrection of old ideas on this issue never resulted in a change of policy, it demonstrates the extent to which British officials at the heart of power in Whitehall continued to include the perception of Basra as a profoundly pro-British area in the policy-making process. That they did so despite the increasingly weak nature of the local separatist movement shows how British officials were prepared to take a sympathetic view of the scheme when it suited their own interests. But by 1929, there was hardly anything left of the Basra separatist movement.

10   Centralisation Logics

When the British promise of independence for Iraq within three years was issued in mid September 1929, the political scene in Basra was void of separatist
influences and filled with many other different projects. Some of them related to
communities much larger than Basra, others to parochial identities within the
city. But none focused on the city – or the Basra division – as a potential focus
for a political community.

Of the pseudo-separatists of the previous year, 'Abbud al-Mallak and 'Abd
al-Kazim al-Shamkhani now promoted anti-Zionist demonstrations in support
of Arab brethren living in Palestinian towns hundreds of kilometres away.[1]
They were joined by teachers of the Rahmaniyya School, which the anti-
separatist Ahmad Hamdi Mullah Husayn had set up in the mid 1920s, as well as
people associated with the anti-British circle at the Naqshbandiyya Library – all
united under slogans against "imperialism", "Zionism" and Arthur Balfour, the
British statesman behind the 1917 promise of a Jewish homeland in Palestine.[2]
Individuals from the lower social strata, particularly Shi'is and non-Muslims,
had started to attend meetings arranged by visitors from Persia, at which communist doctrines were discussed.[3] Ideas from India about boycotting foreign
goods and replacing them with products of local origin circulated.[4] The Jews
had formed societies of their own, while young Christians were among those
who flocked to the local branch of a non-confessional political party headquar-
tered in Syria.[5] 'Abd al-Muhsin al-Sa'dun, formerly the rallying point for the
separatists as a possible second-best option, was busy making a government
coalition with Yasin al-Hashimi, a keen supporter of conscription.[6] The separatists, who had opposed the creation of an expensive army and its deployment for
Iraqi nationalist purposes, were all silent.

Iraqi projects come to Basra, 1929–1932

By 1929, the Basra political scene was thus one of cacophony, brimming over
with projects pointing in diverse directions. These tendencies continued over the
next years – with young teachers organising theatre performances with themes
from the wider Arab world (like *'Uhud al-hubb wa-al-istiqlal* or The Age of
Love and Independence, on resistance to Ottoman rule in Lebanon), local
youngsters joining a local subdivision of the Society for Islamic Youth (an organisation with affiliated branches as far away as Algeria and India), and semi-
clandestine communist activities simmering against a backdrop of sporadic port
visits by Soviet steamers.[7]

Yet, in all of this, one phenomenon stood out: the proliferation of new political parties and organisations with an explicitly national, Iraqi character. In several instances, this took the shape of the establishment of Basra chapters of organisations with a national profile and headquarters in Baghdad, such as the

Ikha movement and the Hizb al-Watani.[8] Both were dominated by strong Baghdad leaderships, and their activities naturally came to revolve around politics in the capital. Also pioneering trade union activity created partnerships between Baghdad and Basra. In April 1930, an organisation of workers in the Baghdad printing industry took the initiative to have a similar union set up in the southern port city; some months later, craftsmen from the capital travelled to Basra to open a union of artisans (*jami'yat ashab al-san'a*).[9]

The discourse of local individuals associated with this new "national" trend put Basra in a greater, Iraqi context. When Iskandar Mansur, a local newspaper editor, wrote about the financial crisis in 1930, his focus was clearly a national one. In discussing the problems affecting the export of grains he used the term "our grains" (*hububna*) – a reference that could have nothing to do with Basra's own harvest, which was negligible for crops other than dates. His article thereby established an association between grains produced in areas further north, in districts such as the Middle Euphrates and Mosul, and the idea of national ownership of these natural resources. Mansur's message to readers in Basra concerned how Iraq, as a "nation" (*umma*), should tackle the crisis.[10]

Another important aspect of the new political discourse in Iraq was modernism, encapsulated in the omnipresent slogan of "progress". When Boy Scouts from Basra went on excursion to neighbouring 'Arabistan in Persia, their itinerary focused on sites associated with modernity like railway stations and a new public park – not on the abundant archaeological sites of the area.[11] Basra's booth at the 1932 national exhibition in Baghdad featured graphic charts of the new port facilities, with a few native river-craft the only possible token of localism and nostalgia for the past.[12] "Education" was another universalistic watchword which most young Iraqi intellectuals could embrace, including religious writers who quoted the Egyptian Islamic modernist Muhammad 'Abduh in support of starting schools for girls.[13] Just as they had done with historiography, the anti-separatists took possession over these new ideals and made them their own, soon equating "education" with "Iraqi education".[14] The Basra separatists, on the other hand, had been unable to make political capital out of what was arguably the epitome of "progress" in the region: The Anglo-Persian Oil Company had transformed nearby Abadan to a showcase of modernity with modern housing and electric street lights, but no propaganda inspired by this "partnership" between the British and local forces ever emerged.[15]

Other processes at the local level in this period reiterated the idea of an Iraqi national community, sometimes by creating new opportunities that brought the local inhabitants closer to the state, sometimes by limiting the number of available options that threatened to pull them elsewhere. In the early 1930s, Basra's educational facilities were expanded to a school with full secondary status; the city saw the establishment of new government services in specially designed buildings (said to be among the most impressive in the new Iraq, in a "Spanish-Arab" architectural style that replaced the cruder British wartime designs); and commercial telephone services to the capital were opened.[16] At the same time, stringent restrictions were imposed on international travel in the Shatt al-'Arab region – putting an end to centuries of virtually unhindered trans-river links – and more effective customs patrols were posted to the Zubayr area.[17] As a result of such policies and measures, key spheres like education, transport and the economy gradually acquired an Iraqi logic where Baghdad was the natural centre. This was a campaign characterised not by an elaborate programme of indoctrination or a decisive major battle, but by a number of small triumphs – the establishment of a local branch of an "Iraqi" society here, or the appearance of yet another symbol of the Iraqi central government there.

These developments also had an impact on the content of the political debate in southern Iraq after 1929. As people became aware of the prospects for early Iraqi independence, several groups in other parts of Iraq with grievances against the central authorities rushed to make a final bid for their preferred alternatives to a unitary state. The British and the League of Nations found themselves inundated with petitions from Kurds, Yazidis, Chaldeans and Assyrians, all presenting schemes that variously challenged the territorial integrity of the mandate end-product.[18] But Basra did not join this chorus, even though the city had pioneered the exploration of territorial alternatives to the three-vilayet model for Iraq.[19]

Instead, Basra's farewell greeting to the British administrators came in 1931 in a form no one had expected. For several days in July, the police lost control of the supposedly apolitical Gulf city as a strike was declared and large crowds of angry demonstrators attacked government property, demanding the abolition of new taxes and calling for a new government in Baghdad.[20] The strike was a response to similar actions organised elsewhere in the country, particularly in the capital, where groups loyal to two leading Iraqi nationalists, Yasin al-Hashimi and Ja'far Abu al-Timman, had initiated the movement.[21] In Basra, Shi'is of the 'Ashar suburb dominated as strike leaders, but descriptions of the ensuing chaos reveal a multitude of modes of expression and agendas: Tribesmen from a village of reed huts on the edge of the urban area performed war dances, orthodox Jews availed themselves of the opportunity to smash the premises of a much disliked theosophical society frequented by young members of their community, and some participants in the strike proclaimed Mahatma Gandhi their great hero. Behind the myriad of motivations, however, one message recurred in the slogans and profited from the surge of popular energy while at the same time stressing the connection between Basra and the wider Iraqi society: the cabinet in Baghdad should resign, and Yasin al-Hashimi should be the new prime minister.[22]

The nationalist message and political non-conformists

The degree of unity between all these various organisations was limited. Factional and sectarian differences remained, and membership data for the various associations reveal the survival of parochial bonds to clans or religious communities.[23] But, importantly, even groups who perceived themselves to be discriminated against in the political process now chose alternatives where the new Iraqi territorial framework was generally accepted. This was an important contrast to the 1920s, when political dissent had been channelled into all sorts of local, particularistic projects.

One example involves developments among the Shi'is. A look at the composition of the Basra delegation invited to travel to Baghdad as official guests as the marking of Iraqi independence finally approached in October 1932 shows that the local Shi'i majority community was not represented on this historic occasion.[24] Nevertheless, and despite conflicts with local Sunni notables on better terms with the authorities in Baghdad, their political activities in Basra over the subsequent years largely focused on the Hizb al-Watani, with its Iraqi nationalist leadership in Baghdad.[25] Similarly, the tiny, secretive communist cells with theoretical links to an internationalist movement had in their rhetoric distinctive elements emphasising Iraq as a national community – as in their references to memories of the 1920 "Iraqi revolution" in an attack on the alliance between the colonial power and the ruling class.[26]

Crucially, rhetorical concepts amplifying the idea of a united Iraq became progressively widespread also among intellectual elites less subservient to the state than the teachers and officials who depended upon it for their salaries. In particular, the adoption among Shi'i ulama of language stressing national territorial unity had a wide-ranging impact on Iraqi political discourse. Although the idea, floated in 1927, that the Shi'is might be better off with a state of their own did sporadically resurface in the shape of rumours, the texts actually published by Shi'i elites during this critical period of transformation – pamphlets, newspaper articles and books on religion – increasingly treated Iraq as a basic of source identity.[27]

This can be seen for instance in the writings of 'Abd al-Amir al-Basri, a Basra Shi'i and *'alim* settled in Najaf. In a booklet written in 1929, he confronted a Lebanese Shi'i cleric in a discussion over Shi'i rituals. He claimed that "all Iraq, from its most distant to its nearest parts" (*kull al-'iraq min aqsahu ila adnahu*) refuted the puritan views held by the Lebanese writer (who had attacked practices such as chest-beating with chains during Muharram processions), and went on to cite the strength of Shi'ism in Iraq since the days of Imam Husayn, "when the movement had started in Kufa". As a contrasting category, he spoke of the Lebanese Shi'is by referring to their particular regional origin – *'amilis* or persons from the southern Jabal 'Amil – but for the group that he himself represented there was clearly no need to use any other nomenclature than "Iraq".[28]

Likewise, even in their most subversive moments, other Shi'i politicians with links to religious circles now reproduced the concept of an Iraqi national entity. In 1932, in a pamphlet widely circulated within Iraq and abroad, a text with strong anti-monarchical connotations emphasised the centrality of the old Mesopotamian civilisations ("from the times of the Greeks and the Babylonians") as well as the glorious medieval Baghdad in the history of the country the writers claimed to represent. This country, it was maintained, had now been handed over to an individual "from the wilderness of the desert" (*wuhush al-badiyya*) and his "Turkish officers from Asia Minor" – a reference to Faysal and his entourage – who were taking over the lands and repressing the "sons of the country".[29]

Also other discontents in Basra politics who in the 1920s had sought alternatives to Iraq now tentatively gravitated towards the new centre in Baghdad. In 1929, a petition from Zubayr (a bastion of support for Ibn Sa'ud) asked for a stronger Iraqi state presence in the area by requesting additional classes in the local government school.[30] In 1930, members of a Kut al-Zayn family with a central role in the 1928 campaign for Persian citizenships took part in Iraqi elections.[31] In 1932, a new team of Boy Scouts recruited in Qurna participated in sports games in Basra, under the auspices of the national scouting association.[32] And even inhabitants of outlying Madina, seen as the most ungovernable place within the Basra region, made efforts to introduce the nationalist Ikha movement to their home district.[33]

Individuals positioned entirely outside the spectrum of local politics, like British capitalist entrepreneurs and other expatriates, succumbed to Baghdad logics in the 1930s as well. Many trading houses relocated from Basra to the Iraqi capital, and in 1931 the printing company Times Press followed suit.[34] At the same time, potential vehicles for the development of a local cosmopolitan patriotism shared by Basrawis and non-natives only grew more and more rusty. Horse races, introduced by wartime officers to forge ties between the British and the Basrawis, saw a sharp drop in spectators, and clubs designed to foster bonds between Europeans and local elites began to disintegrate through disagreements between "Iraqis" and "foreigners".[35] Instead of coming to the rescue of the separatist project during its death throes, members of the local British community in Basra began cultivating their own distinctiveness and their own subdivisions: by the end of 1931, a Caledonian society had become part of Basra's social scene.[36]

Ex-separatists and anti-separatists into the independent Iraq

The feeble state of the Basra separatist movement was only confirmed by developments after 1929. In that year, the man who had enjoyed most success in creating an enduring political movement in Basra in modern times, Sayyid Talib, died in Berlin. Thousands of Basrawis and leaders of every sect in the city later took part in an unprecedented mass gathering when his body was transferred from Basra to Zubayr for burial.[37] The authors of the 1921 petition, whose relations with Talib had remained cool since his attempt at conquering the throne for all of Iraq, had never managed to mobilise anything on a comparable scale.

A sense of resignation now seemed to reign, with a tendency on the part of the separatists to accept the new realities and to enter into alliances with conservatives elsewhere in Iraq in hope of minimising further damage from unpredictable young politicians. A project to protest new tax arrangements in 1931 was hastily shelved when the strike of that year came to threaten the city's economy; the idea of haggling with the state was quickly superseded by a letter of grati- tude to the local authorities for having dealt so effectively with the rebellious urban masses.[38] And just as in the 1920s, the old separatists remained passive at junctures when they could have created a platform for dissent, such as the elec- tion to a new date board, established in 1932 by the government but with seats for local representatives. At the first meeting of this body, no leading represen- tatives of the landowners even bothered to show up.[39]

Separatism was no longer a political movement in Basra. Outsiders would continue to refer to the old project intermittently in the first half of the 1930s, on occasions when it suited them to paint a pessimistic picture of the Iraqi po- litical landscape. But in Basra it was by now, at most, a flight of fancy that only sporadically found expression, generally as a passive reaction to some outside stimulus. After 1929, this happened a few times in response to rumours of changes in British policy, particularly concerning the air-base strategy. The idea that Britain would eventually evacuate all its air installations in central Iraq and concentrate its operations in Basra surfaced repeatedly, leading to accusations from the Baghdad nationalist press that the port city already had the appearance of a "British naval base", and to hopes among the local business community of a return to the economic boom associated with the war and the early 1920s.[40] Although the British eventually decided to hold on to their base also in central Iraq, their position in Basra remained particularly influential for most of the 1930s. One local observer described the head of the Basra Port Directorate, Colonel J.C. Ward, as the "real ruler" (*al-hakim al-haqiqi*) of the city.[41] From such a state of affairs, the pro-British supporters of the old separatist movement may at least have taken some comfort.

In these circumstances, the waning separatist movement was no longer the main challenge to the concept of a unified Iraqi state in the Basra region. In Oc- tober 1932, former separatists and anti-separatists alike participated in inde- pendence celebrations, dramatically marked by the speech of King Faysal in Baghdad being transmitted live via newly opened radio connections to Basra, where it was broadcast to large audiences by means of public address systems.[42] Again, both camps were represented when local subscriptions to a new plane for the Iraqi air force, to be named "Basra", gathered pace during the autumn, sym- bolically sealing the link between the Gulf city and the larger national commu- nity.[43]

The fates of the individuals involved in the separatist project in the new Iraq were diverse. Some of the most important leaders, including Sani', 'Abd al- Ahad and Aga Ja'far, passed away in the early 1930s, the latter having settled in Damascus.[44] Others withdrew from politics or concentrated on local administra- tion, such as Nuh, who was re-elected to the municipality in 1931 and partici- pated in a committee to prepare Basra for a 1932 overhaul of the Iraqi tax sys- tem.[45] The most striking example of a separatist who remained in conflict with the Iraqi state was Sayyid 'Abd 'Ali of Qurna, hailed by the British as a model mayor during the years of occupation, but in the 1930s accused of being in league with outlaws in the marshes between Iraq and Persia.[46]

Other separatists gradually came to terms with the new state and began interacting with it – or their families would do so within a generation or two. 'Abd al-Latif al-Mandil became close to the Iraqi nationalist and modernist Ma'ruf al-Rusafi, who eventually wrote a poem in honour of the Basra notable.[47] 'Abd al-Karim al-Sa'dun entered the established system as a parliamentary deputy in the 1930s, as did others close to the separatist movement, including 'Abdallah al-Khalil and 'Abd al-Razzaq al-Na'ma.[48] The children of Yusuf 'Abd al-Ahad rose to high positions in the Iraqi administration.[49]

In this way, Basra's traditional notable families of landowners and merchants managed to maintain control of local key positions such as the mayorship, as well as most of the area's seats in the Iraqi parliament. Three consecutive elections between 1933 and 1935 returned only a few outspoken nationalists – but the fact that the notables now competed for seats in a Baghdad assembly signified anti-separatist victory in the more basic struggle about how the Ottoman carcass in the region should be handled. Ironically, during the 1930s it was this latter group which, by being much more articulate than the traditional notables, fronted matters of local concern (such as the exorbitant prices charged by the Basra water works) – now put forward in parliament and thus within the confines of the new political system.[50] These young Basrawis were also the ones to make it to the top within the new, emerging Iraqi system in this period: Muhammad Zaki became a great parliamentarian, a teacher of law and minister of justice before he suddenly died in the midst of his advance to positions of influence in Baghdad;[51] 'Abd al-'Aziz al-Mutayr excelled within the judicial branch of government and became a supreme court judge in the Iraqi capital.[52]

The new generation of Iraqi nationalists eventually remodelled even the Basra date industry – the keystone of the Gulf city's local patriotism – in their own image. Promotional materials (another novelty never seized upon by the separatists) from the 1930s boasted of a trade completely reorganised on "modern" and "hygienic" lines, painstakingly pointing out that the "non-complimentary terms" used by wartime British officials to describe packing methods were no longer justified.[53] Photographs showing streamlined packing stations with meticulously groomed packers in chalky-white uniforms were part of the marketing effort, all intended to construct a dichotomy between the old days and the new epoch of Iraqi independence. If the Basra notables managed to hold on to seats and secure government jobs for their sons, it was the young anti-separatists who took the lead in defining the contents of the new Iraq.

There were also those from both camps whose attempts at embracing the new Iraqi state were followed by withdrawal or even tragedy. One of the anti-separatists, Ahmad Hamdi Mullah Husayn, left politics, concentrated on business in the 1930s and eventually became a prolific Baha'i writer.[54] 'Abd al-Muhsin al-Sa'dun's efforts at compromise with the nationalist forces were severely hampered by Britain's unwillingness to accord Iraq anything more than nominal independence, a tension that in the end proved unbearable and led the

prime minister to commit suicide in 1929.[55] And 'Abdallah ibn Ahmad al-Sani',
who had chosen to pursue a career within the system his separatist father
fought, was in 1931 slain at the hands of a Sa'dun shaykh opposed to the marriage between Sani' and a woman of the Sa'dun clan.[56] (The murderer was
eventually pardoned due to the regime's fear of the tribal power of the Sa'duns.)
Such individual disasters notwithstanding, the entire political spectrum in Basra
– as expressed through modern political organisations and media – had by the
early 1930s come to accept the territorial framework of a single state from the
Gulf to the Kurdish mountains. The remaining problem for the Iraqi government concerned more unconventional politicians.

The ultimate act of incorporation: conscription

Ever since Ottoman days, the principal issues in encounters between state and
individual in the Basra region had centred on negotiations over taxes and conscripts. This was certainly the case for the deprived Shi'i majority population in
the area, still toiling as *ta'ab*s or *fallahun* for their rich Basra landlords.

With respect to taxation, the state actually became less visible after Iraq's
independence. With a new consumption tax regime introduced in 1931, government dues on agricultural produce were now collected at the market place. In
theory, this meant better prospects for self-subsistence, as there was no tax to
pay for crops that did not reach the market. In practice, however, peasant de-
pendence upon the market for everyday items like tea and sugar as well as imported textiles was such that the poorest Iraqis were hardest hit by the new regime. And if the state now faded into the background, it did so only by allowing
another force to gain the upper hand: the new arrangements left the relationship
between cultivator and landholder as the main area of dispute in relation to the
annual harvest, and a further piece of legislation in 1933 on the rights and duties
of the cultivators made matters worse for the peasants by theoretically tying
them to the land until they had paid off all debts to the landlord.[57]

On the other hand, the threat of conscription had receded somewhat during
the mandate. Although the population had become accustomed to seeing divisions of a new professional Iraqi army operating in the Basra area, and despite
census manoeuvres in the late 1920s, they themselves had so far not been forced
to enrol. The main factor delaying the government's implementation of the military draft had been fear of reactions from tribal areas in the country, a danger
impossible to overlook even in comparatively placid Basra. Robbers could still
operate quite freely in the Qurna area and had contacts with brigands active in
the marshlands across the Persian border, leading local officials to claim that air
power was the only effective remedy.[58] Rumours circulated that Iraqi independence would mean a relaxation of control in the countryside and a resurgence of
tribal power.[59] The visit to the region in 1931 by 'Ujaymi al-Sa'dun – an old
rebel chief of the Muntafiq and now a resident of Turkey – aroused memories of
a period when the writ of the state was limited to the riverbanks proper, at

best.[60] And in Kut al-Zayn, tribal ties were described as vigorous and robust, with the Persian consul repeatedly showing an interest in reviving the pro-Persian agitation of his predecessors in this traditional fiefdom of the consulate.[61]

It was in this context the government in 1935 decided to press ahead with the scheme for enrolling a national army. Despite the signs of incomplete government control in Basra's rural areas, the new policy was implemented during the course of the summer without major problems. Only in traditionally troublesome Madina did some form of effective resistance materialise, and airplanes, this time from the Iraqi air force, were called in along with troops from Basra. Eventually the tribal leaders surrendered, and it was arranged for sons of some of the chiefs to join the army as officers. Elsewhere in the Basra countryside, calm prevailed throughout the year.[62]

The incorporation of the population into the Iraqi state now had a new quality, for to most people along the banks of the Shatt al-'Arab, it was conscription rather than the precise territorial configuration of administrative entities which had been the main bone of contention in previous confrontations with the state. Still, this capitulation to the central government was probably more a sign of exhaustion than an act that followed a process of genuine integration: school attendance in the countryside was still very low, and the provision of other government services in its infancy.[63] In this sense, it was a victory for the state rather than the Iraqi nation.

What was clear at any rate was that the landowning Basra separatists had drained the rural segment of the population of resources and energy, instead of recruiting them to their own project. In no small measure it was the urban notables who were responsible for both the poverty of the villagers and for thwarting their various grass-roots initiatives to challenge Baghdad. This in turn led to a situation in which the central government managed to obtain conscripts even from localities where the Ottomans had been unable to do so for centuries. If the Basra separatist movement had collapsed by 1929, it was only the successful enforcement of the military draft in 1935 that marked the real end to alternative visions for the state in the Basra area.

11   Separatist Implosion, Nationalist Triumph

By 1935, it was evident that the scheme for turning Basra into a British-sponsored Gulf state had failed completely. The separatist project had become wiped out as a political movement, the independent monarchy was steadily solidifying its hold on the port city, and even local enemies of the Baghdad government had adopted the language of the unitary state, reproducing the idea of Iraq's territorial integrity in the same sentences that criticised the powers of the day.

In the early 1920s, there had been several factors working to the advantage of the separatist project. In the end, however, strategic location, fertile date lands and material wealth all proved inadequate to secure for Basra a special political status. British policy was one central variable that certainly hampered the project – yet, with its frequent detours into emergency scenarios involving some sort of Basra protectorate, it was too ambivalent to single-handedly extinguish the idea of an autonomous Gulf city. The collapse of the bid for secession must be explained with reference to other circumstances, notably the anatomy of the separation movement itself and the outlook of its leadership. But first a closer examination of the British position is warranted, for post-1935 developments only underlined the extent to which Basra had been the real cornerstone for British imperial interests in the region – interests which were ultimately to become another casualty in the separatist debacle.

British policy and imperial interests

That London's policy of supporting a single Iraqi state should endure seems particularly remarkable if a long-term perspective on British imperial interests in the region is employed. During the First World War, it was generally agreed that Basra was the only area in the easternmost provinces of the Ottoman Empire where British strategic interests demanded a permanent post-war presence. Later, various empire-related arguments were constructed for justifying a British sphere that included Baghdad and Mosul as well (first indicating it was necessary to hold the areas north of Basra to prevent a return of the Turks, then suggesting that Baghdad was essential to the new chain of imperial air communications); however, closer scrutiny of these arguments in departmental discussions eventually revealed them to be half-truths at best. When the monarchy in 1941 came under threat as pro-Nazi politicians with links to the Iraqi army staged a coup, London's military response only confirmed that Basra was still the central strategical spot in Iraq that required British intervention. After a swift occupation of Basra, the decision to proceed further northwards appeared more reluctant – and was eventually taken because the British-built airfields near Baghdad could become a threat if they fell to the enemy, not because the Iraqi capital was seen as possessing any intrinsic value to the British Empire.[1] In this manner, the policy of standing by a large political entity instead of concentrating British resources in a coastal enclave almost tipped the balance against London in 1941. And this it did, with full force, as the Iraqi monarchy came to an end in 1958.

It has been maintained that in the early twentieth century the "viability" of states was seen to be so intimately connected to geographical size so as to render alternative visions of small-scale states unrealistic and even ridiculous.[2] Clearly, the size factor had been central to the argument for a unified Iraq ever since the times of Wilson and Cox in the post-war years. Yet, on the other hand, Dobbs's Hanseatic fantasies in the mid 1920s and Hall's visualisation of a British fastness in Basra as late as in 1930 demonstrate that there were no epistemological or conceptual barriers to this sort of reasoning among British bureaucrats.

A more likely explanation involves size as a function of imperial economics and cost-cutting measures. The British preference for larger, if necessary federative, entities wherever possible (and sometimes where it was not possible) is a striking feature of London's imperial policy, both in the interwar period and later. In India, British supporters for a federal state came to dominate over those working for the survival of the potentially more pro-British princely states and the traditional concept of "two Indias"; in Malaysia, London's administrators encouraged several institutions favouring pan-Malay sentiments to the detriment of individual rulers of smaller states who might have been more reliable allies for the future.[3] Federation experiments were launched in British colonies in Africa and in the West Indies during the 1950s. In combination with an absence of what one writer in the 1920s dubbed *drusitis* – excessive interest in local particularisms – such policies created a contrast to other imperial powers like France, which deliberately promoted ethnic enclaves to bolster key strategic territories, for instance along the Syrian and Lebanese coasts.[4] Only in the 1960s did the enthusiasm for federalism as an instrument of imperial devolution show some signs of abating, but even after this point the cases of successful pro-colonial separatism on the part of Lilliputian imperial subunits formed the exception to the rule.[5] Such exceptions included the successful bids by the Cayman Islands and later Anguilla for recognition as separate dependencies of Britain (detached from Jamaica and St. Kitts & Nevis respectively), instances which were characterised by unusual alliances between pro-British natives and British administrators or MPs, and which also exhibited parallels to the local–imperial synergies that enabled Ceuta, Melilla and Mayotte to become special administrative territories within the Spanish and French imperial systems.[6] But in the vast majority of cases – from Basra via Penang and Aden to Nevis (the reluctant junior partner of St. Kitts & Nevis) and Barbuda (in a ditto situation within Antigua & Barbuda) – British imperial officials refrained from becoming bogged down in alliances with local forces that could have had fissiparous consequences.

Inklings of such principled attitudes aside – for an explicit policy it was not – most of the factors that worked against the Basra scheme in London were at first utterly trivial. Shuckburgh did not want to quarrel with Cox about "minor issues" and Churchill was worried that he might "stultify" himself if policies were reversed. The search for internal departmental harmony and consistency may well have been more important than Basra itself and its place in the British Empire: In February 1921, when Cox enquired about the status of the semi-autonomous Pusht-i Kuh in Persia, a newly employed junior official at the India Office drew up an imaginative vision of Basra and Pusht-i Kuh in a larger cluster of pro-British mini-states in the region, only to be rebuked by a senior official who emphasised pragmatism and a continuation along lines already in the making.[7] Just as quarrels with Cox were untimely, the opening of large, new dossiers had limited appeal to an already overworked administration in Whitehall. But over time, the logic of a single Iraqi state became self-perpetuating, and weightier outside forces (particularly in the RAF and the air industry) gradually became its powerful standard-bearers.

In retrospect, the unceremonious departure of the British from all their key assets in the Middle East in the 1950s and the 1960s (Suez, Aden and Abadan in addition to Basra) creates the impression of imperial overeating – that the interests of the British Empire as a system had been forsaken in favour of "men on the spot" with their appetite for large proconsulships. But that is precisely a retrospective mode of thinking. There is much to suggest that, in the 1930s, Britain was so confident in its own position in Iraq that merely raising the issue of Basra's separateness other than in an emergency scenario would be perceived as constructing problems where none existed. Why, after all, let go of Baghdad and the increasingly credible prospects of oil revenues from Mosul if everything could be held, at more or less the same cost? During the treaty negotiations of 1929 and 1930, Colonial Office staff simply did not contemplate the eventuality of Britain becoming abruptly ejected from Iraq – this was to change radically only after 1945.[8]

The solution adopted for Basra shows that in 1930 Britain was convinced that it could control this territory satisfactorily through informal arrangements, without requiring special arrangements for the strategic Gulf coastline. There was no need for a separate Basra because, for all the foreseeable future, an imperial presence in a nominally independent Iraq was already secured (as was a pre-eminent position in commerce) – there was certainly little sign of a faltering "will to imperialism" in this policy.[9] With hindsight, this confidence can rightly be described as overbold, even arrogant. At the time, at least some British officials hinted at this. But for them to convince the whole British imperial machinery about the necessity of a radical change of policy, something more persuasive was required. This is where the Basra notables had an opportunity, and it is where they failed.

Elite ineptitude and strategic shortcomings

The real reasons for the separatist fiasco must be sought within the movement itself, and within its leadership in particular. More than anything else, it was their lack of political dexterity that sealed the fate of their scheme for a city-state in the Persian Gulf and made it possible for groups with fewer material resources to take the lead in defining new, nationalist identities for the post-Ottoman era.

The first failure of the Basra separatist leaders was their inability to cross the bridge from romantic dreams to practical politics. In 1921 they had at least a list of preferences which might over time develop into practical policies. Their priorities included separate treatment of their own region, local control of taxes and law enforcement, and guarantees that the link to the British Empire would remain in place. However, the separatists never managed to adjust their visions to the changing political realities of the 1920s.

The most important political force with which the separatists failed to establish rapport was the British, who never became convinced of the virtues of a separate state in the Basra area. In particular, one item on the separatist agenda diverged from mainstream British thinking on Middle Eastern politics: the separatists preferred a non-dynastic form of government to a monopoly on power vested in a noble local family. In the 1918 plebiscite, the Basra elite had warned against Arab amirs, including two of the local magnates, Khaz'al of Muhammara and Sayyid Talib. According to the arrangements proposed in the 1921 petition, any local ruler should instead emerge from a procedure with democratic elements. Such notions found scant support among the British, who tended to prefer traditional authority in the form of emirates.

In this context, no attempt was made at mollifying the British with a charismatic figure, a shaykh, who could compete with and even outshine Faysal. Indeed, the separatists managed to estrange one of the few notables who stood out because of his family's unique prestige in local society – the head of the Naqib family, Sayyid Hashim, who was educated in India and on good terms with many of the rulers in the Gulf.[10] At the same time, they failed to exploit the noble lineages of Zubayr families who did sympathise with their project, and had ancestors who had been virtual rulers of both Basra and Zubayr for a brief period in the 1830s.[11] Later in the 1920s, rumours surfaced of a possible role for another member of the Naqib dynasty, the newly returned Sayyid Talib, but no close ties were established between the separatist leaders and this dominant figure of pre-war Basra.[12]

Similarly, at successive critical stages during the 1920s, the separatists failed to follow up opportunities for realising their vision within the evolving framework of mandated Iraq. In particular, possibilities for securing a federal solution for the country were jeopardised. In the first half of the 1920s, there were long negotiations related to the constitutional arrangements for a future Iraq, sessions in which Basra notables were invited to take part. In 1927 another suitable occasion for addressing issues related to administrative decentralisation arose with the drafting of a law on provincial government and local administration. But throughout the mandate, the Basra separatists continued to mutter among themselves instead of negotiating, boycotting instead of bargaining. Their failure to engage with political realities was characterised by total inarticulateness in the arenas where decisions were made.

The second shortcoming of the separatist leadership lay in their inability to expand the coalition supporting their project. Remarkably, the separatist delegation in 1921 featured no representatives of Basra's urban Shi'i Arab majority (only the small communities of Persians and rural Qurna were included) – an omission repeated in the governor's council, the power base for the separatists' dominance of local politics in the early 1920s. By contrast, various Iraqi nationalist circles took a much more inclusive approach towards the Shi'is.[13]

The consequences of this became evident when the crucial issue of conscription came on the agenda in 1927 and created an unprecedented surge of political activity in Basra, involving, for the first time in this period, the countryside as well as the city. By now, however, local Shi'i elites had become divided between emerging Iraqi nationalist and more traditional sectarian networks, while hardly anyone had links to the separatist camp. It is perfectly conceivable that the primary motive behind the anti-conscription campaigns of 1927 and 1928 was to keep the state at an arm's length rather than any intense longing for becoming actively involved in the various imagined communities then being sketched out. But, in contrast to external forces like Najd and Persia which acquired footholds in Basra politics during the late 1920s, the separatists were unable to exploit this intense fear of conscription. They had left the Shi'is largely to their own devices during the preceding years, and had no network for propagating their own ideas among new constituencies.

There were also defections from communities with whom the separatists already had initiated some limited elite-level co-operation. The separatists had mostly targeted the traditional elite of Basra's smaller religious communities as coalition partners, but intra-communal relations were in many cases already under considerable strain as economic boom and new educational opportunities were making it increasingly possible for young people to break free from the closed environments into which they had been born. During the 1920s, bitter internal conflicts erupted for instance among the Jews, Chaldeans and Syrian Catholics, with the younger generation complaining about old-fashioned community schools and conservative religious leaders.[14] Many saw politics as a possible arena for transcending the parochial identities of these religious communities. Crucially, it was ideologies like Iraqi nationalism, pan-Arabism or communism that came to attract most of the dropouts from these communities.[15] The separatist leaders, on the other hand, seemed incapable of offering much to the younger generation of political elites.

By the time the separatist leaders finally showed signs of willingness to transform their cliquish grouping into a broader alliance, they had already lost much local influence due to the increasingly assertive policies of the central government and its new-found, anti-separatist local partners. The separatist movement had failed to gain a firm hold even in Zubayr, where a majority of the inhabitants shared the social and geographical background of the two most prominent separatist leaders. Several residents of the desert town had found an alternative hero in the person of Ibn Sa'ud, who during the 1920s had emerged as a figure rather more enterprising than the Basra separatists; others flocked to various Iraqi nationalist camps in Basra or further afield. With the leading Basra separatists unable to disseminate their programme even through traditional elites from their own bailiwick, it would have been a Herculean challenge to build a viable coalition with segments of Basra community with which there had been much less social interaction in the past.

At the root of the separatist failure lay a third distinct weak point in strategy: a complete neglect of the field of symbolic politics. The separatist vision never developed beyond a brief petition, even though the promoters of the scheme evidently continued to cling to their original ideas for several years. Many of Basra's communities were represented at the elite level in the separatist delegation, but few efforts were made to include the popular masses of these communities in the separatist enterprise. No political party in favour of separation emerged, no propaganda in the shape of newspapers or literature was produced, no school which could have become an intellectual centre for the movement was sponsored, and no vista to inspire a broadening of the movement was cultivated. The separatists were simply unable to make any purposeful contribution to the numerous processes that were initiated in cultural, educational and political spheres after the kingdom of Iraq became a reality in 1921. This considerably weakened their chances of success, because the public at large did not share the pro-British spirit so central to the separatist project, and the task of persuasion ahead of them in 1921 was formidable.

The publicity drought in the field of symbolic politics proved fatal for the separatists, even though political processes involving larger audiences were still in their infancy at the time. By remaining passive, the separatists allowed their local competitors to stake out the course in the public domain, tentatively and exploratively at first but with profound ramifications for both the local political process and the evolving political discourse. There emerged individuals who supported visions more compatible with an Arab kingdom for Iraq, who occupied the symbolic space opened up after the Ottoman collapse, and who started to build links with like-minded people in the cities to the north – often on the basis of networks established during Ottoman times. Initially, these politicians favoured a variety of visions for the future themselves, and their heroes ranged from King Husayn of Hijaz to Mustafa Kemal in Ankara. But they all agreed on the necessity of fighting a scheme that threatened to isolate Basra from the areas further north. By being more articulate than their adversaries, they gained a head start in symbolic politics, which made up for the socio-economic advantages of the separatists and ultimately empowered them to oust the separatists from the local administration. In this process, their visions for the future and their political language also came to converge, coalescing into support for the unitary state from the Gulf to Mosul which had served as their career spring-board.

The separatists' problems in coalition-building illustrate how the various crafts within the art of constructing new identities may intertwine. The very concept of building an inter-sectarian coalition suffered a blow when the separatist alternative failed to make headway in the years following the launch of the 1921 petition, and individual separatist leaders subsequently resorted to alternative strategies. In that process, they embraced more well-established packages of symbols and values, connected with identity labels that were mutually antagonistic and also less acceptable to new potential partners. The most evident of these alternative strategies had been the turn to Ibn Sa'ud by Mandil and Sani'. The Najdi ruler and his Wahhabism were anathema for the Shi'is (whom this current of Islam labelled as unbelievers), and the strengthening of links between Ibn Sa'ud and some of the separatist leaders doubtless damaged the prospects for a more broad-based local alliance.[16] Another instance: in 1923, as the educational sphere evolved without any separatist input, one participant in the original separatist delegation chose to sponsor a Persian school to be set up under the auspices of the Persian consulate.[17] And in 1928, the two foremost separatist leaders did not protest or suggest any alternative when landowning merchants from their native Zubayr joined the local campaign for Najdi citizenships, a move which would highlight sectarian differences in Basra society rather than levelling them. Such signals from the separatist elite may have induced others to move further away from the paradigm of a civic, secular partnership based on common local interests – and, in this manner, the failure in coalition-building was ultimately related to the absence of a strong symbolic and ideological framework for the separatist vision, a framework that could have neutralised the attractions of competing identity projects.

Traditional notables in a new epoch

The inefficiency of the traditional Basra notables in the political domain stands out strongly when comparisons are made with local elites of their generation in other areas detached from the Ottoman Empire during the First World War. In Haifa, for instance, well-established local elites supportive of a daring and controversial undertaking – that of creating an alliance with the Zionists – proceeded to back it up at the organisational level by establishing a political party and by building links to journalists sympathetic to their cause.[18] In Alexandria, the traditional socio-economic elite managed to institutionalise their cotton-based commercial activity through the Alexandria General Produce Association, and made good use of the municipality to develop a symbolic superstructure that celebrated their cosmopolitan way of life in museums and public parks.[19] (In Basra, by contrast, the old date bourse – an informal gathering of landowners in Abu al-Khasib assembled annually to fix the prices – had by 1930 been taken over by an American export firm.[20]) In both Haifa and Alexandria, other

political forces eventually came to prevail – but the people behind political visions that challenged the louder and less complex varieties of nationalism at
least made an effort to get their views across. The Basra separatist leaders, on
the other hand, showed little interest in entering negotiations about practical
compromises within the framework of the monarchy, refrained from approaching other segments of the local population who might have provided increased
scope and vitality to the coalition behind the 1921 petition, and apparently did
not even contemplate a more public campaign in support of their scheme. The
contrast to Singapore, where industrious political elites eventually conquered
the local administration and used it as a tool in a state-directed campaign for
multi-ethnic coexistence, could not have been greater.

Why did the notables of Basra fail to even explore avenues that might have
helped transform the vision of a separate Basra into a viable political movement? One possible explanation relates to the social composition of the separatist elite, and its consequences for their outlook on politics. They were mostly
traditional notables of Basra's mercantile and landowning communities with
little formal education or work experience from the Ottoman bureaucracy –
which in turn reflected the fact that the segment of the local elite intimately integrated into the Ottoman system had been comparatively small in Basra. What
the separatist circle lacked was representatives of Basra's intellectuals, in particular the effendis, young men who had been educated in the modern Ottoman
schools and had often worked as government officials. The effendis had spearheaded tentative pre-war experiments of linking culture and religion with larger,
imagined political communities; in Basra, they had formed an important adjunct
to the pre-war reform movement. But in the 1920s, they flocked to the anti-
separatist label or to other projects that had little to do with the 1921 petition.
Some were even busy creating nationalisms for the Christians of northern Iraq,
advocating that they were the heirs to the mighty Assyrians and deserved a
homeland of their own.[21]

It is difficult to tell whether this situation was the result of a deliberate refusal of the separatists to include the young Basra intellectuals in their movement, or if it was the separatist project itself which held no appeal to the local
educated elite. Anecdotal evidence suggests that the traditional notables were
ambivalent about the effendis as a new social group, appreciating their talents
but also viewing them as a threat to the established social order. Armed with the
pile driver of Modern Education, young men of humble origins could advance
rapidly in an environment that was changing faster than ever before; eager to
transcend sectarian and denominational barriers, they created chaos in established patterns of social interaction. Come election time, and they would de-
scend on the coffee shops and bazaars with tales of new political ideologies
which threatened to explode the existing system of social solidarities. The notables' sense of uneasiness about this new societal force had been apparent as
early as in the days of the pre-war reformist movement, when they had settled
for wholesale acceptance of the anti-foreigner ideological facade professed by
the effendis, yet had continued to express pro-British views privately. This had

left the whole enterprise with an uneasy dualist character – and a contradiction impossible to maintain in the post-war period, when Britain became the main local power.

In several cases after the war, Basra notables joined ranks to exclude these young firebrands from the electoral process.[22] Yet, it was also clear that the traditional elite saw the effendis as possessing some kind of undefined magic deriving from their modern education, enabling them to manoeuvre more smoothly within the machinery of the modern state. Thus it was that the Basra landowners, who considered themselves the world's leading experts on date cultivation, would choose an educated highlander from Mosul to write reports for them and represent them when they prepared complaints about a new system of agricultural taxation. But this individual was also feared for his political views, and received no support at elections to the Iraqi parliament. Eventually, he would refuse to act as mediator for the Basra landowners in their dealings with the central government.[23]

This ambivalence may have contributed to a situation in which no decisive alliance was established between the separatist elite and the intelligentsia of Basra. For there were certainly candidates available who had chosen to stay aloof from the circles advocating closer ties with the north. Among them was Jad Ghawi, a Palestinian who had been educated at a British school in Jerusalem and had served in Sudan before becoming appointed assistant to Basra's governor, the separatist Ahmad al-Saniʿ. But in 1923, he chose to leave Basra and reverted to his career as an administrative official in Africa.[24] It would seem that no irresistible job offer had materialised from the Basra separatists. Similarly, the Meccan historian Muhammad al-Nabhani had his home in Basra in the early 1920s, residing in the heart of the old town, close to the houses of many leading separatists.[25] He had already published a history of Bahrain, and was now working on a manuscript of Basra's history.[26] Nabhani had a traditional scholarly background, and was in social terms probably more palatable to the separatist elite than many of the young effendis. But again, no community of interest developed. In the late 1920s, Nabhani was working as a teacher at the government school in Basra.[27]

Even if no suitable candidates for the job as a court poet for the separatist leaders were obtainable locally, the affluent Basra notables could easily have imported one, or at least sponsored a propagandist in some other Middle Eastern city where there was an abundance of unemployed young intellectuals. This was exactly what their neighbour, the shaykh of Muhammara, had done before the war, when he hired a Christian Egyptian journalist to publish propaganda on his behalf in Cairo.[28] Similarly, the example of Kuwait-born ʿAbd al-ʿAziz al-Rushayd demonstrates the wide range of projects these young literati were willing to join, despite the often universalistic ideals that they had received through their education. Rushayd had been trained at traditional religious schools in Mecca before he went on to study with modernist Muslim circles in Egypt, and had travelled widely within the Ottoman Empire.[29] Yet in the 1920s, he emerged as an intellectual supporter of the small Kuwaiti emirate and defended its political legitimacy in a book on Kuwaiti history.[30] Later, in the 1930s, he became a Sa'udi propagandist in Indonesia, now spreading the Salafi creed which militated against divisions within the Islamic umma. Also the intelligentsia needed jobs, and many demonstrated considerable versatility through their careers.

In contrast to the separatists, the supporters of unity with Baghdad treated the young intellectuals as a resource. Indeed, many of the anti-separatists belonged to this group themselves, and made use of their capabilities as orators and writers. Others did not themselves excel in rhetoric but nevertheless used their money to support young intellectuals, poets or journalists who were capable of conquering the public space on their behalf. One anti-separatist had a "secretary" who often delivered speeches for him; others arranged festivities in the honour of some of the local cultural talents.[31]

Beyond the sphere of political artisanship, the 1920s saw certain broader socio-economic developments that contributed to the further marginalisation of the separatist scheme. First, the business strategies pursued by the mercantile Basra separatist elite were unhelpful to their political ambitions. The city had a weak industrial tradition (the handlooms of nineteenth-century Baghdad and Mosul form contrasting examples) and therefore no pool for re-investing agricultural surplus. Instead of stimulating the emergence of an industrial bourgeoisie (a potential vanguard for any project of urban autonomy), the rapidly growing profits from Basra's fertile hinterland were consistently diverted into yet more land development relating to date monoculture and to conspicuous luxury consumption, chiefly in the shape of cars and holidays in Syria or in Europe. As a result, Basra remained a society with an enormous divide between the very rich and the very poor, lacking a socio-economic environment that could support a common, local patriotic spirit among middle-class citizens.

Secondly, changing patterns in Basra's urban geography may have assisted the process whereby the city's traditional leaders lost their grip on local politics. Since the 1880s, 'Ashar had emerged as a suburb to Basra. Its growth had accelerated during the war due to its strategic riverside location, and it was increasingly seen as the real centre of Basra, where more and more mercantile and governmental institutions were located.[32] In political terms, this was virgin territory where the influence of Basra's traditional elite was weaker, and it was in 'Ashar many of the political meetings emphasising Basra's connections with wider communities took place in the 1920s. At the time, the Basra notables maintained that their plan was to keep the old town as a residential centre, with 'Ashar a commercial hub only.[33] But the policies of the central government increasingly favoured the suburb, and eventually most governmental offices were located there.[34] Gradually, the Basra notables involved in business understood that they too would have to reorientate themselves towards the river – and in this process may have discovered how their original separatist project, cultivated in the inner town of old Basra, belonged to what was increasingly seen as urban periphery.

And finally, there are signs that the mercantilist spirit at the heart of the 1921 petition may itself have induced the separatist leaders to put the brakes on for the project during the 1920s. One primary objective of the petition had been to avert potential damage to business caused by the violent rivalries the Basra leaders thought would accompany any attempt at setting up an Arab state. With that state becoming reality in a comparatively peaceful fashion during the early 1920s, the separatist project increasingly assumed a utopian, and therefore un-businesslike, character. It created friction with leading British officials, and caused offence among potential trading partners in Baghdad. Interestingly, some of the most prominent trading houses of Basra – among them the Asfar, Garibian and Salih families – remained neutral during the conflict over separa-tism, opting to continue to do business as usual without becoming embroiled in politics.[35] To them, their compatriots' complaints about the central authorities may have seemed insignificant in comparison with the steady profits that could be generated by uninterrupted trade. Members of the separatist elite may in-creasingly have felt that this course was preferable, although many expressed sentimental feelings for their original project as late as in 1928, and made life difficult for themselves throughout the mandate by sticking to their old ideas.

Elites, manipulations and constraints in the competition over nationalisms

Many studies on ethnicity and nationalism focus on how cunning elites have seemingly endless possibilities of manipulating the populace, goading it in the directions in politics they so desire. By contrast, the story of the separatist Basra notables and their travails during the 1920s is mainly about limitations and con-straints facing elites.

Because the Basra notables barely managed to get their separatist project off the ground, any discussion of how it appealed to wider segments of the local population at the time would be mere speculation. It is the separatists' inability to construct a nationalism and pursue it in real politics – and the consequences of this failure for their own ambitions – that can be traced in the historical sources. However, the information available on the fate of the various sub-separatisms that emerged in Basra in the late 1920s may offer insights concern-ing the actual drawing power and magnetic force of the competing local politi-cal projects in this period, for these initiatives were headed by elites who made more determined efforts to pursue their visions in the public domain.

The 1928 Kut al-Zayn pro-Persian movement was primarily a practical re-sponse by the local population to the threat of conscription. Its territorial dimen-sions were understated, overshadowed by a campaign for naturalisation as Per-sian subjects. Later, as Iraqi investigations were initiated, several of those inter-viewed claimed that they were born on islands in the river; the interviewers saw this as a made-up story aimed at achieving neutrality in the ongoing conflict and prompted by the widely held belief that the international status of islands in the Shatt al-'Arab was undetermined. And when the inhabitants after some time discovered that also the Persian state was on the lookout for conscripts to its own army, the pro-Persian project lost much of its attraction, and their "Persian" identity evaporated.[36] Nevertheless, some elements of their protest were to prove more enduring. In the 1940s, revolts in Muhammara to restore the old shaykhship in the town were initiated from the Iraqi side of the river, once more challenging the established state system in the region. Through the institution of the shaykhship and its symbolic force, this tribal, trans-river tradition could be nurtured more easily than could the abstract urban separatist project, with Khaz'al's descendants and their entourage forming a tangible focus in exile in Basra for many decades.[37]

Similarly, the political campaign in Zubayr in the late 1920s was also connected to a more long-lasting identity project. The Zubayris were unique among the Basrawis in transforming their individual tribal myths of descent (from various locations around the Arabian Peninsula) into a common (Najdi) identity.[38] The secluded environment of their town in the desert west of Basra – a virtual island sheltered from the larger port city – was an important factor in this, for Najdi cultural symbols were reproduced here on a daily basis, in architecture, fashion, poetry and music. The isolated desert town, a living museum of Najdi artefacts, with a population who could narrate how their grandfathers migrated to the area some hundred years ago, was the logical opposite to chaotic Basra in preconditions for cultivating a separate identity: in the port city, everything would have to be constructed and quite literally dug from the earth if a special myth of origin (like a link to the ancient Sumerians) were to be established; in the case of Zubayr, the refusal of the movement's chosen regional patron, Ibn Sa'ud, to play a more active role restrained a movement that in itself was quite successful – and that was to survive in the sense of a distinctive Zubayr identity for some time.[39]

Given the size of its electorate, the Shi'i anti-conscription movement was the one with the greatest potential for achieving something on its own, and it was here that the limits and constraints facing politicians at work were most evident. After the idea of separating the Shi'i south of Iraq had figured prominently at public meetings and religious festivals in 1927, this scheme melted away over the next few years. In this episode, separatism was actually being tested in politics rather than being abandoned at the drawing board. To a greater extent than with the 1921 petition movement, it is here possible to speak of an audience rejecting a project introduced by an intellectual elite – a lack of resonance.[40]

The problem for the Shi'i separatists lay in factors that prevented their own message from reverberating among its intended audience. Competing traditions, competing elites, and competing discourses all added up to form a dense intellectual web in which the separatist idea soon went astray and lost all import. The Shi'i separatists lacked neither resources nor dexterity – instead their project collapsed out of its own sheer meaninglessness.

This phenomenon could be seen for instance in historiography. It was evident that 'Ali al-Sharqi steered clear of exploiting classical Shi'i history to buttress the idea of separating the south, even though community annals from the early years of Shi'i history focus precisely on this area, between the great historical cities of Basra and Kufa (modern Najaf's less famous twin city). But Shi'i history in this region soon became linked up with wider areas, such as Samarra' to the north, part of the Sawad province in classical times, just like Basra and Kufa. Even more importantly, to construe the ordeals of the early Shi'is as anything but an attempt at restoring the family of 'Ali, their first imam, to the position as ruling dynasty of the entire Muslim world would verge on blasphemy. Instead, Sharqi chose to write local histories on more recent developments, and in so doing actually created subdivisions within the Shi'i territories, between the extreme south and the Middle Euphrates. Sharqi's unconventional essays were soon forgotten, whereas Shi'i rituals of a more universalistic character continued to resound in annual celebrations.

An equally weighty contribution to the anti-separation position came from within traditional Shi'i circles. Most advocates of a separate, Shi'i south belonged to a group of young ulama with limited prestige in the hierarchy of learning, but their frequent political twists and turns received much attention from British intelligence staff. Of more consequence among the wider Shi'i population were the grand *mujtahid*s of the holy cities, like Ayatollahs Isfahani and Na'ini. The advice from these circles pulled in two directions – towards anti-sectarianism, and towards political quietism more generally, neither of which favoured a bid for a separate Shi'i entity.[41]

A third force inimical to the project for a Shi'i state was growing Iraqi nationalism, now in evidence also among the Shi'is themselves, who were beginning to use "Iraq" as a natural term of reference in their writings. Romantic accounts of the 1920 uprising have portrayed nationalism among the Shi'is as an almost supernatural, age-old force that inexplicably yet compellingly propelled them towards Iraqi unity.[42] A more mundane interpretation is to view their nationalism simply as another intellectual trend of the day – supported symbolically and materially by a tide of dialogues, processes and logics which stressed Baghdad as the capital of a united Iraq. But the resultant centripetal energy was formidable and made it more and more difficult to challenge the idea of a unified state structure.

The point of departure for this Iraqi nationalism had been the old geographical concept of "Iraq" which covered most of the Basra and Baghdad vilayets, a concept that acquired widespread currency at least among the administrative elites of the late Ottoman era. Even the Basra notables behind the 1921 petition had paid some lip-service to this geographical term. The Arabic translation of their petition somewhat confusingly used the name "Iraq" for their proposed federation (of the two statelets "Iraq" and "Basra"), instead of maintaining the distinction of the original English text between "Mesopotamia" (for the federation) and its two constituent states – an avoidance of the common Arabic translation of Mesopotamia (*ma bayna al-nahrayn*) in favour of "Iraq" that suggests the awkwardness of discarding a term already well established. Analyses of Iraqi history that assume a 1914 cultural tabula rasa (or, alternatively, posit an overpowering Shi'i sectarian/separatist pull towards the Gulf and Persia) overlook this continuity with the recent Ottoman past: If Basra had been a true identity vacuum, even the hapless Basra notables would have been able to dominate it; alternatively, if the population had been unequivocally anti-Baghdad in political orientation, merely the slightest hint from the political elite would have led to an instant separatist take-off.

The main development during the mandate was that the traditional core concept of "Iraq" increasingly became equated with a bigger area, mainly expanding to the north-west, until it finally became undistinguishable from the entity defined as the modern state of Iraq as set out in border delimitations and treaties with neighbouring Najd, Kuwait, Transjordan, Syria, Turkey, and, finally in 1937, Iran. Technically, this modern Iraq was of course the creation of the British, primarily Wilson and Cox, whose personal whims and impulses had a decisive impact on the precise territorial configuration of the new state. But it was the young intelligentsia of the new Iraq, working as schoolteachers, journalists and lawyers – the likes of Sulayman Faydi and Amin 'Ali Basha'yan – who were instrumental in establishing the link between the old geographical term and the new national community and who did the job of coating this link with layers of meaning. To describe Iraq as a purely "British invention" is to underrate both their efforts and the historical roots of their enterprise.[43]

The gradual advances of Iraqi nationalism can be studied through reverting to the counterfactual scenarios created by British officials themselves at various stages during and after the First World War. What if a separate peace with the Ottomans in 1917 had come to fruition along the lines contemplated by Arthur Balfour, with a Baghdad under Ottoman suzerainty, on the pattern of pre-war Egypt? In Basra there would certainly have been no outcry of Iraqi nationalism, and few would have been reluctant to part with Baghdad. Resistance to becoming a British crown colony would have been limited to those few pro-Ottoman individuals who had not already fled northwards, and it would have been as pro-CUP as pro-Iraqi in orientation. Baghdad reactions along "Iraqi" nationalist lines would have been sparse as well: even among the anti-Ottoman officers of Baghdad and Mosul engaged in the Arab revolt no separate "Iraqi" organisation had yet emerged. Next, what if a British decision to withdraw to Basra had been made in the early 1920s, as some circles thought advisable during the military crisis with the Turkish nationalists in 1922? Basra would still have remained largely contented with British rule; the pro-Iraqi factions were much too fragmented to pose a concerted challenge, and even the areas around Baghdad were divided between pro-Ottoman and Iraqi nationalist elites.[44] The memory of "Iraq" as a wider regional entity might have lingered on in some circles, but not in a more substantial way than what was seen later in "Jazira" – the vibrant economic region from Mosul towards Aleppo that was split into two parts by the Anglo-French wartime agreements and where sentimental talk about the regional unity of the past would continue to surface later in the twentieth century, albeit mostly in an innocuous and inconsequential form. But what if John Hall's ideas from the late 1920s of Basra as a British air base in the Gulf had been put into practice? Hall himself certainly believed in the political feasibility of this kind of scheme, but the strike in 1931 showed how wrong he was: By the end of the 1920s there were numerous local political organisations in Basra with distinctly Iraqi profiles, and ideals of Iraqi nationalism were being reproduced on a daily basis as Basra citizens went about their business in schools, government offices and commercial institutions. Any British attempt at isolating the south at that late stage would have been met with strong protests, and the "question of Basra" would have acquired overtones similar to many of the irredentist conflicts that beset Europe in the period – there would also have been obvious parallels to the situation in the Suez Canal Zone (under British control after the 1936 Anglo-Egyptian treaty), where shots were fired against British soldiers long before the 1956 crisis. In short, in 1917 Iraqi nationalism was but one among several ideological test balloons in the inner Gulf region; by 1929 it had been turned into a weighty, pervasive and dominant political force.

The phenomenon of inarticulate separatist elites from a traditional background becoming overwhelmed by younger and more dynamic nationalists is by no means unique to Basra. Such tendencies could also be seen in South East Asia after the Second World War, when British and Dutch colonial powers moved to radically restructure their presence in the region. Although separatists on Penang (in present-day Malaysia) and in the Moluccan archipelago (now in Indonesia) in the late 1940s were marginally more enterprising than their Basra counterparts in backing up their petitions with associations and newspapers, they too seemed to hesitate when it came to mass politics, in some cases even expressing fear of the forces it could unleash.[45] What that in turn could lead to was painfully experienced by the leaders of a third failed separatist movement, that of Aden (Yemen) in the late 1950s and the early 1960s, who took their message to electoral politics and lost.[46] But there is a counter-example to all these stories of separatist failures by traditional notables: Squeezed between hostile nationalist propaganda from Italy and Yugoslavia, Riccardo Zanella nonetheless managed to create enough popular enthusiasm for the idea of an independent free state in Fiume to win parliamentary elections in the small Adriatic enclave in 1921. In that case, only brutal Italian Fascism could bring an end to the localist vision, and the example shows that even in an era when nationalism was the dominant paradigm in international politics, political elites could succeed in rowing against the current if they had the courage and skilfulness to do so.

Parallels to the Iraqi nationalists' advances can also be found globally. The way they took a geographical concept from their days as Ottoman bureaucrats and transplanted it into modern politics as an identity label bears a certain resemblance to those bureaucrat "pilgrimages" and subsequent political activities described by Benedict Anderson for places as diverse as Latin America (explaining the emergence regional subunits within this vast Spanish-speaking area) and the United Kingdom (to account for the historical weakness of Scottish separatism).[47] Of cases where the points of departure and the international environment present a particularly close fit to conditions in Basra and Iraq (i.e. competing regional and larger national visions after the First World War in a territory not distinguished by any pre-existing administrative unity, exclusive language or religion), Iraqi nationalists stand out as rather more successful than their counterparts in Libya (where after the Second World War the persistence of regional loyalties in Tripolitania, Cyrenaica and Fezzan made for a show-down between their respective international patrons in Rome, London and Paris) and to some extent those of Transjordan (where regional and pro-Saudi loyalties remained manifest in certain areas of the south also later in the twentieth century).[48] In Iraq, by contrast, the regionalist discourse of *its* south had been firmly wiped out by the early 1930s because the nationalists had managed to make their mark on the country's educational apparatus, its voluntary associations and its political discourse. The self-confidence of Iraqi nationalists was already comparable to that found among political leaders in Latin American countries with longer but analogous histories of nation-building.

The view of ethnicity and nationalism underlying this interpretation of Iraqi history falls somewhere between the relativism of constructivist scholars (some of whom argue that anything goes as long as political elites are prepared to set nationalist fires ablaze) and the determinism seen among researchers with a more static view of nationalism ("ethno-symbolism" is the most recent label chosen by those who stress the links between pre-modern history and modern-day nationalisms).[49] Clearly there are strong elements of creativity and even invention in Iraqi nationalism. But equally important is the fact that the Iraqi nationalists of the 1920s did not start from scratch. There was an idea about a "geographical Iraq"; there were groups in society who had practical career experiences from Ottoman days that were interwoven with this "Iraq" concept; there existed sediments in historical literature where "Iraq" was the backdrop for stories of life and death. Methodologically, this situation should be distinguished from contexts were there was almost no unique symbolic heritage to build on (as in Transjordan) as well as from settings where the contours of a national society were far more evident (for instance Egypt). Constructivism, with its focus on omnipotent political elites and subservient (but mostly innocent?) popular masses, might disregard such crucial differences in the preconditions for nation-building; scholars who emphasise the pre-modern antecedents of nationalism might find it difficult to account for how nations with comparable starting points have ended up with nationalisms of wildly different calibres. However, if the static "ethnic cores" or "historical cores" of the ethno-symbolist writers were demystified and recast in more tangible terms ("historiography", "theology", "literature", "archaeological objects", "ancient ruins", etc.) they could be conceived of as being dynamic but at the same time not malleable to the extreme. In such an interpretation those "cores" are open to change by enterprising politicians and yet also intellectually dense and sluggish – often requiring that any changes or innovations be made through reference to the existing logic. That is a framework which captures the behaviour of all the participants in the clash over identities in Basra in the 1920s: the mercantile separatists (who did not even dare enter the labyrinth of symbolic politics), the Shi'i separatists of 1927 (who did enter but found themselves stuck in a morass of better-established intellectual traditions hostile to the idea of a Shi'i breakaway state) as well as the Iraqi nationalists (who thrived because they found some recognisable elements from the past and were later able to expand on them even to the point of sheer fantasy). Instrumentalism must have latitude for the pre-modern to make sense of the curious spectacle that faced visitors to the Iraq Museum in Baghdad in the 1930s: At the doorway, Assyrian ("northern") winged bulls formed a symbolic guard, protecting the interior exhibition rooms where show-cases of Sumerian ("southern") antiquities proudly celebrated the achievements of the Iraqi nation. Neither of these features was dictated by history; both had been constructed in dialogue with it.[50]

Into an age of nationalism

In Iraq, the anti-separation logic eventually filtered through to even the sceptical Basra notables associated with the 1921 petition. Most of them established some kind of modus vivendi with the state against which they or their relatives had militated. During the 1930s, the "separatist" label disappeared completely from Basra politics, and it was strikes with a nationalist theme (such as protests against the 1937 border settlement with Iran) that grabbed the headlines in the latter part of the decade.[51] The creation of a company for oil exploration in the Basra area in 1938 did not reverse the new Iraqist trend (actual pumping did not start until after the Second World War), and when the British occupied Basra for a second time in 1941 there was no resurgence of separatist feeling – and indeed little sympathy for the British in general.[52]

But the Iraqi monarchy possessed many of the same weaknesses seen in the separatist movement. In particular, this was the case with respect to the challenge of building broad-based coalitions across social borders. Much later, many of the old Basra families came to suffer when the petrified regime began to crumble and the violence of Iraqi politics intensified, finally exploding in the 1958 revolution. Yet, less than three decades after its inception, this system produced citizens who, despite their misgivings over the increasingly mono-lithic and brutal nature of the modern Iraqi state, had a fundamental acceptance of its territorial framework. Large numbers of Basrawis left for other states in the Middle East after 1958, but this phenomenon of individual migration only demonstrated that tampering with the territorial integrity of Iraq was no longer considered a viable option, and that the very pervasiveness of the idea of "a united Iraq" in the political discourse had become a constraint to politicians contemplating radical alternatives to the Baghdad-based governments of the day.[53] Even Badr Shakir al-Sayyab, the communist poet from Basra who turned so many conventions upside-down during his career, displayed a seemingly un-shakeable faith in the Iraqi nationalist paradigm.[54] And by the 1960s, when the leading quietist Shi'i ulama were challenged by a new generation with a more activist profile, many of these young men of religion had themselves become so accustomed to the idea of a territorially unified Iraq that they came to adopt a profound Iraqist orientation – sometimes even in flagrant violation of their own Islamist and internationalist maxims.[55] Supported by a logic of a centralised state that had become intrinsic to economic, social and intellectual life, the ideal of Iraqi unity was thus in full bloom well before the authoritarian rule of the Ba'th. Throughout the period from 1935 to 2003, tensions between the south and the Iraqi capital came to revolve around the nature of the regimes in power in Baghdad, rather than the territorial framework of the state as such.[56]

12   After 2003: A Second Wave of Separatism?

By early 2003, the date-garden belt from Fao to Qurna – the "Garden of Eden" of imaginative officials of the British mandate – had changed beyond recognition. The population had increased tenfold, with Basra now a city of more than one million inhabitants. What were formerly the rustic townships of Zubayr and Abu al-Khasib had become suburbs of the sprawling Gulf city. The cityscape itself had new characteristics: 'Ashar had become the undisputed city centre, with high-rise buildings and governmental offices, whereas the old town of Basra was a derelict backwater.

The economy of the city once described as "Venice of the Middle East" was in tatters. The 1970s had seen oil boom, growth in tourism from conservative Gulf states, and spin-offs from Basra's location close to Iraq's only deep-water port. But years of war with Iran (1980–1988) as well as with the United States and its allies (1991), followed by a crippling sanctions regime, had almost destroyed the fundament for the city's economy. Infrastructure and millions of date palms had been damaged during fighting, and, because of the sanctions, the state-controlled oil industry was at low ebb. The only significant private-sector avenue for economic growth – date agribusiness – was hurt by the sanctions as well, as it was cut off from its traditional export markets. On top of all of this, the general health of the population was in steep decline, a fact blamed on both a dilapidated sewage system as well as a scrapyard of ordinance left behind around Basra by past invading armies.

Basra was in 2003 a pronouncedly Shi'i city – in fact one of the largest Shi'i cities in the world. The Sunnis had been reduced to a small minority within Basra proper, and did not even dominate their old bastion of Zubayr – from which large-scale emigration to Saudi Arabia had taken place after 1958. The Jewish community had left for Israel, but Christian minorities and small Shi'i sub-sects of Akhbaris and Shaykhis still gave Basra a certain air of religious manifold and coexistence. Political power rested firmly, as before, with Sunnis – now aligned with the Ba'th regime in Baghdad. Shaykhs of the Muntafiq Sa'dun clan and leaders of smaller Sunni tribes had been vested with positions in the regime's security apparatus, and were prominent as apparatchiks in local Ba'th organisations.

What had apparently not changed much between 1935 and 2003 was the notion of Basra's integral place in the Iraqi nation. The anti-separation spirit that had prevailed after the separatist episode of the 1920s had endured for the rest of the twentieth century. It had weathered an Iranian siege in the early 1980s, a traumatic uprising against the regime in 1991 – when the rebels held on to the vision of a unified Iraq even as they briefly managed to take over local government offices – and had survived a subsequent decade of unprecedented anti-Shi'i sectarianism by a regime bent on staying in power by subsidising what it could find of local Sunni collaborators. If any memory of the 1921 petition for a separate Basra survived at all, it did so only in private. The separatist idea had been eradicated from Basra's public domain.

For the first time since the 1920s, some rethinking of the connection between southern Iraq and the rest of the country was nevertheless in the offing. Western schemes for a possible partition of Iraq along sectarian lines had aroused little interest so far, but among Iraqi oppositionists there was growing debate on how their country should be governed if the Ba'th were ousted from power and replaced by a democratic regime. This mounting discussion included new ideas about the relationship between Baghdad and the territory to its south. But in contrast to 1921, the initiative lay not with urban leaders in Basra, but with Shi'i intellectuals in exile – some of them from Basra, others from areas closer to the Iraqi capital.

The federalism debate and the Shi'is

Just as Basra had changed, the Shi'i political scene had undergone a transformation in the twentieth century. At the time of the British mandate, the community had been divided on the question of the preconditions for legitimate government. Quietists had rejected any close links with modern state structures, maintaining than any temporal government would be usurping the authority of the hidden Twelfth Imam.[1] On the other hand, activists had argued that legitimate government was indeed possible in the age of the Hidden Imam's occultation. They had favoured a system where the ulama would exercise a censorial role vis-à-vis modern-day legislatures – a model inspired by the 1906 constitutional revolution in Persia, but a trend still in its infancy in Iraq.[2] Symptomatically, when a tiny minority of young clerics in 1927 had sought to promote the idea of a separate Shi'i state in the south, they had made no attempt whatsoever to prop up their scheme with theories of Islamic government.[3]

The big change in the twentieth century was the emergence of new ideas about Shi'i participation at all levels of politics. From the 1950s onwards, the expanded role for the ulama first witnessed in the constitutional revolution in Persia was taken further by activist ulama like Ayatollah Khomeini. His theory of the rule of the jurisprudent (*wilayat al-faqih*) bestowed legitimacy upon the government of a qualified, just ruler – a *mujtahid* cleric prepared to enter the realm of worldly politics and hold the reins of power himself. Khomeini's ideas became implemented after the revolution in Iran in 1979, automatically making the new Islamic republic a focus for the whole Shi'i world.

However, with the fulfilment of Khomeini's vision came new problems. Quietist clergy, especially outside Iran, denied any special legitimacy to the new Iranian government. Many Shi'is continued to follow the advice of the apolitical Ayatollah al-Khu'i in Najaf in Iraq, who after Khomeini's death in 1989 consolidated his position as the pre-eminent source of emulation (*marja' al-taqlid*) for Shi'is worldwide – an informal leadership role traditionally based on excellence in Islamic scholarship and associated with the cleric with the greatest number of followers. When Khu'i died in 1992, Iran made an aggressive attempt at unifying political and spiritual leadership by sponsoring the candidature of Khomeini's successor, 'Ali Khamene'i, as the new paramount *marja'* – but met with a backlash from traditionalists who scoffed at the Iranian leader's scholarly credentials. Many saw him as more of a politician, unable to compete with the traditional ulama to the extent that Khomeini had managed to. Khamene'i ultimately gave up, and the Najaf-based quietist 'Ali al-Sistani – himself not in favour of Khomeini's doctrines of a political clergy – gradually consolidated his position as the *mujtahid* with the widest backing in the Shi'i world. This left a latent tension between an Islamic republic with an activist ethos based in Tehran and a spiritual centre with a quietist orientation outside its reach, in Najaf in Iraq.[4]

Even ulama sympathetic to the idea of a politicised clergy were uneasy with the new Islamic republic. Several leading clerics outside Iran came to favour theories of Islamic government involving collective religious leadership (vested in a council of qualified clerics) or multiple ruling jurisprudents (each governing a polity of his own independently) as alternatives to the Iranian model of a single, supreme Shi'i leader. Many emphasised competition among ulama and pluralism in the field of legal interpretation as something distinctively positive – an attitude seen for instance in the scholarship of Muhammad Husayn Fadl Allah. Using historical analogy, supporters of this current reasoned that, just as the imams of the classical period could have several representatives, so could the authority of the Hidden Imam in the age of occultation be exercised through a number of individual deputies. In this manner, the pan-Islamic imperative of Khomeini's thinking came up against a second challenge.[5]

Against this backdrop of ideological convolution among the Shi'is, new ideas on the relationship between southern Iraq and Baghdad gradually emerged in the 1990s. The process dated back to the aftermath of the failed 1991 uprising against the Ba'th regime, and intensified in 2002 as the changing international climate made a US-led war against Iraq a likely prospect. Increasingly, the concept of *federalism* captivated the exiled opposition, especially after Washington made the triad "democracy, pluralism and federalism" the platform for uniting the anti-Ba'th forces in preparation for war. This forced the Shi'is to move from passive reiteration of the idea of "Iraqi unity" to an active stance for or against a new system of government that envisaged radical decentralisation of the Iraqi state – and left the federalism debate as a prism through which it is possible to study changing Shi'i ideas about the place of the south in an Iraqi polity.[6]

In the early 1990s, after the Kurds had launched the idea of federalism as a basic principle for new post-Ba'th order in Iraq, many segments of the Shi'i opposition forces reacted with scepticism, seeing it as an attack on their traditional anti-separation position. Shi'i protests against a federal solution hampered the early efforts of the Iraq National Congress (INC) following its foundation in 1992, and federalism remained a divisive issue for the opposition throughout the decade.[7] Shi'i unease about federalism persisted in many circles throughout the flurry of opposition gatherings in the autumn of 2002, with leading figures like Muhammad Husayn Fadl Allah (the Lebanon-based guiding light for many members of the Da'wa party) publicly opposing it.[8] The position of the grand *mujtahid* 'Ali al-Sistani crystallised during the spring of 2003 when the Ba'th regime was finally toppled by US-led forces: From pre-war quietism, he went on to reiterate the existing (unitary) administrative map of Iraq in post-war fatwas, before finally voicing active opposition against federalism in 2004, as part of a protest against any sort of ethnically defined privileges or minority vetoes in the future system of government in Iraq.[9]

A conglomerate of ideals from Shi'i political thought has helped sustain the anti-federalism position in large parts of the community. First, to quietists seeking to avoid close contact with any political powers of the day, there is scant attraction in elaborate debates on the devolution of political structures deemed illegitimate in the first place. This point had been instrumental in diluting Shi'i support for the 1927 sectarian separation project for the south, and remained relevant for many Shi'is after the 2003 war. Secondly, supporters of the view that legitimate government in the absence of the Hidden Imam *can* be achieved tend to subscribe to ideals of greater political unity among Muslims and to shy away from schemes for subdivision. Federalism may seem inimical to the aspirations of those who advocate the indivisibility of the Islamic community, the importance of overcoming sectarian divisions (instead of consecrating them through territorial compartmentalisation), and the need to unite behind strong and viable state entities capable of challenging Israel's dominance in the region.[10] Indeed, some adherents of Khomeini's model of government consider any polity outside the realm of the supreme *faqih* a potential challenger, and on this basis strongly advocate centralisation within an Islamic state.[11]

Resistance against any further political fragmentation among Muslims – including federalisation – makes sense in the context of such pan-Islamist ideals. Not as readily attributable to Islamic traditions is the widespread and robust defence of "Iraqi unity" in these circles, which after all have a declared goal of greater Islamic integration across current state boundaries. In attacks on federalism, Shi'i Islamists have employed the claim that "Iraq as an entity and society has been known for its harmony and cohesiveness for hundreds of years", its alleged territorial links to *bilad al-sawad* of the classical Islamic age, and even the assumed historic continuity of Iraq back to pre-Islamic times and the great Mesopotamian civilisations (*bilad al-rafidayn*).[12] Two of these premises are secular, and the sole Islamic justification presented – the link to *bilad al-sawad* – ignores how the territory of today's Iraq was divided into two separate provinces in the age of the imams. In fact, most of the time the demand for Iraqi unity is simply presented as an axiom, just as it was in the 1930s after Shi'i areas like Basra had come to accept the idea of a single polity centred on Baghdad.[13]

Despite these pressures towards anti-federalism, some enthusiastic Shi'i proponents of federal solutions for Iraq did emerge in the 1990s. Individuals in exile – some affiliated with the INC, others with links to the charitable Khu'i Foundation in London – picked up Kurdish ideas for a bi-national federation and proceeded to create a more comprehensive federal scheme that would encompass all of Iraq, with several constituent states.[14] Subsequently, many Shi'is within the INC came to adopt this formula during the opposition conferences of 2002, and, after much initial hesitation, the main branch of the Da'wa embraced federalism when they entered the Iraqi governing council as one of the "big seven" political parties in May 2003.[15]

The central feature of these Shi'i proposals, often referred to by their authors as "administrative" (*idari*) variants of federalism, is deliberate avoidance of ethnic or sectarian zones as building blocks in a new state model. Borders between federal states are to be drawn according to "geographic" and "demographic" criteria, yielding between five and seven entities in the various proposed political maps. Any kind of sectarian canton, a "Shi'istan", is thus explicitly rejected. Beyond the question of borders, supporters of this current have proposed a radical degree of decentralisation for the entire Iraqi political system – in one variant leaving almost every sphere of government except foreign policy to the federal states. Little, however, has been done to integrate these federal schemes with Islamic political theory, and a veneer of outspoken anti-sectarianism remains the sole feature that distinguishes them from federalism in the Western tradition.[16] In March 2004, Shi'i supporters belonging to this camp played a central role in hammering out a Transitional Administration Law where federalism was made applicable to the whole of Iraq, not only the Kurdish provinces. A clause limiting federal regions to a maximum of three existing governorates at the same time precluded the formation of a large Shi'i unit from Basra to Karbala' – a provision consonant with the fervent opposition to openly sectarian solutions among Shi'i federalists with Islamist backgrounds.

Between these two positions, many Shi'is have remained ambivalent in the question of federalism, often avoiding a definite stand on the issue by using deliberately vague and double-edged language. An example of this is the position of the Supreme Council for the Islamic Revolution in Iraq (SCIRI). On the surface, the organisation was among the earliest and most outspoken Shi'i proponents of a "federal" future for Iraq, with public statements purportedly in a pro-federal direction dating back to the mid 1990s.[17] In 2002, SCIRI repeatedly justified federalism for Iraq with reference to the success of this system of government elsewhere (the United States, Switzerland and Pakistan were among the examples given), and the party later became a prominent actor in the US-sponsored post-war political process in Iraq where embrace of "federalism" was next to mandatory for participating.[18] However, behind this "yes" to federalism, more contradictory tendencies have emerged. In statements in Arabic, SCIRI leaders have often employed terminology that has given ambiguity to the core concept of federalism – including terms such as "decentralisation" (*al-lamarkaziyya*) and "the rule of the provinces" (*hukm al-wilayat*).[19] The use of the Arabic word for "decentralisation" rather than "federalism" (*al-fidiraliyya*) creates equivocality, because this term has historically been applied to a whole range of contexts, including local government in states essentially unitary in structure, such as Egypt, Qatar and Morocco.[20] And the analogy between West-

ern federalism and the system of government in former Islamic empires (Ottoman and Abbasid practices are specifically mentioned) through the concept of
"rule of the provinces" is problematic, as there was hardly any voluntary ces-
sion of legislative powers away from the centre in these empires.[21] Secular federalists among the Iraqis, such as the main Kurdish parties, would certainly object to a "federal" system that implied a unified system of (Islamic) law for all
citizens categorised as "Muslims".

The picture becomes even more complex in the writings of the late Muhammad Baqir al-Hakim, the long-time leader of SCIRI. Hakim's writings render
"federalism" as an option for decentralisation within a political system that is
explicitly Islamic.[22] This is, however, a system based on Khomeini's theory of
wilayat al-faqih, and the logical apex of this kind of state model is the office of
the individual recognised as "supreme jurisprudent" – which for SCIRI's followers since the early 1990s has meant the current spiritual leader of Iran, 'Ali
Khamene'i. Such pan-Islamic ideals stand in stark contrast to SCIRI's record as
a pragmatic actor in Iraqi politics, and give an enigmatic character to their public support for a federal system in Iraq. Vagueness has become SCIRI's norm
also in the question of territorial subdivisions within a federal system: At times
it has portrayed federalism mainly as a concession to Kurds or to non-Muslim
minorities (implying a motive to consider the remaining territory as a single
unit), whereas on other occasions the organisation has indicated a more open
attitude to the question of the number of units in a federal arrangement.[23]

A fourth Shi'i approach to federalism has been distinctive simply for its un-
predictability. Having started as an Iraqi underground movement in the late
1990s, Muqtada al-Sadr and his supporters exploited the security vacuum after
the 2003 war to emerge as a major Shi'i faction with new and radical views on
Islamic politics. Inspired by the activist heritage of Muqtada's father Muhammad (assassinated, probably by the regime, in 1999), some of the supporters of
this new Sadrist trend have gone further than most other Shi'i Islamist parties in
challenging the monopoly of the *mujtahids* in defining the ideals of Shi'ism, by
engaging in unconventional acts and preaching non-conformist ideas. Groups
loyal to Sadr – who is not a qualified *mujtahid* himself – have forcefully taken
over Sunni mosques, issued death threats to individuals engaged in alcohol
trade, and recommended that Christians be subjected to Islamic law under a future Islamic government.[24] Although they have stopped short of severing all
links with the traditional Shi'i hierarchy – in 2003 they briefly adopted the
Qum-based *mujtahid* Kazim al-Ha'iri as spiritual leader and after a rupture in
2004 reverted to the rulings of Muqtada's late father – their capriciousness has
also had an impact on the debate over federalism. On the one hand, Sadr's supporters have defended an Iraqi identity in traditional nationalist terms, and mili-
tantly protested against any federal state model. In early 2004 they enlisted the
support of Shi'i Turkmens in Kirkuk (an area far outside the traditional Shi'i
heartland and targeted by the Kurds for an autonomous Kurdish state) to make
the case for a unitary Iraq with no collective concessions on the basis of ethnicity. Later, they joined the chorus of criticism against the Transitional Admini-

stration Law, condemning its clauses on federalism as an enshrinement of divisions in Iraqi society. And the works on political theory by their sometime ally in the traditional hierarchy of scholars – Ayatollah al-Ha'iri – certainly leave little room for decentralisation ideas, an approach that seemed confirmed when Ha'iri in early 2004 presented a draft constitution for an essentially centralised Islamic government in Iraq.[25] Yet, on the other hand, the Sadrists have at times flirted precisely with the idea of unifying the Shi'is in a territorial bloc. An article in their newspaper *al-Hawza* outlining such a scheme appeared in March 2004, focusing on the need for the Shi'is to retain control over revenue accruing from pilgrims visiting their areas.[26]

The article in *al-Hawza* was radical because it departed from the anti-sectarianism that had accompanied Shi'i rethinking of federalism so far. Here was an indisputable invitation to link "Shi'i areas" to geopolitics, and an urge to set the Shi'i-populated regions apart from the rest of Iraq on the basis of their special historical and sectarian legacy. In isolation, the text might have been dismissed as yet another example of contradictory signals from the Sadrists, who throughout the winter of 2004 had wavered in their stand on the legitimacy of the Iraqi provisional government. But the Sadrists were not the only ones to introduce radical ideas into the Shi'i debate on federalism in 2004. In June, the SCIRI-affiliated Voice of the Mujahidin Radio broadcast a call for the Shi'is to unite in "a federal entity", signalling a new and more sectarian direction of policy.[27] And in the extreme south of the country, the soaring debate on federalism was beginning to make an impact: after having remained loyal to the paradigm of a unitary Iraqi state for more than seventy years, Basrawis were once more concocting new territorial visions for the Gulf city and its hinterland.

Basra and new regionalist trends

After the war in 2003, Basra remained a sideshow of Iraqi politics for some time. Like many other areas in the country, the Gulf city had to cope with immense security and infrastructural problems created by the collapse of Ba'th power and the lack of reconstruction plans on the part of the occupiers – a situation exacerbated in the south due to a decade of deliberate neglect by the Iraqi government following the 1991 uprising. In July 2003, two Basrawis joined the Iraqi governing council, and two others were appointed ministers in the provisional government created one month later. Media portrayed Basra as a relatively calm area, although reports of tensions between Islamists affiliated with Muqtada al-Sadr and secularists surfaced frequently, and the standard description of violent attacks against the British occupying forces as "episodic" became more strained and self-contradictory each time it was repeated.

In December 2003, the picture of Basra as a passive recipient of politics that had been defined in Baghdad and the Shi'i holy cities started to change. In that month, the governor of the city, Wa'il 'Abd al-Latif, a Shi'i lawyer and former judge who was now also a member of the governing council, attended a conference in the north of the country organised by Kurdish leaders eager to demonstrate to other Iraqis the virtues of federal government. By March 2004, it was evident that 'Abd al-Latif had taken up this idea and persuaded other Basrawis to join him. During a visit to Dubai, he hailed the United Arab Emirates' (federal) system of government and commended it as a model for a future Iraq, before proceeding to speak of bilateral links between Basra and Dubai. He envisaged his home region as an entity with wide-ranging autonomies within an 18-state Iraqi federation.

More signs of local interest in federalism came in the summer of 2004. First reported through international and Kurdish media, plans for a federal unit comprising the three southernmost regions of Iraq were said to be under discussion by local governors. Then, on 10 August, came a dramatic threat by local politicians loyal to Muqtada al-Sadr – at the time besieged by US forces in Najaf – that continued aggression against their leader would precipitate the separation of the three southern provinces "from the rest of Iraq". The nature of the ultimatum presented was criticised by Sadr himself, but subsequent events demonstrated that something more than mere roguery on the part of marginal Sadrists was underway in the south: A week later, the whole delegation of Basra representatives to a 1,000-member national conference in Baghdad withdrew en masse from the proceedings, citing dissatisfaction with the proportion of seats offered to the Gulf city in the legislative council to be formed.

The arguments accompanying Basra's protest revealed the existence of vigorous local patriotism. One delegate declared Basra to be "the city of oil, revolution and martyrs"; others protested against the dominance of the large, well-established Iraqi political parties to the detriment of independents representing regional interests. In late August, Hasan al-Rashid, the Basra governor elected to replace Wa'il 'Abd al-Latif (promoted to minister for the provinces in the provisional government), confirmed the intention to create a southern region based on three governorates, repeated 'Abd al-Latif's reference to the United Arab Emirates' federal experience, and went on to quote the oil distribution arrangements in place in Abu Dhabi (where local authorities control 50 per cent of the revenues). Soon, the scheme for a federal canton in the south (referred to variously as "the federalism of the south" – *fidiraliyyat al-janub* – or "the region of the south, *iqlim al-janub*) was being casually discussed in local newspapers, receiving support from a cross-section of the population inclusive of both secularists and independent Islamists.[28]

Basra in a federal Iraq

The growing federalism debate in Shi'i circles thus gave birth in 2004 to a scheme for Basra as the nucleus of an autonomous area within Iraq, only the second such project to occur since the establishment of the state in 1921. It is too early to tell whether the new regionalist trends in the south will prevail, and any categorical anticipation of their future relationship with forces loyal to a unitary state model would be premature. Twentieth-century experience indicates that anti-separation and centralist ideals became thoroughly entrenched in Basra after the first secession attempt and may require extraordinary political talents to challenge; whether Basra federalists of the new millennium possess such qualities remains an open question. The January 2005 elections certainly produced no clarification as regards federalism: no distinctive pro-federal party emerged in Basra, and the local advocates of federation instead chose to run on larger national coalition lists where the whole issue was swept under the carpet in an election campaign short on real content. In the end, it was local supporters of the radical Islamist and centralist Muhammad al-Ya'qubi (an ex-affiliate of Muqtada al-Sadr) who, by a narrow margin, gained control of the Basra governorate, at the expense of some of the independent Islamists who had fronted the federalism demands during the preceding autumn. Still, decisions by the first elected post-Ba'th government – such as their choice in May 2005 of a Shi'i non-southerner (Ibrahim Bahr al-'Ulum) for the post as oil minister – contributed to a situation where the federalism question remained in suspense, and a steady stream of pro-federal meetings showed that popular opinion on the matter remained highly divided.[29]

What can be said is that to the extent the unitary state is coming under pressure, new tracks are in the making. The 1921 vision of a city-state and the 1927 idea of a separate Shi'i political entity are today overshadowed by a new regional project that envisages the southern provinces of Maysan and Dhi Qar (the divisions of 'Amara and Muntafiq during the British mandate) along with Basra as a united entity within a federalised Iraq – separate from the Shi'i heartland further north. In fact, this area corresponds almost perfectly to the vilayet of Basra of Ottoman times. Yet the history of the interwar separatist projects – none of which focused on the old Ottoman province – suggests that any such congruence is spurious and that a genuinely new trend is underway. Basra particularism in the first months of 2005 was clearly regionalist rather than separatist, and a great deal of the rhetoric from almost a century of Iraqi nationalism still remained intact – significantly, the new spokespersons for the south continued to shy away from terms such as "independent" (*mustaqill*) or "separated" (*munfasil*), both of which had been part and parcel of the 1921 petition rhetoric. The pro-British references of the 1920s were absent as well. Nevertheless, here was a vast array of radical new ideas: Basra leaders now looked to the United Arab Emirates as a model, focused on control over oil revenues as a key issue, used the collective suffering endured during decades of Ba'thist misrule as the base for defining a "southern" identity, and referred to the ecological destruction of the marshlands north of Basra as a powerful symbol of regional grievances. The organisational base, consisting of independent politicians and splinter groups from the larger (Shi'i) Islamist parties, also clearly showed that this was a peripheral protest movement in relation *both* to Baghdad and to Iraqi Shi'ism, further underscoring the futility of equating "the south" with Shi'ism as a whole. (When people of the region use the term "the south" (*al-janub*) themselves, this tends to connote the "Deep South" of Iraq at the lower ends of the two great rivers.) On the other hand, despite some lip service to the "federalism" concept, the main Shi'i factions and spiritual leaders elsewhere in the country in practice continued to adhere to the vision of an essentially unitary state structure – although there were growing signs of a split between elites and the grass-roots membership on the issue, and thus indications of ideas in motion in these circles too.[30]

The success of a federalisation of Iraq – including Basra – will depend on the constitutional process for a new democratic regime, which is expected to get underway in earnest during the course of 2005. Hitherto, this process has been characterised by a marked preoccupation with questions such as the number of units in a federal state, how to demarcate boundaries in a new political map of a federal Iraq, the ideal correlation between federal structure and ethnic geography, and the status of hotly contested localities like Kirkuk – claimed by Kurdish leaders but outside the three core Kurdish governorates. This kind of emphasis may be positive in so far as it helps in exploring regional identities that could form the basis for future federal entities, but it has masked a more profound problem: how can secular and Islamist models of federalism be reconciled? For even though oil-rich Basra has seen some cross-party convergence in a pro-federal direction, polarisation on this point remained intense at the national level at the outset of the constitution discussions in 2005: some pro-federalist Shi'is from the religious parties based in Baghdad and Najaf contemplated an "Islamic" version of federalism, where the only exception from a unified system of Islamic law would be the "internal affairs" of non-Muslim minorities; whereas many secular federalists (the Kurds in particular) envisaged a federal system where concessions to Islamism would be limited to the standard fare of existing Middle Eastern systems, such as a provision that the president of the federation be a Muslim, or a role for Islamic jurisprudence in the field of personal status law. Most of the draft constitutions presented in 2003 and 2004 were based on total victories for either secularists or Islamists, with scant efforts to create hybrids capable of bridging the divide (a judiciary combining secular and religious benches might be one relevant subject for debate); hardly any public discussion of the federal experiences of other countries with ethno-religious complexity and sizeable Islamist movements (Nigeria, Pakistan and Malaysia are prominent examples); and few signs of innovations within Islamist political theory that could contribute to a positive and distinctively Islamic justification for federalism.[31] In fact, in spring 2005 it looked as if leading political factions in Iraq were considering another semantic fudge along the lines of the Transitional Administration Law (where there is deliberate ambiguity with regard to the Islamism/secularism debate – "all Iraqis are equal in their rights without regard to gender, sect, opinion, belief, nationality, religion, or origin" is coupled with a prohibition on legislation that "contradicts the universally agreed tenets of Islam"), leaving it to simple parliamentary majorities to work out the exact role of religion in the new Iraq. Such a hazy formula may well satisfy groups jockeying for power in Baghdad or great powers eager to wash their hands of the situation and get out of Iraq. But when vagueness of this kind is to be translated into the practical administration of justice, the casualties may well prove to be those individuals who become subjected to impromptu Sharia courts at the local level – the adultery case against Amina Lawal from northern Nigeria is but the most glaring example of what protracted legal deadlocks of this kind can lead to in a strongly decentralised polity.

Unless more can be done to address the impasse between Islamists and secularists, the prospects for successful federation remain bleak. If the goal is to defuse this polarised situation, entirely new questions will need to be taken up for debate. Shi'i Islamists opposed to federalism (and Shi'i pseudo-federalists) must at some point ask themselves whether it might be permissible to drop the insistence on a unitary, Islamic framework, if that could help avert a civil war in the country. Secular federalists must realise the dangers of creating a second Algeria if they persevere with pushing through a constitution with only token concessions to the Islamists. And both camps should seriously consider the possibilities for a mixed-breed variety of federalism – a system which could open up opportunities to Islamists in certain geographical regions while at the same time guarding against human rights violations of the kind an immature federal system may be particularly vulnerable to (seen in Islamist-controlled areas of federal Pakistan in addition to the more publicised cases from Nigeria), perhaps by luring the office-shy higher ranks of the Shi'i hierarchy into some sort of moderating role. After all, Shi'ism, with so many internal checks and balances embodied in its stratified clerical system, might well offer something of a security valve against boundless extremism. If employed creatively in a federal framework, Shi'ism could sustain a trailblazer Middle Eastern democracy, a polity capable of accommodating conflicts between Islamists and non-religious citizens by means entirely unavailable to unitary states. Basra, where secular and Islamist federalists share a common political environment should be particularly well positioned to pioneer a debate on this kind of problems, and the association of Ayatollah Sistani's representative in Basra with a southern regionalist bloc of deputies in April 2005 suggested the existence of a pathway that could force the highest ranks of the Shi'i clergy to engage in the federalism debate in a much more specific manner in the future.[32] But Basra is at the same time especially vulnerable to a constitutional stalemate: here, local politicians of both secularist and Islamist persuasions have already demonstrated an interest in territory as a bargaining card, and violent fracases on the campus of Basra University in March 2005 between Sadrists and secular students were a reminder that the chasm between the two sides was as deep as in other parts of the country.

Ultimately, Iraqi federalists of the twenty-first century will not find definitive answers about how to overcome the secularist/Islamist divide by studying the 1921 Basra separation project. That enterprise was a wholly secular one, and occurred at a time when there were fewer Islamic political models available than today. What the first Basra separation project does show is that it is indeed possible to conceive of the Iraqi model of coexistence between various ethno-religious groups repeated on a smaller scale, as Iraqi microcosms. If the Iraqi polity could be remodelled on several such medium-sized federal entities, that would serve to remove some of the intense pressure from a single centre of power, and reduce the potential for violent strife over a powder-keg capital in an over-centralised system. As an attempt at doing precisely that, the foundered 1921 separation movement of Basra – along with all its adolescent complexes and vexations – remains acutely relevant, more than eight decades after its inception.

Notes

Chapter 1

1. Whitaker (2003); Fallows (2002); *The Economist* (9 March 1991): 51–52.
2. Kazemzadeh (1998): 77–79; Byman (1997): 15; Dannreuther (1995): 83–84.
3. Sluglett & Farouk-Sluglett (1990): 258; Nakash (1994): 277–278, Visser (2004). In many parts of Iraq, suggestions of links to Iran were angrily rejected by Shiʻi rebels in 1991, al-Salihi (1998): 118–120.
4. For accusations by Iraqi authorities about projects along separatist lines, see al-Bayati (1997): 229–236. An example of the interventionist approach advocating partition is Kazemzadeh (1998): 77–78. After the 2003 Iraq War, similar ideas have been promoted by Gelb (2003) and Anderson & Stansfield (2004): 222–224. See also the solution of confederation advocated by Galbraith (2004).
5. For Jazira, see Khoury (1987): 525–534; for Newfoundland, Walsh (1985) and Neary (1988): 218, 316; for Ambon, van Kaam (1977): 85–87; for Goa, Rubinoff (1998): 85–86 and n.1; for Papua, McKillop (1982): 329–337.
6. For Mayotte, see Caminade (2003); for the Cayman Islands, Craton (2003): 316–317; for Melilla, Driessen (1992) – in particular pp. 139–146 and 169–170 on the tentative (and ultimately unsuccessful) attempts at creating an inter-ethnic enclave identity to reach beyond the Spanish settler segment.
7. Christie (1996): 28–52; Carapico (1998): 90–91, 101.
8. For Fiume, see Zanella (1946): 23–26; for Singapore, Jose & Doran (1997): 476 and Narayanan (2004).
9. Khoury (1987): 470; Kostiner (1984): 39.
10. For an overview of possible uses of counterfactualism in history, see Ferguson (1999).
11. Al-Rasheed (1991); Bang (1996); Yamani (2004).
12. Fuccaro (1999b).
13. The usual cut-off date in historical accounts of relations between Tehran and the Arab-populated areas in the south-west is 1925, when Persian authority was reasserted in the region, see for instance Ghani (1998): 346. However, separatist tension persisted beyond this point, as discussed in chapters 9 and 11 of this book. Khoury (1987) provides an overview of all the areas later incorporated into Syria, but there have not yet been any specialised studies of autonomist aspirations in individual regions except for the Druze mountains – covered for instance in Alamuddin (1993): 147–149.
14. Introduction by Abdul-Haq al-Ani to Saleh (1995): ix.
15. Yapp (1987): 333.
16. Baram (1991): 1.
17. Batatu (1978): 16–17. For an example of its use by a scholar in favour of the constructivist approach, see Shields (2000): 191 n. 12.
18. See for instance Wimmer (2002): 181.
19. Tripp (2002): 29, in particular the remark that "even Sayyid Talib's apparent reference to the autonomy of an entity called 'Iraq' cannot easily be separated from his view that the smaller stage of Basra was inappropriate for his personal ambition and that he needed to control Baghdad as well".
20. See in particular Nakash (1994): 71–72.
21. Fattah (1999). See also Fattah (1997, 2002, 2003).
22. See for instance Mufti (1996): 23–24.
23. For a recent example, see the contribution by Yaphe (2004) in a collective work leaning towards the constructivist approach.

Chapter 2

1 Descriptions of Basra's topography are given in *BSAL* (1308/1890): 86–95, (1318/1900): 200–208; Lorimer (1908): 94–115; General Staff (1923): 13–15.
2 *BSAL* (1308/1890): 86–87.
3 Issawi (1988): 17–18; Owen (1993): 273; *AR* (1918): 258–260.
4 Rousseau (1809): 32; Heude (1819): 48; Fattah (1997): 69; Issawi (1988): 14.
5 Khurshid Effendi (1981): 5.
6 Issawi (1988): 14, 192–193; de Rivoyre (1883): 220; Layard (1846): 31.
7 *BSAL* (1308/1890): 79, (1318/1900): 205–206.
8 *BSAL* (1308/1890): 79, 94; Adamov (1912): 129.
9 *BSAL* (1308/1890): 81, 92.
10 Dowson (1921) I: 20–40; Cursetjee (1918): 139–142; Young (1933): 42–43; al-Qahwati (1980): 354–356.
11 Geary (1878) I: 90–91; Adamov (1912): 26.
12 Based on *RTB* (1887–1913). In the 1890s, the value of date exports in cases (mostly bound for European and American markets) was roughly on par with that of dates packed in skins and palm-leaf baskets (associated with markets in Arabia, Persia and India). However, demand in the new markets gained pace, and after 1906 the annual value of dates exported in cases consistently stayed higher than 300 per cent of the value of shipments in traditional packaging for the old regional markets.
13 *Ibid.* The figures are limited to seaborne trade only and were collected by the British consul from shippers. They thus exclude trade with the Arabian interior, and the claim that they could give a complete picture of all sectors of maritime trade seems dubious – particularly with regard to smaller vessels used in regional trade. Nevertheless, the data do harmonise roughly with figures collected at the receiving end in India, and are also specific to Basra, which contributed the lion's share of dates exported from its port, see Dowson (1921): 44; *RTB* (1896–1898, 1907).
14 Lorimer (1908): 2507–08; al-Qahwati (1980): 354–392; Owen (1993): 274–278; Issawi (1988): 145–147; Fattah (1997): 105–106.
15 *BSAL* (1308/1890): 150; Geary (1878) I: 92; Vadala (1920): 64–65; *RTB* (1891); al-Nabhani (1923): 114; Fattah (1997): 71–72, 195–197.
16 Based on statistics in *RTB* (1887–1913). See also remarks on methodological problems in the discussion of date exports above.
17 Issawi (1986): 173; Issawi (1988): 209, 260.
18 These aspects of trade in the Gulf region in the late nineteenth century are discussed in detail in Fattah (1997), a study which covers both regional and long-distance commerce and the linkages between them.

Chapter 3

1 The most enduring and important of these autonomous principalities were the Afrasiyab emirate, based in Basra, from around 1610 to 1668, and the government of the Georgian freedmen of Baghdad from 1747 to 1831, disrupted by a Persian occupation between 1776 and 1779. Longrigg (1925): 99–122; Nieuwenhuis (1982): viii. A comprehensive study of Basra in the period prior to the restoration of Ottoman power in 1831 is Abdullah (2001).
2 Issawi (1988): 215.
3 In theory, also Kuwait formed part of this *sancak*, but no Ottoman soldiers or administrators were ever posted to the town.
4 Historical background on these peripheral groups can be found in two anthropological studies. For the Dafir, see Ingham (1986); for conditions north of Qurna, Salim (1962).

5   *BSAL* (1308/1890): 89, (1318/1900): 205; Adamov (1912): 91; Lorimer (1908): 805; Dieu-
    lafoy (1990): 158–159.
6   Fernea (1970): 60; Ansari (1974): 15.
7   YEE/9/3: Memo by Mehmed 'Ali Bey (8 Kanun-i sani 1304/20 January 1889). In the south-
    ern and western direction there was theoretically no border at all. Yet, in practice, no areas
    beyond Qatar in the south and the district of Hasa' in the west (euphemistically referred to
    as the *sancak* or district of "Najd" – a geographical name that traditionally connoted a much
    wider area) were included in the administrative system, *SAL* (1323/1905): 646. Çetinsaya
    (1994) includes much information on developments in the Basra vilayet as a whole, with
    particular emphasis on security problems related to the tribes north of Basra *sancak* as well
    as the Ottoman perception of a threat from Britain in the region. The latter issue (along with
    Ottoman counter-strategies) is analysed in detail for Najd *sancak*, Kuwait and Qatar by
    Anscombe (1997).
8   Al-Qahwati (1980): 96–101; Anscombe (1997): 74–85.
9   Kelly (1968): 34, 399–400, 763, 810; Lorimer (1915): 1373, 1446, 1492; de Rivoyre (1883):
    195–196.
10 Adamov (1912): 10; retrospect in FO/195/2341: J.G. Lorimer to G.A. Lowther (5 December
    1910); FO/195/2055: P. Melville to N.R. O'Conor (8 August 1899).
11 Some data on the origins of local administrators are available in materials on Ottoman pris-
    oners from the First World War, IO/L/PS/10/534: *Note verbale* from the Ottoman govern-
    ment (7 June 1916).
12 Names and geographical origin of gazetted marines are given in *BSAL* (1308/1890): 65–69,
    (1309/1891): 134–145, (1317/1899): 118–122. For later periods, the indexes of correspon-
    dence for the navy are useful because of the systematic practice of using surnames denoting
    place of origin (e.g. Aksaraylı Hasan Effendi etc.), a feature quite unique to this branch of
    the Ottoman armed forces.
13 Anscombe (1997): 170.
14 Fattah (1997): 146; Wallis Budge (1920) I: 167.
15 FO/195/2020: I.A. Forbes to Baghdad residency (26 February 1898).
16 *SAL* (1326/1908): 712.
17 FO/602/49: S.G. Knox to E. Mockler (9 August 1895); Anscombe (1997): 129. Zubayr
    stands out among the localities around Basra by being endowed with several works on local
    history, some of which also cover developments in the late Ottoman era. These include al-
    Sani' (1985–89), Humaydan (1996) and al-Samarra'i (2001).
18 BEO/VGG/263 (24 Teşrin-i sani 1310/6 December 1894, 8 Teşrin-i sani 1311/20 November
    1895); *BSAL* (1308/1890): 168; al-Nabhani (1923): 27; al-'Azzawi (1988):163; Badi'
    (1914): 59.
19 BEO/VGG/263 (29 Mart 1311/10 April 1895); *BSAL* (1308/1891: 66); Jwaideh (1953):
    163–176. For a discussion about the penetration of the state's authority in matters related to
    trade, see the analysis of "government towns" (such as Basra) versus "tribal suqs and free
    ports" (such as Zubayr) in Fattah (1997): 185–206.
20 Jwaideh (1953): 117.
21 Al-Wardi (1969–79) III: 61–63.
22 FO/195/2274: F.E. Crow to O'Conor (21 February 1908).
23 Retrospect in *Awqat* (27 January 1922); Jwaideh (1953): 163–171.
24 Al-'Azzawi (1935–56) VII: 203–205; al-Nabhani (1923): 320; FO/195/2188: Crow to
    O'Conor (1 September 1905); Faydi (1998): 89–92; Badi' (1914): 67.
25 FO/195/2164: J.H. Monahan to O'Conor (21 June 1904).
26 BEO/VGG/266 (30 Kanun-i sani 1293/11 February 1878); BEO/VGG/267 (4 Temmuz
    1322/17 July 1906).
27 BEO/VGG/263 (8 Teşrin-i sani 1311/20 November 1895); FO/195/1885: Mockler to P.
    Currie (22 October 1895); al-Shaykhli (1972): 256–257.

28   BEO/VGG/263 (12 Temmuz 1311/24 July 1895); Hedgecock and Hedgecock (1927): 116–118.

29   FO/195/2164: Monahan to O'Conor (21 June 1904). See also Badi' (1914): 74–75; de Rivoyre (1883): 229–230.

30   Faydi (1998): 67–68; al-Khalidi (1981): 201 n.1; retrospect in *AR* (1917): 201.

31   Bell (1917b): 1.

32   Retrospect in *AR* (1915): 1–2.

33   BEO/VGG/263 (21 Teşrin-i sani 1310/3 December 1894); *BSAL* (1309/1891): 2.

34   Geary (1878) I: 90–91; Lorimer (1908): 98–114; Wilson (1911): 114; Salim (1962): 37.

35   FO/195/1885: Mockler to W.J. Cunningham (18 September 1895); FO/195/2164: Monahan to O'Conor (23 December 1904).

36   FO/371/3407(189788): Note by A.L. Gordon Walker (31 May 1918); Dowson (1931): 16–22.

37   Sluglett (1976): 237–238; Issawi (1975): 168; IO/L/PS/10/617 (P4528): Note by H. Dobbs (1916).

38   *BSAL* (1308/1890): 167–169; Jwaideh (1963): 121–133; Philby (1948): 115; Issawi (1975): 167.

39   BEO/VGG/264 (16 Eylul 1322/29 September 1906); Jwaideh (1963): 131–132; Batatu (1978): 74–75; al-Najjar (1971): 134–135; Issawi (1975): 167. On Muhammara in this period more generally, see al-Hilw (1972); Ansari (1974); Strunk (1977).

40   Al-Ansari (1969): 20–25; Adamov (1912): 55; Bell (1917b): 3.

41   FO/195/2338: Crow to G.A. Lowther (15 March 1910); FO/195/2096: A.C. Wratislaw to O'Conor (2 February 1901); al-'Azzawi (1935–56) VII: 203–204; Faydi (1998b): 314; Jwaideh (1963): 119, 133.

42   BEO/220795: Telegram from Muhammad al-Mishri (29 Teşrin-i evvel 1322/11 November 1906); BEO/VGG/264 (27 Haziran 1322/10 July 1906).

43   Ottoman figures for revenue income from the 1890s were not significantly lower than those of the early years of British administration, belying frequent British accusations that the Ottoman practices had been inefficient. For comparisons on the *sancak* and *kaza* levels, see *BSAL* (1318/1900): 152 and FO/195/2242: Crow to O'Conor (28 March 1907), compared with *AR Qurna* (1916–17): Appendix II and *AR* (1917): 29.

44   *BSAL* (1308/1890): 152; al-Nabhani (1923): 122; *AR Qurna* (1916–17): 6.

45   MV/11/130: Ministry of Defence to Council of Ministers (17 Safer 1323/22 April 1905); BEO/VGG/264 (8 Mart 1321/21 March 1905).

46   Faydi (1998b): 317, 323–325; IO/L/PS/10/617 (P4528): Note by H. Dobbs (1916); FO/371/3407 (189788): Note by A.L. Gordon Walker (31 May 1918): 36–37.

47   FO/602/49: G.W. Mungavin to C.G.F. Fagan (18 March 1897); retrospect in *IRP* (1917): 68.

48   Issawi (1988): 13; Geary (1878) I: 91.

49   Al-Bazi (1970): 45; al-Sani' (1985–89) I: 110–112, 148.

50   Y/MTV/34/20: Abu al-Huda al-Sayyadi to Yıldız (10 Zilkade 1305/20 July 1888); Y/MTV/37/67: Ministry of War to Yıldız (26 Kanun-i sani 1304/7 February 1889); Eich (2003): 136.

51   AIR/23/439: Note by Ja'far al-'Askari (20 November 1920); Longrigg (1925): 314; Longrigg (1953): 38; Faydi (1998): 71–72.

52   *BSAL* (1308/1890): 79–81.

53   Retrospect in FO/371/10143 (E346): H. Dobbs to the Duke of Devonshire (24 November 1923).

54   Retrospect in CO/730/132/2: H. Dobbs to L.S. Amery (30 June 1928).

55   DKK/319/10 (11 Rebiülevvel 1306/15 November 1888); FO/195/2243: J. Ramsay to O'Conor (30 November 1907).

56   Retrospect in FO/195/2275: Crow to Lowther (31 December 1908).

57   *BSAL* (1308/1890): 75–76; *BSAL* (1318/1900): 231.

58   Barakat (1977): 46–47 n. 2; Faydi (1998): 79–83; al-Nabhani (1923): 100–101.

59 Y/PRK/UM/72/59: Fakhri Pasha to Yıldız (7 Teşrin-i sani 1320/20 November 1904).
60 On the growth of secondary schools in other parts of the empire, see Fortna (2002): 124.
61 Faydi (1998b): 301; Abdullah (2001): 92–93.
62 Khurshid Effendi (1981): 14.
63 Al-Haydari (1962): 161–162.
64 *BSAL* (1308/1890): 91–92, 94; FO/602/42: P.J.C. Robertson to Baghdad residency (30 October 1882).
65 Adamov (1912): 39–40.
66 The main study of conversion to Shi'ism in this region, Nakash (1994), focuses on areas further north, closer to the holy cities of Karbala' and Najaf. Here, the process of mass sedentarisation among the previously nomadic tribes was a central variable, and the relative recency of the conversion one of the important findings in the analysis.
67 *BSAL* (1308/1890): 80–81.
68 Buckingham (1829): 370.
69 Lorimer (1908): 276; Adamov (1912): 39.
70 Al-Nabhani (1923): 103; al-Kutubi (1951): 75 On Basra's relations with Hasa' and Bahrain in this period, see Salum (1989): 541; Issawi (1988): 14.
71 Hirz al-Din (1964–65) III: 177–182.
72 Al-Fadli (1991): 169; FO/602/42: Robertson to Baghdad residency (30 October 1882); Dieulafoy (1990): 162.
73 For local usage of this term, see Ingham (1976): 64.
74 Nakash (1994): 37–42.
75 Al-Tahir (1972): 143 n. 1.
76 The Jaza'ir region north of Basra was an important recruitment zone for leading Shi'i ulama during the seventeenth and eighteenth centuries, see Momen (1985): 122–123. For Shi'i ulama from Basra before the late nineteenth century, see al-'Alawi (1989): 36; Litvak (1998): 131; al-Tihrani (1937–) I: Entry no. 572, XIII: Entries no. 1211, 1471.
77 Momen (1985): 189–199.
78 For the links between Shi'ism, Shaykhism and Babism (and later Baha'ism), see Amanat (1989): 33–69; Smith (1987): 56–71.
79 YEE/9/3: Memo by Mehmed 'Ali Bey (8 Kanun-i sani 1304/20 January 1889). For Ottoman views on the Shi'i challenge in the easternmost provinces of the empire more generally, see Deringil (1990).
80 Y/PRK/UM/12/108: Sha'ban Pasha to Yıldız (1 Ağustos 1304/13 August 1888); Mehmed Süreyya Bey (1890–98) IV: 859; al-Haydari (1962): 174; al-Khalidi (1981): 217; al-Nabhani (1923): 100–103.
81 Deringil (1990); Çetinsaya (1994): 237–239, 276; *Neglected Arabia* 52 (1904).
82 BEO/VGG/263 (26 Haziran 1312/8 July 1896, 27 Temmuz 1313/8 August 1897). Many of the students of tribal origin who actually took up their study places found life in the imperial capital difficult, and only a relatively small proportion succeeded in graduating, BEO/VGG/263 (2 Kanun-i evvel 1308/14 December 1892); Akpınar (1997): 70.
83 Al-Nabhani (1923): 108; al-Kutubi (1951): 43.
84 FO/195/2020: W. Loch to Currie (23 April 1898).
85 In addition to biographies of leading ulama, the best sources on the sectarian geography of late Ottoman Basra are lists of mosques such as those in al-Nabhani (1923): 93–105. From the 1920s onwards, local newspaper announcements giving details of cases before the personal status law courts provide data on urban quarter residence and sectarian affiliation.
86 *Neglected Arabia* 79 (1910); Raunkiær (1913): 26; Badi' (1914): 85–86.
87 Lorimer (1908): 269–270.
88 Al-Nabhani (1923): 103; Van Ess (1961): 122.
89 Al-Nabhani (1923): 107–109.
90 Retrospect in FO/195/2310: Crow to Lowther (9 December 1909).
91 Buckingham (1829): 373–375; Fontanier (1844–46) I: 211–214; Longrigg (1953): 11, 61.

92   Adamov (1912): 41; Scudder (1998): 220.
93   FO/195/2188: L.S. Newmarch to O'Conor (3 August 1905); *Field Report* 1 (1892).
94   Drower (1937): 15.
95   FO/195/1935: J.F. Whyte to Mockler (23 June 1896).
96   On the efforts to open Ottoman museums outside Istanbul, see Shaw (2003): 169–171.
97   Al-Nabhani (1923): 71; Longrigg (1925): 316; Barakat (1984): 62–70; al-Shaykhli (1972): 265.
98   Jwaideh (1953): 155, 161, 185; Butti (1955): 165.
99   BEO/VGG/266 (20 Teşrin-i sani 1291/2 December 1876); FO/195/2215: Crow to G. Barclay (22 September 1906); *BSAL* (1309/1891): 66 compared with FO/195/2309: Crow to Lowther (6 September 1909).
100 FO/602/22: Crow to Barclay (15 April 1908).
101 BEO/VGG/263 (22 Nisan 1307/5 May 1891).
102 A/MKT/MHM/432/30: File on silk cultivation in Basra (8 Şevval 1285/21 January 1869).
103 Issawi (1988): 409–410, 468–469; Batatu (1978): 17.
104 *RTB* (1891); FO/602/42: Robertson to Baghdad residency (15 November 1882); Lorimer (1908): 96; Pearson and Proud (1996): 191–192.
105 Al-'Azzawi (1935–56) VIII: 56–57; *BSAL* (1308/1890): 164–166; Badi' (1914): 61.
106 Çetinsaya (1994): 154–155 n. 134, 158 n. 143.
107 Y/A/HUS/164/24: Copy of governor of Basra to Sublime Porte (22 Kanun-i evvel 1295/3 January 1880), copy of governor of Hijaz to Sublime Porte (10 Mart 1296/22 March 1880); FO/602/42: Major Jennings to W. Tweedie (23 February 1891).
108 Ottoman *tezkere* (travel document) for Aga Ja'far from private collection (16 Teşrin-i evvel 1326/29 October 1910); BEO/VGG/263 (12 Mart 1311/24 March 1895); FO/195/2215: Crow to Barclay (22 September 1906); FO/602/42: Robertson to Baghdad residency (5 October 1882).
109 BEO/VGG/267 (19 Mart 1321/1 April 1905).
110 BEO/VGG/263 (15 Eylul 1310/27 September 1894); FO/195/1935: Mockler to Currie (24 November 1896).
111 Jwaideh (1953) and Barakat (1984) provide details of Basra's municipal administration in this period.
112 *BSAL* (1308/1890): 77; Barakat (1984): 38; al-Nabhani (1923): 325; Longrigg (1925): 315–316; Ra'uf (1983): 226.
113 Y/MTV/234/86: General Mustafa to Yıldız (1 Ağustos 1318/14 August 1902); *BSAL* (1318/1900): 289; *IRP* (1917): 45
114 Y/MTV/301/61: General Tahir to Yıldız (6 Ağustos 1323/19 August 1907).
115 Abdullah (2001): 33–34.
116 Al-Matba'i (1995–98) III: 278–279; al-Wardi (1969–79) III: 62–63; al-Haydari (1962): 165; Lorimer (1908): 2372–2373.
117 FO/195/2214: Crow to O'Conor (9 June 1906); historical note in IO/L/PS/10/535 (P3505): P.Z. Cox to India Office (24 July 1916).
118 Bell (1940): Extract from *Arab Bulletin* (7 October 1917).
119 Al-Wardi (1969–79) III: 61–62; FO/195/2020: I.A. Forbes to Baghdad consulate (18 April 1898).
120 Retrospect in FO/195/2308: Crow to Lowther (10 March 1909).
121 Developments in Kuwait are discussed in chapter 5.
122 Al-Shaykh Khaz'al (1962–70) III: 15; Raunkiær (1913): 60; Lorimer (1908): 535–540.
123 FO/195/2139: Crow to O'Conor (8 July 1903)
124 Y/PRK/HR/31/74: File on Kuwait (24 Şevval 1319/3 February 1902).
125 FO/195/1935: Mockler to Currie (24 November 1896); Eich (2003): 95–97, 191–193.
126 Y/PRK/UM/57/76: General Mustafa Nuri to Yıldız (19 Şubat 1317/4 March 1902); BEO/VGG/264 (6 Ağustos 1317/19 August 1901, 14 Kanun-i evvel 1317/27 December 1901, 7 Mart 1321/20 March 1905).

127 Yusuf Zade (1904): 12, 36–40.
128 Y/MTV/233/33: Telegram from governor of Aydin (28 Temmuz 1318/10 August 1902); *BSAL* (1308/1890): 77; DKK/698/184 (3 November 1912); Faydi (1998): 72–73; al-Wardi (1969–79) III: 34.
129 Y/PRK/AZJ/30/121: Ibrahim Effendi to Yıldız (6 Mart 1311/18 March 1895). For examples of participation in the pilgrimage to Hijaz even by Shi'is living in remote rural areas, see Badi' (1914): 108–110.
130 Y/PRK/AZJ/24/85 and Y/PRK/AZJ/25/63: Undated letters from Ahmad al-Zuhayr submitted to the sultan's office (both files dated 29 Zilhicce 1310/14 July 1893); YEE/8/8: Undated report by Zuhayr (file dated 21 Rebiülevvel 1308/4 November 1890). Zuhayr's father and the local *naqib* were the only contemporary Basrawis included in a "Who is Who" of the Ottoman Empire published in Istanbul in the 1890s, Mehmed Süreyya Bey (1890–98) IV: 51, 859.
131 BEO/VGG/267 (22 Şubat 1321/7 March 1906); de Rivoyre (1883): 215–216; retrospect in *Awqat* (23 May 1929).
132 Al-Qahwati (1980): 292–296; *Lughat al-'Arab* (1911–12): 179.
133 Lorimer (1908): 797.
134 Hirz al-Din (1964–65) I: 39, II: 222; Litvak (1998): 82; al-Kanani (n.d.): Entry no. 14.
135 Hirz al-Din (1964–65) II: 123; al-Tihrani (1937–) XVII: Entry no. 211; al-Fadli (1991): 164–165, 169, al-Maktaba al-Adabiyya al-Mukhtassa (1997): 31–32.
136 Y/PRK/UM/67/111: General Mustafa to Yıldız (24 Kanun-i evvel 1319/6 January 1904).
137 Faydi (1998): 153; Ingham (1997): 45–46; photographs in al-Sani' (1985–89) I: 123, *Quarterly Letter from the Field* 23 (1897): 5, al-Nabhani (1923): 343 and in Faydi (1998): 156.
138 Retrospect in *Basrah* (1 September 1923).
139 Lorimer (1908): 793.
140 Khurshid Effendi (1981): 15; Ingham (1997): 46–47.
141 FO/195/2074: Wratislaw to O'Conor (9 January 1900, 21 March 1900).
142 Barakat (1977): 12–18.
143 Al-Nabhani (1923): 87–88; Majid (1989): 587–594; al-'Azzawi (1949): 4.
144 Al-Kutubi (1951): 43. On the *ma'tam* institution, see Fuccaro (1999) and Khuri (1980): 154–173.
145 Al-Tabataba'i (1966): 1–46.
146 FO/195/2139: Crow to O'Conor (30 June 1903); FO/195/2138: Crow to O'Conor (9 April 1903, 11 May 1903).
147 Y/MTV/291/15: Ministry of Justice to Yıldız (11 Teşrin-i sani 1322/24 November 1906); FO/195/2188: Monahan to O'Conor (22 January 1905).
148 Balaghi (2002).
149 Faydi (1998): 71; FO/195/2116: Wratislaw to O'Conor (13 June 1902); BEO/VGG/264 (20 Kanun-i sani 1319/2 February 1904, 2 Şubat 1319/15 February 1904).
150 BEO/71141: Governor of Basra to Ministry of Foreign Affairs (12 Kanun-i sani 1312/25 January 1897).
151 Y/PRK/MK/9/46: Mukhtar Pasha to Yıldız (12 Teşrin-i sani 1315/24 November 1893); BEO/229387: File on article from *al-Liwa'* (20 Safer 1325/4 April 1907).

Chapter 4

1 Retrospect in *Basrah* (24 December 1931).
2 FO/195/2275: F.E. Crow to G.A. Lowther (4 December 1908).
3 On Faydi's manifold contributions to Basra's political and cultural life in this period and later, see Laftah (2003).
4 Faydi (1998): 79–83.

5   DH/MUİ/29-1/44: Sublime Porte to Ministry of Interior (27 Kanun-i evvel 1324/9 January 1909).

6   Barakat (1977) details the emergence of a press in Basra in this period.

7   *İkaz* (4 October 1909, 15 December 1909).

8   *İkaz* (17 May 1909, 4 October 1909).

9   DH/MUİ/14/1/85: Sulayman Faydi and others to Ministry of Interior (10 Eylul 1325/23 September 1909).

10 Relations between Arab elites in general and the Ottomans are thoroughly analysed in Prätor (1993) and Kayali (1997).

11 *MMZC* (25 Şubat 1324/10 March 1909): 223–224.

12 *MMZC* (4 Mart 1325/17 March 1909): 329.

13 *MMZC* (28 Şubat 1324/13 March 1909): 289.

14 DH/MUİ/44-2/1: File on demolition works at Basra (4 Muharrem 1328/16 January 1910).

15 DH/EUM/VRK/8/82: File on Basra police (8 Zilhicce 1329/29 November 1911).

16 DKK/674/99–106 (12 May 1910); FO/195/2338: Crow to Lowther (25 April 1910).

17 MV/138/55: Minutes of proceedings (25 Mart 1326/7 April 1910).

18 Faydi (1998): 89–91.

19 FO/195/2338: Crow to Lowther (15 March 1910); FO/195/2368: W.D.W. Matthews to Lowther (27 May 1911)

20 Faydi (1998): 81–83.

21 Laftah (2003): 36.

22 *BSAL* (1309/1891): 66.

23 DH/MUİ/5/117/62: 'Abd al-Muhsin al-Zuhayr to Ministry of Interior (10 Temmuz 1326/23 July 1910), Süleyman Nazif Bey to Ministry of Interior (18 Temmuz 1326/31 July 1910).

24 *Al-Basra al-Fayha'* (27 Mart 1327/9 April 1911); FO/602/52: Crow to Lowther (13 April 1911).

25 FO/195/2368: Matthews to C.M. Marling (8 July 1911); FO/195/2369: Matthews to Lowther (28 October 1911).

26 FO/195/2340: Crow to Lowther (15 September 1910).

27 Prätor (1993): 250.

28 FO/195/2340: J.G. Lorimer to Lowther (12 September 1910); FO/195/2368: Matthews to Lowther (19 August 1911).

29 *MMZC* (29 Teşrin-i sani 1325/12 December 1909): 273.

30 *MMZC* (28 Teşrin-i sani 1325/11 December 1909): 249; FO/195/2338: Crow to Marling (5 January 1910).

31 *MMZC* (11 Kanun-i sani 1325/25 January 1910): 639–642. The rapidly growing independent press in Istanbul created another channel where Basrawis could put pressure on the government through letters to the editor. One example is a telegram from the Mishri family of Basra to *Sabah* (7 Teşrin-i sani 1326/20 November 1910), with a complaint about the state of security in rural areas.

32 *İkaz* (19 January 1910, 8 April 1910, 29 September 1910).

33 FO/195/2368: Matthews to Lowther (19 August 1911).

34 FO/195/2369: Crow to Lowther (22 December 1911).

35 Faydi (1998): 122–123.

36 FO/602/52: Crow to Lowther (22 March 1912); Birru (1991): 380–381.

37 Barakat (1984): 152.

38 DH/ID/144-1/45: Governor's council Basra to Ministry of Interior (7 Haziran 1328/20 June 1912).

39 For the recruitment of Ottoman officials to the reform movement, see FO/602/52: Crow to Lowther (27 March 1912).

40 DH/ID/79/19: 'Umar Fawzi to Sublime Porte (20 Haziran 1328/ 3 July 1912), office minute (6 Temmuz 1328/19 July 1912).

41 Barakat (1984): 157–158.

42   Laftah (2003): 66–67.
43   FO/602/21: Crow to Lowther (29 November 1912).
44   Birru (1991): 491.
45   IO/L/PS/10/617 (P3504): P.Z. Cox to A. Hirtzel (23 July 1916) enclosing extract of Baghdad diary March 1913.
46   A transcript of the petition is given in FO/602/52: Crow to Lowther (24 February 1913).
47   *Lughat al-'Arab* (1912–13): 474–475; Birru (1991): 489–490.
48   FO/195/2451: Crow to Lowther (8 May 1913); al-Sa'dun (1987): 105; al-Shaykh Khaz'al (1962–70) II: 266.
49   FO/602/52: Crow to Lowther (24 February 1913).
50   For the elections results, see Barakat (1984): 163.
51   A copy of the original programme is preserved in FO/195/2451: Crow to Marling (28 August 1913). It was also published in local newspapers, *Lughat al-'Arab* (1913–14): 273.
52   For the original pamphlet, see FO/602/52: Crow to Lowther (30 August 1913)
53   FO/195/2451: Crow to Lowther (28 January 1913); IO/L/PS/10/535 (P76a): Memorandum by Crow (3 January 1915).
54   *IRP* (1917): 46; GB diaries (26 November 1913).
55   FO/602/52: Crow to Lowther (24 February 1913); IO/L/PS/10/462 (P3938): L. Mallet to E. Grey (31 August 1914); Dowson (1921) I: 56–57; *RTB* (1913): 1. The position of the date-exporters is given less prominence in two studies which emphasise the anti-British dimension of the movement and its connection to the situation of merchants trading in general goods, Haddad (1991) and Fattah (2002). The pre-war attitude of this vital segment of Basra's elite is, however, a key to understanding the background for political developments in Basra over the subsequent decades.
56   DH/EUM/EMN/41/6&49/7: Monthly reports for September, October and November 1913; FO/195/2451: Crow to Mallet (22 December 1913).
57   IO/L/PS/11/75: Istanbul embassy to India Office (6 March 1914).
58   DH/ID/178/21: File on reforms in Basra vilayet (28 Cumadelâhire 1332/24 May 1914).
59   Al-Shaykh Khaz'al (1962–70) II: 270–271; Faydi (1998): 153.
60   Al Zulfa (2001).
61   *İkaz* (17 November 1909).
62   Butti (1976): 29.
63   Extracts from *al-Dustur* in *Lughat al-'Arab* (1912–13): 588, (1913–14): 111.
64   IO/L/PS/10/617 (P3504): P.Z. Cox to A. Hirtzel (23 July 1916), enclosing extract of Baghdad diary March 1913; Van Ess (1974): 62.
65   *İkaz* (4 October 1909).
66   FO/195/2451: Crow to Marling (28 August 1913): *Barnamach* [sic] *jam'iyyat al-islah al-basriyya*, article 14.
67   FO/602/52: Cutting from Baghdad newspaper (apparently taken from *al-Riyad*, around October 1910). See also *İkaz* (29 September 1910); *Lughat al-'Arab* (1911–12): 122–123.
68   *İkaz* (12 January 1910).
69   FO/195/1935: J.F. Whyte to E. Mockler (26 May 1896) enclosing petition from the Mandaean community.
70   Al-Tihrani (1937–) VIII: Entry no. 1086.
71   *Lughat al-'Arab* (1912–13): 4–5.
72   One example is a pamphlet entitled *al-'Iraq, al-'Iraq* which circulated in Baghdad in 1910. The more standard usage was reflected in expressions such as "the deputies of Iraq", used as a heading for a list of deputies from Baghdad and Basra (but not including Mosul), *Lughat al-'Arab* (1911–12): 491, FO/195/2340: Lorimer to Lowther (26 August 1910).
73   Al-Haydari (1962): 120–121.
74   Al-Tabataba'i (1966): 70–74.
75   Badi' (1914): 72; al-Maktaba al-Adabiyya al-Mukhtassa (1997): 32; biography of Habib ibn Qirayn from www.awhad.org.

76   See for instance Basha'yan (1890): 40; al-Khalidi (1981): 216.
77   Al-Shaykh Khaz'al (1962–70) II: 267; FO/195/2451: Crow to Marling (19 July 1913); Singer (1901–06) II: 586; FO/195/2309: Crow to Lowther (11 September 1909); retrospect in *Awqat* (29 November 1923). The tendency of local non-Muslim communities to use foreign states as patrons should not be exaggerated. The elites of these communities participated in Ottoman institutions and, in some cases, regarded European powers as a possible threat. The British consul manumitted slaves belonging to Jewish notables, and local Christians were sceptical of American protestant missionaries, FO/195/1842: Note by S.G. Knox (23 November 1894); FO/195/1799: F.G. Beville to Mockler (28 September 1893).
78   Van Ess (1974): 70–71.
79   *Lughat al-'Arab* (1913–14): 277–278.
80   Faydi (1998): 226; Burj (1990): 105; retrospects in IO/L/PS/11/95 (P2891): P.Z. Cox to A.H. McMahon (18 March 1915).
81   BEO/VGG/263 (3 Haziran 1311/16 June 1895); FO/195/1885: Mockler to P. Currie (2 October 1895).
82   FO/195/2339: Crow to Lowther (23 April 1910).
83   The claim which is sometimes made that the participation of members of the Tabataba'i family in the pre-war reform movement represented an example of inter-sectarian co-operation, is misleading. These individuals belonged to an old Sunni family of Zubayr, see al-Haydari (1962): 167–168; al-Ansari (1969): 58–59. While Shi'is were not excluded in principle, their contributions were much more sporadic, for one example see *İkaz* (17 May 1909).

Chapter 5

1   A comprehensive analysis of the development of British policy towards the Gulf region is given in Busch (1967 and 1971).
2   Busch (1967): 24; Kelly (1968): 768.
3   Kumar (1965): 120, 137; Busch (1967): 94.
4   For these suggestions, see Alghanim (1990): 59–61; Anscombe (1997): 110.
5   FO/371/148(10680): Memorandum by A. Parker (10 March 1906).
6   WO/106/42(C3/37): A.H. McMahon to the Marquess of Crewe (15 February 1912).
7   FO/602/53: F.E. Crow to N.R. O'Conor (2 May 1907); FO/195/2309: Crow to G.A. Lowther (12 July 1909).
8   FO/195/2308: Crow to Lowther (25 April 1909); FO/195/2451: Crow to Lowther (28 January 1913); FO/195/2451: Crow to Lowther (15 March 1913).
9   FO/195/2341: Crow to Lowther (30 December 1910).
10   Marlowe (1967): 53.
11   FO/195/2339: Crow to Lowther (20 May 1910); FO/195/2340: Crow to Lowther (27 October 1910).
12   IO/L/PS/11/88 (P408): Office minute (undated, around February 1915); Cohen (1976): 298–309; Ireland (1937): 24–29; Kent (1976): 118–119.
13   WO/95/5122: War diary 6th division/17th brigade (15 March 1915).
14   Busch (1971): 52.
15   Evans (1926): 18. For an account from the Ottoman perspective, see al-Shaykhli (1972): 328–340.
16   General Staff (1923): 354.
17   Al-Tahir (1972): 329–331 n.1.
18   Al-Khalidi (1981): 125–126, 131–132; al-Shaykhli (1972): 341; General Staff (1923): 354; *IRP* (1917): 30.

19 The only local tribe known to have participated were the Bani Mansur, ADM/137/205: Report by W. Nunn on river operations 1914–1917 (appendixes) p. 155; al-Matbaʻi (1995–98) III: 128.

20 WO/95/4965 (War diary vol. IV): Note by C. Stack (29 January 1915); al-Shaykh Khazʻal (1962–70) IV: 73–74.

21 ADM/137/204: Report by W. Nunn on river operations 1914–1917 II pp. 7–8; Wilson (1931): 20.

22 WO/95/5122: War diary 6th division/17th brigade/First Oxfordshire and Buckinghamshire Company (9 May 1915); WO/106/891: E.C. Cookson to C. Mackenzie (9 May 1915); Barker (1967): 61–62; *The Oxfordshire and Buckinghamshire Light Infantry Chronicle* (1914–15): 60; Reynardson (1919): 135–136.

23 Similar flags were used at Shuʻayba, Barker (1967): 71.

24 WO/157/776: Report by Kalash ibn Diwin (10 April 1915); WO/95/4965: War diary, general officer commanding (5 May 1915); FO/602/42: C.W. Ravenshaw to Baghdad residency (30 September 1888); General Staff (1923): 348–349; Admiralty (1917): 116; al-ʻAzzawi (1937–56) IV: 66–67, 287–288.

25 ADM/137/205: Report by W. Nunn on river operations 1914–1917 (appendixes) p. 108.

26 WO/95/4965: War diary, general officer commanding (5 May 1915).

27 Bell (1917): 76–77; IO/L/PS/11/168 (P1194): Zubayr diary (October 1919); WO/157/776: General staff intelligence to Dirhamiyya intelligence officer (12 June 1915).

28 *AR Qurna* (1916–17): Appendix I; Wilson (1931): 28–29, 295; IO/L/PS/10/751 (P5471): A.T. Wilson to India Office (16 July 1918).

29 Luizard (1991): 324.

30 Al-Wardi (1969–79) IV: 151; Wilson (1931): 13, 35.

31 Goold (1976): 926–931.

32 IO/L/PS/11/88 (P552): Wilson to C.E. Yate (28 November 1914); Busch (1971): 22, 54 n. 104.

33 Atiyyah (1973): 129; retrospect in FO/371/5230 (E12461): C. Hardinge's minutes (12 October 1920).

34 ADM/137/432: E. Barrow's minutes (14 December 1914) Wilson (1931): 38, 50–51; Sluglett (1976): 10–12, 51–52 n. 13.

35 Wilson (1931): 311.

36 As cited in Rothwell (1970): 275.

37 CAB/27/37 (EC2525): Foreign Office memorandum (21 November 1918): 6.

38 Wilson (1931): 16–17; Longrigg (1953): 82.

39 See excerpts in Schofield (1993): 48–49; Wilson (1931): 9 n. 1.

40 CAB/27/1: Report of the De Bunsen committee, maps I–V (30 June 1915); Klieman (1970): 4–6; Kent (1976): 121.

41 Rothwell (1970): 279; Adelson (1995): 129.

42 FO/371/3042(69123): A. Chamberlain to A.H. Grant (29 March 1917).

43 FO/371/3042(74511): P.Z. Cox to Chamberlain (7 April 1917).

44 Mejcher (1976): 24; Busch (1971): 188–189.

45 Wilson (1931): 71.

46 Wilson (1931): 13; *AR* (1917): 200.

47 Ireland (1937): 83–84; IO/L/PS/10/617 (P3042): Note by G.L. Bell (22 July 1916).

48 *AR* (1918): 255–265.

49 *AR* (1917): 205, 234; Moberly (1924–27) II: 279–281.

50 Young (1933): 49–53. Many aspects of British administrative practices in Basra in this period are covered in al-Tamimi (1979).

51 IO/L/PS/10/617 (P3042): Note by G.L. Bell (22 July 1916); *AR* (1917): 18; Garbett (1919): 412.

52 *AR* (1918): 301; IO/L/PS/11/171 (P2643): Qurna report (November 1919).

53 *AR Basra Sanjaq* (1916–17).

54 *AR* (1917): Qurna section.
55 FO/371/3407(189788): Note by A.L. Gordon Walker (31 May 1918); Ireland (1937): 118; al-Khalidi (1981): 192; al-Mubadir (1978): 205; al-Tamimi (1976): 71–79.
56 Sluglett (1976): 274.
57 Ireland (1937): 124–125; Diskin (1971): 208–212, 234–239, 350 n. 3; *AR* (1917): 134–135.
58 Al-Tamimi (1976): 71–74; Barakat (1977): 77 n. 1.
59 *AR Basra Sanjaq* (1916–17): 4; *AR Qurna* (1916–17): 1.
60 IO/L/PS/10/619 (P816): Wilson to E.S. Montagu (30 December 1918); *AR* (1917): 202; IO/L/PS/10/617 (P5119): Cox to India Office (6 November 1917); *AR* (1918): 255.
61 *AR* (1917): 201–202.
62 Wilson (1931): 147; Young (1933): 49; Faydi (1998): 207.
63 Wilson (1931): 286.
64 *AR* (1918): 279.
65 *AR* (1918): 303; IO/L/PS/10/732 (P4280): Fortnightly report (10 July 1918).
66 IO/L/PS/10/617 (P5119): Enclosure in Cox to India Office (6 November 1917).
67 IO/L/PS/10/686 (P617): Cox to Montagu (14 February 1918).
68 IO/L/PS/10/732 (P1208): Fortnightly report (22 December 1917); *Basrah* (8 January 1918, 19 April 1918).
69 Süleyman Nazif (1918).
70 Egerton (1974, 1991); Adelson (1995): 104.
71 CAB/27/23 (MEC24): Note by A. Hirtzel (11 January 1918) and (MEC68): Note by India Office (31 January 1918).
72 CAB/27/24: EC minutes (24 April 1918); CAB/27/25: Note by Cox (22 April 1918).
73 CAB/27/35 (EC2030): Note by Political Department, India Office (21 October 1918).
74 CAB/27/35 (EC2135): Note by G.M.W. Macdonogh (28 October 1918).
75 CAB/27/24: EC minutes (18 July 1918); CAB/27/24: EC minutes (3 October 1918).
76 IO/L/PS/10/755 (P26): Cox to India Office (24 December 1918). Despite having been conceived partly with war propaganda aims in mind, the declaration was not actually issued until 8 November 1918, shortly after the armistice of Mudros between the Ottomans and the Allies. Busch (1971): 188–199.
77 IO/L/PS/10/686 (P4150): Wilson to India Office (15 September 1918).
78 *Ibid.*
79 CAB/27/35 (EC2002): Wilson to India Office (16 October 1918); Mejcher (1976): 28–42; Yapp (1987): 332.
80 CAB/27/35 (EC2030): Note by the Political Department, India Office (21 October 1918).
81 IO/L/PS/11/142 (P5441): Note by H.V. Cox (29 October 1918).
82 FO/371/4148 (E13298): Notes of EC meeting (27 November 1918).
83 *Ibid.*
84 Ireland (1937): 161–162.
85 A record of this consultation is given in FO/248/1249 (Mesopotamian affairs, 29): A.S. Meek to Wilson (21 December 1918), on which the subsequent discussion of the results is based.
86 For one interviewee no sectarian affiliation can be established with certainty.
87 *IRP* (1917): 7; al-Sani' (1985–89) I: 271; FO/248/1250 (Mesopotamian affairs, 69): Husayn al-Kashani to Cox (9 May 1919).
88 Wilson (1931b): 114.
89 IO/L/PS/10/755 (P663): T. Holderness's minutes (14 February 1919); FO/371/4148 (E15406): H.W. Young's minutes (30 January 1919).
90 IO/L/PS/10/821 (P4943): A.G. Phillips to A.L. Gordon Walker (27 June 1919), (P7983): Gordon Walker to Wilson (4 June 1919).
91 IO/L/PS/10/821 (P5398): Wilson to India Office (1 June 1920).
92 IO/L/PS/10/756 (P3319): Wilson to Montagu (19 June 1919); Ireland (1937): 185–187.

93 FO/371/4148 (E57002): Young's minutes (12 April 1919) and (E13298): Foreign Office to the British delegation at the peace conference in Paris (26 January 1919).

94 While publicly supportive of the government's policy, Curzon in private continued to waver as to the feasibility of the one-state scheme well into 1920, FO/371/5226 (E3322): Curzon's minutes (undated, mid April 1920).

95 CAB/27/24: EC minutes (24 April 1918): 4; IO/L/PS/10/750 (P5083): Extract from *The Times* (no date given, early August 1919).

96 House of Lords (10 February 1920); House of Commons (25 March 1920): 644–645, 662–664.

97 IO/L/PS/10/757 (P2463): Note of cabinet meeting (23 March 1920).

98 FO/371/4148 (E17477): Memorandum by Young (undated, written at the end of January 1919); FO/371/5071 (E2464): Young's minutes (6 April 1920); FO/371/5227 (E7395): Young's minutes (1 July 1920); Young papers: Young to W.H. Deedes (30 December 1920).

99 FO/371/5227 (E7395): Young's minutes (1 July 1920).

100 FO/371/4148 (E17477): R. Cecil's minutes (31 March 1919); FO/371/5227 (E7395): Hardinge's minutes (undated, around July 1920).

101 *AR* (1918): 254.

102 *AR* (1919): 25 (written in early 1920).

103 Atiyyah (1973): 290–291; Khoury (1983): 85–86.

104 Tauber (1995): 179.

105 IO/L/PS/10/897c: Basra Sanjaq diaries (January and March 1920).

106 IO/L/PS/10/622 (P6716): Basra Sanjaq diary (April 1920); GB (23 February 1920, 29 February 1920).

107 IO/L/PS/10/821 (P5398): Wilson to India Office (1 June 1920), (P6804): Wilson to India Office (27 July 1920); Diskin (1971): 357 n. 2.

108 IO/L/PS/10/821 (P2145): Wilson to India Office (10 February 1920).

109 IO/L/PS/10/821 (P7750): Wilson to India Office (10 September 1920).

110 IO/L/PS/10/757 (P6326): Wilson to A. Hirtzel (9 July 1920).

111 IO/L/PS/10/622 (P7537): G.V.B. Gillan to Wilson (24 July 1920).

112 FO/371/5227 (E7395): A. Trevor to Foreign Office (29 June 1920).

113 Faydi (1998): 425–516; GB (26 July 1920, 2 August 1920, 8 August 1920).

114 Faydi (1998): 504–505.

115 IO/L/PS/10/839 (P3467): AI (3 July 1920, 21 August 1920, 28 August 1920); IO/L/PS/10/622 (P7537): G.V.B. Gillan to Wilson (24 July 1920).

116 IO/L/PS/10/839 (P3467): AI (24 July 1920). In contrast to the areas further north, the Basra countryside remained calm.

117 House of Commons (23 June 1920, 20 July 1920); Mejcher (1976): 71.

118 House of Commons (23 June 1920): 2253.

119 House of Lords (25 June 1920): 888.

120 House of Commons (23 June 1920): 2267.

121 FO/371/5230 (E12461): G.N. Curzon's minutes (12 October 1920).

122 IO/L/PS/10/911 (P6125): R.G. Vansittart to G.N. Curzon (2 August 1920), J.E. Shuckburgh's minutes (11 September 1920).

123 On the drafting of the British mandate, see Busch (1971): 419, 443–444.

124 FO/371/5232 (E16336): Cox to India Office (26 October 1920). In contrast to Wilson, Cox was able to appreciate the strength of Iraqi nationalist feeling in other places, such as Baghdad.

125 IO/L/PS/11/192 (P8850): Cox to India Office (11 December 1920).

126 *Ibid.* Shuckburgh's minutes (20 December 1920).

127 FO/371/5232 (E15762): K. Cornwallis's and Young's minutes (20 December 1920).

128 IO/L/PS/11/192 (P244): Cox to India Office (8 January 1921).

129 FO/371/6349 (E277): Cox to India Office (2 January 1921). For the concerns of the British military about "scattered" garrisons and the need for greater "concentration", see Jeffery (1984): 151–154.
130 GB (18 December 1920).
131 GB (10 January 1921).
132 IO/L/PS/11/192 (P244): Shuckburgh's minutes (13 January 1921).
133 Klieman (1970): 105–124.
134 Klieman (1970): 110; Busch (1971): 469.

Chapter 6

1   Philby papers VIII (*Mesopotage* manuscript): 575; Ireland (1937): 320–321.
2   CO/537/819 (18699): P.Z. Cox to W.S. Churchill (13 April 1921); GB (12 April 1921).
3   BHCF/7/15/3/I: AI (16 April 1921).
4   CO/730/2 (34955): Cox to Churchill (11 June 1921); CO/730/2 (31864): IR (15 May 1921); BHCF/27/195: W.C.F.A. Wilson to H.StJ.B. Philby (18 May 1921).
5   CO/730/18 (37926): W.C.F.A. Wilson to Cox (14 June 1921).
6   *Basrah* (19 June 1921).
7   GB (23 June 1921).
8   BHCF/7/15/3/I: AI (25 June 1921); CO/730/3 (34298): Cox to Churchill (9 July 1921).
9   For the official, printed version in English, see CO/730/18 (37926): W.C.F.A. Wilson to Cox (14 June 1921). Almost identical Arabic versions were later published in *al-Rafidan* (19 May 1922) and al-Basir (1924): 233–236.
10   CO/730/3: IR (1 July 1921); BHCF/7/15/3/I: AI (16 April 1921).
11   CO/730/2 (32697): R.W. Bullard's minutes (4 July 1921).
12   CO/730/2: IR (15 May 1921).
13   CO/730/18(37926): W.C.F.A. Wilson to Cox (14 June 1921).
14   CO/730/2 (32697): Cox to Churchill (29 June 1921).
15   GB (23 June 1921, 7 July 1921).
16   Ireland (1937): 327 n. 4; Longrigg (1953): 132; Kedourie (1959): 64; Sluglett (1976): 4, 8 n. 10, 77; Dodge (2003): 183 n. 70.
17   By far, the most common approach to the petition among Iraqi writers has been to ignore its appearance, see for instance al-Adhami (1989) I: 149–150, where resistance against Faysal is seen as limited to the Kurds, as well as to individuals who themselves were striving for the Iraqi throne.
18   *Al-Rafidan* (19 May 1922, 21 May 1922).
19   *Al-Istiqlal* (18 May 1922).
20   Al-Basir (1924): 232–236.
21   Al-Basir (1924), second page of unpaginated preface.
22   'Abd al-Husayn (1933): 14–18.
23   Faydi (1952): 269–273.
24   Al-Hasani (1953–61) I: 69–70.
25   Based upon a reprint of the 1974 edition, al-Hasani (1988) I: 100–105.
26   Batatu (1978): 188–189, 328–329. The related developments of 1922 discussed by Batatu on p. 118 are covered in chapter 8. Luizard (1995) is based on Batatu.
27   *Ibid.*: 329.
28   Al-Tamimi (1979): 632–648.
29   *Ibid.*: 586.
30   Barakat (1980): 232, 233–234 n. 5.
31   Al-Suwaydi (1987): 117.
32   Al-Pachachi (1989): 36–41.

33   Al-'Umar (1989): 390–393 is a pot-pourri of quotes from the works discussed above and concludes that the separatist movement "did not represent the people of Basra". On the contrary, "nationalists" and "educated citizens" (*muthaqqafun*) had united against a separatist petition organised by people who had profited from the British wartime regime.

34   *Al-Zaman*, Basra edition (11 January 2004, 19 April 2004).

35   CO/537/819 (18699): Cox to Churchill (13 April 1921).

36   CO/730/2 (28897): Cox to Churchill (29 June 1921).

37   GB (12 April 1921, 23 June 1921).

38   CO/730/2 (32697): J.H. Hall's minutes (1 July 1921).

39   CO/537/819 (18699): J.E. Shuckburgh's minutes (19 April 1921).

40   CO/730/2 (32697): Hall's minutes (1 July 1921).

41   CO/730/1 (13125): Bullard's minutes (21 March 1921).

42   CO/537/819 (18699): H.W. Young's minutes (18 April 1921).

43   CO/730/2 (32697): Young's minutes (5 July 1921); CO/730/3 (33549): Draft telegram; CO/730/3 (34298): Young's minutes (18 July 1921).

44   CO/730/3 (33549): Churchill's minutes (9 July 1921), (34298): Bullard's minutes (18 July 1921).

45   *Basrah* (19 June 1921).

46   CO/730/3 (33549): Churchill to Cox (9 July 1921).

47   Balfour papers 303/1: A.T. Wilson to F.C.C. Balfour (20 October 1921), enclosure of excerpt of letter to Wilson from a political officer in the occupied territories (anonymised by Wilson).

48   CO/730/2 (32697): Bullard's minutes (4 July 1921); CO/730/3 (34955): Bullard's minutes (15 July 1921).

49   CO/537/819 (18699): Cox to Churchill (13 April 1921); GB (12 April 1921).

50   *IGG* (March 1921).

51   Philby (1948): 195–201.

52   Philby papers VIII (*Mesopotage* manuscript): 456, 503, 514.

53   Philby (1948): 201; Philby papers VIII (*Mesopotage* manuscript): 588.

54   GB (26 June 1921).

55   GB (30 June 1921, 7 July 1921).

56   Philby (1948): 201–202; GB (19 June 1921, 7 July 1921).

57   GB (5 June 1921, 10 July 1921); al-Wardi (1969–79) VI: 76.

58   Philby (1948): 199–203; Philby papers VIII (*Mesopotage* manuscript): 593–594.

59   GB (12 April 1921); Philby (1948): 196–197. French sources based on discussions with Philby corroborate this point, MAE/Irak/18: E.L.H. Chauvet to A. Briand (18 April 1921).

60   Philby (1948): 186–187.

61   Philby papers XII: Pocket diary 1921. His last visit to Basra prior to this was in February 1921.

62   Philby papers VIII (*Mesopotage* manuscript): 482, 496.

63   Al-Sani' (1985–89) I: 235–236, 269–270; al-Haydari (1962): 170; al-Qahwati (1980): 294.

64   Al-Shaykh Khaz'al (1962–70) II: 236–237; FO/195/2367: F.E. Crow to G.A. Lowther (25 February 1911); Faydi (1998): 155–156.

65   Al-Hasani (1988) I: 46; GB (29 November 1920, 4 December 1920).

66   IO/L/PS/11/192 (P244): Cox to India Office (11 December 1920).

67   Y/MTV/301/61: General Tahir to Yıldız (6 Ağustos 1323/19 August 1907); BEO/VGG/264 (21 Haziran 1314/3 July 1898); FO/195/2243: J. Ramsay to N.R. O'Conor (30 November 1907); FO/195/2339: F.E. Crow to G.A. Lowther (27 May 1910); al-Qahwati (1980): 290; information supplied by Aga Ja'far's granddaughter, Tamara Agha-Jaffar.

68   Al-Qahwati (1980): 295; FO/195/2116: A.C. Wratislaw to N.R. O'Conor (8 October 1902); *Commercial and Trades Directory of Iraq* (1925): 27; information supplied by Meer S. Basri and David Sagiv.

69   FO/195/2368: W.D.W. Matthews to G.A. Lowther (18 August 1911); Faydi (1998): 87; *IRP* (1917): 2.
70   'Abdallah (1978): 26–27; al-'Azzawi (1935–56) VII: 145–151, 221, VIII: 19; al-Nabhani (1925): 96–99, 108–109; Rogan (1996): 89, 97–98, 106 n. 46; Faydi (1998): 126–127.
71   *AR Qurna* (1916–17, 1919); General Staff (1923): 353.
72   CO/730/3 (41185): Cox to Churchill (12 July 1921).
73   GB (15 May 1921).
74   Al-Ansari (1969): 23–25. *Bash al-a'yan* (Ottoman: *baş-i ayan* or *başayan*) literally means "chief of the notables", and although the importance of this seventeenth-century honorific later diminished, it still made sense to a Basrawi in Istanbul in the late nineteenth century to sign a petition using the title "son-in-law of the *basha'yan* of Basra vilayet" as a way of underlining his own importance, Y/PRK/AZJ/30/121: Ibrahim Effendi to Yıldız (6 Mart 1311/18 March 1895).
75   Basha'yan (1890); *Lughat al-'Arab* (1913–14): 56–68, 676; al-'Abbasi (1961): 102–103; Ra'uf (1983): 295; al-Basri (1949): 15–16; Barakat (1977): 25–27; *IRP* (1917): 16–17.
76   WO/157/778: Intelligence summary (19 August 1915); al-'Abbasi (1961): 103
77   Al-'Azzawi (1937–56) IV: 192; BHCF/7/15/3/II: AI (15 April 1922).
78   IO/L/PS/10/839: AI (24 July 1920); *Awqat* (18 October 1922).
79   DH/ID/79/19: 'Umar Fawzi to Ministry of Interior (15 Temmuz 1328/28 July 1912); Barakat (1977): 38–45; Faydi (1998): 133, 155; 'Ali (1981): 88.
80   Al-Ward (1978): 78–79; Muhsin and 'Aliwi (1989): 696–697; Barakat (1977): 31–36; al-Hasani (1957): 54, 56.
81   *BSAL* (1318/1900): 288; *SAL* (1328/1910): 611, (1333–34/1914–15): 562; IO/L/PS/10/534: *Note verbale* from the Ottoman government (7 June 1916); Faydi (1998): 73; *Awqat* (17 May 1922).
82   Al-'Umari (1955): 137–146; Basri (1987): 167; Faydi (1998): 122–123.
83   IO/L/PS/10/622 (P7537): G.V.B. Gillan to A.T. Wilson (24 July 1920); IO/L/PS/11/192 (P8050): Cox to India Office (11 December 1920); Ireland (1937): 296–297.
84   CO/730/1: IR (15 April 1921).
85   FO/371/5230(124561): Note by I.N. Clayton (22 August 1920).
86   GB (1 November 1920, 24 February 1921).
87   Al-Wardi (1969–79) VI: 56–62.
88   GB (12 April 1921).
89   GB (17 April 1921); Sluglett (1976): 93 n. 4.
90   GB (12 April 1921).
91   GB (23 June 1921).
92   FO/248/1249 (Mesopotamian affairs, 29): A.S. Meek to A.T. Wilson (21 December 1918).
93   GB (29 November 1920).
94   GB (28 August 1921).
95   CO/537/819 (18699): Cox to Churchill (13 April 1921).
96   Al-Bazi (1970): 40–41; al-Nabhani (1923): 331; Barakat (1984): 126–129.
97   Y/PRK/ASK/237/75: Ministry of War to Yıldız (26 Şubat 1321/11 March 1906); FO/195/2139: F.E. Crow to N.R. O'Conor (4 November 1903); FO/195/2242: Crow to O'Conor (22 February 1907).
98   Al-Wardi (1969–79) III: 62; Faydi (1998): 66; al-Khalidi (1981): 201–202.
99   GB (14 June 1920).
100   *IGG* (February 1921).
101   CO/730/3 (41185): Cox to Churchill (12 July 1921).
102   *IRP* (1917): 45; al-Sani' (1985–89) I: 236; Van Ess (1961): 67–68. See also chapter 3.
103   Jwaideh (1953): 155 n. 1.
104   FO/248/1249 (Mesopotamian affairs, 29): A.S. Meek to A.T. Wilson (21 December 1918).
105   BHCF/7/15/3/I: AI (4 June 1921).

106 BHCF/7/15/3/I: AI (21 May 1921); Hirz al-Din (1964–65) II: 71–72; al-Matba'i (1995–98) III: 167; al-Khaqani (1954) I: 396.

107 The following account is based on newspaper reports from *Awqat* (26 June 1921, 27 June 1921).

108 'Abd al-Husayn (1933): 16–17; al-Wardi (1969–79) VI: 86; al-Tamimi (1979): 642–643.

109 Van Ess (1943): 172. On his work in Basra, see Van Ess (1974); Scudder (1998): 165–166.

110 MAE/Irak/18: E.L.H. Chauvet to A. Briand (1 July 1921, 13 September 1921).

111 GB (30 June 1921); al-Tamimi (1979): 629.

Chapter 7

1 CO/730/33 (4465): Memorandum by H.W. Young (28 January 1922); CO/730/20 (13465): P.Z Cox to W.S. Churchill (3 March 1922). The reply was informally communicated to Mandil in January 1922, but apparently never officially issued.

2 Dickson (1949): 272–275; Olson (1989): 82–85; Eskander (2001).

3 CO/730/40 (22919): H. Dobbs to the Duke of Devonshire (5 May 1923).

4 CAB/27/206: Report by Iraq committee (23 March 1923).

5 CO/730/41 (43904): Young's minutes (12 September 1923).

6 Yapp (1987): 331–333.

7 CO/730/73 (15758): Draft report (6 April 1925).

8 Grayson (1997): 224–230.

9 BHCF/27/38: W.C.F.A. Wilson to K. Cornwallis (16 December 1922).

10 *AR* (1921): 1.

11 *AR* (1921): 9.

12 CO/730/21 (19350): Cox to Churchill (22 April 1922); CO/730/23 (40582): Cox to Churchill (1 August 1922); House of Commons (31 May 1922).

13 CO/730/21 (19350): Young's minutes (25 April 1922), Churchill to Cox (27 April 1922); CO/730/23 (40582): Young's minutes (15 August 1922), Churchill to Cox (19 August 1922).

14 IO/L/PS/10/919 (P2494): Cox to Churchill (14 June 1922).

15 CO/730/40: IR (15 May 1923).

16 *Basrah* (15 August 1922).

17 Cox papers: Curzon to Cox (3 January 1922); CAB/23/31: Cabinet conclusions (15 September 1922); Ireland (1937): 377–378; Sluglett (1976): 79–80.

18 CO/730/64 (57600): R.V. Vernon's minutes (14 January 1925). See also Raglan (1925): 481–482.

19 CO/730/40 (30136): Young's minutes (16 June 1923).

20 CO/730/58 (12946): Dobbs to J. Thomas (5 March 1924).

21 CAB/23/48: Cabinet conclusions (1 May 1924).

22 Marrs (1918): 20; al-Sani' (1985–89) I: 80–82, 97–103, 106–107; al-Shaykh Khaz'al (1962–70) II: 264–265; al-Rubay'i (1978): 73.

23 Marrs (1918): 21; *IRP* (1917): 32.

24 Bowman papers: Diary (22 August 1918); *AR* (1919): 23.

25 As quoted in Philby (1922): 240.

26 This quotation as well as the subsequent ones are taken from BHCF/27/195: Shaykh Ibrahim to Cox (2 Jumada al-Akhira 1339/10 February 1921, 11 Sha'ban 1339/20 April 1921). Ibrahim's analogy to Kuwait is known also from other sources, see al-Shaykh Khaz'al (1962–70) IV: 78.

27 BHCF/27/195: Undated petition, received around April 1921.

28 Several undated petitions from inhabitants of Zubayr were received by British authorities between March and April 1921, BHCF/27/195.

29 *Al-Awqat al-Basriyya* (20 February 1921).

30   Some of the families now campaigning against Ibrahim had tried to persuade the British to restore the shaykhship to their own candidate since the early days of the occupation, BHCF/27/195: Cox to 'Abd al-Karim al-Mishri (10 May 1915).

31   Al-Ansari (1969): 23.

32   Raunkiær (1913): 24–26, 63, 269; General Staff (1923): 37–38.

33   Al-Sani' (1985–89) IV: 160. For early twentieth-century views on the potential of Umm Qasr, see Schofield (1993): 25, 29, 76, 78; Anscombe (1997): 129.

34   On Zubayr families involved in Basra trade, see al-Sani' (1985–89) II: 242–244.

35   *BSAL* (1308/1890): 77, (1318/1900): 288; al-Sani' (1985–89) III: 43; *Lughat al-'Arab* (1913–14): 388.

36   BEO/VGG/263 (7 Eylul 1310/20 September 1894).

37   DH/KMS/33/20: Sulayman al-Zuhayr to Ministry of Interior (26 Haziran 1331/9 July 1915); CO/730/2: W.C.F.A. Wilson to Cox (14 June 1921); Tu'ma (1984): 361–362.

38   CO/730/4: IR (15 August 1921); *Basrah* (29 July 1921).

39   *Awqat* (21 August 1921).

40   On the procedure for appointing the council, see BHCF/8/151: C.J. Edmonds to Dobbs (6 October 1925).

41   *Basrah* (2 November 1921, 13 July 1922, 12 July 1923); BHCF/7/23/58: E.S. Berry to K. Cornwallis (16 September 1928).

42   *Awqat* (16 December 1924); BHCF/7/23/58: Berry to Cornwallis (16 September 1928); al-Bazi (1970): 37.

43   Another key member of the council with a minority background was 'Abd al-Nabi Mir Mu'allim, the Jewish executive clerk (*mudir tahrirat*) who had held a similar position during the Ottoman regime, Basri (1983–93) I: 62–63; Jawdat (1967): 190–192.

44   Sayyid 'Abd 'Ali remained mayor in Qurna until 1926, AIR/23/272: SSO-Basra (3 April 1926), and one of the sons of Taha al-Salman was *mudir* in Hartha from 1922 to 1926, *IGG* (15 March 1922, 15 April 1926).

45   BHCF/27/195: AHC to G.V.B. Gillan (9 March 1921).

46   BHCF/27/195: Gillan to AHC (3 March 1921).

47   BHCF/27/195: Cox to W.C.F.A. Wilson (19 April 1921); Cox to Shaykh Ibrahim (23 April 1921).

48   BHCF/27/195: Cox to Shaykh Ibrahim (6 June 1921).

49   The opinion of the Basra authorities was conveyed to Cox by the Ministry of Interior, BHCF/27/195 (5 August 1921).

50   *IGG* (15 September 1921); al-Sani' (1985–89) I: 175–178; BHCF/27/195: Shaykh Ibrahim to Cox (13 December 1921).

51   BHCF/27/195: Cornwallis to Cox (21 April 1923), W.C.F.A. Wilson to Cornwallis (3 February 1925); *Awqat* (21 April 1925).

52   AIR/20/533: SSO-Basra (25 November 1921).

53   AIR/20/533: Cornwallis to Cox (10 January 1922).

54   AIR/20/533: W.C.F.A. Wilson to Cornwallis (8 November 1921); SSO-Basra (10 December 1921).

55   AIR/20/533: B.H. Bourdillon to GHQ (10 January 1922).

56   AIR/20/533: RAF-Basra to AHQ (16 January 1922).

57   CO/730/19: IR (15 January 1922, 1 February 1922).

58   *Awqat* (4 January 1922).

59   BHCF/7/15/3: AI (19 August 1922, 3 February 1923, 3 March 1923).

60   *Basrah* (1 March 1922).

61   *Awqat* (7 April 1922).

62   *Awqat* (3 November 1922).

63   *Awqat* (7 February 1922).

64   All the speeches delivered during the reception for Rihani have been reproduced in Butti (1923): 162–180.

65   On the emergence of "pro-Eastern" or "pan-Asian" currents in the late Ottoman Empire, see
      Worringer (2004).
66   *Awqat* (2 October 1922); BHCF/7/15/3/III: (27 January 1923). On Dawudi, see Basri (1994)
      II: 376–377; al-Matbaʻi (1995–98) I: 67.
67   FO/371/7772: IR (1 December 1922); CO/730/40: IR (1 June 1923).
68   Retrospects in BHCF/7/23/58: Berry to Cornwallis (16 September 1928).
69   Details of scenes of the procession were given in an advertisement by a local photographer
      who produced a series of images of the event, *Basrah* (27 August 1923).
70   *Basrah* (14 August 1924); *Awqat* (15 August 1924). The consulate was also instrumental in
      establishing a Persian school in Basra, *Awqat* (4 May 1923); al-Barrak (1984): 110.
71   CO/730/77: IR (6 August 1925).
72   See textual excerpts in al-Wardi (1969–1979) VI: 201–204. Claims about Shiʻi separatism
      after the First World War have sometimes been made on the basis of a quotation from Elie
      Kedourie in Vinogradov (1972): 124, referring to "the establishment of a Shiʻa state inde-
      pendent from the rest of Iraq". But the original source, Kedourie (1959): 62, renders no terri-
      torial specificity to the revolt at all. It relates to a demand for a "theocratic government"
      more generally, and is in fact a translation into French of an easily available British report.
73   *Awqat* (29 January 1923); *RAI* (1926): 125–126.
74   Retrospects in *Awqat* (15 December 1921, 4 June 1922).
75   *Awqat* (15 December 1921).
76   Al-Khalidi (1981): 214–215, 217–218; al-Suhrawardi (1933) II: 377–380, 416–417.
77   Al-Khalidi (1981): 192–195.
78   Al-Khalidi (1981): 172–175.
79   Al-Saniʻ (1985–89) III: 271; al-Humaydan (1996): 64.
80   *Awqat* (4 January 1923); al-Khalidi (1981): 175–177.
81   *Awqat* (12 August 1922).
82   Al-Saniʻ (1985–89) III: 273–274, 278.
83   *Lughat al-ʻArab* (1928–29): 276. Hanbali *fiqh* (jurisprudence) was among the subjects
      taught at the school, al-Saniʻ (1985–89) III: 278. On Shinqiti, see al-Khalidi (1981): 95–96,
      100.
84   Al-Khalidi (1981): 218; al-Saniʻ (1985–89) III: 272.
85   *Neglected Arabia* 86 (1913); Scudder (1998): 245–246; al-Hilali (1959): 204.
86   *Neglected Arabia* 89 (1914): 4. Among the pupils were the sons of separatist leaders such as
      Saniʻ and Mandil; the children of both Shaykh Khazʻal of Muhammara and Sayyid Talib;
      members of the prominent Shiʻi landowning ʻAtiyya family of Qurna; and youth from the
      local Christian and Jewish communities. Al-Hilw (1969–72) III: 61; CO/730/38: IR (1 Feb-
      ruary 1923); biographical article on ʻAbdallah al-Saniʻ in *Awqat* (9 November 1931); Batatu
      (1978): 488; Scudder (1998): 246.
87   *Neglected Arabia* 144 (1928): 9, 148 (1929): 15; *Awqat* (5 May 1925).
88   Van Ess (1943): 172–174; Van Ess (1974): 113.
89   *Neglected Arabia* 137 (1926): 13.
90   Van Ess (1974): 112–113, 118; GB (24 February 1921).
91   *Neglected Arabia* 161 (1932): 10; Van Ess (1974): 117.
92   *Neglected Arabia* 137 (1926): 13, 149 (1929): 11.
93   For an overview of the historiography of this revolt, see Popovic (1999): 159–188.
94   Kennedy (1986): 287–292.
95   Many of the available sources on this period are mentioned in al-Hamdani (1984); Gibb
      (1960). For an overview of the period, see Longrigg (1925): 99–119.
96   Sumer was casually referred to as *shummar* in the contemporary Arabic press, *Awqat* (10
      March 1924). The exact location of Characene remains unknown today although a point be-
      tween Basra and Qurna is suggested by historians, Hansman (1967): 42; Schuol (2002):
      198–199.

97   On the background of this publication, see Diskin (1971): 297 n.1. For Karmali, see Basri
      (1994) I: 267–268.
98   Al-Karmali (1919): 22.
99   *Basrah* (8 March 1925).
100   A historiography of Ottoman works on this region is provided in Longrigg (1925): 327–330.
      The local notables held copies of some manuscripts written from pro-Ottoman perspectives,
      for instance the works of 'Abd al-Ghaffar al-Akhras (circa 1805–1874). See al-Madamagha
      (1981): 129, al-Wa'ili (1961): 255–258 and al-'Azzawi (1949): 4–6 for Akhras's back-
      ground.
101   Nazmi Zade (1730): 248.
102   Ibn al-Ghamlas (1962): 57; *BSAL* (1318/1900): 182, 196.
103   Al-Karmali (1919): 200–203.
104   Tavernier (1678) II: 88–89; La Boullaye Le Gouz (1657): 291–293; de Thévenot (1727) IV:
      557–584; Murray (1820) I: 395.
105   Browne (1902–24) IV: 354, 363.
106   Al-Khaqani (1961–62) I: 46, II: 9, 75.
107   Basha'yan's role in publishing this material is emphasised in the preface to the book, al-
      Ka'bi (1924): 2.
108   Al-Ka'bi (1924): 3.
109   *Ibid.*:18–20.
110   *Ibid.*: 38–39, 43.
111   See particularly the passages in al-Ka'bi (1924): 18–20. Outside Basra, two copies of the
      manuscript, dating from 1799 and 1824 respectively, have been preserved in the British Li-
      brary (ADD 23,450 and 23,451), and the discussion of the editing of the manuscript is based
      on comparisons between these two and al-Ka'bi (1924). According to Colin Baker at the
      Arabic section of the British Library, the two manuscripts were bought by the British Mu-
      seum around 1860.
112   Al-Karmali (1919): 10, 17–18.
113   *Awqat* (1 August 1922).
114   Iraq Museum (1926): 1; GB (9 June 1926).
115   Dougherty (1927): 2, 73–74.

Chapter 8

1   *AR* (1921): 14; *Basrah* (23 December 1922); LN/MAN/S1630 (4): Note on revenue affairs,
      undated, around 1927.
2   *RAI* (special report for the period 1920–31): 216; Dowson (1921) I: 42; statistics from *AR*
      Customs (1923–28).
3   *RAI* (1923–24): 57–58, 60; *Awqat* (5 March 1925); Barakat (1984): 390–391.
4   *Basrah* (25 June 1923); *RAI* (1925): 36.
5   *Awqat* (2 December 1922).
6   *RAI* (1928): 129.
7   CO/730/145/11: G.F. Clayton to L.S. Amery (29 April 1929).
8   *Basrah* (11 July 1922); Geere (1916): 22.
9   *Awqat* (25 August 1922, 20 April 1923).
10   AIR/23/273: SSO-Basra (6 June 1926); al-Badr (1987): Chapter entitled *al-'awda ila al-*
      basra (unpaginated Internet edition).
11   General Staff (1923): 388–391.
12   Al-Hasani (1988) I: 75.
13   Retrospect in CO/730/64 (57600): W. Ayton's minutes (January 1925); FO/371/6353: IR (1
      October 1921); T/161/959 (11146/1): S.H. Slater to P.Z. Cox (27 March 1922).

14 T/161/959 (11146/1): C.C. Garbett to J.E. Shuckburgh (6 June 1921); FO/624/40: E.J.W. Slade to Cox (5 April 1922).
15 CO/730/21 (15891): Cox to W.S. Churchill (2 April 1922); al-Hasani (1988) I: 82–88, 101.
16 Al-Hasani (1988) I: 83.
17 CO/730/21: IR (15 April 1922).
18 CO/730/25: IR (1 October 1922).
19 Dickson (1949): 274–275.
20 Dickson papers 2A/4B: Note by H.R.P. Dickson (30 September 1922).
21 *Awqat* (30 December 1922).
22 *Basrah* (29 June 1923, 30 June 1923); CO/730/42: IR (20 September 1923).
23 *Awqat* (6 March 1924).
24 CO/730/58: IR (17 April 1924).
25 FO/371/10094 (E4350/232): H. Dobbs to J. Thomas (11 May 1924).
26 CO/730/60: IR (12 June 1924).
27 *Basrah* (20 June 1924); CO/730/62: IR (2 October 1924).
28 CO/730/59: IR (1 May 1924). See also al-Hasani (1988) I: 219.
29 Al-Adhami (1989) II: 310; CO/730/59: IR (15 May 1924).
30 Al-Hasani (1988) I: 236.
31 Al-Hasani (1988) I: 101.
32 *Al-Istiqlal* (18 June 1922); *al-Mufid* (19 June 1922, 24 June 1922); Batatu (1978): 118; GB (22 June 1922); al-Basir (1924): 238–239.
33 AIR/23/546: Mutasarrif Muntafiq to Ministry of Interior (11 August 1923).
34 *AR* (1921): 9, CO/730/20: Cox to Churchill (3 March 1922).
35 MAE/Irak/20: Vicomte de La Panouse to A. Maginot (13 July 1922).
36 *Al-Istiqlal* (18 May 1922).
37 CO/730/40: IR (15 May 1923); Longrigg (1953): 148.
38 BHCF/7/15/3: AI (19 January 1924, 26 January 1924).
39 Al-Hilw (1972): 129.
40 *Awqat* (20 May 1925).
41 CO/730/75: IR (28 May 1925). See also résumé in *Basrah* (5 June 1925).
42 *Awqat* (27 May 1925).
43 *Awqat* (28 May 1925).
44 *Awqat* (29 May 1925).
45 *Al-Rafidan* (22 May 1922); BHCF/7/15/3: AI (25 March 1922, 9 September 1922).
46 GB (28 August 1921); *Awqat* (25 August 1921); al-Pachachi (1989): 49.
47 CO/730/57: IR (21 February 1924).
48 CO/730/60: IR (12 June 1924).
49 *Awqat* (2 April 1923, 21 April 1925). The anti-treaty activities of one of the organisations supported by Shamkhani are covered in al-Tamimi (1996): 198; for Hashimi, see Marr (1985): 65.
50 *Awqat* (24 April 1923, 5 August 1925).
51 *Awqat* (6 March 1924); retrospect in AIR/23/275: SSO-Basra (31 March 1928); al-'Umari (1955): 138–139.
52 CO/730/61: IR (8 August 1924).
53 *Awqat* (15 August 1922).
54 *Awqat* (28 September 1922).
55 *Awqat* (9 September 1924); Basri (1994) II: 389.
56 'Abdallah (1978): 45–47.
57 GB (25 May 1922).
58 *Awqat* (6 March 1924).
59 *Awqat* (15 March 1923, 20 April 1923).
60 Almana (1980): 191.
61 CO/730/37: IR (1 January 1923).

62 CO/730/21 (13552): Sketch map (1922).

63 *Awqat* (15 January 1922, 23 February 1922, 14 March 1922).

64 CO/730/4: IR (15 August 1921); CO/730/42 (49230): Dobbs to the Duke of Devonshire (22 September 1923).

65 For this system of seasonal migrations, see Ansari (1974): 25–26. Attempts were made to enhance border control in 1922, but the new regulations were ignored for many years, *Basrah* (19 July 1922); *AR Customs* (1923–24): 5–6; retrospect in CO/730/132/2: Dobbs to C. Empson (20 February 1928).

66 Faydi papers: Declaration of loyalty from tribesmen of Khaz'al (15 Muharram 1343/16 August 1924).

67 Al-Najjar (1971): 317.

68 *Awqat* (23 October 1921).

69 *Awqat* (14 May 1925); AIR/23/269: SSO-Basra (31 May 1925); retrospect in AIR/23/275: SSO-Basra (21 April 1928).

70 CO/730/76: IR (9 July 1925).

71 FO/371/10833: IR (25 June 1925).

72 CO/730/78: IR (3 September 1925).

73 Examples of Basrawis who in the second half of the 1920s began participating within the Iraqi system are given in al-Adhami (1978): 190; Shubbar (1989): 107–108, 310; *Awqat* (29 May 1927).

74 FO/371/10143: Dobbs to the Duke of Devonshire (24 November 1923); *Awqat* (27 October 1922).

75 CO/730/75: IR (28 May 1925); FO/248/1373: Mushar al-Mulk to P. Loraine (17 June 1925).

76 FO/460/5 (25): Karguzar Khuzistan to Dr. Lincoln (27 July 1925); *ibid.*: Note on interview with Haji Ya'qub ibn Haji Adhbi (July 1925).

77 Al-Hilw (1969–72) III: 64–65, V: 12–15; *Awqat* (30 July 1925); AIR/23/270: SSO-Basra (25 July 1925).

78 CO/730/75: IR (28 May 1925); FO/460/5 (25): Note by A.T. Wilson (24 July 1925).

79 *Awqat* (1 May 1925); CO/730/75: IR (14 May 1925).

80 AIR/23/263: SSO-Baghdad (16 December 1925); CO/730/105/1: IR (24 December 1925).

81 GB (1 April 1924). On Mustafa Kemal as a hero for Iraqi youth, see Simon (1986): 103.

82 Al-Hasani (1988) II: 45.

83 Shubbar (1989): 112–113; al-Hasani (1988) II: 60–62, 82–83; al-Adhami (1978): 202.

84 Among the Basra supporters of Gaylani were Amin 'Ali Basha'yan, while Shamkhani and 'Abbud al-Mallak continued to follow Hashimi, CO/730/107/68: IR (24 November 1925); AIR/23/274: SSO-Basra (6 November 1926).

85 Retrospect in BHCF/7/23/58: E.S. Berry to K. Cornwallis (16 September 1928); *IGG* (15 January 1927).

86 *Basrah* (12 December 1926); AIR/23/274: SSO-Basra (2 January 1927, 9 January 1927, 15 January 1927).

87 Jawdat (1967): 190–192; BHCF/7/23/60: R.F. Jardine to Cornwallis (28 October 1928).

88 For developments concerning the *qa'im-maqam*ate of Abu al-Khasib, see *IGG* (4 June 1927, 2 July 1927). A career official of northern origin had been installed at Qurna already in the summer of 1925, and in accordance with the practice of frequent reshuffling of administrative officials, was in 1927 replaced by an official who had previously served in Baghdad, *IGG* (31 August 1925, 9 July 1927). Similar developments took place in Zubayr in this period, *IGG* (16 July 1927); al-Sani' (1985–89) I:179–180.

89 *Awqat* (1 May 1926, 3 May 1926).

Chapter 9

1 *Awqat* (26 May 1925); CO/730/74: IR (16 April 1925).

2   BHCF/7/15/3/VI: AI (20 May 1926); *Awqat* (3 June 1925).
3   *Awqat* (15 July 1926); *Basrah* (21 July 1926); al-Khalili (1963) II: 20–21, 208–209; see also al-Zanjani (1967): 289–91.
4   AIR/23/432: SSO-Basra (19 November 1927).
5   AIR/23/432: SSO-Basra (12 November 1927, 3 December 1927); AIR/23/274: SSO-Basra (26 March 1927).
6   BHCF/7/15/3/VII: AI (8 October 1927); AIR/23/275: SSO-Basra (15 October 1927); al-Khalili (1963) II: 205–210.
7   AIR/23/274: SSO-Basra (12 February 1927).
8   Al-'Umari (1969): 160–162.
9   AIR/23/274: SSO-Basra (6 March 1927). Many studies on Iraqi Shi'ism (and certainly the majority of studies whose authors are themselves Shi'is) tend to bypass the 1927 sectarian strife. Ende (1978 and 1979) are important exceptions.
10 Key references to the vision of a decentralised (or divided) Iraq are FO/371/12259 (E3220): Note by H. Dobbs (27 June 1927); FO/371/12264: IR (5 July 1927); CO/730/123/10: Extract of letter from E.L. Ellington (4 October 1927); FO/371/12265: IR (1 October 1927); BHCF/7/15/3: AI (1 October 1927, 12 November 1927); AIR/23/267: SSO-Baghdad (19 December 1927).
11 BHCF/7/15/3: AI (2 July 1927).
12 AIR/23/432: SSO-Baghdad (23 August 1927).
13 BHCF/7/15/3: AI (18 June 1927); AIR/23/267: SSO-Baghdad (19 December 1927).
14 AIR/23/267: SSO-Baghdad (19 December 1927). For Sharqi, see al-Khalili (1963) II: 48–84; Nakash (1994): 113–114.
15 *Lughat al-'Arab* (1926–27): 526–530, 575–579, (1927–28): 535–539 and (1928–29): 275–279, on which the subsequent discussion is based.
16 AIR/23/432: SSO-Basra (17 December 1927).
17 The *ma'tam* of one of the families which played a leading role in the Nahda party is described in al-Kutubi (1951): 50–51.
18 *Awqat* (11 July 1927); *Basrah* (17 July 1927).
19 AIR/23/432: SSO-Basra (25 August 1927). On this newspaper, see Butti (1955): 106–109.
20 *Awqat* (28 February 1927); AIR/23/274: SSO-Basra (12 February 1927, 6 March 1927).
21 AIR/23/432: SSO-Basra (27 November 1927).
22 *Lughat al-'Arab* (1926–27): 527, (1928–29): 279; al-Sharqi (1929): 5–47; al-Khalili (1963) II: 59.
23 AIR/23/275 (17 December 1927); Batatu (1978): 328–329.
24 AIR/23/432: SSO-Basra (9 July 1927).
25 Ende (1978): 26–29; al-Qazwini (1923): 186–191. As a result of the disagreement between Muzaffar and Qazwini, only the Shi'is of 'Ashar (where Muzaffar had the upper hand) celebrated Muharram with processions in 1927, see *Awqat* (11 July 1927); *Basrah* (17 July 1927).
26 See for instance al-Qazwini (1928): 392–395.
27 BHCF/7/15/3/VIII: AI (3 March 1928); AIR/23/275: SSO-Basra (5 November 1927).
28 The Nahda candidates failed to transform their increased popularity into electoral success in Basra as well, *Awqat* (10 May 1928, 11 May 1928); Edmonds papers 26: Diary (4 May 1928).
29 AIR/23/267: SSO-Basra (20 August 1927).
30 Descriptions of the agitation in Zubayr are given in BHCF/7/15/3/VII: AI (1 October 1927); AIR/23/267: SSO-Basra (20 August 1927, 17 September 1927); AIR/23/275: SSO-Basra (22 October 1927).
31 *Awqat* (3 May 1926).
32 Almana (1980): 187–191.

33   *Basrah* (7 December 1926); CO/730/126/6: Dobbs to L.S. Amery (19 January 1928); Wahba
     (1960): 89–91. For examples of pro-Saudi movements elsewhere in the Gulf, see Wilkinson
     (1987): 267.
34   Al-Hasani (1988) I: 81; AIR/23/272: SSO-Basra (24 November 1925).
35   *Awqat* (17 November 1927); al-Hasani (1988) II: 108–109; AIR/23/276: SSO-Basra (15
     June 1928, 10 December 1928).
36   Al-Hasani (1988) II: 162–163; Glubb (1960): 193; *Awqat* (30 May 1927).
37   CO/730/116/12: Extract from *al-'Iraq* (17 August 1927); al-Hasani (1988) II: 112.
38   Glubb (1960): 191–192; al-Nabhani (1925): 13–14; Ingham (1986): 19–20.
39   BHCF/7/15/3/VII: AI (22 October 1927).
40   Almana (1980): 240; AIR/23/274: SSO-Basra (6 November 1926).
41   AIR/23/267: SSO-Basra (5 June 1927); Dickson (1949): 276–277.
42   A detailed account of these events is given in CO/730/132/2: Note by C. Empson (1 March
     1928). See also *Awqat* (24 January 1928, 30 January 1928); BHCF/7/15/3/VIII: AI (26 May
     1928, 9 June 1928); CO/730/132/2: Dobbs to Amery (15 February 1928), on which the sub-
     sequent discussion is based.
43   On relations between Persia and Iraq in the late 1920s, see al-'Alawi (1989): 336.
44   BHCF/7/15/3/VIII: AI (11 August 1928). For some of the ulama involved, see Hirz al-Din
     (1964–65) II: 57–58, 153; al-Hilw (1969–72) I: 90.
45   BHCF/7/15/3/VIII: AI (18 August 1928); Edmonds papers 7/5: Note by C.J. Edmonds (11
     February 1927); AIR/23/276: SSO-Basra (4 July 1928); Khadduri (1951): 241.
46   *Awqat* (14 June 1928); CO/730/130/10: Dobbs to R.C. Parr (12 July 1928);
     BHCF/7/15/3/VIII: AI (23 June 1928); al-Bakka' (1987): 45.
47   CO/730/132/2: B.H. Bourdillon to Empson (18 February 1928).
48   Examples of this attitude are given in CO/730/60: IR (21 August 1924); FO/371/16011
     (E6888/4478): F. Humphrys to J. Simon (1 December 1932); Porath (1984): 76; Ahmad
     (1994): 197. Kashani-Sabet (1999) provides background to Persian perspectives on the dis-
     puted frontier areas. For attempts to construct a link between the border areas and pre-
     Islamic civilisations considered to belong to the sphere of ancient Persia, see Mirza Sayyid
     Ja'far Khan (1969): 51.
49   CO/730/132/2: Dobbs to Amery (3 March 1928); *RAI* (1928): 48–49.
50   *Awqat* (14 August 1928); AIR/23/276: SSO-Basra (2 August 1928).
51   AIR/23/106: SSO-Basra (26 July 1928, 27 July 1928); CO/730/130/10: Dobbs to Amery (14
     August 1928).
52   CO/730/132/2: Dobbs to Amery (7 August 1928).
53   AIR/23/106: SSO-Basra (2 August 1928).
54   *RAI* (1928): 40.
55   *RAI* (1927): 204–211.
56   AIR/23/267: SSO-Basra (12 June 1927); BHCF/7/15/3/VIII: AI (25 August 1928).
57   AIR/23/275: SSO-Basra (21 April 1928).
58   *Awqat* (16 July 1928, 11 October 1928).
59   *Basrah* (26 June 1928).
60   *RAI* (1926): 129.
61   *Awqat* (24 January 1929).
62   FO/371/10833: IR (20 August 1925); *Basrah* (11 January 1927); IO/L/PS/10/547 (P2400):
     Memorandum by C. Wills (11 January 1928).
63   Trade statistics are given in *AR Customs* (1923–28).
64   AIR/23/272: SSO-Basra (27 March 1926).
65   CO/730/145/11: G.F. Clayton to Amery (25 April 1929).
66   *Basrah* (18 June 1928); Faydi (1998b): 313–321.
67   AIR/23/271: SSO-Basra (3 October 1925).
68   *Awqat* (14 January 1927); AIR/23/274: SSO-Basra (22 January 1927).

69 BHCF/7/23/58: E.S. Berry to K. Cornwallis (16 September 1928). The enclosure to this despatch, framed as an annual report on personalities, had evidently been written around March 1928, shortly before the parliamentary elections.

70 *Awqat* (23 November 1927).

71 *Awqat* (20 May 1927, 29 June 1927); Barakat (1977): 98. *Al-fayha'* (literally, "the sweet-smelling") is an epithet of Basra.

72 *Awqat* (30 September 1924); al-Badr (1987): Chapter *bidayat al-'am al-dirasi al-jadid 1923–1924* (unpaginated Internet edition).

73 For examples of individual experiences, see al-Matba'i (1995–98) III: 142, 158, 234–235. See also Marr (1985b): 95 on how this centralisation affected all of Iraq.

74 *Awqat* (7 March 1926, 16 March 1926).

75 Dougherty (1927): 67-72, Dougherty (1927b): 157. The author later changed his theory and his focus moved away from the Basra region, Dougherty (1930): 19, Williams (1994).

76 AIR/23/276: SSO-Basra (10 December 1928); BHCF/7/15/3/VIII: AI (17 November 1928).

77 *Awqat* (29 July 1929).

78 *The Times* (16 October 1928): 15.

79 *Awqat* (11 May 1928); CO/730/145/11: Clayton to Amery (25 April 1929); AIR/23/276: SSO-Basra (10 December 1928).

80 BHCF/7/15/3/VIII: AI (8 September 1928); AIR/23/276: SSO-Basra (31 January 1929).

81 *Basrah* (7 November 1928, 23 November 1928, 28 November 1928); *Awqat* (6 November 1928); BHCF/7/15/3/VIII: AI (8 December 1928).

82 Al-Tamimi (1979): 648.

83 BHCF/7/15/3/V: AI (8 August 1925, 22 August 1925).

84 AIR/23/263: SSO-Baghdad (16 December 1925).

85 BHCF/7/23/58: Berry to Cornwallis (16 September 1928); Edmonds papers 26: Diary (29 July 1927).

86 Batatu (1978): 188–191.

87 Retrospect in *Awqat* (30 July 1929).

88 AIR/23/276: SSO-Basra (10 December 1928).

89 CO/730/148/1: Cabinet paper 214 by S.W. Passfield (1929); CO/730/151/5: J.E. Shuck-burgh's minutes (early January 1930).

90 CO/730/78(42269): Dobbs to Amery (16 September 1925); CO/730/105/5: Shuckburgh to Dobbs (13 January 1926) and Shuckburgh's minutes (16 December 1926); CO/730/120/1: Dobbs to Amery (14 June 1927).

91 Sluglett (1976): 156, 174 n. 43.

92 FO/371/12259 (E3220): Note by Dobbs (27 June 1927); CO/730/120/3: Note by Dobbs (20 November 1927).

93 BHCF/27/183: Office note, probably by Bourdillon, early 1928.

94 CO/730/124/6: Bourdillon to Amery (15 July 1927).

95 Al-Tamimi (1979): 647.

96 CO/730/145/11: Clayton to Amery (25 April 1929); BHCF/7/23/60: R.F. Jardine to Cornwallis (28 October 1928).

97 On the implementation of this strategy, see Silverfarb (1986), particularly pp. 23–32 on the British air bases.

98 CO/730/151/12: Humphrys to Passfield (11 June 1930).

99 On the RAF's promotion of "air policing" as a strategy to keep itself alive as an organisation, see Omissi (1990) where the phenomenon is discussed in an empire-wide context.

100 AIR/8/94: Note by H. Trenchard (June 1927).

101 AIR/8/94: Trenchard to Air Ministry (18 January 1929); CO/730/151/5: J.H. Hall's minutes (undated, around March 1930).

102 AIR/8/94: Note by E.L. Ellington (19 January 1929).

103 Al-Adhami (1978): 268.

104 CO/730/138/2: Note of a meeting at the Foreign Office (24 January 1929).

105 CO/730/148/8: Hall's minutes (6 September 1929).
106 CO/730/151/7: Hall's minutes (28 April 1930); CO/730/151/9: Hall's minutes (15 May 1930), CAB/27/206: Iraq Committee report (18 December 1922).
107 CO/730/151/7: Record of interdepartmental conference (30 April 1930); CO/730/151/9: Hall's minutes (15 May 1930).

Chapter 10

1   *Awqat* (5 September 1929); BHCF/7/15/3: AI (5 September 1929); CO/730/150/1: Translation of petition from Ja'far ibn 'Isa al-Muzaffar (25 November 1929).
2   AIR/23/277: SSO-Basra (4 September 1929, 11 September 1929, 1 October 1929). Some of the Basra participants were members of the Baghdad-based Hizb al-Istiqlal, see al-Tamimi (1996): 270.
3   AIR/23/276: SSO-Basra (5 January 1929); AIR/23/102: SSO-Basra (16 March 1929); Batatu (1978): 404–410.
4   AIR/23/276: SSO-Basra (8 April 1929).
5   AIR/23/276: SSO-Basra (23 April 1929); BHCF/7/15/3: AI (10 August 1929); 'Abbas (1969): 18–19.
6   *RAI* (1929): 14–15; 'Abdallah (1978): 320, 327.
7   *Awqat* (29 November 1929, 13 December 1930, 8 February 1932).
8   Faydi (1998): 410 n.1; AIR/23/276: SSO-Baghdad (26 July 1930).
9   *Awqat* (1 April 1930, 17 April 1930).
10 *Awqat* (24 July 1930).
11 *Basrah* (3 April 1931).
12 *Basrah* (5 April 1932).
13 *Awqat* (24 June 1924).
14 *Basrah* (11 June 1923).
15 On Abadan in this period, see Kasravi (1983): 215.
16 *Awqat* (30 August 1930); *Basrah* (13 January 1932, 13 October 1932).
17 *Basrah* (27 June 1930); *Awqat* (27 August 1932).
18 *RAI* (1930): 24–30; Stafford (1935): 89–98; Silverfarb (1986): 37; Fuccaro (1999b): 160–165; al-Hilw (1969–72) V: 30.
19 In the summer of 1930, "rumours" of separatism once more featured briefly in intelligence reports, but as earlier, local investigations failed to uncover anything substantial, BHCF/7/15/3/XI: AI (2 August 1930, 23 August 1930); *Near East and India* (7 August 1930).
20 AIR/23/277: SSO-Basra (23 July 1931); *Basrah* (17 July 1931, 23 July 1931); *Awqat* (17 July 1931).
21 Batatu (1978): 200–201.
22 Faydi (1998): 398 n.1; BHCF/7/15/3: AI (18 July 1931); retrospect in AIR/23/383: SSO-Basra (10 May 1932).
23 On Shi'i dominance of one of the local factions with a nationalist profile, see AIR/23/589: AI (30 September 1933).
24 *Basrah* (4 October 1932).
25 AIR/23/589: AI (2 September 1933).
26 See excerpts in Batatu (1978): 432–433.
27 For the episodic revival of separatist rumours related to Shi'is (chiefly in the Middle Euphrates area, well to the north of Basra), see AIR/23/589: AI (22 April 1933, 19 August 1933). Just as in 1927, the names of certain members of the lower ranks of the Shi'i clergy cropped up in relation to these kinds of episodes, see for instance al-Hilw (1969-72) V: 30. The position of Muhmmad Husayn Kashif al-Ghita' is particularly interesting: Whereas he in the 1920s had been involved in sectarian politics and still in 1930 allegedly claimed that

the Shi'is should work for "a purely Shi'i government in Shi'i areas", his subsequent rise in the hierarchy of ulama (aided by a deliberate policy by King Faysal to support him because of his Arab origin) was paralleled by a turn to pan-Islamist rhetoric. Although he later again became involved in Shi'i politics, there were few signs of his erstwhile separatist ideas and he focused instead on securing a more equitable share for the Shi'is in the government of Iraq. BHCF/7/15/3/XI: AI (26 July 1930); IO/L/PS/10/1313: IR (11 January 1932).

28   Al-Basri (1929): 2–5, 31.
29   LN/MIN/R2176 (35957): *Sawt min al-'iraq* (undated, circa August 1932).
30   *Awqat* (2 November 1929).
31   *Awqat* (26 September 1930).
32   *Awqat* (4 April 1932).
33   AIR/23/589: AI (23 December 1933).
34   *Basrah* (16 April 1931).
35   *Basrah* (9 March 1931, 6 October 1932).
36   *Basrah* (7 October 1931).
37   *Awqat* (17 August 1929).
38   Laftah (2003): 136.
39   *Awqat* (22 August 1932).
40   *Basrah* (17 April 1931, 18 May 1931).
41   Shabandar (1993): 255–256.
42   *Basrah* (8 October 1932).
43   *Awqat* (2 November 1932).
44   *Basrah* (22 May 1930, 16 June 1932); information from Tamara Agha-Jaffar.
45   *Awqat* (12 January 1931, 13 May 1932).
46   AIR/23/277: SSO-Basra (25 September 1931).
47   Al-Rusafi (1931): 472. On Rusafi, see al-Qaysi (1958): 185–205; Izzedien (1962): 16, 23–27, 45, 51–53.
48   For Basra representatives to Iraqi parliaments during the monarchy, see al-Hasani (1988) X: 292–314.
49   Byford (1935): 53.
50   *Awqat* (26 May 1931).
51   Al-'Umari (1955): 140–146.
52   Safwat (1988): 93; al-Pachachi (1989): 168.
53   Basra Date Board (1937).
54   Al-Khalidi (1981): 206–208 n.1; 'Awwad (1969) III: 511–512; Al Muhammad (1947–52): I and II.
55   'Abdallah (1978): 345–361.
56   BHCF/7/17/168: A.H. Ditchburn to K. Cornwallis (14 November 1931).
57   Dowson (1939): 258–259; Sluglett (1976): 251–252; Batatu (1978): 105–108, 133.
58   AIR/23/277: SSO-Basra (25 September 1931).
59   AIR/23/277: SSO-Basra (14 October 1931).
60   *Awqat* (15 January 1931).
61   AIR/23/589: AI (28 October 1933); AIR/23/590: *Political Gazette* (25 May 1935).
62   FO/624/4 (29 August 1935, 4 September 1935); WO/252/1195: *The Tribes of Iraq* (1942): 3–30.
63   Young (1934): 278–279; Dowson (1939): 253. On the development of the Iraqi education system in the 1930s and the nationalist message it promoted, see Simon (1986): 74–114.

Chapter 11

1   See Silverfarb (1986): 125, 133.
2   See the discussion in Hobsbawm (1977).

3   On these comparative examples, see Copland (1997): 97; Andaya & Andaya (2001): 235–237.

4   The term "drusitis" was derived from the name of the Druze community in Syria. Longrigg (1968): 208 n. 2.

5   The second attempt at a (shrunken) Caribbean/West Indies federation in the late 1960s failed to receive London's wholehearted support, Flanz (1968): 123 n. 53.

6   Kenneth Blackburne (British colonial administrator) and Nicholas Ridley (MP) became involved in separatist campaigns on the Cayman Islands and Anguilla respectively.

7   IO/L/PS/10/932 (P680): P.Z. Cox to E.S. Montagu (25 January 1921), R. Marrs's minutes (6 February 1921), J.E. Shuckburgh's minutes (9 February 1921).

8   For a perspective on changes in British imperial policy as a consequence of the Second World War, see Darwin (1991): 117–122.

9   One British official suggested in 1930 that after the British bases in Iraq had been held "for the first twenty-five years" they would probably remain "indefinitely", CO/730/151/7: J.H. Hall's minutes (28 April 1930).

10   CO/730/18 (37926): W.C.F.A. Wilson to Cox (14 June 1921); *Awqat* (8 February 1923, 29 July 1925); al-Matba'i (1995–98) III: 278–279.

11   *Al-Istiqlal* (22 May 1922); Fontanier (1844–46) I: 218–229, 354.

12   BHCF/7/15/3: AI (17 January 1924).

13   See for instance *Awqat* (26 June 1921); Faydi papers: Petition to King Faysal (April 1926); retrospect in AIR/23/275: SSO-Basra (29 December 1927).

14   *Basrah* (2 February 1926); *Awqat* (16 June 1927, 25 February 1928). The Jewish representative in the separatist delegation, Ya'qub Nuh, was among those who came under attack.

15   BHCF/7/15/3: AI (9 August 1928); AIR/23/383: SSO-Basra (10 May 1932); Batatu (1978): 409 n. 17.

16   It was not only the Shi'is of Basra who were worried about Ibn Sa'ud. Sunnis of the city who were non-Wahhabis repeatedly expressed worries about the attacks directed from Najd against Hijaz and voiced solidarity with King Husayn instead, FO/371/10833: IR (1 October 1925); Husayn and Sa'id (1978): 14.

17   *Awqat* (8 May 1923).

18   Seikaly (2002): 183–185.

19   Ilbert (1996): 185.

20   *Basrah* (26 August 1930).

21   CO/730/62: IR (2 October 1924).

22   AIR/23/277: SSO-Basra (28 October 1930).

23   Faydi papers: Sulayman Faydi to 'Ali Jawdat al-Ayyubi (26 April 1929); Faydi (1998): 402–403 n. 3 and (1998b): 313–321.

24   *Awqat* (4 January 1923, 5 January 1923).

25   *Awqat* (6 June 1922).

26   Al-Nabhani (1914); al-Nabhani (1923).

27   Al-Badr (1987): Chapter *al-intiqal ila maqarr al-madrasa al-thanawiyya* (unpaginated Internet edition).

28   Antaki (n.d.); al-Hilw (1969–72) III: 52; Kasravi (1983): 212. Khaz'al repeated the exercise after the war when he briefly and unsuccessfully made a bid for the Iraqi throne, Antaki (1920); al-Zirikli (1927–28): 593–594.

29   For a biographical note, see Al al-Shaykh (1973): 339.

30   Al-Rushayd (1926).

31   BHCF/7/15/3/III: AI (27 January 1923); *Awqat* (5 November 1924).

32   *Neglected Arabia* 105 (1918).

33   *Basrah* (23 December 1922).

34   Barakat (1977): 80–81 n.1; *RAI* (1927): 158; *Dalil al-mamlaka al-'iraqiyya* (1935): 914.

35   *Commercial and Trades Directory of Iraq* (1925): 20–31 gives details of several prominent Basra merchant families who generally stayed aloof from politics in the 1920s.

36 CO/730/132/2: Report by C. Empson (1 March 1928); AIR/23/276: SSO-Basra (4 November 1928).

37 Al-Hilw (1969–72) V: 38–41.

38 Of the other regional identity labels mentioned in chapter 4, "Hasawis" and "Bahrainis" became less important later in the twentieth century, although Hasawis continued to be disproportionately represented among the Shaykhis, as did the Bahrainis among the Akhbaris – suggesting the possibility of ethnic sentiment lingering on within a religious-sectarian framework.

39 Later in the twentieth century, Basra's urban expansion eventually brought an end to Zubayr's isolation, and because of Shi'i immigration the Sunni stronghold lost some of its distinctiveness. Still, even today, Zubayris stand out among the Basrawis in continuing to articulate a sense of special identity, as seen in several websites devoted to Zubayr – many created by Zubayris in exile in Saudi Arabia. Examples from the period 2001–2004 include www.alzubair-online.net and www.alzubair.net.

40 For an application of the concept of nationalist "resonance" in neighbouring Syria in this period, see Gelvin (1998): 158–160.

41 Na'ini's universalistic attitude had been visible as early as in 1909 when he wrote about constitutional issues in Persia and consistently quoted arguments specific to Sunnism alongside Shi'i justifications for a constitutional regime, see al-Na'ini (1909), paragraphs before footnote 12 and after footnotes 51 and 61. The basic dichotomy in his treatise is between "Muslims" and "foreigners" (*ajanib*) rather than between different Muslim sects.

42 Al Fir'awn (1952): 27.

43 If it is reductionistic to portray the exterior territorial framework of modern Iraq as London's fabrication, the British certainly made their mark on the inner surface of the new Iraqi polity and its political culture, as shown for instance by Dodge (2003).

44 Related to the discussion of this scenario is the question of whether Turkey really would have made a dash for Baghdad in the event of a British withdrawal, as predicted the standard nightmare in Whitehall at the time. In fact, Turkish foreign policy soon stabilised along exemplarily pragmatic lines, with its chief guiding principle the 1918 ceasefire lines, not any megalomanous pan-Islamic or pan-Turanian irredenta. Throughout the early 1920s Ankara aimed at recouping the territories that fell "within the borders of the [1920] national pact" (*Misak-ı Milli hudutları içinde*) such as Alexandretta and Mosul – not former Ottoman lands in general. By 1925, there was a Turkish consulate in Damascus; by 1928 the change to the Latin alphabet signified a point of no return as far as an Ottoman-like resurrection was concerned. Briefly put, Aleppo, Mosul or Kirkuk might well have been valuable additions to Turkey, but Baghdad or Damascus would have rendered the new republic overstretched, bent out of shape during the most critical phase of its efforts to redefine Turkish national identity. And so even though scattered cries for expansion towards old Ottoman lands in the Gulf region could be heard in certain quarters in Turkey as late as during the 1930s, this clearly remained a minority direction within Turkish nationalism as a whole. For Turkish perspectives on the settlement of the Mosul question, see Demirbaş (1991): 30–31, 35, 47, 64; Türkmen (2003): 28, 72–74

45 Christie (1996): 45–47, 112–120.

46 Carapico (1998): 90–91.

47 Anderson (1991): 55–58, 90.

48 For Libya, see Davis (1987): 25–26; for Transjordan and (later) Jordan, International Crisis Group (2003): 8, Center for Strategic Studies at the University of Jordan (2003).

49 Smith (2000): 62–76.

50 The debate among archaeologists on the precise course of the coastline in the region during Sumerian times exemplifies this idea of fluctuation within certain parameters in the construction of modern nationalisms. Whereas some scholars have claimed that Basra proper was actually submerged during the time of the old Mesopotamian civilisations (in contrast to nearby sites such as Ur), others have challenged this position, see Lees and Falcon (1952).

51 For these strikes, and their links to wider Arab nationalist agendas, see Tripp (2000): 91.
52 One observer maintained that only the non-Muslim communities of Basra expressed delight at the arrival of the British forces, FO 371/27065 (E1593): Report (19 April 1941). See also Longrigg (1953): 290, 292.
53 The magnitude of the exodus from Zubayr to Saudi Arabia was such that the remaining inhabitants spoke of it as "the reverse migration" (*al-hijra al-mu'akisa*), an allusion to the initial immigration to Zubayr from Najd in the nineteenth century which had been the main factor in the growth of the desert town, see al-Sani' (1985–89) I: 7.
54 See for instance the poem "Stranger at the Gulf" (*gharib 'ala al-khalij*) in al-Sayyab (1960).
55 For examples of Shi'i rhetoric from this era, see for instance Abdul-Jabar (2003): 134–137.
56 The most significant exception to this general trend occurred in the 1960s, when young Shi'is of religious backgrounds briefly contemplated imitating Kurdish demands for local autonomy. The very existence of such a project has been dismissed by Shi'i writers as Ba'thist propaganda, but British reports (which expressed disinterested surprise at the new development) contain substantial information on the supporters of the scheme. Still, quite as in 1927, the movement proved ephemeral, lacking the support of the higher echelons of the Shi'i hierarchy. See FO371/17571 (EQ1017/2): S.L. Egerton to W. Marsden (22 February 1964); Abdul-Jabar (2003): 140–141.

Chapter 12

1   See chapter 3.
2   For examples from Iraq, see Hairi (1977): 193–197.
3   See chapter 9.
4   For the significance of transnational links among the Shi'is during this struggle in the 1990s, see Buchta (1995); Mallat (1997): 154–160.
5   Khurasan (1999): 420; al-Husayni (1996); Sakai (2001): 43.
6   A more detailed overview of Shi'i ideas about federal state models for Iraq is given in Visser (2004).
7   *Sawt al-Da'wa* (15 October 1992: 1–2, 1 December 1992: 2–3, 1 September 1993: 1 and 3); al-Samarra'i (1993): 369–370.
8   Interview in *al-Shira'* (17 March 2003); transcript of interview from al-'Arabiyya Television (23 March 2003) from www.bayynat.org.lb.
9   *Al-Hayat* (20 April 2003): 3, (22 March 2004): 3.
10 *Al-Jihad* (27 May 2002: 2, 2 December 2002: 1).
11 Undated fatwa by Kazim al-Ha'iri on political participation by Shi'is within the political system of Bahrain, www.alhaeri.org.
12 *Al-Jihad* (27May 2002): 2; *al-Milaff al-'Iraqi* no. 75 (1998): 72.
13 If no specifically Islamic justification for the maintenance of a unitary state in Iraq can be found, utilitarian arguments (such as the virtue of federalism as a means of preventing bloodshed among the Iraqis) should theoretically be valid for Islamists as well.
14 *Dialogue* (February 1992): 2–3; *Iraqi Issues* vol. 1 no. 4 (1992): 4–6; Allawi (1994); Kubba (n.d.).
15 For the changing attitude to federalism among Da'wa leaders, see transcripts of interviews with Abu Bilal al-Adib (Iran 2 Television, December 2002) and Jawad al-Maliki (Sahr Television, 24 December 2002), from www.daawaparty.com.
16 *Taqrir 'an al-tahawwul ila al-dimuqratiyya fi al-'iraq* (2002): 3 n. 1 and appendix p.118, 184–195, *al-Nahar* (9 November 2002): 10
17 Ra'uf (2000): 327–329; *al-Hayat* (1 April 1996): Interview with Muhammad Baqir al-Hakim.
18 *Al-Hayat* (13 August 2002): 2.

19   Federal News Service: Transcript of a discussion held at the American University Center for
      Global Peace Forum, 8 June 2002.
20   Arab writers sometimes distinguish between political (*siyasi*) and administrative (*idari*)
      decentralisation, and these two terms often correspond to the dichotomy between a federal
      and a unitary state structure as employed in Western terminology. The use of terms such as
      "administrative federalism/decentralisation" (*al-fidiraliyya/al-lamarkaziyya al-idariyya*) can
      therefore give rise to differing interpretations, as the emphasis on "administrative" used by
      some writers to underline the "non-political" criteria for demarcating the federal units
      (rather than to qualify the degree of devolution), by others can be seen as a concession to a
      state logic which is essentially unitary in spirit.
21   For a reading of "political" decentralisation within the Islamic empires as a destructive force
      resisted by the centre, see Mustafa (1990).
22   See al-Hakim (n.d.), published during the 1990s.
23   *Kayhan* (8 June 2003): "Ayat allah hakim: shura-yi muntakhab-i amrika bara-yi idarah-i
      'iraq namashru' ast".
24   *Al-Zaman* (28 May 2003): "Al-sadr yad'u min al-najaf ila dawla islamiyya tulzimu al-
      masihiyyin bi-al-islam"; *al-Sharq al-Awsat* (17 May 2003): "Imam shi'i 'iraqi yatawa'adu
      nisa' wa-ashab dur sinima wa-ba'at al-khamr"; *al-Zaman* (5 May 2003): "Al-sadr yad'u min
      al-najaf ila dawla islamiyya tulzimu al-masihiyyin bi-al-islam".
25   Al-Ha'iri (2004). On Ha'iri's approach, see also al-Ha'iri (1998) part 3.
26   *Al-Hawza* (18 March 2004).
27   Voice of the Mujahidin Radio (21 June 2004, Foreign Broadcast Information Service tran-
      script).
28   *Al-Manara* (22 August 2004: 1, 29 August 2004: 3); *al-Mada* (16 October 2004).
29   *Al-Manara* (10 April 2005: 2, 24 April 2005: 2).
30   After the growing sectarian violence in Iraq during 2004, some Shi'i exiles in Europe even
      launched Internet discussions about outright separatism for all the Shi'i lands of Iraq, on
      websites like www.dc.turkuamk.fi/users/qalramma/shi3at. Still, this new trend seemed af-
      flicted with some of the problems that had obstructed similar attempts in the past (like those
      of 1927, and the 1960s, see chapters 9 and 11). No Shi'i framework of political theory was
      available to back it up, the established clergy remained disinterested or hostile – and the
      very concept of "Iraq" had the appearance of a millstone which even these renegades were
      unable to shake off: To denote the Shi'i-inhabited territories singled out for separation, they
      used the term "the historical Iraq" (*al-'iraq al-ta'rikhi*, as opposed to the existing "political"
      one) rather than coining an alternative name for the proposed Shi'i homeland. It is also
      noteworthy that in central Iraq, Shi'i federalist initiatives remained comparatively subdued
      during 2004, and failed to progress beyond the level of unsubstantiated and disavowed ru-
      mours. Nevertheless, these trends (just like the rise of the Sadrist movement) are interesting
      indications of attempts by Shi'is to circumvent the traditional ulama, and as such remins-
      cent of processes seen among the Sunnis ever since the rise of Islamism as a political force.
31   *Al-Zaman* for September and October 2003 featured a separate column for constitutional
      issues; most of these contributions were presented within a secular framework. For Islamist
      proposals, see for instance *al-Da'wa* (31 December 2003).
32   "Kutlat nuwwab min ajl fidiraliyyat al-janub", www.aljeeran.net, (22 April 2005). The ac-
      tions and statements of this representative, 'Ali 'Abd al-Hakim al-Safi, do raise the delicate
      question of who really speaks for Sistani. There were in 2005 signs that several components
      of Sistani's worldwide network were becoming increasingly autonomous, issuing statements
      quite independently and not necessarily on the basis of consultations with the grand ayatol-
      lah.

Glossary

aga	Honorific title with a wide range of connotations: among Persians in Basra, used for landowners and wealthy merchants; in Ottoman terminology frequently employed by army officers who did not have a military college education.
Akhbarism	Direction within Shi'ism which emphasises an orthodox approach to legal questions, with a highly conservative attitude to the use of free logical reasoning and analogy in questions of legal interpretation.
'alim	Muslim scholar, singular of *'ulama'*.
amir	Literally, "commander": in Islamic history usually reserved for minor rulers who did not aspire to spiritual leadership by becoming caliph or *amir al-mu'minin* (commander of the faithful).
ashraf	Collective term for descendants of the Prophet.
'Ashura	Tenth day of the month of Muharram, holy to Shi'is.
awqaf	Real estate property set aside as a charitable endowment.
Babism, Babi	Religious splinter group from Shaykhism (q.v.) which further developed the concept of human interaction with the Hidden Imam, to the point where its leaders themselves claimed a role as Mahdis (q.v.) Also a forerunner for Baha'ism.
bey	Multivalent Ottoman honorific title: Basrawis holding it were usually the sons of *pasha*s, whose male offspring automatically acquired *bey* status.
diwan	Informal social gathering of men in a specifically designated guest house or other reception facility.
effendi	Polite title associated with literate and educated males who held no other honorific; in late Ottoman times perhaps comparable to "Esquire", by the 1920s increasingly used simply to express "Mr."
fallahun	Agricultural tenant workers.
faqih	Person trained in Islamic jurisprudence (*fiqh*).
ghayba	Literally, "absence" or "disappearance", among the Shi'is used to refer to the power vacuum brought about by the Twelfth Imam's disappearance and his entry into a state of occultation in AD 874.
Hanbalism	The Islamic tradition of jurisprudence associated with the medieval scholar Ibn Hanbal. Hanbalism is one of the four universally recognised schools of legal interpretation within Sunni Islam, and is seen as the most orthodox one.
Hajji	Honorific title assigned to anyone who has performed the pilgrimage to Mecca.
Hidden Imam	See *ghayba*.
hizb	Political party.
ibn	"Son", used in names to mean "son of".
Ikhwan	Literally, "brethren", as a proper noun used to refer collectively to militant tribes of Arabia professing Wahhabism, q.v.
jarib	Measure for land holdings, in Basra usage the approximate equivalent of an acre.
kaza	Subdistrict in the Ottoman Empire, the next administrative level after *sancak*.
lamarkaziyya	Decentralisation (literally "non-centralisation").
liwa'	The largest administrative division in monarchical Iraq, in practice often corresponding to Ottoman *sancak*s. The English term "division" was established as an official translation during the British mandate; in later Iraqi history these units became *muhafazat*s, often referred to in English as "governorates" or "provinces".
Mahdi	Divinely inspired leader expected to appear to lead the Muslims before the end of the world, a concept particularly central to Shi'i theology.
Mandaeans	Members of a syncretic sect who often describe themselves to outsiders as "followers of John the Baptist". Their religion features rituals that celebrate vivifying powers like running water and the sun.

208

marja' al-taqlid	"Source of emulation": the cleric chosen by each individual Shi'i believer as his or her spiritual point of reference, required for all members of the laity and everyone who is not a *mujtahid*, q.v.
ma'tam	Social gathering among the Shi'is, associated with designated "funeral houses" but with a wide scope of social functions.
mirî	Government land.
müdir	Chief official of a *nahiye*, the administrative unit below the subdistrict in the late Ottoman Empire as well as in monarchical Iraq (*mudir*).
Muharram	First month of the Muslim calendar, commemorated by Shi'is as the holy month in which Imam Husayn died as a martyr.
mujtahid	In Shi'ism: cleric who has reached the level of erudition required for practising legal interpretation (*ijtihad*) and has received formal authorisation by an established *mujtahid* to this effect.
mullah	Member of the Islamic clergy, among Shi'is in Iraq often reserved for the lower echelons of the religious hierarchy.
mülk	Private property.
mutasarrif	Ottoman Empire: governor of a *sancak*. Monarchical Iraq: governor of a *liwa'*.
nahiye	(Arabic: *nahiya*.) Subordinate administrative unit within a *kaza* (Ottoman Empire) or *qada* (monarchical Iraq).
Najdi	Relating to Najd, the central plateau region of the Arabian Peninsula.
pasha	A formal grade in the upper Ottoman military-administrative hierarchy, used in the civilian, military and naval branches of government. Also bestowed on provincial notables as a honorific title.
qada	Sub-governorate or district in monarchical Iraq.
qa'im-maqam	Head of a sub-governorate/district (*qada*) in monarchical Iraq.
naqib	Formally appointed chief of the *ashraf* (q.v.) in an Islamic city.
Ramadan	The Muslim holy month.
Salafism	Islamic modernist movement with a focus on the use of reasoning and interpretation to renew Islam in the modern world.
sancak	Sub-governorate or district in Ottoman administrative terminology.
sanjaq	Arabic form of *sancak*, in use as administrative term from 1914 to 1920.
sayyid	Descendant of the Prophet (used in this sense mainly among Shi'is).
sharif, sharifian	"Highborn": denoting a descendant of the Prophet. Since Ottoman times used in a specialised sense to refer to the governor of Mecca. The British used the derivative "sharifian" about the Arab dynasty which controlled this post at the time of the outbreak of the First World War.
Shaykhism	Sub-current within Shi'ism distinguished by the belief that human intermediaries may serve as an interface between mankind and the Hidden Imam.
ta'ab	In the Basra area: tenant with life-long and hereditary tenancy rights.
tapu	Land registration process whereby tenants obtained personal and hereditary usufructuary rights to state lands.
ulama	Collective term for the clergy in Islam.
'Usuli	The main branch of Shi'ism, distinguished by the central role accorded to *mujtahid*s (q.v.) in the interpretation of Islamic law.
vilayet	The largest administrative unit in the Ottoman Empire, a province.
Wahhabism	Puritan Islamic current associated with the eighteenth-century Arabian scholar Muhammad ibn 'Abd al-Wahhab and based on Hanbalism, q.v.
Yazidis	Members of a syncretic religious community based mostly in rural parts of the Mosul area. Yazidism includes elements from several religions including Christianity and Islam; the belief in manifestation of divinity through angels capable of blending with human souls is one of its basic features.

Sources

In the twentieth century, Basra experienced a tumultuous journey – from being an outpost of the Ottoman Empire, via British military and mandated rule, to a position as the second city of a country chronically ravaged by war and war-like conditions. This rough ride left its mark on the historical sources available for research, with decimations of records in 1914, 1941 and 2003. Today, the main classes of surviving historical materials are spread as far away from Basra as Britain, Turkey and India.

For the Ottoman period, the primary governmental sources are Ottoman and British archives. The Ottoman registers of correspondence covering communications between Basra and the grand vizier's office are useful points of entry for more detailed documents, and are helpful in cases where the original letters no longer exist. These sources have been employed together with materials from the sultan's archives at Yıldız, the Ministry of Interior (particularly useful for post-1908 developments) and the Ottoman navy – which had a regional base in Basra and therefore a special interest in the area. Among the published Ottoman sources, the annual yearbooks issued by the local authorities in Basra in the late nineteenth and early twentieth centuries contain a wealth of information. British consular records are also informative for the late Ottoman period, and are noteworthy for the fact that most of them were produced by a consul who favoured a policy of preserving the integrity of the Ottoman Empire. They can thus counterbalance reports by visitors from British-Indian administrative circles, where there was support for an interventionist policy in the Gulf, and where perceptions of local politics may have been biased accordingly. Additionally, the British sources are central for analyses of segments of the population with whom the Ottomans had limited direct contact – examples include renegade tribal shaykhs, heterodox religious sects and slaves of African origin.

For post-1914 developments, British governmental archives are the main source. In addition to the files of the India Office and the Colonial Office (which held titular responsibility for the administration of Basra during most of the period of British rule), the archives of the Royal Air Force and the Baghdad High Commission (files evacuated to Delhi in 1941 and now in the National Archives of India) provide extensive coverage of local-level developments. Representing two separate tiers of intelligence on local politics connected with opposite poles in British policy-making circles, the abstracts of the intelligence of the Iraqi police and the reports of the RAF special service officers in these archives can be employed in combination to obtain a more balanced picture of controversial political incidents. London's influence over Iraq's police forces persisted even after the country's formal independence in 1932 through British inspectors, and the British intelligence reports created in this period are useful for the politics of the early years of the Iraq monarchy.

Private papers and books by officials working for the British administration form an important complement to the official archives. The collections of Gertrude Bell, John Philby and Cecil Edmonds are replete with materials relating to Basra as well as to the larger Shi'i community. The writings of Valentine Dowson have proven indispensable for their coverage of Basra's date industry, and the accounts by S.E. Hedgecock and his wife on the Marsh Arabs are among the few contemporary descriptions of this peripheral segment of Basra society.

Of materials created by people outside the Ottoman and the subsequent British administrations, Basra's newspapers are an especially informative source. The most enduring of the post-1908 local newspapers, *İkaz*, has been used for this study in a complete run covering most of 1909 and 1910. For the British period, *Basrah Times* and the Arabic *Al-Awqat al-'Iraqiyya*, both preserved for the duration of the mandate (technically forming the combined broadsheet *Times of Mesopotamia*), are mines of information. Of biographical materials, the memoirs of Sulayman Faydi, a lawyer from Mosul who practised in Basra during the late Ottoman and early British period, stand out. Also autobiographies by other individuals who lived in Basra for shorter intervals (Badr Khalif al-Badr, Muhammad Ra'uf Taha al-Shaykhli and 'Ali Jawdat) have been helpful, as has a historical work by Muhammad al-Nabhani, a Hijazi historian who took up residence in Basra during the war and covered the recent past extensively in his writings. To counterpoise the dominance of reports created by the powers of the day, writings and documents created by non-British foreign representatives in Basra can be of benefit; these include works by foreign consuls in Basra (Muhammad Hasan Khan Badi', of Persia; Aleksandr Adamov, a Russian; and Ramire Pie Maxime Vadala, French representative), as well as a whole archive of French consular correspondence from the post-war period. Finally, a non-governmental organisation heavily involved in Basra in the first half of the twentieth century, the Reformed Church of America, created archival materials, a periodical (*Neglected Arabia*) and books written by its leading administrators (Dorothy and John Van Ess), providing a different perspective on local affairs.

Archival sources

References are given with an abbreviation indicating which collection the document belongs to, followed by the code of the relevant archival item. If the location of the document in question within the archival piece is not immediately evident, i.e. if the documents are not bound in a chronological sequence, further information such as the relevant file number is given in parentheses. Archival references are in all caps acronyms, for italicised all caps acronyms see under official publications.

The following abbreviations are used across several groups of archives:

AHC   Acting high commissioner.
AHQ   Air headquarters.
AI   Abstract of intelligence.
AR   Administrative report.
EC   Eastern Committee.
GHQ   General headquarters.
IR   Intelligence report.
MEC   Middle East Committee.
SSO   Special service officer.

France

Archives du Ministère des Affaires étrangères, Paris
MAE: Files from "série correspondence et commerciale, série 'E', Levant 1918–40".

India

National Archives of India, New Delhi
BHCF: Files of the British high commissioner which were evacuated from Baghdad to India in 1941.
FPD: Files of the Foreign and Political Department of the Indian government.

Switzerland

Archives of the League of Nations, Geneva
LN/MIN: Secretariat files, Section des minorités.
LN/MAN: Section files, Section des mandats.

Turkey

Ottoman section of the Prime Ministry State Archives, Istanbul
A/MKT/MHM: Sadaret Mektubî Kalemi Mühimme Kalemi Odası (files of a special chancellery within the grand vizier's office devoted to urgent high-priority matters).

BEO: Bab-i Âli Evrak Odası (The Sublime Porte or office of the grand vizier, numerical files).
BEO/VGG: Bab-i Âli Evrak Odası, vilayet gelen giden defterleri (précis of correspondence with the provinces).
DH: Dahiliye Nezareti (Ministry of Interior files).
DH/EUM/EMN: Emniyet-i Umumiye Müdiriyeti Emniyet Kalemi (files from the internal security department of the Ministry of Interior, including political intelligence).
DH/EUM/VRK: Emniyet-i Umumiye Müdiriyeti Evrak Odası (files from the internal security department of the Ministry of Interior, especially relating to police matters).
DH/İD: Dahiliye Nezareti, İdarî Kısım (miscellanea from the administrative department of the Ministry of Interior).
DH/KMS: Dahiliye Nezareti, Kalem-i Mahsus Müdüriyeti (files from a special department of the Ministry of Interior established in 1913 and operative during the First World War).
DH/MUI: Dahiliye Nezareti, Muhaberat-ı Umumiye İdaresi (Intelligence files of the Ministry of Interior).
DKK: Deniz Kuvvetleri Komutanlığı Genel Arşivi (archives of the Ottoman navy, registers of correspondence).
MV: Meclis-i Vükelâ (council of ministers files).
Y/A/HUS: Yıldız, sadaret hususi maruzat evrakı (documents from Yıldız, the sultan's palace: correspondence from the grand vizier).
Y/PRK/AZJ: Yıldız perakende evrakı, arzuhal ve jurnaller (miscellanea: petitions, reports).
Y/PRK/HR: Yıldız perakende evrakı, Hariciye Nezareti maruzati (correspondence with the Ministry of Foreign Affairs).
Y/PRK/MK: Yıldız perakende evrakı, müfettişlik ve komiserlikler tahriratı (miscellanea: correspondence with inspectors and commissioners).
Y/PRK/UM: Yıldız perakende evrakı, umum vilayetler tahriratı (miscellanea: correspondence with the provinces).
Y/MTV: Yıldız, mütenevvi maruzat (a collection of various reports from sources outside the grand vizier's office).
YEE: Yıldız esas evrakı (the sultan's private collection of files of particular interest to himself).

<u>United Kingdom</u>

Basil S. Faidhi Collection
Personal papers of Sulayman Faydi.

British Library, Manuscript Collections
Personal papers of Arnold Talbot Wilson.

British Library, Oriental and India Office Collections
ADD: Oriental manuscripts collection.
IO/EURMSS: European manuscripts collection.
IO/L/PS/10 and 11: Files of the Political Department, India Office.
IO/R/15/5: Records of the Kuwait Political Agency.

Public Record Office
ADM/137: Admiralty papers used by Historical Section of the Committee of Imperial Defence.
AIR/8: Records of the chief of Air Staff.
AIR/20: Air Ministry, unregistered papers of the Air Historical Branch.
AIR/23: Records of the Royal Air Force.
CAB/23: Conclusions of cabinet meetings.
CAB/27: Papers of cabinet committees.
CO/537: Colonial Office records, supplementary secret correspondence.
CO/730: Colonial Office records on Iraq.
CO/781: Colonial Office, registers of correspondence.

CO/813: Colonial Office, Iraqi government gazettes.
FO/195: Records of the British Embassy, Istanbul.
FO/248: Records of the British Embassy, Tehran.
FO/371: Foreign Office, general political correspondence.
FO/460: Records of the British Consulate, Muhammara.
FO/602: Records of the British Consulate, Basra.
FO/624: Records of the British Embassy, Baghdad.
T/161: Records of the Treasury, Supply Department.
WO/95: War Office, war diaries, First World War.
WO/106: War Office, Directorate of Military Operations and Intelligence.
WO/157: War Office, intelligence summaries.
WO/252: War Office, records of libraries and joint intelligence agencies.
WO/302: War Office, maps from the Mesopotamian campaign, First World War.

School of Oriental and African Studies, London
Personal papers of Arthur Rhuvon Guest.

University of Durham
Personal papers of Francis Cecil Campbell Balfour.

University of Newcastle
GB: Personal papers of Gertrude Lowthian Bell, published by the University of Newcastle upon Tyne Library as an Internet archive (www.gerty.ncl.ac.uk). The references are to the letters within this collection unless additional information (diaries etc.) has been given.

University of Oxford, the Middle East Centre at St. Antony's College
Personal papers of Humphrey Ernest Bowman.
Personal papers of Percy Zachariah Cox.
Personal papers of Harold Richard Patrick Dickson.
Personal papers of Cecil John Edmonds.
Personal papers of Harry St. John Bridger Philby.
Personal papers of Hubert Winthrop Young.

Theses and unpublished manuscripts

Abbas, Hasan Ali Turki (1997): *Imam Kashif al-Ghita, the Reformist Marji' in the Shi'ah School of Najaf*, Ph.D. thesis, University of Arizona.
Abdullah, Thabit A.J. (1992): *The Political Economy of Merchants and Trade in Basra, 1722–1795*, Ph.D. thesis, Georgetown University.
al-Adhami, Muhammad Muzaffar (1978): *Political Aspects of the Iraqi Parliament and Elections Processes*, Ph.D. thesis, School of Oriental and African Studies.
Alghanim, Salwa Muhammad Ahmad (1990): *The Reign of Mubarak al-Sabah: Shaikh of Kuwait, 1896-1916*, Ph.D. thesis, School of Oriental and African Studies.
Ansari, Mostafa (1974): *The History of Khuzistan, 1878–1925: A Study in Provincial Autonomy and Change*, Ph.D. thesis, University of Chicago.
Balaghi, Shiva (2002): " 'Law is the Language and Power of Justice:' The Persian Press and the Debate on Constitutionalism and Islamic Law in Turn of the Century Iran", paper presented at the 10th annual conference on "The Individual vs the State", Budapest, June. [*The author advises that a final version is to be published at a later stage and should be used for purposes of reference.*]
Çetinsaya, Gökhan (1994): *Ottoman Administration of Iraq, 1890–1908*, Ph.D. thesis, University of Manchester.

Diskin, John Joseph (1971): *The Genesis of the Government Educational System in 'Iraq*, Ph.D. thesis, University of Pittsburgh.

Jwaideh, Albertine (1953): *Municipal Government in Baghdad and Basra from 1869 to 1914*, B.Litt. thesis, University of Oxford.

al-Khattab, 'Adil 'Abdallah (1972): *Basra City. A Study in Urban Geography*, Ph.D. thesis, School of Oriental and African Studies.

Mahallati, Haydar (1998): *'Abd al-mun'im al-fartusi. Hayatuhu wa-adabuh*, thesis presented at the University of Isfahan, made available at www.al-shia.com.

al-Nakib, Haifa Ahmed (1973): *A Critical Study of Saiyyid Talib Pasha al-Nakib in the Setting of His Time and Environment, on the Basis of Arabic and Foreign Documents*, M.Phil. thesis, University of Leeds.

al-Qaysi, Abdul Wahhab Abbas (1958): *The Impact of Modernization on Iraqi Society during the Ottoman Era: A Study of Intellectual Development in Iraq, 1869–1917*, Ph.D. thesis, University of Michigan.

Strunk, William Theodore (1977): *The Reign of Shaykh Khaz'al Ibn Jabir and the Suppression of the Principality of 'Arabistan: A Study in British Imperialism in Southwestern Iran*, Ph.D. thesis, Indiana University.

Townsend, John (1996): *A Great Man: The Life of Sir Percy Cox*, manuscript in the Private Papers Collections of the Middle East Centre, St. Antony's College, University of Oxford.

Wilson, Arnold T. (1911): *Précis of the Relations of the British Government with the Tribes and Shaikhs of Arabistan*. Typewritten report (Bushire).

Official and semi-official publications

Iraq
IGG: *Iraq Government Gazette* (1921–).

Iraq. Basra Date Board
Dates and the Date Industry of Iraq (1937).

Iraq. Department of Customs and Excise
AR Customs: *Administration report* (titles vary slightly, 1923–28).

Iraq. Directory General of Census
Census of Iraq (1947).

Iraq. Iraq Museum
Iraq Museum (1926): *Babylonian Stone Room*.

Iraq. Ministry of Interior
AR (1921): *Annual Report of the Basrah Liwah* [sic] *for the Year 1921–1922*.

Iraq. Opposition in exile. Democratic Principles Working Group
Taqrir 'an al-tahawwul ila al-dimuqratiyya fi al-'iraq (2002).

Ottoman Empire
MMZC: *Meclis-i mebusan zabıt ceredesi* (1325 h./1909–1334 h./1918).
SAL: *Salname-yi devlet-i aliye-yi osmaniye* (1313 h./1895–1333 h./1914).

Ottoman Empire. Governor of Basra
BSAL: *Basra vilayeti salnamesi* (1308 h./1890–1320 h./1902).

United Kingdom. Admiralty War Staff, Intelligence Division
Admiralty (1917): *A Handbook of Mesopotamia. Vol. II: Irak, the Lower Karun, and Luristan.*

United Kingdom. Arab Bureau, Basra branch
[Bell, Gertrude] (1917): *The Arab of Mesopotamia.*
[Bell, Gertrude] (1917b): *Tribes round the Junction of the Euphrates and the Tigris.*
IRP (1917): *Iraq Personalities.*

United Kingdom. British authorities in Iraq
AR (1915): *Administration Report. January–March 1915* [Revenue Department].
AR Qurna (1916–17): *Administration Report of Qurnah and District for Year 1916–17.*
AR Basra Sanjaq (1916–17): *Administration Report of Basrah Sanjaq.*
AR (1917): *Review of the Reports on the Administration of the Basrah Vilayat from April to December 1917.*
AR (1918): *Mesopotamia Administration Report 1918.*
AR (1919): *Basrah Division Annual Report for 1919.*
AR Qurna (1919): *Administrative Report for the Qurnah Area for the Year 1919.*
[Bell, Gertrude] (1920): *Review of the Civil Administration of Mesopotamia.*

United Kingdom. Colonial Office
RAI: *Report by His Britannic Majesty's Government to the Council of the League of Nations on the Administration of Iraq for the Year . . .* (titles vary slightly, 1922–31).

United Kingdom. General Staff, British forces in Iraq
General Staff (1923): *Military Report on Iraq (Area 6).*
General Staff (1923b): *Military Report on Iraq (Area 7).*

United Kingdom. Parliament
RTB: *Report on the Trade of Basra for the Year . . .* (titles vary slightly, 1887–1913).
House of Commons: *The Parliamentary Debates: Official Report.*
House of Lords: *The Parliamentary Debates: Official Report.*

Newspapers and journals

Awqat: al-Awqat al-'Iraqiyya (Basra).
al-Awqat al-Basriyya (Basra).
Basrah: Basrah Times (Basra).
al-Da'wa (Baghdad).
Dialogue (London).
Field Report [of the Arabian Mission, Reformed Church of America, New York].
al-Hawza (Baghdad).
al-Hayat (London).
İkaz (Basra).
Iraqi Issues (Washington, D.C.)
al-Istiqlal (Baghdad).
al-Jihad (Tehran).
Kayhan (Tehran).
al-Khalij al-'Arabi (Basra).
Lisan al-'Arab (Baghdad).
Lughat al-'Arab (Baghdad).
al-Mada (Baghdad).
al-Manara (Basra).

al-Milaff al-'Iraqi (Surbiton, Surrey).
al-Mufid (Baghdad).
al-Nahar (Beirut).
Near East and India (London).
Neglected Arabia (New York).
Oxfordshire and Buckinghamshire Light Infantry Chronicle (London).
Quarterly Letter from the Field [of the Arabian Mission, Reformed Church of America, New York].
al-Rafidan (Baghdad).
Sabah (Istanbul).
Sawt al-Da'wa (United Kingdom).
al-Sharq al-Awsat (London).
al-Shira' (Beirut).
Times, The (London).
al-Zaman (Baghdad).
al-Zaman, Basra edition (Basra).

Directories

Commercial and Trades Directory of 'Iraq (Basra and Baghdad: The Times Printing and Publishing Co., 1925).
Dalil al-mamlaka al-'iraqiyya (Baghdad: Mahdi Husayn al-Amin, 1935).
The Iraq Directory (Baghdad: Dangoor's Printing and Publishing House, 1936).

Books, articles and other published materials

'Abbas, Ihsan (1969): *Badr shakir al-sayyab: dirasa fi hayatihi wa-shi'rih* (Beirut: Dar al-Thaqafa).
al-'Abbasi, 'Abd al-Qadir Basha'yan (1961): *Al-basra fi adwariha al-ta'rikhiyya* (Baghdad: Matba'at Dar al-Basri).
'Abd al-Husayn, Muhammad (1933): *Dhikra faysal al-awwal* (Baghdad).
'Abdallah, Lutfi Ja'far Faraj (1978): *'Abd al-muhsin al-sa'dun wa-dawruhu fi ta'rikh al-'iraq al-siyasi al-mu'asir* (Baghdad: Wizarat al-Thaqafa wa-al-Funun).
Abdul-Jabar, Faleh (2003): *The Shi'ite Movement in Iraq* (London: Saqi).
Abdullah, Thabit A.J. (2001): *Merchants, Mamluks, and Murder: The Political Economy of Trade in Eighteenth-Century Basra* (Albany: State University of New York Press).
Abu-Hakima, Ahmad Mustafa (1983): *The Modern History of Kuwait, 1750–1965* (London: Luzac & Co.)
Adamov, Aleksandr (1912): *Wilayat al-basra fi madiha wa-hadiriha.* 1982 translation from Russian by Hashim Salih al-Takriti (Basra: Markaz Dirasat al-Khalij al-'Arabi).
Adelson, Roger (1975): *Mark Sykes: Portrait of an Amateur* (London: Jonathan Cape).
——— (1995): *London and the Invention of the Middle East: Money, Power, and War, 1902–1922* (New Haven: Yale University Press).
al-Adhami (1978): see theses and unpublished manuscripts.
al-Adhami, Muhammad Muzaffar (1989): *Al-majlis al-ta'sisi al-'iraqi* (Baghdad: Dar al-Shu'un al-Thaqafiyya al-'Amma).
Admiralty (1917): see official publications.
Ahmad, Ibrahim Khalil (1982): "Al-salnamat al-'uthmaniyya masdaran li-ta'rikh al-basra al-hadith" in *al-Khalij al-'Arabi* vol. 14 no. 3.
Ahmad, Kamal Madhar (1994): *Kurdistan in the First World War Years* (London: Dar al-Saqi).
[Ahmad], Khan Bahadur Agha Mirza Muhammad (1927): "Some News Notes on Babiism" in *Journal of the Royal Asiatic Society of Great Britain and Ireland*.
Akpınar, Alışan (1997): *Osmanlı Devletin'de Aşiret Mektebi* (Istanbul: Selçuk Kitabevi).

Al al-Shaykh, 'Abd al-Rahman (1973): *Mashahir 'ulama najd wa-ghayruhum* (Riyadh: Dar al-Yamama).

Alamuddin, Najib (1993): *Turmoil: The Druzes, Israel and the Arab-Israeli Conflict* (London: Quartet Books).

al-'Alawi, Hasan (1989): *Al-shi'a wa-al-dawla al-qawmiyya fi al-'iraq* (Paris: CEDI).

Al Fir'awn, Fariq al-Muzhir (1952): *Al-haqa'iq al-nasi'a fi al-thawra al-'iraqiyya sannat 1920 wa-nata'ijiha* (Baghdad: Matba'at al-Najah).

Alghanim (1990): see theses and unpublished manuscripts.

'Ali, 'Abd al-Husayn Yunis (1981): *Qa'ima bi-al-kutub al-masadir al-'arabiyya 'an al-basra* (Basra: Markaz Dirasat al-Khalij al-'Arabi).

Allawi, Ali (1994): "Federalism" in Fran Hazelton (ed.), *Iraq since the Gulf War* (London: Zed Books).

Al Mahbuba, Ja'far al-Shaykh Baqir (1955–58): *Madi al-najaf wa-hadiruha* (Najaf: Matba'at al-Adab).

Almana, Mohammed (1980): *Arabia Unified: A Portrait of Ibn Saud* (London: Hutchinson Benham).

Al Muhammad, A.H. (1947–52): *Al-tibyan wa-al-burhan 'ala anna 'isa nasala wa-zahara mahdi akhir al-zaman* (Baghdad: Matba'at Baghdad).

Al Zulfa, Muhammad ibn 'Abdallah (2001): "Min rudud fi'l al-sultat al-'uthmaniyya tujaha isti'adat al-malik 'abd al-'aziz li-al-ahsa' 'am 1331 h./1913 m." in *al-Jazira* 17 March.

Amanat, Abbas (1989): *Resurrection and Renewal: The Making of the Babi Movement in Iran, 1844–1850* (Ithaca: Cornell University Press).

al-Amin, Muhsin (1986): *A'yan al-shi'a*. New edition edited by Hasan al-Amin (Beirut: Dar al-Ta'arruf).

al-'Amiri, Thamir 'Abd al-Hasan (1992–95): *Mawsu'at al-'asha'ir al-'iraqiyya* (Baghdad: Dar al-Shu'un al-Thaqafiyya al-'Amma).

Andaya, Barbara Watson & Leonard Y. Andaya (2001): *A History of Malaysia*. Second edition (Basingstoke: Palgrave).

Anderson, Liam & Gareth Stansfield (2004): *The Future of Iraq: Dictatorship, Democracy or Division* (Basingstoke: Palgrave Macmillan).

al-'Ani, Shuja' Muslim (1989): "Al-haraka al-adabiyya al-haditha fi al-basra (1920–1980)" in *Jami'at al-Basra: Mawsu'at al-basra al-hadariyya: al-mawsu'a al-fikriyya* (Basra: Matba'at Dar al-Hikma).

al-Ansari, Ahmad Nur (1969): *Al-nusra fi akhbar al-basra*. Edited by Yusuf 'Izz al-Din (Baghdad: al-Majma' al-'Ilmi al-'Iraqi).

Ansari (1974): see theses and unpublished manuscripts.

Anscombe, Frederick F. (1997): *The Ottoman Gulf: The Creation of Kuwait, Saudi Arabia and Qatar* (New York: Columbia University Press).

Antaki, 'Abd al-Masih (n.d.): *Al-durar al-hisan fi manzumat wa-mada'ih mawlana mu'izz al-saltana sirdar arfa' sumuw al-shaykh khaz'al khan* (Egypt: Matba'at al-'Arab).

———— [1920]: *Al-qasida al-'alawiyya al-mubaraka* (Egypt: Matba'at Ra'amsis).

Atiyyah, Ghassan R. (1973): *Iraq 1908–1921: A Socio-Political Study* (Beirut: Arab Institute for Research & Publishing).

'Awwad, Gurgis [Hanna] (1944): "Ma sullima min tawarikh al-buldan al-'iraqiyya" in *al-Muqtataf* no. 105.

———— (1969): *Mu'jam al-mu'allifin al-'iraqiyyin fi al-qarnayn al-tasi' 'ashar wa-al-'ishrin, 1800–1969* (Baghdad: Matba'at al-Irshad).

al-'Azzawi, 'Abbas (1935–56): *Ta'rikh al-'iraq bayna ihtilalayn*. 1990 reprint (Qum: Intisharat al-Sharif al-Radi).

———— (1937–56): *'Asha'ir al-'iraq* (Baghdad: Matba'at Baghdad and Sharikat al-Tijara wa-al-Tiba'a).

———— ed. (1949): *Majmu'at 'abd al-ghaffar al-akhras fi shi'r al-ustadh 'abd al-ghani al-jamili wa-ma qalahu al-akhras fih* (Baghdad: Sharikat al-Tijara wa-al-Tiba'a).

al-'Azzawi, Muhammad 'Abdallah (1988): "Al-zubayr fi al-'ahd al-'uthmani 1571–1914", review essay in *al-Khalij al-'Arabi* vol. 20 no. 3.

Badi', Muhammad Hasan Khan [1914]: *Tarikh-i basra* [Calcutta].

al-Badr, Badr Khalif (1987): *Rihla ma'a qafilat al-haya*. Internet edition (www.b-albadr.net).

al-Bakka', Tahir Khalaf Jabr (1987): "Al-'alaqat al-'iraqiyya al-iraniyya fi sahifatayn 'iraqiy-yatayn: al-istiqlal wa-al-'alam al-'arabi 1920–1932" in *al-Mu'arrikh al-'Arabi* vol. 13 no. 36.

Balaghi (2002): see theses and unpublished manuscripts.

Balfour-Paul, Glen (1994): *The End of Empire in the Middle East: Britain's Relinquishment of Power in Her Last Three Arab Dependencies* (Cambridge: Cambridge University Press).

Bamberg, J.H. (1994): *The History of the British Petroleum Company. Vol. II: The Anglo-Iranian Years, 1928–1954* (Cambridge: Cambridge University Press).

Bang, Anne K. (1996): *The Idrisi State in 'Asir, 1906–1934* (Bergen: Centre for Middle Eastern and Islamic Studies).

Barakat, Rajab (1977): *Min ta'rikh al-sihafa fi al-khalij al-'arabi 1889–1973: sihafat al-basra* (Baghdad: Matba'at al-Irshad).

———— (1980): "Al-basra fi 'ahd al-ihtilal al-baritani, 1914–1921", review essay in *al-Khalij al-'Arabi* vol. 12 no. 2.

———— (1984): *Baladiyyat al-basra, 1869–1981* (Basra: Markaz Dirasat al-Khalij al-'Arabi).

———— (1988): "Sirr rihlat al-sayyid talib al-naqib ila najd" in *al-Khalij al-'Arabi* vol. 20 no. 3.

Baram, Amatzia (1991): *Culture, History and Ideology in the Formation of Ba'thist Iraq, 1968–89* (Basingstoke: Macmillan).

Barker, A.J. (1967): *The Neglected War: Mesopotamia, 1914–1918* (London: Faber and Faber).

al-Barrak, Fadil (1984): *Al-madaris al-yahudiyya wa-al-iraniyya fi al-'iraq: dirasa muqarina* (Baghdad: al-Dar al-'Arabiyya).

Basha'yan, 'Abdallah (1890): *Al-futuhat al-kawwaziyya fi al-siyaha ila al-aradi al-hijaziyya* (Basra: Matba'at al-Basra).

al-Basir, Muhammad Mahdi (1924): *Ta'rikh al-qadiyya al-'iraqiyya*. 1990 reprint (London: Laam).

al-Basri, 'Abd al-Amir (1929): *Lahjat al-sidq wa-lisan al-haqq* (Najaf: al-Matba'a al-Haydariyya).

al-Basri, Hasun Kazim (1949): *Dhikra . . . al-shaykh salih basha'yan al-'abbasi* (Beirut: Dar al-Kashshaf).

Basri, Mir (1983–93): *A'lam al-yahud fi al-'iraq al-hadith* (Jerusalem: Rabitat al-Jami'iyyin al-Yahud al-Nazihin min al-'Iraq).

———— (1987): *A'lam al-siyasa fi al-'iraq al-hadith* (London: Riyad el-Rayyes).

———— (1991): *A'lam al-kurd* (London: Riyad el-Rayyes).

———— (1994): *A'lam al-adab fi al-'iraq al-hadith* (London: Dar al-Hikma).

al-Bassam, 'Abdallah ibn Muhammad (2000): *Tuhfat al-mushtaq fi akhbar najd wa-al-hijaz wa-al-'iraq* (Kuwait: Sharikat al-Mukhtalif).

Batatu, Hanna (1978): *The Old Social Classes and the Revolutionary Movements of Iraq: A Study of Iraq's Old Landed and Commercial Classes and of its Communists, Ba'thists, and Free Officers* (Princeton: Princeton University Press).

al-Bayati, Hamid (1997): *Shi'at al-'iraq bayna al-ta'ifiyya wa-al-shubhat fi al-watha'iq al-sirriyya al-baritaniyya 1963–1966* (London: Al-Rafid).

Bayhum, Muhammad Jamil (1931): *Al-intidaban fi al-'iraq wa-suriyya* (Sayda: Matba'at al-'Irfan).

al-Bazi, Hamid (1970): *Al-basra fi al-fatra al-muzlima* (Baghdad: Dar Manshurat al-Basri).

al-Bazzaz, 'Abd al-Rahman (1997): *Al-'iraq min al-ihtilal hatta al-istiqlal*. Fourth edition (London: Dar al-Barraq).

Bell, Gertrude (1917, 1917b, 1920): see official publications.

[Bell, Gertrude] (1940): *The Arab War: Confidential Information for General Headquarters, Being Despatches from the Secret 'Arab Bulletin'*. With an introduction by Kinahan Cornwallis (London: The Golden Cockerel Press).

Bengio, Ofra (1995): "The Challenge to the Territorial Integrity of Iraq" in *Survival* vol. 37 no. 2.

Birru, Tawfiq (1991): *Al-'arab wa-al-turk fi al-'ahd al-dusturi al-turki, 1908–1914* (Damascus).

Brass, Paul R. (1991): *Ethnicity and Nationalism: Theory and Comparison* (London: Sage).

Browne, E[dward].G. (1890): *A Traveller's Narrative Written to Illustrate the Episode of the Bab.* 1930 reprint (New York: Baha'i Publishing Committee).

——— (1902–24): *A Literary History of Persia in Four Volumes.* 1928–30 reprint (London: Cambridge University Press).

Buchta, Wilfried (1995): "Die Islamische Republik Iran und die religiös-politische Kontroverse um die *marja'iyat*" in *Orient* vol. 36, no. 3.

Buckingham, James Silk (1829): *Travels in Assyria, Media and Persia* (London: Henry Colburn).

Burj, Muhammad 'Abd al-Rahman (1990): *Muhibb al-din al-khatib wa-dawruhu fi al-haraka al-'arabiyya, 1906–1920* (Cairo: al-Hay'a al-Misriyya al-'Amma li-al-Kitab).

Busch, Briton Cooper (1967): *Britain and the Persian Gulf, 1894–1914* (Berkeley: University of California Press).

——— (1971): *Britain, India and the Arabs, 1914–1921* (Berkeley: University of California Press).

Butti, Fa'iq (1971): *A'lam fi sihafat al-'iraq* (Baghdad: Matba'at Dar al-Sa'a).

——— (1976): *Al-mawsu'a al-suhufiyya al-'iraqiyya* (Baghdad: Matba'at al-Adib al-Baghdadiyya).

Butti, Rafa'il (1923): *Amin al-rihani fi al-'iraq* (Baghdad: Matba'at Dar al-Salam).

——— (1955): *Al-sihafa fi al-'iraq* (Cairo: Jami'at al-Duwal al-'Arabiyya).

Byford, Cecil (1935): *The Port of Basrah* (Basra: Port of Basra Directorate).

Byman, Daniel L. (1997): "Divided They Stand: Lessons about Partition from Iraq and Lebanon" in *Security Studies* vol. 7 no. 1.

Caminade, Pierre (2003): *Comores – Mayotte: une histoire néocoloniale* (Marseille: Agone).

Carapico, Sheila (1998): *Civil Society in Yemen: The Political Economy of Activism in Modern Arabia* (Cambridge: Cambridge University Press).

Carnegie Endowment for International Peace (1924): *The Treaties of Peace 1919–1923* (New York).

Carter, J.R.L. (1984): *Merchant Families of Kuwait* (London: Scorpion Books).

Center for Stategic Studies at the University of Jordan (2003): *Ma'an: An Open-Ended Crisis* (Amman).

Çetinsaya (1994): see theses and unpublished manuscripts.

Chirol, Valentine (1903): *The Middle Eastern Question or Some Political Problems of Indian Defence* (London: John Murray).

Christie, Clive J. (1996): *A Modern History of Southeast Asia: Decolonization, Nationalism and Separatism* (London: I.B. Tauris).

Cohen, Stuart A. (1976): *British Policy in Mesopotamia 1903–1914* (London: Ithaca Press).

——— (1978): "Mesopotamia in British Strategy, 1903–1914" in *International Journal of Middle East Studies* vol. 9 no. 2.

Cole, Juan R.I. (1989): *Roots of North Indian Shi'ism in Iran and Iraq: Religion and State in Awadh, 1722–1859* (Berkeley: University of California Press).

Copland, Ian (1997): *The Princes of India in the Endgame of Empire, 1917–1947* (Cambridge: Cambridge University Press).

Craton, Michael (2003): *Founded upon the Seas: A History of the Cayman Islands and Their People* (Kingston: Ian Randle).

Crawford, Harriet (1991): *Sumer and the Sumerians* (Cambridge: Cambridge University Press).

Cuinet, Vital (1890–1895): *La Turquie d'Asie. Géographie administrative, statistique descriptive et raisonnée de chaque province de l'Asie-Mineure* (Paris: E. Leroux).

[Cursetjee, C.M.] (1918): *A Voyage in the Gulf. C.M. Cursetjee's 'The Land of the Date'.* 1991 reprint with an introduction by Paul Rich (Cambridge: Allborough Publishing).

Dannreuther, Roland (1995): *The Middle East in Transition* (Oslo: Institutt for forsvarsstudier).

Darwin, John (1980): "Imperialism in Decline? Tendencies in British Imperial Policy between the Wars" in *The Historical Journal* vol. 23 no. 3.

———— (1981): *Britain, Egypt and the Middle East: Imperial Policy in the Aftermath of War, 1918–1922* (London: Macmillan).

———— (1991): *The End of the British Empire: The Historical Debate* (Oxford: Basil Blackwell).

Davis, Eric (1995): " 'Ali 'Abd al-Raziq" in John L. Esposito (ed.): *The Oxford Encyclopedia of the Modern Islamic World* vol. I (Oxford: Oxford University Press).

Davis, John (1987): *Libyan Politics: Tribe and Revolution* (London: I.B. Tauris).

Demirbaş, Bülent (1991): *Musul Kerkük Olayı ve Osmanlı İmparatorluğunda Kuveyt Meselesi* (Istanbul: Arba).

Deringil, Selim (1990): "The Struggle against Shiism in Hamidian Iraq. A Study in Ottoman Counter-Propaganda" in *Die Welt des Islams* vol. 30.

———— (1999): *The Well-Protected Domains: Ideology and the Legitimation of Power in the Ottoman Empire, 1876–1909.* Paperback edition (London: I.B. Tauris).

Dickson, H.R.P. (1949): *The Arab of the Desert: A Glimpse into Badawin Life in Kuwait and Sa'udi Arabia* (London: George Allen & Unwin).

Dieulafoy, Jane (1990): *L'Orient sous le voile.* With an introduction by Jean-Pierre Sicre (Paris: Éditions Phébus).

Diskin (1971): see theses and unpublished manuscripts.

Dodge, Toby (2003): *Inventing Iraq: The Failure of Nation Building and a History Denied* (New York: Columbia University Press).

Dougherty, Raymond P. (1927): "Searching for Ancient Remains in Lower Iraq" in *Annual of the American Schools of Oriental Research* vol. 7.

———— (1927b): "Survivals of Sumerian Types of Architecture" in *American Journal of Archaeology* vol. 31.

———— (1930): "The Sealand of Arabia" in *Journal of the American Oriental Society* vol. 50.

Dowson, Ernest (1931): *An Inquiry into Land Tenure and Related Questions. Proposals for the Initiation of Reform* (Letchworth: The Garden City Press).

Dowson, Valentine Hugh Wilfred (1921): *Dates and Date Cultivation of the 'Iraq* (Cambridge: W. Heffer).

———— (1939): "The Date Cultivation and Date Cultivators of Basrah" in *Journal of the Royal Central Asian Society* vol. 26 no. 2.

Driessen, Henk (1992): *On the Spanish-Moroccan Frontier: A Study in Ritual, Power and Ethnicity* (New York: Berg).

Drower, E.S. (1937): *The Mandaeans of Iraq and Iran: Their Cults, Customs, Magic, Legends, and Folklore.* 1962 reprint (Leiden: E.J. Brill).

Duman, Hasan (1982): *Osmanlı yıllıkları (salnameler ve nevsaller): bibliyografya ve bazı İstanbul kütüphanelerine göre bir katalog denemesi* (Istanbul: İslâm Tarih, Sanat ve Kültürü Araştırma Merkezi).

Egerton, George W. (1974): "The Lloyd George Government and the Creation of the League of Nations" in *The American Historical Review* vol. 71 no. 2.

———— (1991): "Imperialism, Atlanticism and Internationalism: Philip Kerr and the League of Nations Question, 1916–1920" in *Annals of the Lothian Foundation* vol. 1 no.1.

Eich, Thomas (2003): *Abu l-Huda as-Sayyadi. Eine Studie zur Instrumentalisierung sufischer Netzwerke und genealogischer Kontroversen im spätosmanischen Reich* (Berlin: Klaus Schwarz Verlag).

Eldem, Edhem; Daniel Goffman & Bruce Masters (eds.) (1999): *The Ottoman City between East and West* (Cambridge: Cambridge University Press).

Ende, Werner (1978) "The Flagellations of Muharram and the Shi'ite 'Ulama'" in *Der Islam* vol. 55.

———— (1979): *Arabische Nation und islamische Geschichte. Die Ummayaden im Urteil arabischer Autoren des 20. Jahrhunderts* (Wiesbaden: Franz Steiner Verlag).

Eskander, Saad (2001): "Southern Kurdistan under Britain's Mesopotamian Mandate: From Separation to Incorporation, 1920–23" in *Middle Eastern Studies* vol. 37 no. 2.

Evans, R. (1926): *A Brief Outline of the Campaign in Mesopotamia, 1914–1918* (London: Sifton Praed & Co.)

Evans, Stephen F. (1982): *The Slow Rapprochement: Britain and Turkey in the Age of Kemal Atatürk, 1919–38* (Beverley: The Eothen Press).

al-Fadli, 'Abd al-Hadi (1991): "Dhikra al-shaykh mirza muhsin bin al-shaykh sultan al-'abbad al-fadli al-ahsa'i (1309–1409 h.)" in *al-Mawsim* no. 9–10.

Fallows, James (2002): "The Fifty-first State?" in *The Atlantic Monthly*, November.

Fattah, Hala (1997): *The Politics of Regional Trade in Iraq, Arabia, and the Gulf, 1745–1900* (Albany: State University of New York Press).

——— (1999): "Culture and Identity in the Work of an Ottoman Historian of Basra" in *ISIM Newsletter* no. 3.

——— (2002): "Islamic Universalism and the Construction of Regional Identity in Turn-of-the-Century Basra: Sheikh Ibrahim al-Haidari's Book Revisited" in Leila Tarazi Fawaz & C.A. Bayly (eds.): *Modernity and Culture from the Mediterranean to the Indian Ocean* (New York: Columbia University Press).

——— (2003): "The Question of the 'Artificiality' of Iraq as a Nation-State" in Shams C. Inati (ed.): *Iraq: Its History, People, and Politics* (Amherst: Humanity Books).

Faydi, Basil Sulayman (ed.): (1998): *Mudhakkirat sulayman faydi. Min ruwwad al-nahda al-'arabiyya fi al-'iraq* (London: Dar al-Saqi).

——— ed. (1998b): *Mu'allafat mukhtara* (London: Dar al-Saqi).

Faydi, Sulayman (1952): *Fi ghamrat al-nidal* (Baghdad).

Ferguson, Niall (1999): "Virtual History: Towards a 'chaotic' theory of the past" in *idem* (ed.): *Virtual History: Alternatives and Counterfactuals*. Paperback edition (New York: Basic Books).

Fernea, Robert A. (1970): *Shaykh and Effendi: Changing Patterns of Authority among the El Shabana of Southern Iraq* (Cambridge, Mass.: Harvard University Press).

Ferrier, R.W. (1982): *The History of the British Petroleum Company. Vol. I: The Developing Years, 1901–1932* (Cambridge: Cambridge University Press).

Fisher, John (1999): *Curzon and British Imperialism in the Middle East, 1916–19* (London: Frank Cass).

Flanz, Gisbert H. (1968): "West Indian Federation" in Thomas M. Franck (ed.): *Why Federations Fail: An Inquiry into the Requisites for Successful Federalism* (New York: New York University Press).

Fontanier, V. (1844–1846): *Voyage dans l'Inde et dans la Golfe Persique* (Paris: Paulin).

Fortna, Benjamin C. (2002): *Imperial Classroom: Islam, the State and Education in the Late Ottoman Empire* (Oxford: Oxford University Press).

Fuccaro, Nelida (1999): "Islam and Urban Space: Ma'tams in Bahrain before Oil" in *Magazine: ISIM Newsletter*, July.

——— (1999b): *The Other Kurds: Yazidis in Colonial Iraq* (London: I.B. Tauris).

Galbraith, John S. (1960): "The 'Turbulent Frontier' as a Factor in British Expansion" in *Comparative Studies in Society and History* vol. 2 no. 2.

——— (1984): "No Man's Child: The Campaign in Mesopotamia, 1914–1916" in *The International History Review* vol. 6 no. 3.

Galbraith, Peter W. (2004): "How to Get Out of Iraq" in *New York Review of Books* vol. 51 no. 8.

[Garbett, C.C.] (1919): "Turkish Rule and British Administration in Mesopotamia" in *The Quarterly Review* no. 232.

Gavin, R.J. (1975): *Aden under British Rule 1839–1967* (London: C. Hurst).

Geary, Grattan (1878): *Through Asiatic Turkey* (London: S. Low, Marston, Searle & Rivington).

Geere, H. Valentine (1916): "Lower Mesopotamia" in *United Empire* vol. 7 no. 1.

Gelb, Leslie (2003): "The Three-State Solution" in *New York Times*, 25 November.

Gelvin, James L. (1998): *Divided Loyalties: Nationalism and Mass Politics in Syria at the Close of Empire* (Berkeley: University of California Press).

General Staff (1923, 1923b): see official publications.

Ghani, Cyrus (1998): *Iran and the Rise of Reza Shah: From Qajar Collapse to Pahlavi Power* (London: I.B. Tauris).

Gibb, H.A.R. (1960): "Afrasiyab" in H.A.R. Gibb *et al.* (eds.): *The Encyclopaedia of Islam* vol. I (Leiden: E.J. Brill).

Gilmour, David (1995): *Curzon*. Paperback edition (London: Papermac).

Glubb, John B. (1960): *War in the Desert: An RAF Frontier Campaign* (London: Hodder and Stoughton).

Goldstein, Erik (1987): "British Peace Aims and the Eastern Question: The Political Intelligence Department and the Eastern Committee, 1918" in *Middle Eastern Studies* vol. 23 no. 4.

Goold, Douglas (1976): "Lord Hardinge and the Mesopotamia Expedition and Inquiry, 1914–1917" in *The Historical Journal* vol. 19 no. 4.

Graves, Philip (1941): *The Life of Sir Percy Cox* (London: Hutchinson & Co.)

Grayson, Richard S. (1997): *Austen Chamberlain and the Commitment to Europe: British Foreign Policy, 1924–29* (London: Frank Cass).

Haddad, Mahmoud (1991): "Iraq before World War I: A Case of Anti-European Arab Ottomanism" in Rashid Khalidi *et al.* (eds.): *The Origins of Arab Nationalism* (New York: Columbia University Press).

Hairi, Abdul-Hadi (1977): *Shi'ism and Constitutionalism in Iran. A Study of the Role Played by the Persian Residents of Iraq in Iranian Politics* (Leiden: E.J. Brill).

al-Ha'iri, Kazim (1998): *Al-marja'iyya wa-al-qiyada* (Qum).

——— (2004): *Labina awwaliyya muqtaraha li-dustur al-jumhuriyya al-islamiyya fi al-'iraq* (Qum, Internet edition from www.alhaeri.org).

Hakim, Muhammad Baqir (n.d.): *'Aqidatuna wa-ru'yatuna al-siyasiyya* (published on www.al-hakim.com).

Hall, H.R. (1930): *A Season's Work at Ur* (London: Methuen & Co.)

al-Hamdani, Tariq Nafi' (1984): "Al-'alaqat bayna afrasiyab wa-al-dawla al-'uthmaniyya" in *al-Khalij al-'Arabi* vol. 16.

Hansman, John (1967): "Charax and the Karkheh" in *Iranica Antiqua* vol. 7.

Hasan, Muhammad Salman (1965): *Al-tatawwur al-iqtisadi fi al-'iraq* (Sayda: al-Maktaba al-'Asriyya).

al-Hasani, 'Abd al-Razzaq (1930): *Mujaz ta'rikh al-buldan al-'iraqiyya* (Baghdad: Matba'at al-Najah).

——— (1953–61): *Ta'rikh al-wizarat al-'iraqiyya*. Second edition (Sayda: Matba'at al-'Irfan).

——— (1957): *Ta'rikh al-sihafa al-'iraqiyya* (Baghdad: Matba'at al-Zahra').

——— (1988) : *Ta'rikh al-wizarat al-'iraqiyya*. Seventh edition (Baghdad: Dar al-Shu'un al-Thaqafiyya al-'Amma).

al-Hashimi, Rida (1968): "Thabat bi-asma' al-mawaqi' al-athariyya wa-al-ta'rikhiyya fi liwa' al-basra" in *al-Mirbad* vol. 1 no. 1.

al-Haydari, Ibrahim Fasih (1962): *'Unwan al-majd fi bayan ahwal baghdad wa-al-basra wa-najd*. 1998 reprint (London: Dar al-Hikma).

Hedgecock, S.E. & Mrs. Hedgecock writing as "Fulanain" (1927): *Haji Rikkan. Marsh Arab* (London: Chatto & Windus).

Heude, William (1819): *A Voyage up the Persian Gulf and a Journey Overland from India to England in 1817*. 1993 reprint (Reading: Garnet).

al-Hilali, 'Abd al-Razzaq (1959): *Ta'rikh al-ta'lim fi al-'iraq* (Baghdad: Sharikat al-Tab' wa-al-Nashr al-Ahliyya).

al-Hilw, 'Ali Ni'mat (1968): *Ta'rikh imarat ka'b al-'arabiyya* (Najaf: Matba'at al-Ghura al-Haditha).

——— (1969–72): *Al-ahwaz* (Baghdad: Dar al-Basri).

——— (1972): *Al-muhammara. Madina wa-imara 'arabiyya* (Baghdad).

Hirz al-Din, Muhammad (1964–65): *Ma'arif al-rijal fi tarajim al-'ulama' wa-al-udaba'* (Najaf).

——— (1992): *Maraqid al-ma'arif* (Tehran: Manshurat Sa'id ibn Jabir).

Hobsbawm, E.J. (1977): "Reflections on 'The Break-Up of Britain' " in *New Left Review* no. 105.

Hopwood, Derek (1993): "Social Structures and the New State 1921–1958" in Derek Hopwood *et al.* (eds.): *Iraq: Power and Society* (Reading: Ithaca Press).

Hotz, A., ed. (1907): *Cornelis Cornelisz Roobacker's scheepsjournaal Gamron-Basra (1645).* (Leiden: Brill).

al-Humaydan, Muhammad (1996): *Al-mukhtasar min ta'rikh madinat al-zubayr fi suwar* (Dammam).

Husayn, 'Abd al-Jabbar Hamid and Muhammad 'Ali Hamza Sa'id (1978): *Fihris watha'iq al-basra wa-al-khalij al-'arabi al-mutawaffira fi markaz dirasat al-khalij al-'arabi* (Basra: Jami'at al-Basra).

al-Husayni, Muhammad (1996) "Al-takyif al-dusturi li-shakl al-dawla al-islamiyya", *al-Fikr al-Jadid* vol. 11–12.

Husry, Khaldun S. (1974): "The Assyrian Affair of 1933 (II)" in *International Journal of Middle East Studies* vol. 5 no. 3.

[al-Huwayzi], Ibn Ma'tuq (1862): *Diwan* (Egypt: Mahmud Effendi Halim).

Ibn al-Ghamlas, [Ibrahim] (1962): *Wulat al-basra wa-mutasallimuha.* Edited by 'Ali al-Basri (Baghdad: Dar al-Basri).

Ibn Bishr, 'Uthman (1983): *'Unwan al-majd fi ta'rikh najd* (Riyadh: Darat al-Malik 'Abd al-'Aziz).

Ibn 'Isa, Ibrahim ibn Salih (1966): *Ta'rikh ba'd al-hawadith al-waqi'a fi najd* (Riyadh: Dar al-Yamama).

Ibrahim, Ferhad (1997): *Konfessionalismus und Politik in der arabischen Welt: Die Schiiten im Irak* (Münster: LIT Verlag).

Ilbert, Robert (1996): *Alexandrie, 1830–1930: histoire d'une communauté citadine* (Cairo: Institut français d'archéologie orientale).

Ingham, Bruce (1976): "Regional and Social Factors in the Dialect Geography of Southern Iraq and Khuzistan" in *Bulletin of the School of Oriental and African Studies* vol. 36 no. 1.

——— (1986): *Bedouin of Northern Arabia: Traditions of the Al-Dhafir* (London: KPI).

——— (1997): *Arabian Diversions: Studies on the Dialects of Arabia* (Reading: Ithaca Press).

International Crisis Group (2003): *Red Alert in Jordan: Recurrent Unrest in Maan* (Amman/Brussels).

Iraq Museum (1926): see official publications.

Ireland, Philip Willard (1937): *'Iraq. A Study in Political Development* (London: Jonathan Cape).

Issawi, Charles (1975): *The Economic History of the Middle East, 1800–1914* (Chicago: University of Chicago Press).

——— (1986): "Notes on the Trade of Basra, 1800–1914" in *Journal of Turkish Studies* vol. 10.

——— (1988): *The Fertile Crescent 1800–1914: A Documentary Economic History* (Oxford: Oxford University Press).

Izzedien, Yousif (1962): *Poetry and Iraqi Society, 1900–1945* (Baghdad).

Jansen, Godfrey (1992): "Why a Shi'istan could not work" in *Middle East International* 11 September.

al-Jasir, Hamad (1981): *Jamharat ansab al-usar al-mutahaddira fi al-najd* (Riyadh: Dar al-Yamama).

Jawdat, 'Ali (1967): *Dhikrayat 'ali jawdat 1900–1958* (Beirut: Matabi' al-Wafa').

Jeffery, Keith (1984): *The British Army and the Crisis of Empire, 1918–22* (Manchester: Manchester University Press).

Jose, Jim & Christine Doran (1997): "Marriage and Marginalisation in Singaporean Politics" in *Journal of Contemporary Asia* vol. 27 no. 4.

Joseph, John (1983): *Muslim-Christian Relations and Inter-Christian Rivalries in the Middle East: The Case of the Jacobites in an Age of Transition* (Albany: State University of New York Press).

Jwaideh (1953): see theses and unpublished manuscripts.

Jwaideh, Albertine (1963): "Midhat Pasha and the Land System of Lower Iraq" in Albert Hourani (ed.): *Middle Eastern Affairs No. 3* (London: Chatto & Windus).

——— (1965): "The Sanniya Lands of Sultan Abdul Hamid II in Iraq" in George Makdisi (ed.): *Arabic and Islamic Studies in Honor of Hamilton A.R. Gibb* (Leiden: E.J. Brill).

———— (1996): "The Al Sa'dun Emirate and Its Decline" in *Arab Historical Review for Ottoman Studies*, no. 13–14.

Jwaideh, Albertine & J.W. Cox (1988): "The Black Slaves of Turkish Arabia during the Nineteenth Century" in *Slavery and Abolition* vol. 9 no. 3.

al-Ka'bi, Fath Allah ibn 'Alwan (1924): *Zad al-musafir wa-lahnat al-muqim wa-al-hadir fi ma jara li-husayn basha ibn afrasiyab hakim al-basra*. Edited by Khalaf Shawqi Amin al-Dawudi (Baghdad: Matba'at al-Furat).

al-Kanani, Ahmad (n.d.): *Man allifa fi al-hajj min ahl hajar*. Internet edition (www.hadj.ir).

al-Karmali, Anastas Mari (1919): *Khulasat ta'rikh al-'iraq* (Basra: Matba'at al-Hukuma).

Kasaba, Resat (2001): "Edhem Eldem, Daniel Goffman and Bruce Masters, 'The Ottoman City between East and West' ", book review in *International Journal of Middle East Studies* vol. 33 no. 3.

Kashani-Sabet, Firoozeh (1999): *Frontier Fictions: Shaping the Iranian Nation, 1804–1946* (Princeton: Princeton University Press).

Kasravi, Ahmad (1983): *Tarikh-i pansad salah-i khuzistan* ([Tehran]: Intisharat-i Khvaju).

al-Katib, Ahmad (1998): *Tatawwur al-fikr al-siyasi al-shi'i min al-shura ila wilayat al-faqih* (Beirut: Dar al-Jadid).

Kayali, Hasan (1997): *Arabs and Young Turks: Ottomanism, Arabism, and Islamism in the Ottoman Empire, 1908–1918* (Berkeley: University of California Press).

Kazemzadeh, Masoud (1998): "Thinking the Unthinkable: Solving the Problem of Saddam Hussein for Good" in *Middle East Policy* vol. 6, no. 1.

Kedourie, Elie (1959): "Réflexions sur l'histoire du Royaume d'Irak, 1921–1958" in *Der Orient* vol. 11.

———— (1978): *England and the Middle East: The Destruction of the Ottoman Empire 1914–1921* (Hassocks: The Harvester Press).

Kelly, J.B. (1968): *Britain and the Persian Gulf, 1795–1880* (Oxford: The Clarendon Press).

Kennedy, Hugh (1986): *The Prophet and the Age of the Caliphates: The Islamic Near East from the Sixth to the Eleventh Century* (London: Longman).

Kent, Marian (1976): *Oil and Empire: British Policy and Mesopotamian Oil, 1900–1920* (London: Macmillan).

———— (1984): "Great Britain and the End of the Ottoman Empire, 1900–1923" in *idem* (ed.): *The Great Powers and the End of the Ottoman Empire* (London: George Allen & Unwin).

Keyder, Caglar; Y. Eyüp Özveren & Donald Quataert (1993): "Port-Cities in the Ottoman Empire: Some Theoretical and Historical Perspectives" in *Review* (Fernand Braudel Center) vol. 16 no. 4.

Khadduri, Majid (1946): *Nizam al-hukm fi al-'iraq* (Baghdad: Matba'at al-Ma'arif).

———— (1951): *Independent Iraq: A Study in Iraqi Politics since 1932* (London: Oxford University Press).

al-Khal, Muhammad, ed. (1961): *Ta'rikh al-imara al-afrasiyabiyya* (Baghdad: Matba'at al-Majma' al-'Ilmi al-'Iraqi).

al-Khalidi, 'Abd al-Latif al-Dulayshi (1981): *Min a'lam al-fikr al-islami fi al-basra: al-shaykh muhammad amin al-shinqiti 1293–1351 h./ 1876–1932 m.* (Baghdad: Wizarat al-Awqaf wa-al-Shu'un al-Diniyya).

al-Khalili, Ja'far (1963): *Hakadha 'araftuhum* (Baghdad: Matba'at al-Zahra').

al-Khaqani, 'Ali (1961–62): *Makhtutat al-maktaba al-'abbasiyya fi al-basra* (Baghdad).

———— (1954): *Shu'ara' al-ghari, aw, al-najafiyyat*. 1988 reprint (Tehran: Maktabat Ayat Allah al-'Uzma al-Mar'ashi al-Najafi).

al-Khattab, 'Adil 'Abdallah (1978): "Madinat al-qurna. Dirasa fi jughrafiyyat al-mudun" in *al-Khalij al-'Arabi* vol. 9.

Khoury, Philip S. (1983): *Urban Notables and Arab Nationalism: The Politics of Damascus, 1860–1920* (Cambridge: Cambridge University Press).

———— (1987): *Syria and the French Mandate: The Politics of Arab Nationalism, 1920–1945* (Princeton: Princeton University Press).

Khubruy Pak, Muhammad Riza (1998): *Naqdi bar fidiralism* (Tehran: Shirazah).

al-Khurasan, Salah (1999): *Hizb al-da 'wa al-islamiyya* (Damascus: Al-Mu'assasa al-'Arabiyya li-al-Dirasat wa-al-Buhuth al-Istiratijiyya).

Khuri, Fuad I. (1980): *Tribe and State in Bahrain* (Chicago: University of Chicago Press).

——— (1990): *Imams and Emirs: State, Religion and Sects in Islam* (London: Saqi).

Khurshid Effendi (1981): *Wilayat al-basra*. Excerpted from *Siyahatnamah-i hudud* and translated from Persian by Nuri al-Samarra'i (Basra: Jami'at al-Basra).

Klieman, Aaron S. (1970): *Foundations of British Policy in the Arab World: The Cairo Conference of 1921* (Baltimore: The Johns Hopkins Press).

Kostiner, Joseph (1984): *The Struggle for South Yemen* (London: Croom Helm).

Krüger, K. (1932): *Kemalist Turkey and the Middle East* (London: George Allen & Unwin).

Kubba, Laith (n.d.): *The Plight of the Shi'a of Iraq* (London).

Kuklick, Bruce (1996): *Puritans in Babylon: The Ancient Near East and American Intellectual Life, 1880–1930* (Princeton: Princeton University Press).

Kumar, Ravinder (1965): *India and the Persian Gulf Region, 1858–1907: A Study in British Imperial Policy* (London: Asia Publishing House).

al-Kutubi, Muhammad Rida (1951): *Ta'rikh al-ma'atim al-husayniyya: madiha wa-hadiruha. 1: Fi liwa' al-basra* (Najaf: Maktabat Dar al-Kutub al-Tijariyya).

La Boullaye Le Gouz, François de (1653): *Les voyages et observations du Sieur de La Boullaye Le Gouz* (Paris: G. Clousier).

Laftah, Khawla Talib (2003): *Sulayman faydi wa-dawruhu al-siyasi wa-al-thaqafi wa-al-ijtima'i fi al-'iraq 1885–1951* (Baghdad: Matba'a al-Adib al-Baghdadiyya).

Layard, A.H. (1846): "A Description of the Province of Khuzistan" in *Journal of the Royal Geographical Society* vol. 16.

Lees, G.M. and N.L. Falcon (1952): "The Geographical History of the Mesopotamian Plains" in *The Geographical Journal* vol. 118.

Litvak, Meir (1998): *Shi'i Scholars of Nineteenth Century Iraq: The 'Ulama' of Najaf and Karbala'* (Cambridge: Cambridge University Press).

Longrigg, Stephen Hemsley (1925): *Four Centuries of Modern Iraq*. 1968 reprint (Farnborough: Gregg).

——— (1953) *'Iraq, 1900 to 1950: A Political, Social and Economic History* (Oxford: Oxford University Press).

——— (1958): *Syria and Lebanon under French Mandate*. 1968 reprint (Beirut: Libraire du Liban).

Lorimer, J.G. (1908): *Geographical and Statistical Gazetteer of the Persian Gulf, 'Oman and Central Arabia*. 1970 reprint (Farnborough: Gregg).

——— (1915): *Gazetteer of the Persian Gulf, 'Oman and Central Arabia*. 1970 reprint (Farnborough: Gregg).

Luizard, Pierre-Jean (1991): *La formation de l'Irak contemporain: Le rôle politique des ulémas chiites à la fin de la domination ottomane at au moment de la construction de l'État irakien* (Paris: Centre national de la recherche scientifique).

——— (1995): "Des Muntafik: Une representation en miniature de la 'question irakienne'" in *Monde arabe Maghreb Machrek* no. 147.

——— (1999): "Les confréries soufies en Irak arabe" in Frederick de Jong & Bernd Radtke (eds.): *Islamic Mysticism Contested: Thirteen Centuries of Controversies and Polemics* (Leiden: E.J. Brill).

Lukitz, Liora (1995): *Iraq: The Search for National Identity* (London: Frank Cass).

McCarthy, Justin (1981): "The Population of Ottoman Syria and Iraq, 1878–1914" in *Asian and African Studies* vol. 15.

McKillop, Bob (1982): "Papua Besena and Papuan Separatism" in R.J. May (ed.): *Micronationalist Movements in Papua New Guinea* (Canberra: Australian National University).

al-Madamagha, Mustafa Kazim (1981): *Nusus min al-watha'iq al-'uthmaniyya 'an ta'rikh al-basra fi sijillat al-mahkama al-shar'iyya fi al-basra (1188–1330 h.)* (Basra: Jami'at al-Basra).

Majid, Muhammad Hasan 'Ali (1989): "Funun al-nathr fi al-basra fi al-'asr al-nahda" in Jami'at al-Basra: *Mawsu'at al-basra al-hadariyya: al-mawsu'a al-fikriyya* (Basra: Matba'at Dar al-Hikma).

al-Maktaba al-Adabiyya al-Mukhtassa (1997): *Sayyid al-nakhil al-muqaffa mustafa jamal al-din: fi dhikrahu al-sanawiyya al-ula* (Qum: al-Maktaba al-Adabiyya al-Mukhtassa).

Mallat, Chibli (1997): *The Middle East into the 21st Century* (Reading: Ithaca Press).

Mansfield, Peter (1992): "Why the Arabs Want to Keep Iraq Intact" in *Middle East International*, 9 October.

al-Mansur, Nizar (2004): *Al-nusra li-shi'at al-basra* (Cairo: Maktabat Madbuli).

Marlowe, John (1967): *Late Victorian: The Life of Sir Arnold Talbot Wilson* (London: The Cresset Press).

Marr, Phebe (1985): *The Modern History of Iraq* (Boulder: Westview Press).

———— (1985b): "The Development of a Nationalist Ideology in Iraq, 1920–1941" in *The Muslim World* vol. 75.

Marrs, R. (1918): *Notes on the Country Traversed by the Basra-Nasiriyah Railway* (Calcutta: Government Press).

al-Matba'i, Hamid (1995–98): *Mawsu'at a'lam al-iraq fi al-qarn al-'ishrin* (Baghdad: Wizarat al-Thaqafa wa-al-I'lam).

Mehmed Süreyya Bey (1890–1898): *Sicill-i osmani* (Istanbul: Maarif Nezareti).

Mejcher, Helmut (1973): "British Middle East Policy 1917–1921: The Inter-Departmental Level" in *Journal of Contemporary History* vol. 8 no. 4.

———— (1976): *Imperial Quest for Oil: Iraq 1910–1928* (London: Ithaca Press).

Midhat, Ali Haydar (1903): *The Life of Midhat Pasha* (London: John Murray).

Mignan, Robert (1829): *Travels in Chaldæa, Including a Journey from Bussorah to Bagdad, Hillah and Babylon, Performed on Foot in 1827* (London: H. Colburn and R. Bentley).

Mirza Sayyid Ja'far Khan, Mushir al-Dawla (1969): *Risalah-i tahqiqat-i sarhaddiyya*. Annotated by Muhammad Mushiri (Tehran: Bunyad-i Farhang-i Iran).

Moberly, F.J. (1924–27): *The Campaign in Mesopotamia 1914–1918*. 1930 reprint (London: His Majesty's Stationery Office).

Momen, Moojan (1985): *An Introduction to Shi'i Islam* (New Haven: Yale University Press).

Monroe, Elizabeth (1963): *Britain's Moment in the Middle East, 1914–1956* (London: Chatto & Windus).

Morgan, Kenneth O. (1986): *Consensus and Disunity: The Lloyd George Coalition Government, 1918–1922* (Oxford: The Clarendon Press).

al-Mubadir, Salim Sa'dun (1978): *Qada' al-faw. Dirasa fi al-jughrafiyya al-zira'iyya* (Baghdad: Matba'at al-Irshad).

Mufti, Malik (1996): *Sovereign Creations: Pan-Arabism and Political Order in Syria and Iraq* (Ithaca: Cornell University Press).

Muhsin, Rahim 'Abbud & Muhammad 'Awda 'Aliwi (1989): "Al-tiba'a wa-al-nashr fi al-basra qadiman wa-hadithan" in Jami'at al-Basra: *Mawsu'at al-basra al-hadariyya: al-mawsu'a al-fikriyya* (Basra: Matba'at Dar al-Hikma).

Murphey, Rhoads (1987): "The Ottoman Centuries in Iraq: Legacy of Aftermath?" in *Journal of Turkish Studies* no. 11.

Murray, Hugh (1820): *Historical Account of Discoveries and Travels in Asia* (Edinburgh: A. Constable).

Mustafa, Mas'ud Ahmad (1990): *Aqalim al-dawla al-islamiyya* (Cairo).

al-Nabhani, Muhammad (1914): *Al-tuhfa al-nabhaniyya fi imarat al-jazira al-'arabiyya* (Baghdad: Dar al-Salam).

———— (1923): *Al-basra. Al-tuhfa al-nabhaniyya fi ta'rikh al-jazira al-'arabiyya*. 1980 reprint (Basra: Markaz Dirasat al-Khalij al-'Arabi).

———— (1925): *Al-tuhfa al-nabhaniyya fi ta'rikh al-jazira al-'arabiyya . . . Al-juz' 10 – al-muntafiq*. Reprint (n.p., n.d.).

al-Nafisi, 'Abdallah Fahd (1990): *Dawr al-shi'a fi tatawwur al-'iraq al-siyasi al-hadith*. Second edition (Kuwait: Dhat al-Salasil).

al-Na'ini, Muhammad Husayn (1909): *Tanbih al-umma wa-tanzih al-milla*. Internet edition (www.bahrainonline.org).

al-Najjar, Mustafa 'Abd al-Qadir (1971): *Al-ta'rikh al-siyasi li-imarat 'arabistan al-'arabi 1897–1925* (Egypt: Dar al-Ma'arif bi-Misr).

——— (1974): *Al-ta'rikh al-siyasi li-mushkilat al-hudud al-sharqiyya li-al-watan al-'arabi fi shatt al-'arab* (Basra: Jam'iyyat al-Difa' 'an 'Urubat al-Khalij al-'Arabi).

Nakash, Yitzhak (1994): *The Shi'is of Iraq* (Princeton: Princeton University Press).

Narayanan, Ganesan (2004): "The Political History of Ethnic Relations in Singapore" in Lai Ah Eng (ed.): *Beyond Rituals and Riots: Ethnic Pluralism and Social Cohesion in Singapore* (Singapore: Eastern Universities Press).

Nayfeh, Samir (1992): "Iraqi Contras?" in *Middle East International* 11 September.

Nazif: See Süleyman Nazif.

Nazmi Zade, Murtaza (1730): *Gülşen-i hulefa*. 1971 translation from Ottoman Turkish to Arabic by Musa Kazim Nawras (Najaf: Matba'at al-Adab).

Neary, Peter (1988): *Newfoundland in the North Atlantic World, 1929–1949* (Kingston: McGill-Queen's University Press).

Nevakivi, Jukka (1969): *Britain, France and the Arab Middle East, 1914–1920* (London: The Athlone Press).

Nieuwenhuis, Tom (1982): *Politics and Society in Early Modern Iraq: Mamluk Pashas, Tribal Shayks and Local Rule between 1802 and 1831* (The Hague: Martinus Nijhoff).

Olson, Robert (1989): *The Emergence of Kurdish Nationalism and the Sheikh Said Rebellion, 1880–1925* (Austin: University of Texas Press).

Omissi, David E. (1990): *Air Power and Colonial Control: The Royal Air Force, 1919–1939* (Manchester: Manchester University Press).

Owen, Roger (1993): *The Middle East in the World Economy, 1800–1914* (London: I.B. Tauris).

al-Pachachi, 'Adnan (1989): *Muzahim al-pachachi: sira siyasiyya* (London: Centre for Historical Documents and Studies).

Pearson, Patrick C. & Edward B. Proud (1996): *The Postal History of Iraq* (Heathfield: Proud Bailey Co.)

Philby, H.StJ.B. (1922): *Heart of Arabia* (London: Constable).

——— (1928): *Arabia of the Wahhabis*. 1977 reprint (London: Cass).

——— (1948): *Arabian Days: An Autobiography* (London: Robert Hale).

Piscatori, James P. (1986): *Islam in a World of Nation-States* (Cambridge: Cambridge University Press in association with the Royal Institute of International Affairs).

Pool, David (1979): "From Elite to Class: The Transformation of Iraqi Political Leadership" in Abbas Kelidar: *The Integration of Modern Iraq* (London: Croom Helm).

Popovic, Alexandre (1999): *The Revolt of African Slaves in Iraq in the 3rd/9th Century*. Translated from French by Léon King, with an introduction by Henry Louis Gates Jr. (Princeton: Markus Wiener).

Porath, Yehoshua (1984): "Nuri al-Sa'id's Arab Unity Programme" in *Middle Eastern Studies* vol. 20 no. 4.

Prätor, Sabine (1993): *Der arabische Faktor in der jungtürkischen Politik: Eine Studie zum osmanischen Parlament der II. Konstitution (1908–1918)* (Berlin: Klaus Schwarz Verlag).

al-Qahwati, Husayn Muhammad (1980): *Dawr al-basra al-tijari fi al-khalij al-'arabi 1869–1914* (Basra: Markaz Dirasat al-Khalij al-'Arabi).

al-Qassab, 'Abd al-'Aziz (1962): *Min dhikrayati* (Beirut: Manshurat 'Uwaydat).

al-Qaysi (1958): see theses and unpublished manuscripts.

al-Qazwini, Muhammad Mahdi al-Kazimi (1923): *Khasa'is al-shi'a* (Baghdad: Matba'at Dar al-Salam).

——— (1928): *Minhaj al-shari'a fi al-radd 'ala ibn taymiyya* (Najaf: al-Matba'a al-'Alawiyya).

Raglan, [Fitzroy Richard Somerset, Baron] (1925): "The Situation in Iraq" in *The English Review* vol. 41.

al-Rahimi, 'Abd al-Halim (1985): *Ta'rikh al-haraka al-islamiyya fi al-'iraq* (Beirut: al-Dar al-'Alamiyya).

al-Rasheed, Madawi (1991): *Politics in an Arabian Oasis: The Rashidis of Saudi Arabia* (London: I.B. Tauris).

Ra'uf, 'Adil (2000): *Al-'amal al-islami fi al-'iraq bayna al-marja'iyya wa-al-hizbiyya* (Damascus).

Ra'uf, 'Imad 'Abd al-Salam (1983): *Al-ta'rikh wa-al-mu'arrikhun al-'iraqiyyun fi al-'asr al-'uthmani* (Baghdad: Dar Wasit).

Raunkiær, Barclay (1913): *Gennem Wahhabiternes Land paa Kamelryg.* (Copenhagen: Gyldendalske Boghandel).

Reynardson, Henry Birch (1919): *Mesopotamia, 1914–15: Extracts from a Regimental Officer's Diary* (London: Andrew Melrose).

Reynolds, David (1991): *Britannia Overruled: British Policy and World Power in the Twentieth Century* (London: Longman).

al-Rihani, Amin (1972): *Ta'rikh najd wa-mulhaqatih.* Fourth edition (Beirut: Dar al-Rihani).

Rivoyre, Denis de (1883): *Obock, Mascate, Bouchire, Bassorah* (Paris: E. Plon).

Robinson, Ronald & John Gallagher, with Alice Denny (1961): *Africa and the Victorians: The Official Mind of Imperialism.* 1965 paperback edition (London: Macmillan).

Rogan, Eugene L. (1996): "Aşiret Mektebi: Abdülhamid II's School for Tribes (1892–1907)" in *International Journal of Middle East Studies* vol. 28 no. 1.

——— (1999): *Frontiers of the State in the Late Ottoman Empire: Transjordan, 1850–1921* (Cambridge: Cambridge University Press).

Rothwell, V.H. (1970): "Mesopotamia in British War Aims, 1914–1918" in *The Historical Journal* vol. 13 no. 2.

[Rousseau, Jean Baptiste] (1809): *Description du Pachalik de Bagdad suivie d'une notice historique sur les Wahabis, et de quelques autres pièces relatives à l'histoire et à la litterature de l'Orient* (published anonymously, Paris: Treuttel et Würtz).

al-Rubay'i, Dawud Jasim (1978): *Qada' al-zubayr. Dirasa fi al-jughrafiyya al-bashariyya* (Baghdad: Matba'at al-Irshad).

Rubinoff, Arthur G. (1998): *The Construction of a Political Community: Integration and Identity in Goa* (New Delhi: Sage).

al-Rusafi, Ma'ruf (1931): *Diwan al-rusafi* (Beirut: Matba'at Dar al-Ma'rid).

al-Rushayd, 'Abd al-'Aziz (1926): *Ta'rikh al-kuwayt* (Baghdad: al-Matba'a al-'Asriyya).

al-Sa'dun, Khalid (1987): "Sirr rihlat al-sayyid talib al-naqib ila najd fi muharram 1333 h./ tishrin al-thani – kanun al-awwal 1914 m." in *al-Khalij al-'Arabi* vol. 19 no. 1.

——— (1989): "Al-sayyid talib al-naqib marra ukhra" in *al-Khalij al-'Arabi* vol. 21 no. 2.

Safwat, Najdat Fathi (1988): *Mudhakkirat rustum haydar* (Beirut: al-Dar al-'Arabiyya li-al-Mawsu'at).

Sakai, Keiko (2001): "Modernity and Tradition in the Islamic Movements of Iraq" in *Arab Studies Quarterly* vol. 23, no. 1.

Saleh, Zaki (1995): *Britain and Iraq: A Study in British Foreign Affairs.* Second edition (London: Books & Books).

al-Salihi, Najib (1998): *Al-zilzal* (London).

Salim, S.M. (1962): *Marsh Dwellers of the Euphrates Delta* (London: The Athlone Press).

Salum, Dawud (1989): "Shi'r al-basra fi 'asr al-nahda" in Jami'at al-Basra: *Mawsu'at al-basra al-hadariyya: al-mawsu'a al-fikriyya* (Basra: Matba'at Dar al-Hikma).

al-Samarra'i, Qasim (ed.) (2001): *Masajid al-zubayr* (Riyadh: Dar al-Faysal al-Thaqafiyya).

al-Samarra'i, Sa'id (1993): *Al-ta'ifiyya fi al-'iraq* (London: Al-Fajr).

al-Sani', 'Abd al-Razzaq 'Abd al-Muhsin [and 'Abd al-'Aziz 'Umar al-'Ali] (1985–89): *Imarat al-zubayr bayna hijratayn* (Kuwait).

Sassoon, David S. (1927): "The History of the Jews in Basra" in *The Jewish Quarterly Review* vol. 17 no. 4.

al-Sayyab, Badr Shakir (1960): *Unshudat al-matar* (Beirut: Dar Majallat Shi'r).

Schoff, Wilfred, ed. (1914): *Parthian Stations by Isidore of Charax* (Philadelphia: Commercial Museum).

Schofield, Richard (1993): *Kuwait and Iraq: Historical Claims and Territorial Disputes.* Second edition (London: The Royal Institute of International Affairs).

Schulze, Reinhard (1990): *Islamischer Internationalismus im 20. Jahrhundert. Untersuchungen zur Geschichte der islamischen Weltliga* (Leiden: E.J. Brill).

Schuol, Monika (2002): *Die Charakene: Ein mesopotamisches Königreich in hellenistisch-parthischer Zeit* (Stuttgart: Franz Steiner Verlag).

Scudder, Lewis R. (1998): *The Arabian Mission's Story: In Search of Abraham's Other Son* (Grand Rapids: W.B. Eerdmans).

Seikaly, May (2002): *Haifa: Transformation of an Arab Society, 1918–1939.* Paperback edition (London: I.B. Tauris).

al-Shabandar, Musa (1993): *Dhikrayat baghdadiyya. Al-'iraq bayna al-ihtilal wa-al-istiqlal* (London: Riyad el-Rayyes).

al-Shalah, Husayn Hadi (2002): *Talib basha al-naqib al-basri wa-dawruhu fi ta'rikh al-'iraq al-siyasi al-hadith* (Beirut: Al-Dar al-'Arabiyya li-al-Mawsu'at).

al-Sharqi, 'Ali (1929): *Dhikra al-sa'dun, aw, ta'rikh batal al-tadhiya wa-al-ikhlas* (Baghdad).

———— (1963): *Al-'iraq wa-al-'arab* (Baghdad: Sharikat al-Tab' wa-al-Nashr al-Ahliyya).

Shaw, Wendy M.K. (2003): *Possessors and Possessed: Museums, Archaeology, and the Visualization of History in the Late Ottoman Empire* (Berkeley: University of California Press).

Shawkat, Naji (1974): *Sira wa-dhikrayat* (Baghdad: Maktabat al-Yaqza al-'Arabiyya).

al-Shaykh Khaz'al, Husayn Khalaf (1962–70): *Ta'rikh al-kuwayt al-siyasi* (Beirut: Dar al-Kitab).

al-Shaykhli, Muhammad Ra'uf Taha (1972): *Marahil al-haya fi al-fatra al-muzlima wa-ma ba'daha* (Basra).

Shields, Sarah D. (2000): *Mosul before Iraq: Like Bees Making Five-Sided Cells* (Albany: State University of New York Press).

Shubbar, Hasan (1989): *Al-'amal al-hizbi fi al-'iraq 1908–1958* (Beirut: Dar al-Turath al-'Arabi).

Silverfarb, Daniel (1986): *Britain's Informal Empire in the Middle East: A Case Study of Iraq 1929–1941* (Oxford: Oxford University Press).

Simon, Reeva S. (1986): *Iraq between the Two World Wars: The Creation and Implementation of a Nationalist Ideology* (New York: Columbia University Press).

———— (1991): "The Education of an Iraqi Ottoman Army Officer" in Rashid Khalidi *et al.* (eds.): *The Origins of Arab Nationalism* (New York: Columbia University Press).

Singer, Isidore, ed. (1901–06): *The Jewish Encyclopedia* (New York: Funk and Wagnalls).

Sluglett, Peter (1976): *Britain in Iraq, 1914–1932* (London: Ithaca Press).

———— (1999): "Formal and Informal Empire in the Middle East" in Robin W. Winks (ed.): *The Oxford History of the British Empire. Vol. V: Historiography* (Oxford: Oxford University Press).

Sluglett, Peter & Marion Farouk-Sluglett (1990): *Iraq since 1958: From Revolution to Dictatorship* (London: I.B. Tauris).

Smith, Anthony D. (2000): *The Nation in History: Historiographical Debates about Ethnicity and Nationalism* (Hanover: University Press of New England).

Smith, Peter (1987): *The Babi & Baha'i Religions: From Messianic Shi'ism to a World Religion* (Cambridge: Cambridge University Press).

Soysal, İsmail (1991): "Seventy Years of Turkish-Arab Relations and an Analysis of Turkish-Iraqi Relations (1920–1990)" in *Studies on Turkish-Arab Relations* vol. 6.

Stafford, R.S. (1935): *The Tragedy of the Assyrians* (London: George Allen & Unwin).

Strunk (1977): see theses and unpublished manuscripts.

al-Suhrawardi, Muhammad Salih (1933): *Lubb al-albab* (Baghdad: Matba'at Dar al-Ma'arif).

Süleyman Nazif (1918): *Firak-i irak* (Istanbul: Mehmed Bey Matbaası).

al-Suwaydi, 'Abd al-Rahman ibn 'Abdallah (1978): *Ta'rikh hawadith baghdad wa-al-basra min 1186 ila 1192 h. 1772–1778 m.* Edited by 'Imad 'Abd al-Salam Ra'uf (Baghdad: Wizarat al-Thaqafa wa-al-Funun).

al-Suwaydi, Tawfiq (1987): *Wujuh 'iraqiyya 'abra al-ta'rikh* (London: Riyad el-Rayyes).

al-Tabataba'i, 'Abd al-Jalil (1966): *Diwan* (Cairo: al-Matba'a al-Salafiyya).

Tachau, Frank (1963): "The Search for National Identity among the Turks" in *Die Welt des Islams* vol. 8 no. 3.

al-Tahir, 'Abd al-Jalil (1972): *Al-'asha'ir al-'iraqiyya* (Beirut: Dar Lubnan).

al-Taliqani, Muhammad Hasan (1999): *Al-shaykhiyya: nash'atuha wa-tatawwuruha wa-masadir dirasatiha* (Beirut: al-Amal li-al-Matbu'at).

[al-Tamimi], Hamid Ahmad Hamdan (1976): "Nazra 'ala mawqi' ba'd al-khidmat al-'amma fi al-basra khilal fitrat al-ihtilal al-baritaniyya 1914–1921" in *al-Khalij al-'Arabi* vol. 6.

———— (1979): *Al-basra fi 'ahd al-ihtilal al-baritani, 1914–1921* (Baghdad: Markaz Dirasat al-Khalij al-'Arabi).

al-Tamimi, Khalid (1996): *Muhammad ja'far abu al-timman. Dirasa fi al-za'ama al-siyasiyya al-'iraqiyya* (Damascus: Dar al-Warraq).

Tauber, Eliezer (1993): *The Emergence of the Arab Movements* (London: Frank Cass).

———— (1995): *The Formation of Modern Syria and Iraq* (London: Frank Cass).

Tavernier, Jean Baptiste (1678): *The Six Voyages of John Baptista Tavernier.* Translated from French by J[ohn] P[hillips] (London).

Thesiger, Wilfred (1967): *The Marsh Arabs.* Paperback edition (Harmondsworth: Penguin Books).

Thévenot, Jean de (1727): *Voyages de M. de Thévenot en Europe, Asie et Afrique.* Third edition (Amsterdam: M.-C. Le Cène).

Tidrick, Kathryn (1989): *Heart-Beguiling Araby: The English Romance with Arabia.* Revised edition (London: I.B. Tauris).

al-Tihrani, Muhammad Muhsin Aga Buzurg (1954–58): *Tabaqat a'lam al-shi'a* (Najaf: al-Matba'a al-'Ilmiyya).

———— (1937–): *Al-dhari'a ila tasanif al-shi'a.* Internet edition (www.ahl-ul-bayt.org).

Times Printing and Publishing Co. (1922): *Historical Mesopotamia* (Basra: Times Printing and Publishing Co.)

Townshend, Charles (1986): "Civilization and 'Frightfulness': Air Control in the Middle East between the Wars" in Chris Wrigley (ed.): *Warfare, Diplomacy and Politics: Essays in Honour of A.J.P. Taylor* (London: Hamish Hamilton).

Tripp, Charles (2002): *A History of Iraq.* Second edition (Cambridge: Cambridge University Press).

Tu'ma, Hadi (1984): *Al-ihtilal al-baritani wa-al-sihafa al-'iraqiyya: dirasa fi al-hamla al-di'aiyya al-baritaniyya, 1914–1921* (Baghdad: Wizarat al-Thaqafa wa-al-I'lam).

Türkmen, Zekeriya (2003): *Musul Meselesi: Askerî Yönden Çözüm Arayışları, 1922–1925* (Ankara: Atatürk Araştırma Merkezi).

al-'Umar, Jihad Salih (1989): "Al-basra bayna al-harbayn al-'alamitayn, 1918–1939" in Jami'at al-Basra: *Mawsu'at al-basra al-hadariyya: al-mawsu'a al-ta'rikhiyya* (Basra: Matba'at al-Ta'lim al-'Ali).

al-'Umari, Khayri (1955): *Shakhsiyyat 'iraqiyya* (Baghdad: Dar al-Ma'rifa).

———— (1969): *Hikayat siyasiyya min ta'rikh al-'iraq al-hadith* (Cairo: Dar al-Hilal).

Vadala, Ramire Pie Maxime (1920): *Le Golfe persique* (Paris: Librairie Arthur Rousseau).

Van Ess, John (1943): *Meet the Arab* (New York: John Day).

Van Ess, Dorothy F. (1961): *Fatima and Her Sisters* (New York: John Day).

———— (1974): *Pioneers in the Arab World* (Grand Rapids: W.B. Eerdmans).

van Kaam, Ben (1977): *Ambon door de eeuwen.* (Baarn: In den Toren).

Vinogradov, Amal (1972): "The 1920 Revolt in Iraq Reconsidered" in *International Journal of Middle East Studies* vol. 3.

Visser, Reidar (2004): "Shi'i Perspectives on a Federal Iraq: Territory, Community and Ideology in Conceptions of a New Polity" in Daniel Heradstveit & Helge Hveem (eds.): *Oil in the Gulf: Obstacles to Democracy and Development* (Aldershot: Ashgate).

Von Oppenheim, Max (1939–68): *Die Beduinen* (Leipzig and Wiesbaden: Otto Harrassowitz).

Wahba, Hafiz (1960): *Khamsun 'aman fi jazirat al-'arab* (Cairo: Mustafa al-Babi al-Halabi).

———— (1964): *Arabian Days* (London: Arthur Barker).

al-Wa'ili, Ibrahim (1961): *Al-shi'r al-siyasi al-'iraqi fi al-qarn al-tasi' 'ashar* (Baghdad: Matba'at al-'Ani).

Wallis Budge, E.A. (1920): *By Nile and Tigris: A Narrative of Journeys in Egypt and Mesopotamia on Behalf of the British Museum between the Years 1886 and 1913* (London: John Murray).

Walsh, Bren (1985): *More than a Poor Majority: The Story of Newfoundland's Confederation with Canada* (St. John's: Breakwater).

al-Ward, Baqir Amin (1978): *A'lam al-'iraq al-hadith, 1869–1969: qamus tarajim* (Baghdad: Matba'at al-Ufsit al-Mina').

al-Wardi, 'Ali (1969–79): *Lamahat ijtima'iyya min ta'rikh al-'iraq al-hadith.* 1992 reprint, (n.p.).

Warman, Roberta M. (1972): "The Erosion of Foreign Office Influence in the Making of Foreign Policy, 1916–1918" in *The Historical Journal* vol. 15 no. 1.

Whitaker, Brian (2003): "The Ayatollah: Iraq's Archduke" in *The Guardian*, 1 September.

Wilkinson, John C. (1987): *The Imamate Tradition of Oman* (Cambridge: Cambridge University Press).

Williams, Ronald J. (1994): "The Two Careers of Raymond P. Dougherty" in *Telescope – Messenger* vol. 4 no. 2.

Wilson (1911): see theses and unpublished manuscripts.

Wilson, Arnold T. (1931): *Loyalties: Mesopotamia, 1914–1917.* Second edition. 1936 reprint (Oxford: Oxford University Press).

———— (1931b): *Mesopotamia, 1917–1920: A Clash of Loyalties.* Second edition. 1936 reprint (Oxford: Oxford University Press).

Wilson, Keith M. (1983): "Constantinople or Cairo: Lord Salisbury and the Partition of the Ottoman Empire 1886–1897" in Keith M. Wilson (ed.): *Imperialism and Nationalism in the Middle East: The Anglo-Egyptian Experience, 1882–1982* (London: Mansell Publishing).

Wimmer, Andreas (2002): *Nationalist Exclusion and Ethnic Conflict: Shadows of Modernity* (Cambridge: Cambridge University Press).

Winstone, H.V.F. (1980): *Gertrude Bell.* Paperback edition (London: Quartet Books).

Worringer, Renée (2004): "Sick Man of Europe or Japan of the Near East?" in *International Journal of Middle East Studies* vol. 36 no. 2.

Yamani, Mai (2004): *Cradle of Islam: The Hijaz and the Quest for an Arabian Identity* (London: I.B. Tauris).

Yaphe, Judith S. (2004): "The View from Basra: Southern Iraq's Reaction to War and Occupation, 1915–1925" in Reeva Spector Simon & Eleanor H. Tejirian (eds.): *The Creation of Modern Iraq, 1914–1921* (New York: Columbia University Press).

Yapp, M.E. (1987): *The Making of the Modern Near East 1792–1923* (London: Longman).

———— (1989): "The Euphrates Expedition" in C.E. Bosworth *et al.* (eds.): *The Islamic World from Classical to Modern Times: Essays in Honor of Bernard Lewis:* (Princeton: The Darwin Press).

———— (1991): *The Near East since the First World War* (London: Longman).

Young, Ernest (1934): "In the Date Gardens" in *Journal of Geography* vol. 33.

Young, Gavin (1977): *Return to the Marshes: Life with the Marsh Arabs of Iraq* (London: Collins).

Young, Hubert (1933): *The Independent Arab* (London: John Murray).

Yusuf Zade, 'Ali ibn Sulayman (1904): *Asna matalib al-arib fi mada'ih al-sayyid talib al-naqib* (Cairo: Matba'at al-Mu'ayyid).

al-Za'arir, Muhammad (1997): *Imarat al rashid fi ha'il* (Beirut: Bisan).

al-Zanjani, Ibrahim al-Musawi (1967): *'Aqa'id al-imamiyya al-ithna 'ashariyya* (Najaf: Matba'at al-Adab).

Zanella, Riccardo (1946): *L'État Libre de Fiume* (Bureau de Fiume).

al-Zirikli, Khayr al-Din (1927–28): *Al-a'lam* (Cairo: al-Matba'a al-'Arabiyya).

Index